REGINALD HARGREAVES

BEYOND THE RUBICON: A HISTORY OF EARLY ROME

A lively survey—social and political—of the development of an empire, based upon historical and military accounts of the time.

BEYOND
THE RUBICON

The Romans created an unparalleled empire that bestowed upon the civilized world two hundred years of orderly rule and peace. Who were these people and what were the events that cast them in their unique historical role?

A distinguished British scholar answers these questions through a close examination of ancient commentaries and chronicles. Major Hargreaves begins with an intriguing interpretation of myth and fact as he describes the founding of Rome, the rule of Romulus, the rape of the Sabines. He explores the expanding powers of Rome—its military campaigns, its political and social structure—as he recounts the land reforms of the Gracchi, the rise of Caesar, the surrender of Vercingetorix.

His provocative narrative ends with the defeat of a rebellious Roman general at Pharsalus—perhaps the most decisive battle in history, since it was to lead to the establishment of Pax Romana.

Other MENTOR Books on Ancient Rome

BEYOND THE RUBICON

A History of Early Rome

by REGINALD HARGREAVES

MENTOR

A MENTOR BOOK

Published by
The New American Library, New York and Toronto
The New English Library Limited, London

OTHER BOOKS BY REGINALD HARGREAVES: *Red Sun Rising, The Narrow Seas, The Enemy at the Gate, This Happy Breed, Women at Arms, Onlooker at War*

IN COLLABORATION: *"Mr. Crofts the King's Bastard," Famous Duels and Assassinations, In the Days of Queen Anne, John Gay*

IN CO-EDITORSHIP: *Great English Short Stories, Great French Short Stories, Great German Short Stories*

Library of Congress Catalog Card Number: 66-28978

MENTOR TRADEMARK REG. U.S. PAT. OFF. AND FOREIGN COUNTRIES
REGISTERED TRADEMARK—MARCA REGISTRADA
HECHO EN CHICAGO, U.S.A.

MENTOR BOOKS are published *in the United States* by
The New American Library, Inc.,
1301 Avenue of the Americas, New York, New York 10019,
in Canada by The New American Library of Canada Limited,
295 King Street East, Toronto 2, Ontario,
in the United Kingdom by The New English Library Limited,
Barnard's Inn, Holborn, London E.C. 1, England

PRINTED IN THE UNITED STATES OF AMERICA

CONTENTS

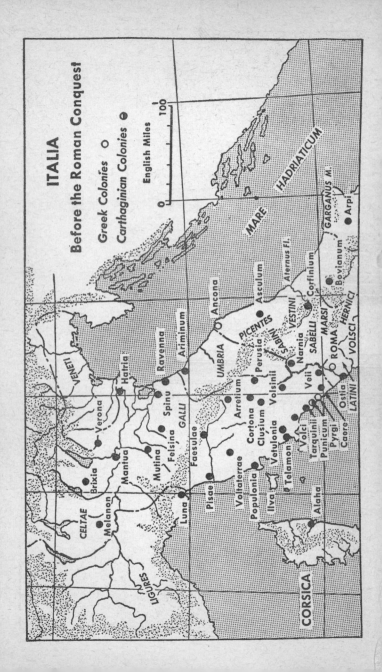

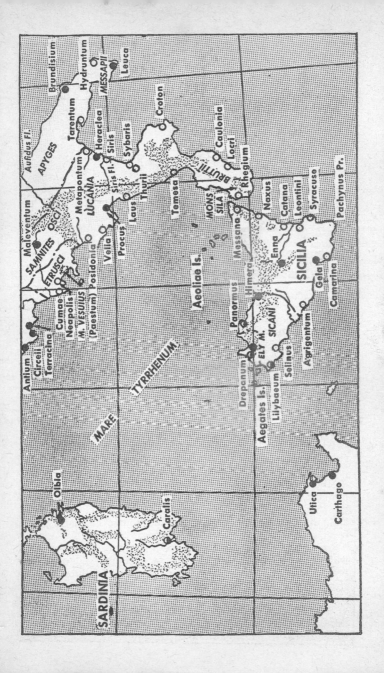

INTRODUCTION

The story of the rivalry between Gaius Julius Caesar and Gnaeius Pompeius Magnus (Pompey the Great) epitomizes the erratic, turbulent history of the Roman people from the time of their emergence as the dominant tribal group in their particular sector of the Italian peninsula, to the day when Rome's future greatness was determined by the outcome of the battle of Pharsalus.

As a battle Pharsalus was as swift and uncomplicated an encounter as James Wolfe's astoundingly speedy victory over Montcalm on the Plains of Abraham in A.D. 1759, and without doubt it was equally far-reaching in its consequences.

For centuries the Roman people had sought in vain for a form of governance in which all classes of the community could assent and by which they would be content to abide. At the outset, for a small agrarian hill tribe encompassed by inimical and predatory neighbors, a war leader—the "man on the shield"—had been essential to insure the clan's survival, and, understandably enough, in due course he had assumed regal status.

Not every successful Warrior-King, however, is endowed with those qualities needed to rule a country equitably and progressively in times of peace. With the failure of their later Monarchs to cope with the manifold responsibilities with which they had been entrusted, the Roman people turned to a republican form of government as more likely to fulfill the task of guiding the nation along the expansionist path to which it was so patently committed.

Republicanism is perhaps the most difficult apparatus of governance to turn into a success, since its satisfactory operation demands a maturity of outlook, a sense of responsibility, an integrity, and an innate bias in favor of equilibrium in all strata of the community rarely to be found in any people. (It is worthy of note that among the nations of the Old World Switzerland is the only republic to have continued as such for over two hundred years.)

In the event, Rome's essay into republicanism failed almost completely. In no sense could it match up to the country's phenomenal rate of expansion, while at the same time it opened the door to a corruption and abuse of power on the part of the elected rulers, and an inconsequent lawlessness and snarling class-consciousness among those who defied any attempt to govern them, which kept the whole land in a turmoil of unrest that culminated in a succession of blood-boltered civil wars.

The Romans had demonstrated equally their ability to conquer an empire and their complete incapacity to rule their own land. An effervescent, extremely umbrageous people, they would neither themselves exercise the reasonable self-control which true liberty demands nor permit restraint to be imposed upon them by their rulers. Everybody demanded an entirely partisan say in the operation of the machinery of state, so it is little wonder that it broke down hopelessly. Indeed, George Washington might well have had ancient Rome in mind when he pronounced that "mankind when left to themselves are quite unfit for their own government."

Political chaos such as prevailed so persistently in Rome invariably throws up a spume of impractical ideologists with as many nostrums for creating heaven upon earth as there are roads to hell. Even more numerous are the political charlatans who perceive in human gullibility a sure means of self-advancement and ready access to the public coffers. But should the land be fortunate, somewhere in the tumult there waits *the Man,* the man who in due season will stamp his will upon the people at large and by sheer force of personality bring order out of chaos.

> ". . . Often do the spirits
> Of great events stride on before the events,
> And in today already walks tomorrow."

From the moment the Gracci resorted to blatant demagogy to introduce reforms whose undoubted overall value was invalidated by the vengeful nature of their subsidiary clauses, the writing on the wall spelled out the name of Caesar. Caesar, in effect, was the end product of a whole concatenation of misguided attempts at governance. For the Gracci paved the way for an even worse type of greedy, power-hungry Jacobin in Marius, who in turn evoked that savagery in Sulla which conferred so indelible a blemish on his name. They were the lords of misrule whose crude political surgery so prostrated a chronically ailing Rome that it demanded all Caesar's healing arts to restore the sufferer to reasonable health.

Caesar's campaign against his rival reached its climax at the battle of Pharsalus, which undoubtedly qualifies as a "decisive" victory since, as Hallam put it, "a contrary outcome would have essentially varied the drama of the world in all its subsequent scenes." Victory at Pharsalus enabled Caesar to reshape the Roman gubernatorial system into something not only acceptable to the majority of the people but of inestimable value to the world at large.

I am under the very greatest obligation to Miss Kathleen M. Withy, B.A., for her invaluable help in preparing the manuscript and Index.

My thanks are also due to Messrs. Longmans, Green & Company for their help in tracking down A. H. Beesly—author of *The Gracci, Marius and Sulla*—and to Captain G. H. Stanning, D.S.O., R.N., Bursar of Marlborough College, who also assisted in the quest.

In the following pages I have resorted to quotations from contemporary or near-contemporary chronicles and commentaries, as well as from acknowledged authorities on the period, deliberately and on an uninhibited scale. Even Caesar himself has been laid under contribution, although it is well to bear in mind that his writings, aimed as they were at posterity, cannot entirely be absolved from the charge of making propaganda. The labor of many other authors not actually quoted in the text has gone into the making of this volume, and in common gratitude the titles of their works have been included in the Bibliography.

REGINALD HARGREAVES

PROLOGUE

❧ ❧

A Pride of Empires

"Cities and Thrones and Powers
Stand in Time's eye
Almost as long as flowers,
Which daily die."

—Kipling

History is not an aimlessly meandering chronicle of chance events; its rhythm has a discernible pattern based upon certain fundamentals which recur with every successive generation.

The spectrum of human society reveals a panorama of constant strife interspersed with a few widely separated intervals of peace. Investigation reveals that since 3600 B.C. the world has known less than three hundred years that were free from the clash of arms. Even during so recent a period as that of 1800 to 1940 the number of conflicts waged amounted to two hundred and eighty-seven.

From the earliest ages of mankind the strong have resorted to armed force to wrest something they coveted from the weak. Communities came into being when families joined together for mutual protection or for the purpose of overpowering and plundering another clan. By attaining at least temporary superiority in arms, expanding tribal groups succeeded in establishing themselves in rich, open countrysides such as the valleys of the Nile and the Euphrates and in similar fertile areas in India and China. The rivers, forming ready means of intercommunication, rendered each community, however widely distributed, a single homogeneous unit.

With expansion a community's boundaries came into contact with those of a neighbor, and each sought enlargement at the expense of the other. The stronger overcame the weaker, annexed its territory, and enslaved its inhabitants, for whereas at the outset primordial man had unfrugally massacred the male survivors of a vanquished tribe, later generations of conquerors had perceived in them, and in the forced labor to which they could be put, a form of property, an expendable means of enhancing the general wealth of the dominant element in the community.

Since war leaders invariably failed to deal equitably with the consequences of conquest, a premium was put on revolt by that part of the populace held in servitude, aided, as like as not, by one of the community's jealous neighbors. With servitude the predestined fate of the vanquished, it was a rotation which underwent constant repetition.

It was not until the days of Philip, King of Macedon (c. 382-336 B.C.), that this traditional pattern of conquest underwent radical modification. Philip not only succeeded in overcoming Athens, Thebes, and other independent Greek city-states, but by a policy of conciliation actually contrived to unite them. Panhellenism had replaced the isolated city-state with the territorial realm; and if Philip's cherished dream of realizing *Homonoia* (unity in concord) through the creation of a centrally controlled world empire was fated to go unfulfilled in his own lifetime it was destined to be almost fully realized in that of his son, the superbly accomplished Alexander.

Prodigally endowed with all the qualities that made for leadership both in war and peace, "Alexander loved polite learning, and his natural thirst for knowledge made him a man of extensive reading and wide humanity." [1] Both an idealist and a hardheaded realist, "he believed he had a mission to harmonize men generally and be the reconciler of the world, mixing men's lives and customs as in a loving cup, and treating the good as his kin and the bad as strangers." [2]

But reconciliation could only be the outcome of victory in arms. So in 334 B.C. Alexander set out on that epic blend of conquest and assimilation that brought under his sway the people of Persia, Palestine, Assyria, Egypt, Babylon, Susa, and

[1] Plutarch, *Lives*.
[2] W. W. Tarn, *Alexander the Great and the Unity of Mankind*.

Sagdiana, and established Greek colonies as far to the east
as the Punjab.

Having marched and fought his way for eight years through
seventeen thousand miles of alien territory, the King of Kings
prepared to set out on his journey homeward, first erecting
twelve great altars on the banks of the Hypasis (Sutlej) and
a tall column of bronze bearing the inscription "Here Alexander halted." [3]

Conquest had everywhere marked his progress, but in every
instance conquest had been followed by the most painstaking
efforts at conciliation; the intermarriage of men and women
of different ethnic stock—together with the introduction of
a unified financial system—was regarded as the most likely
solvent for racial prejudice and animosity.

By the spring of 324 B.C. Alexander was back in Babylon,
having been met on the line of march by embassies from the
Ethiopians, Libyans, Lucanians, Carthaginians, Bruttians,
Etruscans, Iberians, and Gauls, and even by emissaries from
the fledgling city-state of Rome—all bent on rendering hom-
age to him as the Great Conciliator and Lord of the East.

Restless and moody, Alexander was only too well aware
that, stupendous as his achievement had been, his master
plan still fell far short of full realization. There were still
worlds to conquer and then to be reconciled to the principle
of "unity in concord."

Still absorbed in gigantic designs for global conquest and
conciliation, Alexander was stricken down with malaria, in
June of 323 B.C. and within eleven days of his first seizure
he was dead.

Alexander's untimely death in his thirty-third year was of
less significance to posterity than the fact that he had lived
as he had lived and dreamed as he had dreamed, striving
always to give form and substance to the lofty concept of
Homonoia in which he so passionately believed. Indeed, *"the
whole subsequent course of history, the political and cultural
life of after-times, cannot be understood apart from the career of Alexander."* [4] Alexandria, the greatest of the cities
he had founded, became the venerated center of the new

[3] At Baklogh, the erstwhile depot of the 4th Prince of Wales's Own
Gurkha Rifles, there are three clumps of date palms. Tradition avers
that these mark the line of Alexander's outposts, the clumps having
been raised from the dates his soldiery brought with them from the
banks of the Tigris.

[4] Ulrick Wilcken, *Alexander the Great.*

culture he had inspired, "the meeting place of the world."
But nowhere did the Hellenic ethos take firmer hold than
in the emergent city-state of Rome. "It was the Romans who
first gave Alexander the title of 'the Great,' " [5] the Romans
who ultimately strove to revitalize the concept of *Homonoia*
with which his name will always be associated. After the
First Punic War, Roman society adopted Greek standards and
refinements as embodying all that was desirable in the way
of a civilized *modus vivendi*. Thereafter, it was the Greek
historians who drew a parallel between Alexander Magnus
and Scipio Africanus, the conqueror of Hannibal and the
founder of the Roman world empire. And when the curve of
time brought Julius Caesar his victory over Pompeius at the
battle of Pharsalus, it became the conqueror's fixed design to
emulate the fabled Alexander by extending Roman rule and
the principle of *Homonoia* over domains which stretched
from ancient Britain to the Parthian territories in distant
Bactria. It was under the sway of the Rome of the Caesars
that Alexander's dream of "unity in concord" came nearest
to realization, when for two centuries and more the known
world enjoyed the blessing of international tranquillity under
the benevolent autocracy of the Pax Romana.

[5] Wilcken, *op. cit.*

PART I

Portend in the West

"Lowliness is young ambition's ladder,
Whereto the climber-upward turns his face."
—Shakespeare

Chapter I

THE FLEDGLING STATE

"A people . . . still, as it were, but in the gristle
and not yet hardened into the bone of manhood."

—Edmund Burke

In the early years of the eighth century B.C. the boot-shaped peninsula of Italia was inhabited by a large number of scattered and extremely diverse communities. Tribes from the north, sweeping over the Alps, had successively forced their predecessors to move on further down the mainland, which was divided by the spinal cord of the Apennines, running with little irregularity from the Lombardy plain to northern Umbria. Thence the massif swings to the south, ribbing the narrow "toe" and reappearing beyond the sea-gap separating the mainland from Sicily.

Italia,[1] the central peninsula of the three land masses thrusting out into the Mediterranean, together with the islands which formed its natural appanages, occupied a position singularly favorable to independent development. If the Alps and

[1] It was not until the closing years of the Roman Republic that the name of Italy came into general use.

the river Po offered no more than an easily penetrable barrier to hostile invasion, the territory's great depth and the narrow front it presented lent powerful aid to its northern defenses, while its central position constituted a formidable barrier between East and West.

Bounded to the southwest by the tideless Tyrrhenian Sea and to the northeast by the Adriatic, the peninsula's coast lines are not fretted by many deep indentations save between the "heel" and "toe," where the Gulf of Taranto lies, while the Gulf of Euphemia breaks the curve of the "instep." On the "heel" itself Hydruntum (Otranto) served as a reasonable haven for shipping, as did Brundusium (Brindisi) a little farther up the Adriatic coast. Above this port the bulge, crowned by Mount Garganus, overlooked the open roadstead of Ancona.

Among the many tribes settled in the peninsula the Ligurians occupied the northeast Apennines; the sturdy, rather bovine Etruscans, the area bounded by the central mountain ridge and the river Tiber. There were Gauls, or Celts, in the north, Oscans in the south, and in central Italia the "men of the plain" (*Latium*), the hill tribes known as the Sabellians and the Aequi, together with the lesser clans of the Volsci and Hernici. The Latins were thickly distributed over what is now the Roman Campagna, the open terrain lying between the Tiber and the Anio and reaching up into the Volscian hills. A confederacy of thirty townships, their capital was the stronghold of Alba Longa.

In southern Italia the highlands were notable as the homeland of three branches of the tough, resilient Oscan race, of which by far the most important were the Samnites; the Lucanians and Bruttians qualified as slightly inferior offshoots of the same stock.

The proximity of the "heel" of Italia to the Greek Adriatic coast had inevitably resulted in the incursion of races of Hellenic origin, while Sicily, the largest and most fertile of the Mediterranean islands, had early undergone colonization by the Phoenicians and Greeks.

In the midst of this complex of warring or warily friendly tribes a community had taken root on the Campus Martius, athwart the slopes of the last spur of a range of hills running out from the Alban Mountains along the left bank of the river Tiber. The origins of this virile, dynamic tribal group cannot factually be determined, so obscured have they been by legend. But since myth may be accepted as no more than the truth in masquerade, the version of events accepted by the people of Rome itself cannot entirely be ignored.

When Troy was taken by the Greeks, so the story goes, the Trojan Prince Aeneas fled together with his father Anchises, taking with him his few worldly possessions. After a voyage of seven years he and his handful of followers reached the mouth of the Tiber, where Latinus, King of the Aberrigines inhabiting the neighboring territory, received him kindly, even bestowing his daughter Lavinia upon him in marriage. The singular instance of a white sow farrowing to throw the prodigious number of thirty young was interpreted as an indication that the fugitive Trojans were fated to settle in this smiling, fertile land and found a race destined gloriously to increase and multiply.

Establishing an embryonic city on the spot where the sow had farrowed, Aeneas gave it the name of Lavinium. But "Lavinia had been betrothed to Turnus, the young chief of the Rutulians of Ardea. He, wrathful with disappointment, made war upon the strangers. Aeneas sought the aid of Evander, the Arcadian, who had founded a city on the Palatine Hill, which afterwards became Rome. In this struggle the Trojans prevailed and Turnus fell." [2] But three years later a new war broke out, during the course of which Aeneas was drowned in the waters of the Numicius, a small river running between Lavinium and Ardea.

Responsibility for the welfare of the newcomers as well as his own followers now fell on the shoulders of Aeneas's son Ascanius. Warned by omens that Lavinium was not to be the abiding place for his people, after thirty years—as foretokened by the prophetic sounder of swine—the whole community was removed to the ridge of a hill some fifteen miles from what was to become the site of Rome. Here was built a city destined to achieve considerable fame under the name of Alba Longa.[3] Silvius, a son of Lavinia and Aeneas, succeeded Ascanius; the eleven Kings who followed him all bore the selfsame patronymic.

The last of these Monarchs left two sons, Numitor and Amulius; the latter seized the inheritance of an elder who had no desire to assume the responsibilities of kingship. But Numitor had a son and daughter whose future attitude towards a usurper the scheming Amulius was careful to take into account. The son was put to death and the daughter, Rhea Silva, was dedicated to the service of the goddess Vesta to ensure that she should die unwed. But the gods have their own way of dealing with the overweening plans of mortals.

[2] Henry G. Liddell, D.D., *A History of Rome.*
[3] "The Long White City."

The sacred Vestal Virgin was found to be with child by the god Mars, and in due course she gave birth to male twins.

The punishment for incontinence in a Vestal Virgin was to be buried alive, and Amulius was under no temptation to spare his niece. It was ordained that the twins should be thrown into the Tiber. As it chanced, the river had overflowed its banks, covering the ground that one day was to house the Forum with shallow pools. As the shoal water ebbed away the two infants were left unharmed on a patch of dry ground near a wild fig tree, long preserved with becoming reverence under the name of the *Ficus Rumanalis*. Suckled by a wolf and fed by a woodpecker, the boys were found and adopted by a simple herdsman, with whose family they shared a humble cot on the Palatine. They were known by the names of Romulus and Remus.[4]

Grown to manhood, the twins were recognized and accepted as of the legitimate line by the aging Numitor. It was with his consent and support that they attacked Amulius in his palace at Alba and there slew him. With this, Numitor consented to assume the responsibilities of kingship.

Three hundred years had passed since the foundation of Alba, and it was from a habitation defiled by memories of Amulius that the brothers set out to build a new city on the banks of the Tiber. When the question arose as to who should be the founder, "they sought answer of the gods by the flight of birds, watching the heavens all night. At sunrise Remus beheld from the Aventine Hill six vultures, but Romulus from the Palatine saw twelve. So he built the city there and called it by his own name: and when Remus leaped the unfinished wall and scorned the work, he smote him so that he died; 'So be it with any who dare to cross this wall.' And the city was called Rome." [5]

With the city built the only thing lacking was a sufficient population to inhabit it and afford it protection. To swell its numbers welcome was given to all those under the necessity of seeking sanctuary—runaway slaves, freebooters, and even those guilty of the civic crime of shedding blood. The outcome was a hardy, individualistic aggregation of humanity which at least was not lacking in vitality. As a community, however, they nurtured as little hope of reproduction as an assemblage of eunuchs, since the people of the neighboring cities regarded them as entirely unworthy of marriage

---

[4] Livy (Titus Livius), *A History of Rome.*

[5] *Ibid.* The generally accepted date for the foundation of Rome is 453 B.C.

with their nubile womenfolk. To rationalize a situation that threatened the whole of Rome's future destiny, Romulus determined to ensure by unscrupulous stratagem what fairer means had failed to secure. He invited the people of the Sabines and the neighboring Latin towns to attend the celebrations in honor of the god Consus, and when the festivities were at their height a number of Rome's lusty newcomers seized all the marriageable women on whom they could lay their hands and bore them away.

The rape of the Sabine women would have had infinitely more sanguinary repercussions but for the fact that its victims appeared to harbor singularly little resentment for the lot that had befallen them. There was scant support from the newly wedded wives for the campaign embarked upon by the outraged Sabine bachelors, whose armed protest was easily defeated by Romulus and a host of Benedicts only too ready to defend their newfound connubial happiness.

The conflict with the Sabines of Cures was less easily dealt with, and the defenders of Rome were hard pressed until the Sabine women flung themselves between their uxorious Roman husbands and their own kinsmen, demanding peace between them. It was a reconciliation which led in due course to the amalgamation of the Romans and the Cures in one community; certain collaterals of the Etruscan clan, who had come to the Romans' support in their quarrel with the Sabines, also added their quota to generate a common stock.

Under Romulus a system of governance arose which divided the community into two classes—the burgesses, or citizens, and their dependents, or clients, as they were termed. It was the responsibility of the burgess patrons to shield their dependents from all wrong and oppression on the part of others, while the dependents were under obligation to render service to their protectors. Since all political rights were reserved to the burgesses, the relationship between them and their clients very largely anticipated that which pertained in later days between the feudal lord and his vassal.

The burgesses themselves were divided into tribal groups, while each community was subdivided into ten *Curiae,* with each *Curia* under a *Curio,* or chieftain, supported by a *Flamen Curialis,* or priest. In all there were thirty *Curiae,* which met in an assembly [6] termed the *Comitia Curiata* to deliberate on all matters of state brought before it; no enact-

[6] By 241 B.C. the number of tribes had been increased to thirty-five.

ments had legal validity unless they had been approved by a majority of the aforesaid sederunt.

With the regal title Romulus had assumed went the chief command in time of war and the final judgment in matters of life and death. In token of his sovereign power the Roman leader went attended by twelve lictors bearing *fasces* consisting of bundles of elm or birch rods bound tightly together, from which projected a keen-bladed ax head, symbolizing strength through union.

In addition to the *Comitia Curiata,* a Council of Elders, or Senate, constituted a select body to whom the King could turn for counsel,[7] although with two hundred members it was a considerably larger assemblage than the *Curia Regis* of medieval days.

A military establishment was founded to which each of the three communities contributed 100 Horse and 1,000 Foot, the combined force being known as the Legion. The Horse of each clan was known as a Century and was recruited from among the most patrician of the men of suitable age. The corps, which acted as a regal bodyguard, was known by the collective name of *Celeres* and was commanded by three divisional leaders, *Tribuni celerum,* while the Foot were led by three *Tribuni militum.* At the outset the Romans adopted the phalanx formation favored by the Greeks, and it was not until *circa* 326 B.C. that it was realized that the phalanx could neither maintain its ranks against shock tactics nor achieve the mobility needed to come properly to grips with an agile enemy. Ever adaptable, the contemporary leaders promptly put the necessary combat reorganization in hand.[8] But for Romulus and his immediate successors the phalanx, sternly disciplined and with its ranks made up of men toughened by their labor in the fields and vineyards, sufficiently fulfilled the purpose for which it was intended.

Such were the people, and such was the compound of fact and legend in which their early history was enshrined to form the basis of a religious code which, if little more than an abracadabra of superstition embalmed in ritual, at least served "the furtherance of civil order and morality." [9]

---

[7] In effect, the Senate and the *Comitia Curiata* very largely anticipated the House of Lords and the Commons of the British Parliament and the Senate and the House of Representatives of the United States Congress.

[8] See page 34.

[9] Theodor Mommsen, *The History of Rome.* (4 vols.)

Virile, aggressive, yet not so intemperate as to scorn negotiation entirely, the Romans themselves, together with the tribal groups they had assimilated, were obviously destined to multiply and expand, to gain in significance and import as cohesion and a growing sense of unity served progressively to fortify their burgeoning self-confidence.

With the death of Romulus the powers of government passed temporarily into the hands of the Senate. In effect, this was rule by committee, and since a committee is a contrivance by which those who can separately take no decisive action collectively decide that no effective action need be taken, the demand for a single ruler became so insistent as to lead to the elevation of the just and upright Sabine Numa Pompilius to the status of Sovereign. Under his benign rule Rome enjoyed forty-three years of peaceful expansion.

A far more ensanguined period followed with the accession of Tullus Hostilius, who was quick to espouse the cause of his people against the neighboring Albans, ever prone to raid and pillage the Roman settlements of the borderlands. Defiant but eventually overcome, the Albans were forced to submit to the dismantling of their capital; their burgesses and attendant clients migrated to Rome, being assigned the Caelian Hill for their settlement. To console them and facilitate the process of assimilation Tullus made their principal citizens burgesses of Rome, while increasing the élite among his troops by the addition of three hundred of Alba's proudest warriors.

The Sabines were still a power in the land, and although Tullus successfully took the field against them, he was not destined to bring them to submission. Perishing in a sudden outbreak of plague, he was succeeded by Ancus Marcius, grandson of the pious Numa Pompilius.[10]

The reign of Ancus Marcius is chiefly memorable for the war waged by the Romans against the Latins, a conflict in which the latter were soundly beaten. Their lands were divided among the conquerors; the forest territory hard by the sea was declared public property, while a Roman colony was founded at Ostia, by the mouth of the Tiber. The survivors among the vanquished Latins were welcomed into the Roman confederation and given the Hill of Aventinus on which to found their settlement. Conquest followed

[10] Livy, *op. cit.*

by assimilation—Alexander's constructive formula had not been entirely forgotten.

The balance of King Ancus's reign of three-and-twenty years was devoted to the expansion of the city of Rome. A fortress was constructed on the hill known as Janiculum, which was joined to the city by a bridge over the intervening river. In the low ground between the hills a great dike—the dike of the Quirites—helped materially to ensure the inhabitants' security. And since "as the people grew in numbers offenders against the laws became more numerous," King Ancus also built a prison under the hill Saturnius.

During the reign of King Ancus the Sovereign had shown much favor to a certain Lucius Tarquinius, although he was the son of an Etruscan and an immigrant who had chosen to settle in Rome. He was wealthy and in exceedingly good favor with the people, and with the death of Ancus the populace chose him to reign over them rather than one of the sons of the departed Monarch. Victorious in his wars against the stubborn survivors among the Latins and the rump of the inextinguishable Sabines, Tarquinius was equally famed for the many additions he made to secure the capital and improve its amenities. Having drained the paludal area between the Palatine and Aventine Hills, he built the Circus, the great arena for chariot and horse races. Then in the open space between the Palatine and the Capitoline he constructed a forum, or market place, parcelling out the ground abutting on it to accommodate permanent stalls. Laying the foundations of a great temple on the Capitoline Hill, he also set about the building of a stone wall to enclose the entire city.

In recognition of the need for the populace to be more fully represented, Tarquinius added a hundred new members to the Senate. At the same time he doubled the number of the Horse in the Centuries of the auxiliary Ramnes, Tities, and Luceres, his experience in the field having convinced him that the value of well-disciplined cavalry could scarcely be overestimated.

Serving in the King's household was a youth of whose birth,

some told wonderful tales, declaring that he was the son of a god; while others said that his mother was a slave and his father one of the King's clients. But he served the King well, and was in favor with the people, and the King promised him his daughter in marriage. And the youth was called Servius Tullius. But when the sons of

King Ancus saw that Servius Tullius was so loved by
the King Tarquinius, they resolved to slay the King, lest
he should make this stranger his heir, and so they
should lose the crown forever. So they set on two shepherds to do the deed, and these were sent to the King's
palace and pretended to be quarreling with each other.
The King sent for them to hear their story; and while
he was hearing one of them speak, the other struck
him on the head with his hatchet, and then both of them
fled. But Tanaquil, the King's wife, pretended that he
was not dead, but only stunned by the blow; and she
said that he had appointed Servius Tullius to rule in his
name, till he should be well again. So Servius went forth
in royal state, and judged causes amidst the people, and
acted in all things as if he were the King, till after a
while it was known that the King was dead, and Servius
was suffered to reign in his place. Then the sons of
Ancus saw that there was no hope left for them; and
they fled from Rome, and lived the rest of their lives
in a foreign land.[11]

On all counts the adventitious Servius Tullius can be esteemed a just and farsighted monarch. As a sequel to his
successful war with the Etruscans, he divided the territory
he had won among the commonalty. Furthermore, he induced many new immigrants to settle on the Esquiline Hill,
officially including the Quirinal and Viminal Hills within
the city limits and adding appreciably to the capital's defenses. But perhaps his most notable achievement was his
structural reorientation of the populace. The people of the
city were divided into four tribal groups, those of the countryside into six-and-twenty, everyone being assigned to a definite class according to his possessions. These categories were
split up into Centuries, each furnished with arms of their
own providing according to their respective ranks, thus
forming a useful emergency force of militia.

An inveterate legislator, Servius Tullius dimly envisioned
a future wherein kingship would be abandoned in favor of
the rule of a duad or triumvirate, chosen by the people to
"govern them year by year." It was a prospect which, however it might be welcomed by *hoi polloi*, was thoroughly distrusted by the Patrician classes, since the formula obviously
ruled out any continuity in governance.

- *This search for a gubernatorial system which would prove*

11 Livy, *op. cit.*

generally acceptable—regal absolutism, autocracy, or plain unqualified pollarchy—posed a problem which was to haunt, and frequently to bedevil, the whole of Roman history till the age of the Augustans.

At this particular juncture in the country's destiny Servius Tullius unfortunately was without male descendants and his two daughters had been given in marriage to the sons of King Tarquinius. "These two daughters were of very unlike natures, and so were their husbands; for Aruns Tarquinius was of meek and gentle spirit, but his brother Lucius was proud and full of evil; and the younger Tullia, who was the wife of Aruns, was more full of evil than his brother Lucius; and the elder Tullia, who was the wife of Lucius, was as good and gentle as his brother Aruns." [12] In the outcome, "Lucius slew his wife secretly, and the younger Tullia slew her husband; and then they were married to one another, that they might work all the evil of their hearts, according to the will of fate." [13]

The rather nebulous utopianism of Servius Tullius had long been a cause of complaint among the more hardheaded of the patricians, so Lucius Tarquinius experienced no difficulty in gathering support for his design to seize the throne; Servius's attempts to assert his wilted authority ended in his callous slaughter at the hands of a number of the usurper's hotheaded supporters.

"Then the wicked Tullia mounted her chariot, and drove into the Forum, nothing ashamed to go amidst the multitude of men, and she called Lucius out from the Senate House, and said to him, 'Hail to thee, King Tarquinius!' . . . Thus Lucius Tarquinius and the wicked Tullia reigned in the place of the good King Servius." [14]

Rome had exchanged a would-be millenarian for a bloodboltered tyrant, who glowered from the midst of a heavily armed bodyguard. Callously despoiling men of their possessions, he banished those who dared to defy him, outlawing those of the rebellious whom he refrained from slaying. As a matter of policy, however, Tarquinius deliberately cultivated the Latins, even bestowing his daughter on one of their chieftains, for the Latins were needful as allies in Rome's war against the Volscians. Once this enemy was defeated, Tarquinius could devote himself to the tasks of draining the city's more marshy lowlands and erecting a new and

[12] Livy, *op. cit.*
[13] *Ibid.*
[14] *Ibid.*

even more splendid temple on the Capitoline Hill, sweating the poorer folk at this labor "so that many slew themselves for very misery; for in the time of Tarquinius the Tyrant it was happier to die than to live." [15]

But the days of Tarquinius's arbitrary rule were numbered, his expulsion from Rome being precipitated by the unhallowed passion of his son Sextus for his cousin's wife, the lady Lucretia. Determined to possess her, in the absence of her husband with the army besieging the city of Ardea, Sextus surreptitiously made his way to her home at Collatia and swore that "if she yielded not to him, he would slay her and one of her slaves with her, and say to her husband that he had slain her in her adultery." Having accomplished his fell purpose Sextus returned whence he had come.

Then Lucretia sent to Rome for her father, and to the camp at Ardea for her husband, and they came in haste, and with them Brutus,[16] the nephew of the King. And they came in and asked if all were well. Then she told them what was done. "But," she said, "my body only has suffered the shame, for my will consented not to the deed. Therefore," she cried, "avenge me on the wretch Sextus. But though my heart has not sinned, I can live no longer. Lucretia will not set an example of living in unchastity." So she drew forth a knife and stabbed herself to the heart.

When they saw that, her father and her husband cried aloud, but Brutus drew the knife from the wound, and, holding it up aloft, spoke thus: "By this pure blood I swear before the gods that I will pursue Lucius Tarquinius the Proud and all his bloody house with fire and sword, or in whatsoever way I may, and that neither they nor any other shall hereafter be Kings in Rome." [17]

With the rape of Lucretia the long-simmering resentment at Tarquinius's tyrannous rule came to a head. Brutus, supported by Lucretius, Prefect of the City, found himself at the head of a popular movement whose purpose was the banishment of the whole brood of the Tarquinii. With the army turned against him and the gates of Rome shut in his

---

[15] Dionysius (Dionysius Helicarnassensis), *The Roman Antiquities.*

[16] Lucius Junius, whom men misguidedly called Brutus—that is, the dullard.

[17] Vergil (Publius Vergilius Maro), *The Aeneid.*

face, Tarquinius Superbus had no choice but to accept the inevitable. Accompanied by his unendearing sons, Titus and Aruns, he went into sullen exile at Caere in Etruria; the repellent Sextus fled to Garbii, where he had once exercised local authority. It was their memory of his former abuse of power which impelled the inhabitants of Garbii to slay the unrepentant fugitive before he could work further mischief.

Thus in 510 B.C. Rome finally rejected a monarchical system of governance in favor of Patrician rule based upon the popular vote; and the inhabitants of the City of the Seven Hills were left to resolve the problem whether any government, not too strong for the liberties of its people, can be powerful enough to function efficiently in times of grave emergency.

Chapter II

GROWING PAINS

"It is not the beginning, but the continuing the same until the end, until it be thoroughly finished, that yields the true glory."

—Sir Francis Drake

"All power tends to corrupt," Acton pronounced, "and absolute power corrupts absolutely"—whether wielded arbitrarily by an autocratic sovereign or irresponsibly by an ochlocracy.

In the natural revulsion following on the banishment of the Tarquinii Rome underwent a phase of that social unrest and uncertainty which invariably characterizes the aftermath of any major political upheaval. The general feeling of being dangerously adrift was temporarily allayed, however, by the adoption of a republican form of government and the election by the Great Assembly of the *Curies* of two Consuls, who were to hold sovereign power alternately for a month at a time. The first pair to be elevated to this high office were L. Junius Brutus and L. Tarquinius Collatinus. The

State had become the *Senatus Populusque Romanus,* and its leaders were so fixedly resolved to stamp out all memory of the abhorred tyranny of Tarquinius the Proud that the Consul Collatinus, being remotely of the same blood as the oppressor, was speedily forced to relinquish his office in favor of Valerius Publicola, who was entirely free of the taint.

A forlorn attempt on the part of Tarquinius to regain his lost kingdom by force of arms was defeated, although at the cost of Brutus, who fell in the act of dispatching the tyrant's son, Aruns, riding in the forefront of the hostile cavalry. A second attempt by Tarquinius to gain the City of Rome was supported by forces under Lars Porsena of Clusium, a town on the river Clanis, a tributary of the Tiber. So swift was the rejected King's approach to his objective that the Sublican Bridge was reached before it was possible to sound the general alarm. But for the gallantry of Horatius Cocles and two comrades, who held the bridge against all comers, the position would have been lost and Rome itself penetrated.

Siege operations ensued which reduced the citizens of Rome to sorry straits from hunger, since they had failed to stock their stronghold with the necessary victuals to withstand a long investment. But Porsena was no less weary of the protracted beleaguerment and only too ready to come to terms with the city's stubborn defenders. So once again Tarquinius's attempt to win his way back to power was decisively frustrated.[1]

Experience throughout the siege had brought it painfully home to the Senate that Consuls chosen by the people for their administrative and gubernatorial abilities in times of peace might well lack the military skill required of them in time of conflict. It was determined, therefore, to appoint, for six-month periods, a single war-leader, to be called Dictator, or Master of the People, armed with sovereign power, free to act on his own judgment, and required only to justify himself by results. An assistant—the equivalent of a modern Chief of Staff—was also sanctioned and given the title of Master of the Horse. Thus the need, under war conditions, to give priority to the decisions of the military, unhampered by ill-formed and stultifying civilian interference, was clearly and unreservedly accorded recognition.

The measure was completely justified with Tarquinius's

---

[1] Some chroniclers insist that for a time' Porsena was in actual possession of Rome, from which he was ultimately driven by force of arms.

final attempt to regain what he still regarded as his rightful heritage. Supported by a numerous Latin host, the exile met the Roman Legions in head-on battle at Lake Regillus, in the land of the Tuscans. A vicious struggle ended in the complete rout of the Latins, with the loss of their chieftain and the death in action of Tarquinius's last surviving son. Defeated and dismayed, the Latins hastened to come to terms with a triumphant but exhausted Rome, while Tarquinius fled to the Greek city of Cumae, where he died four years after his defeat in the battle of Lake Regillus.

Rome's struggle to preserve her national integrity had committed all classes of the community to the fray, Plebeians being called from their farmsteads and vineyards to fight side by side with the Patricians and their clients. And a "people's war" invariably has the after-effect of subtly proletarianizing the victor nation, since its lower orders are apt to demand a greater return for their exertions than are those who regard service to the country in its hour of need, not as a bargaining point, but as a moral obligation. To this state of affairs the Rome of early Consulate days was no exception. As an outcome of the recent years of intermittent strife the borderlands had been brought to such ruin that their Plebeian inhabitants were convinced that the central authorities owed them substantial compensation. Furthermore, it was a long-standing grievance of the lower orders that, despite the wealth some of them had contrived to accumulate, the Patricians still regarded themselves as belonging to so superior a class that none of their members could contemplate marriage with any individual born out of the pale of their own caste.[2] Lastly, the law of debtor and creditor pressed with considerable severity on the Plebeian who defaulted on a loan or failed to repay it with absolute punctuality. Any borrower who neglected to meet his obligation could be summoned before the Patrician Praetor who was legally authorized to assign the defaulter as a bondsman to his creditor. Were a debt incurred without formal contract and subsequently not met, after a lapse of thirty days the creditor was empowered to arrest the debtor, and, if the money still remained unpaid after sixty days, put the wretched creature to death or sell him as a slave to the highest bidder.

For fifteen years the Plebeians continued to air this par-

[2] Liddell, *op. cit.* This was expressed by the Roman dictate that there was no right of *connubium* between Patricians and any inferior class.

ticular grievance without success; the haughty Consul Appius Claudius, and the Senate, refused all concessions. It was not until the Plebeians threatened to secede from the general community and build a city for themselves on an eminence overlooking the junction of the Tiber and the Anio that steps were taken to placate them. Ultimately it was agreed that "the debtors who could not pay should have their debts cancelled, and that those who had been given into bondage should be restored to freedom. This for the past. As a security for the future, it was conceded that two Plebeians should be appointed for the sole purpose of protecting the people from the Patrician magistrates. These two officers were to be called Tribunes of the Plebs; their persons were to be sacred and inviolable during their year of office; their houses were to be open continually, that all who needed their aid might demand it without delay." [3] In due course the number of these Tribunes was increased to five, and eventually to ten; and although they did not take rank as members of the Senate, they early gained the privilege of attending its deliberations. Above all, "they acquired the great and perilous power of the Veto, by which any one of their number might stop any law, impede the action of any magistrate, or arrest any degree of the Senate, without cause assigned." [1]

Rule by an élite had been modulated into rule under a code of laws whose provisions applied equally to all sections of the community; a form of governance only possible with a populace possessed of a balance, sophistication, and stability to which, as yet, the Romans could in no sense pretend.

Matters did not rest, therefore, with the appointment of the Tribunes. The Plebeians had flexed their muscles and, having learned something of their strength, were determined to use, if not to abuse, it. And there was no lack of opportunist politicians to curry favor with this rising class in the hope that self-advancement would accrue from posing as its champions.

A significant development in the elaboration of the constitution was the inauguration, under the supervision of the Tribunes, of local assemblies, not unlike the town meetings common to Colonial America, at which matters of regional interest could be thrashed out in a manner which in itself

[3] Dionysius, *op. cit.*
[4] *Ibid.*

constituted a practical education in the give-and-take of politics. By 471 B.C. the forceful Tribune Volero Publilius had secured the passage of a law providing that the election of the Tribunes should be ratified by the tribunal assemblies. Thus these bodies were elevated to a position analogous to that of the national assembly as an organ of the state, enjoying a specific responsibility with regard to national legislation. The right of the Plebeians to deliberate and render decisions in their respective assemblies was thus given unqualified recognition, the Tribunes and the Senate being jointly charged to review and give full consideration to the petitions forwarded by the regional assemblies. If approved by this reviewing body—in which the Plebeians' interests were, of course, the Tribunes' first concern—the resolution acquired the sanctity of law.

In their persistent quest for the unattainable, a perfect system of governance, in 451 B.C. the Romans appointed a Decemvirate to frame and codify a comprehensive corpus of laws whereby justice could be assured to all elements in the State. But although the Decemvirate, which included several Plebeians, completed their work, the Twelve Tables they produced left many openings for class-conscious dissatisfaction and rancorous dispute. And Rome was in no position to indulge in domestic discord, since her people were still under constant threat from their neighbors, whose greed or malice brought them again and again in arms across her borders.

During the sixty years between the fall of the monarchy and the Decemvirate, Rome had been closely beset on all sides. In the century after the Decemvirate the scope of operations gradually expanded while slowly but surely turning in Rome's favor. The Aequians, who in 446 B.C. had laid waste the countryside almost to the gates of the Eternal City, had been reduced to submission by 414 B.C., thus securing the line of communications between Rome and her allies the Hernicans. But from their hill-fortresses the Volscians still raided the more fertile of the Roman lower slopes and campagna, although the northern border gave little trouble since the Etruscans were deeply engaged in a losing struggle with the many roving bands of Samnites. Then, as more and more Gauls poured over the Alps, the settlers already in occupation were swept out of existence by the wave of new immigrants, and the whole area became a Celtic province. With the northern Etruscans so painfully engrossed, Rome was free, in company with her allies, the Latins and the

Hernicans, to set about the conquest of the Veii of southern Etruria. It proved a much longer and more bitterly contested venture than the Roman leaders had anticipated, and one, moreover, which kept the troops in the field the whole year round. Since this meant that the bulk of the soldier-husbandmen were unable to return to their homesteads in time to harvest their crops, they had to be furnished with regular pay. This in turn involved the imposition of a land tax (*tributum*) to produce the necessary funds, a levy sharply resented by the Plebeian landowners, who had no hesitation in voicing their objection to it. Only the defeat in the field of the Plebeian Consular Tribunes Genucius and Titinius served to avert an immediate political crisis over the levy, the whole question of its acceptance being deferred while the Senate anxiously sought a Dictator skilled enough to restore the worsening military situation. He emerged in the person of the Patrician M. Furius Camillus, but his achievement in restoring the army's wilted morale and leading it to victory did not suffice to absolve him from the charge that he had retained more of the booty won from the Veii than was his due. In high dudgeon, he withdrew to Ardea, "praying that, if he were unjustly condemned, Heaven might cause his ungrateful country to rue his loss." [5]

The ministers of vengeance were already at hand: the Gauls, whose conquests had brought them within striking distance, were only too ready to challenge a power whose subjugation they looked forward to with arrogant self-assurance.

The Gauls were a people whose preference had always been for a nomadic, predatory way of life that utterly scorned the establishment of stable communities subsisting on the fruits of the soil they had sown and reaped with their own hands. To support themselves on the spoils they had captured and then move on to further profitable conquests spared them the drudgery of toiling for the means of keeping themselves alive, which they infinitely preferred to secure at swords'-points.

Having trampled the unhappy Etruscans of the Po Valley underfoot, the intruders crossed the Apennines into southern Etruria, laying siege to the Etruscan city of Clusium, whose people promptly applied to Rome for succor. A common enemy makes friends even of erstwhile foes, so the Senate lost no time in sending envoys to warn the Gauls that they would molest the comrades and allies of the Republic at their

[5] Mommsen, *op. cit.*

peril; the emissaries followed up this admonition by actively joining the Clusians in the defense of their city. It was a departure from the customary usages of war deeply resented by Brennus and his savage Senones,[6] who demanded that the offending envoys should be surrendered to them forthwith. But the people of Rome, far from heeding the Gaulish demands, promptly elected all three of their representatives military Tribunes.

On learning of this deliberate affront, Brennus broke up his camp at Clusium and marched his infuriated warriors direct on Rome. The river Clanis, on whose banks Clusium had been built, led the savage horde down to the Tiber beneath Volsinii, and they were within twelve miles of the city before a hastily mustered Roman army could be got together to confront them. The Senones were entirely an infantry force. There were no war chariots nor any cavalry among them, and the tribesmen relied on the impetus of their assault and the paralyzing fury of their onset to bring them victory. Armed with their heavy swords and covered by their huge rawhide shields, they were not easily to be turned back.

Having crossed the Clanis, Brennus and his followers found the Romans drawn up on the banks of the Allia, a little stream that rises in the Sabine Hills to empty itself in the Tiber. With the Allia to their front, the Legions' right had taken up position on some tumbled hilly ground, while their left rested on the Tiber.

Avoiding a frontal assault, Brennus threw the whole weight of his attack on the Roman right, which gave under the impetus and crushing weight of the hammer blows rained upon it. Finding their position turned, the balance of the forces were seized with sudden panic and fled; those on the left of the position plunged headlong into the Tiber in the hope of escaping across the stream to Veii. Many were pierced by Gaulish javelins, many more were drowned; the remnant of the defeated host staggered into Rome to spread news of the disaster. Had the Gauls possessed sufficient military acumen to follow up their success hotfoot Rome could have been theirs almost for the trouble of entering it. But being the wild undisciplined rabble that they were, they were far too happily employed in gloating over their booty and carousing in celebration of their victory to grasp that a battle has not only to be won, but that it has also to be

[6] The Senones were a Celtic tribe in which Gaelic and Cymri elements fought side by side.

kept won—in some instances an even harder task than the attainment of victory itself.

In Rome all was consternation and dismay. Frenzied hordes of fugitives fled over the Tiber and the Hill of Janiculum, Patricians and their clients, Vestal Virgins and their *Flamen,* or priests, of Quirinus, stall-holders and husbandmen—all heading for refuge in the friendly city of Caere. In all the panic and confusion, however, there was a sufficient number of Patricians to band together for a desperate attempt to defend the hill of the Capitol, "the acropolis of Rome, the true home of its citizens and its gods."

Thus when the Gauls belatedly put in an appearance, three days after the encounter on the Allia, they found the walls undefended and the city gates wide open. Fearing some trap, they hesitated a whole day further before stealing into the empty streets, another military blunder since it afforded time for the defenders to provision the Capitol and rally even more volunteers to strengthen its garrison. Thus fortified, the Patricians were able to throw back a Gaulish assault on their defenses to such good purpose that a moiety of the invaders settled down to blockade their objective, while roving bands of their comrades set industriously about the pillage of the countryside.

Meanwhile, such of the fugitives as had reached Veii took heart to deal out swift punishment to certain of the marauding enemy bands, thereafter sending posthaste to Ardea to beg the voluntarily expatriated Camillus to lead them against the main body of the Gauls. It was a plea to which even the deeply aggrieved Camillus could scarcely turn a deaf ear, and he readily agreed to take the field. Yet even in the dire straits prevailing, the demands of protocol had to be observed: the exile must first secure authority to assume command from such members of the Senate as were gathered on the Capitol.

The dangerous errand of getting in touch with the garrison on the Hill was confided to a lusty youth named Pontius Cominius, who swam the Tiber under cover of darkness and climbed up the cliff to the Capitol by a precipitous and therefore unguarded path. Returning unhurt by the same route, he bore the tidings to Veii that the Senate solemnly recalled Camillus and appointed him Dictator.

"But with the morning the Gauls had observed the tracks of his ascent, and resolved that with nightfall they would follow the same path. And when the time came the sentinels were asleep and the watch dogs heard them not. But in the

Capitoline temple the sacred geese of Juno, which Roman piety, even in the day of need had spared, cackled with fear. Roused by the sound, M. Manlius seized sword and shield and rushed to the top of the cliff just in time to dash the foremost Gaul down the rock. The Gaul, as he fell, bore down those behind him; the other Romans coming up slaughtered those few that stood to fight. Thus the cackling of the geese and the courage of Manlius saved the Capitol." [7]

Such is the record of events handed down to posterity, and whatever its degree of truth or falsity, the fact is not to be gainsaid that, thwarted in their attempt to overwhelm the Romans' "last ditch" defense, Brennus and his shaggy followers withdrew whence they had come, leaving a shambles where once had stood the proud City of the Seven Hills.

The shock of the shameful defeat on the banks of the Allia and the humiliation of seeing their gleaming city reduced to smoking ruin might well have demoralized a people less resilient and fundamentally stouthearted than the Romans past all hope of revitalization. But it was not in their nature to be long cast down. Indignantly refusing to countenance any suggestion that they should turn their backs on their ravished capital and seek a new home in Veii, they stolidly set about the task of rebuilding and restoring the metropolis on its original foundations.

With equal determination they put in hand the reorganization of their armed forces, and it is from this point that there can be traced the abandonment of the phalanx, originally adopted from the Etruscan model, in favor of a far less vulnerable battle order based upon the division of the Legions into *maniples,* or units, of an average strength of one hundred twenty men. These were made up of heavily armed infantry, on whom fell the main burden of the fighting. They were preceded into action by *velites,* light troops who acted as skirmishers and as guardians of the main body's flanks. The battle formation adopted by the heavy infantry was one which deployed them in three lines, the first two of which were equipped with a shield, a short heavy stabbing sword, and two or three *pila*—the *pilum* being a six-foot-six javelin capable of being hurled up to thirty paces by a strong, practiced thrower. The third line employed the *hasta,* or thrusting spear.

[7] Such is the legend as related by Livy; other chroniclers aver that the Gauls decamped on learning that their temporary abiding place in the north had been harried by the Veneti.

In action the troops moved in what might best be described as a chessboard formation with an interval the width of the average *maniple* between each of the *maniples*. Thus when the *hastati* [8] of the first line had made contact with the enemy, they could either fall back into the intervals between the *maniples* of the second line (*principes*) or the latter could push forward to fill the gaps between the front line *maniples*. It was an extremely flexible and adaptable formation, equally effective against the massed onrush of the Gauls or an assault by an adversary drawn up in phalanx.

Thus through trial and error, and as the outcome of far-reaching reorganization and rigorous training, Rome created a sternly disciplined fighting force which was destined in the fullness of time to win her the mastery of Italy—and of the known world.

The years of Rome's rebuilding were marked by a number of political developments of no less significance than the reconstruction of the Eternal City itself.

The defensive alliance and loose confederation between Rome and Latium showed unmistakable signs of having worn thin, and as the flood tide of the Gaulish invasion receded, the Latins and even the faithful Hernicans repudiated their association with the Romans, the Hernicans temporarily going to the length of leaguing themselves with a wandering tribe of Celts. Such restless attempts to throw off the Roman yoke proved altogether unavailing. The Senate, with the formidable armed force at its disposal, sternly reasserted its authority, even extending it to secure suzerainty over the Volscians, who had been progressively weakened by the attacks on their flanks and rear by the Samnites, with whom Rome presently concluded a formal treaty of alliance. By 348 B.C. Rome's prestige and predominance throughout the Italian peninsula found significant recognition, when the great North African maritime power of Carthage ratified an agreement with the Senate by which the "barbarians" bound themselves to spare the coastal cities of Latium as long as they remained faithful to Rome. At the same time they guaranteed to restore to the suzerain power any revolted city that might fall into their hands.

Even so, there were some still prepared to dispute Rome's claim to supremacy in Italia, the most prominent of whom

---

[8] They still retained this title although no longer armed with the *hasta,* or thrusting spear.

were to be found among the hardy shepherds of Mount Matese, who with their scattered kindred bore the common name of Samnites. A loose confederation of tribes, owing nothing more than token allegiance to the parent stock in Samnium, huge waves of them had swarmed down from their uplands to drive the Etruscans from Capua and the Greeks from Cumae; while others, turning southward, over-ran Magna Graecia while establishing themselves in Lucania and Campania. Here they lorded it as conquerors, treating the original inhabitants as little more than helots, but in the process turning themselves into flaccid townsmen, so that they speedily lost the virility and self-reliance needed to fend off fresh waves of their kith and kin, eager to despoil—if necessary, by conquest—even those of their own race.

A vain attempt on the part of the Capuans to protect some of their dependents from abuse at the hands of the Samnites drove the Campanians to implore the intercession of the Romans, whose suzerainty over Campania the "hill wolves" had never officially recognized.

Rome's response was prompt and unstinting. The Consuls set forth at the head of two separate armies; that of M. Valerius Corvus entered Campania, to be met by a Samnite host which scattered its opponents' cavalry and fought stub-bornly against the Legions until superior discipline and sheer fighting tenacity forced them to turn and flee. Aban-doning their entrenched camp during the night, the Samnites fell back on the fortified city of Suessula.

The other Roman force, under the command of the Consul A. Cornelius Cossus, having been directed to invade Samnium, set out for Saticula, the nearest Samnite town to Capua. Hereabouts the Apennines run north and south in parallel ranges towering over fertile valleys; the rough roads to be followed by the troops passed through the low-lands. The Consul, pressing on without taking the necessary military precautions, had crossed the first range and reached the intervening valley when, looking back, he saw to his horror that the wooded heights to his rear had disgorged a formidable body of the Samnite foe. To advance into un-known territory with the enemy treading on his heels was almost as dangerous as to turn about and try to dislodge the foe from their position of advantage.

In this perplexity a Tribune named P. Decius pro-posed to occupy with the *hastati* and *principes* of one Legion (that is, sixteen hundred men) an eminence over the way along which the Samnites were coming. The

Consul gave permission; Decius seized the height, which he maintained against all the efforts of the enemy till their favorable moment was lost, and the Consul had led back his army and gained the ridge. When night came, the Samnites remained on the hill and went to sleep. In the second watch Decius led down his men in silence, and they took their way through the slumbering foes. They had got halfway through when one of the Romans in stepping over the Samnites struck against a shield. The noise awoke those at hand; the alarm spread; the Romans then raised a shout, fell on all they met, and got off without loss. They reached their own camp while it was yet night, but they halted outside it till the day was come. At dawn, when their presence was announced, all poured forth to greet them, and Decius was led in triumph through the camp to the Consul, who began to extol his deeds. But Decius interrupted him, saying that now was the time to take the enemy by surprise. The army was then led out, and the scattered Samnites were fallen upon and routed with great slaughter.[9]

Such bleakly ironic situations were bound to arise, of course, as long as the qualifications for appointment to the consulship were political rather than military. Fortunately, among the lesser commanders there was invariably someone of sufficient ability and experience to deal with such perilous developments as the military naïveté of their seniors were so liable to occasion.

The Romans, while strong and able enough to deal with the Samnites when they encountered them in level country, were entirely wanting in experience of mountain warfare, for which, indeed, they were without any tactical doctrine. With their enemies withdrawn to their mountain fastnesses, they were very much at a loss as to how best to follow up such advantage as they had achieved. The situation was further complicated by a mutinous demand on the part of a large number of troops for a more equitable division of such war booty as had so far been accumulated. For at this period—as for long after—service in the Legion entitled the citizen-soldier to share in the spoils of conflict, in addition to his pay and a gratuity in the way of a land grant. Discharge of the principal malcontents only had the effect of inciting their comrades to march on Rome to press their

9 Dionysius, *op. cit.*

demands. So ominously did the situation develop that the Consul M. Valerius Corvus was forced to agree to an amnesty by the terms of which it was conceded that in future no military tribune should be degraded and no soldier discharged from the ranks at the arbitrary direction of a Consul; while all citizen-soldiers were guaranteed a due reward for their service to the State. At the same time a further measure was passed for the relief of debtors, a number of whom had been unable to discharge their liabilities owing to the fact that they had been called up for service with the army. In effect, a common danger inclined the Patricians to concession and the Plebeians to a less grudging sense of loyalty.

Rome had barely recovered from the disaffection and discontent among her own people when her leaders were confronted by the threat of conflict with the combined strength of Latium and Campania. The Latins were determined no longer to tolerate the role of humble dependents, but to assert their equality and, if need be, to support it by force of arms. As they were at pains to emphasize, even when a distracted Rome had left them to sustain the war alone, they had still kept the field against the Samnites, and in so doing won the support of the Campanians. Their demand, therefore, was nothing less than union with Rome on an absolutely equal footing. This was far more than brittle Roman pride was prepared to concede, so both sides hastened their preparations to determine the issue by an appeal to arms.

It was a contest in which the Romans were confronted by adversaries whom they themselves had trained in the technique of warfare. But if militarily the Latin League was strong, politically it was dangerously weak. The cities might favor defiance but the colonies founded outside Latium came solidly to the support of Rome; the Hernicans promptly rallied to their suzerain, and even the turbulent Samnites threw in their lot in defense of their erstwhile opponents. Better Rome than an upstart Latium!

The issue was not long in doubt, and in the final encounter at Trifanum superior generalship ensured victory for the Roman Consul Manlius Torquatus. As the outcome of this defeat the Latin League as a political federation ceased to exist. Those Latin cities not absorbed into the Roman State were completely isolated from one another, with nothing in common but their dependence on their suzerain. Each subject community was bound to the central authority by separate treaty, retaining the privilege of local self-government but without any control over foreign policy. "The old rights of *connubium* (intermarriage) and *commercium* (commerce and settlement) were retained by the Latins only in Rome; all similar intercourse between one Latin town and another was prohibited." [10] Even the strongest communities were under obligation to accept Roman leadership in time of war, while the Volscian port of Antium was designated a Roman burgess colony. A single system of law was introduced, while the same language and similar customs prevailed throughout the whole of Latium. Despite certain rumblings of discontent on the part of the Samnites, it was clearly indicated that local autonomy must content Rome's subjects for the time being, with the hope of full Roman citizenship at some unspecified date in the future to encourage them in their fidelity.

Strong as Rome's leaders had proved themselves to be, their position was not so unassailable that they could afford to disdain a policy which can only be termed unscrupulously opportunist. When the wealthy Greek merchants of Tarentum called in their fellow countrymen of Epirus to help them deal with the Samnite and Lucanian marauders who so constantly plagued them, Rome coldbloodedly took the side of her dependents' opponents. Leaving the Lucanians to carry on their running war with the Greek settlements, the Samnites thereupon turned their whole strength toward challenging the Romans in a life-and-death struggle to determine who should achieve the mastery of Italy.

Roman diplomacy having ensured the support of a number of the tribes with small occasion to cherish the unpredictable Samnites, operations in the field went so much in favor of the Legions that their opponents opened negotiations designed to bring the conflict to a close. But when they found that nothing but unconditional submission would satisfy Roman pride, the Samnites resolved to continue the struggle under their indomitable leader, Gavius Pontius.

Unfortunately for the Romans, the year 321 B.C. brought to consular office two men, T. Venturius and Sp. Postumius, who were utterly without experience of war. Enticed into the defiles of the Apennines by false intelligence, they

10 W. W. How and H. D. Leigh, *A History of Rome.*

found the narrow pass of the Caudine Forks blocked by a strong hostile force. Nor was there any hope of retirement by the way they had come, the pass in rear also being occupied by the enemy. "To advance or to retreat was now equally impossible; they therefore threw up entrenchments in the valley, and remained there, the Samnites not attacking them, in reliance on the aid of famine. At length, when their food was spent and hunger began to be felt, they sent deputies to learn the will of the Samnite leaders. . . . The terms accorded by Pontius were the restoration of the ancient alliance between Rome and Samnium, the withdrawal of Roman colonies from places belonging to the Samnites, and the giving back of all places to which they had a right. The arms and baggage of the vanquished army were, as a matter of course, to be given up to the conquerors." [11]

Under the circumstances the Consuls had no option but grudgingly to accept the terms offered, and after being stripped of all but a single garment and made to undergo the humiliating ceremony of "passing under the yoke," the bulk of the Legionaries were set free to return to Rome, leaving only hostages in the Samnites' hands.

The Roman Senate, however, refused to ratify the convention, pronouncing with a casuistry only too characteristic that it was impossible for them to be bound by Consuls who had exceeded their authority. Negotiations having reached an impasse, active operations were renewed in which Rome was hard put even to keep her hold on Latium and Campania. In 315 B.C. the inhabitants of Nuceria, Nola, Atella, and Calatia came out openly on the side of the Samnites; Sora, on the Upper Liris, expelled its Roman colonists, and fresh hordes of Samnites poured down from their arid heights to oppose the Legions.

It was a contest between the hardy mountain clansmen and the sternly disciplined men of the plains, and slowly but surely discipline and rigorous training got the upper hand. Nola entered into alliance with Rome on favorable terms, and as the other Campanian towns followed Nola's example the Samnites were soundly beaten in the open field and doggedly pursued over the Apennines into Bovianum.

With the Samnites temporarily quiescent, attention could be diverted to deal with the almost equally unruly Etruscans, whose forty-year peace treaty with Rome had expired in 311 B.C. Operations were entrusted to Q. Fabius Maximus

---

[11] Mommsen, *op. cit.* Mommsen justly comments, "How rarely has Rome ever granted a vanquished enemy terms as mild as these!"

Rullianus, who, having lured his opponents into embarking on a war of movement, was successful in securing a series of brilliant victories which entirely justified the bold "forward policy" he had elected to pursue. At the same time a band of Samnites, who had taken advantage of the Roman authorities' preoccupation elsewhere to start a separate uprising, were sternly dealt with by the veteran commander Papirius Cursor.

The dying flames of war were temporarily fanned into vigorous life by the rebellion of Rome's ancient allies, the Hernicans, while the unquellable Samnites took advantage of the general state of unrest to organize a march on Rome by way of the valleys of the Liris and Trerus. Three of the Hernican cities had refused to take the field against their former comrades in arms, and the remainder of the clan quickly abandoned a struggle the only outcome of which could be the loss of such independence as had previously been left them. Sullenly the Samnites also sued for, and were granted, peace. Forced to resign all their conquests, they were permitted to retain their traditional liberties only within their native mountains, to which they were henceforth to be confined.

Rome's resources had been put to very severe strain, but the issue of the struggle had demonstrated her superiority past any peradventure and had made it clear that no single nation could hope to prevail against the indomitable Eternal City.

Rome had granted peace to Samnium very largely to gain the leisure to strengthen her hold on central Italy. A girdle of fortresses ensured the good behavior of the Campanians, while the Hernicans were in no position to indulge in anything more dangerous than *sotto voce* grumblings. In the Volscian district the cities of Arpinum and Trebula had had the burdens of citizenship imposed upon them without its corresponding political privileges. The central hills and the line of communications with them had been carefully secured, while by 299 B.C. more Roman colonists, settled in the old Umbrian town of Nequinum, helped to make good the valley of the Tiber.

In the prevailing circumstances, the Etruscans were of two minds whether to try and persuade the Gauls, who threatened their northern frontier, to lend their swords for the defense of their regional freedom, or to invoke the protection of Rome against the Celtic barbarians.

To the irrepressible Samnites, the prospect of a solid alliance between Rome and Etruria forboded nothing less than the abandonment of their last hope of winning back their independence. Accordingly, while certain Roman forces were intent on watching the approach of a band of wandering Gauls, the Samnites threw themselves into Lucania, and the final struggle between the age-old antagonists was speedily in full spate. The conflict was bitter and protracted, the Samnites gradually losing the aid of such few allies as they had persuaded to support them in arms. With victory for the Romans in the battle of Sentinum (295 B.C.), the task of rounding off the campaign was carried through by Manius Curius, who in 290 B.C. granted Rome's ancient foes an honorable peace. Thereafter, fortresses were built and manned at Minturnae and Sinuessa, on the coast of Campania; the Sabines were subjugated and compelled to accept Roman citizenship without the right of the franchise. A settlement was established at Venusia, on the confines of Samnium, Apulia, and Lucania, to which, in 291 B.C., as many as 20,000 Latin colonists were persuaded to remove themselves.

Tarentum was the one city left to defy the Roman might, and by calling on Greece to redress the balance of power in the peninsula, Tarentum was to give the vanquished yet one more chance of pricking the bubble of Rome's soaring pretensions.

Rome's external policy—to conquer and then to conciliate—admitted of no ambiguity and enjoyed the support of the bulk of the Plebeians as well as the Patricians and their clients. But internally her people had yet to evolve a form of government that would find acceptance with and harmonize all classes of the community. It was a fumbling search for the ideal, which was to offer equal opportunity to the political charlatan and power-hungry *arriviste,* as to men whose sole ambition was to serve their country to the best of their ability. But throughout the agelong quest, Rome's overriding strength resided in the fact that no matter how the various parties in the state might differ on domestic issues, all were prepared broadly to subscribe to the same foreign policy.

Chapter III

༄ ༄

EXPANSION AND ITS CONSEQUENCES

"Such were the times when wild wars broke,
And the mad people of the windy ways
Laid spears against us like a sea."

—Atalanta in Calydon

With the death of Alexander the Great in 323 B.C. the fabulous empire he had created swiftly disintegrated. A number of militaristic Hellenic dynasties arose, forever warring one with the other, forever the prey of the barbarians seeking to win back the territories they had lost in earlier times. Eventually, four great monarchies succeeded in establishing themselves and attaining some degree of stability: the empire of Chandragupta in India, Egypt under the Ptolemies, Asia under the Seleucids, and Macedonia under the Antigonids.

In 287 B.C. Alexander the Great's nephew Pyrrhus, King of Epirus, expelled Demetrius, son of Antigonus, from Macedonia, only in his turn to be driven out of his heritage by Lysimachus, with whom he had temporarily shared dominion over the territory.

With Rome deeply preoccupied in establishing her authority over the Samnites, Etruscans, and other local communities, Sicily's admirable port of Syracuse had been seized by the audacious soldier of fortune Agathocles, son of a humble potter. An opportune marriage had brought him wealth, a glib tongue the support of the gullible, so that by 317 B.C. he had experienced little difficulty in seizing supreme power. Rule in Sicily, however, had brought him into collision with the Carthaginians. A people of Semitic stock, descendants of the Phoenicians, who had colonized Tunisia and founded settlements in Spain, the Carthaginians had long cast predatory eyes on Sicily, possession of which was for many years to remain a matter of bitter warlike dispute. The struggle in which Agathocles temporarily gained the advantage was no more than the prelude to even sterner conflict.

In all of Rome's efforts to establish her hegemony in the Italian peninsula the thriving Graeco-Italian settlement of Tarentum had been left very largely undisturbed. Hemmed in on all sides by Roman satellites, the port was not without a strong infusion of those who favored closer ties with the Eternal City. Yet when a squadron of ten Roman war vessels suddenly appeared in the bay, the majority of the port's inhabitants were easily aroused to retort to this breach of Greek international law by manning their own galleys and putting the intruders to flight. In the course of the encounter four of the Roman craft were sunk and one taken, and the Admiral, Valerius, was numbered among the fallen. Such prisoners as were captured were either put to death or sold into slavery.

The die had been cast. The people of Tarentum were at last committed to the conflict they had so long avoided. To follow up their first successful stroke they marched on the Roman outpost of Thurii, compelling the garrison to withdraw and heavily penalizing those of its citizens who were known to favor the Roman cause.

This was open defiance; but for once the Romans were prepared to temporize, since they were extremely reluctant to drive Tarentum into the arms of Pyrrhus, who had contrived to maintain his regal sway over his petty kingdom of Epirus and was eager for any chance to increase his influence and better his prospects.

Rome's attempt to deal with the prevailing situation by diplomacy was completely thwarted by the activities of the "popular" party, whose leaders in 280 B.C. committed Tarentum to the guardianship of 3,000 Epirots headed by their world conqueror *manqué.* Pyrrhus was speedily followed by additional forces which brought the troops under his command to a total of 20,000 heavily armed Foot, 3,000 Horse, 2,500 archers and slingers, and 20 war elephants. Yet even with this formidable array to give the lead, the Epirot Sovereign found the hopes and promises of a general uprising against Rome to be entirely without substance.

There was nothing sluggish about Rome's countermoves to meet the Epirot challenge. Incipient signs of revolt among the restless Etruscans, Lucanians, and Samnites were sternly suppressed and garrisons were strengthened in the predominantly Grecian towns of Lower Italy, while the main army, under P. Valerius Laevinus, hastened to meet the invader before he could effect junction with the smoldering Samnites or foster insurrection in Magna Graecia.

At the outset the fortune of war favored the Epirot, who soundly beat a Roman force in an encounter at Heraclea. But losses on both sides had been exceptionally heavy, and Pyrrhus was far too cautious a soldier lightly to discount the formidable nature of the task he had undertaken. "Another victory such as this," he was heard to comment, "will send me back to the Epirus without a man!"

Indeed, Pyrrhus was so impressed by the quality of his opponents that he sent an embassy to Rome to try and negotiate terms of settlement. But the indomitable spirit of the Eternal City found voice in the greatest man of her proudest house, the blind, aged, but ever-venerated Consul Appius Claudius. Declaring that Rome would never negotiate while enemy troops defiled her soil, he easily persuaded the Senate to reject the Epirot's proposals. Pyrrhus, who had advanced into Campania in support of his envoy's mission, was therefore goaded into organizing an immediate march on Rome.

But the Senate had not been idle. Rome itself was strongly garrisoned; a reinforced Consul hung doggedly on the Epirot's flank. Hastily plundering that part of Campania in which he was cantoned, Pyrrhus retired to winter quarters in Tarentum, determined, when conditions again allowed, once more to put his fortunes to the test of war.

The second and decisive campaign was fought out in Apulia, where Pyrrhus met his opponents on the plain of Ausculum. The intervention of the Epirot's war elephants just sufficed to turn the tide of battle in his favor.

Wearying of fruitless victories which led to nothing better than another contest of strength, Pyrrhus eagerly responded to the Syracusians' plea to deliver their city-haven from the hands of the Carthaginians, into which it had fallen.

A community of interests, however transitory, will make allies of powers almost as distrustful of each other as they are of their common enemy. Thus Rome and Carthage, temporarily veiling their mutual enmity, bent their joint endeavors to ensuring the Epirot's frustration. With considerable guile the Carthaginians offered to resign all claims to sovereignty over the island on condition that they should be allowed to retain their hold on the port of Lilybaeum. This haven was on the west coast of the island within easy reach of Carthage, its geographical position giving it command of the Tyrrhenian Sea and the easterly approach routes to Sardinia, as well as to Corsica. Pyrrhus scornfully rejected the proposal, since it was clear that if Carthage were allowed to keep a foot in Sicily, it would be perfectly easy for her to regain her dominion over the island once the Epirot had left it for his own kingdom. But the fickle Sicilians were weary of the Epirot's autocratic rule. Negotiating secretly to come to terms with their enemies, their pusillanimity and perverted genius for double-dealing so disgusted Pyrrhus that, declaring the islanders unworthy of salvation, in 278 B.C. he withdrew once more to Tarentum.

With the Epirot's return to the mainland he engaged in a final encounter with the Roman forces on the field of Beneventum. With his troops thrown into demoralized disarray, Pyrrhus was driven to the bleak conclusion that no force he was capable of organizing could confront the sternly disciplined Roman army with any hope of securing decisive victory. Adventurers only become really dangerous when they start to believe in their luck, and in Pyrrhus's case he had the wit to recognize that he had wooed the fickle goddess all in vain.

With the Epirot's departure to his own land [1] the insurrectionary garrison in Tarentum, hemmed in by a Roman army to landward and with a Carthaginian fleet before the harbor, speedily came to terms. The city, deprived of its ships, its army, and even of its walls, had the mortification of losing its prosperity with its independence. Once again it had been demonstrated to Rome's restless satellites that defiance of her authority would promptly be met with pitiless restinguishment.

Rome's struggle for existence had, in effect, expanded into a struggle for predominance throughout the territory which encompassed her, and with unfaltering confidence she had achieved her aim. The years ahead would put her to even sterner tests; but through toil and sweat and even greater sacrifice she would emerge triumphant to wear the diadem which bore witness to her undisputed mastery of the western world.

Although mutual interests had brought Rome and Carthage together temporarily to deal with Pyrrhus's attempt to establish himself in Sicily, rivalry for predominance throughout the Mediterranean portended an inevitable clash between them to determine which of the twain should prevail.

[1] Failing to secure the Crown of Macedon, Pyrrhus fell ingloriously in a street brawl in Argos, struck down by a tile thrown at him by an infuriated harridan.

An industrious yet highly adventurous trading race, the Carthaginians had seamed the lands with their caravan routes and, in pursuit of profitable commerce, had traversed the seas from the spice-laden coast of Coromandel to the rock-girdled shores of Cornwall. Based on Carthage, built a hundred years before the foundation of Rome, on a compact, hilly peninsula elbowing out into the Bay of Tunis, these sturdy, thrusting Phoenicians of the West had possessed the foresight to conclude treaties [2] with Rome which virtually excluded her from western waters and from trading freely either with Libya or Sardinia. Without any pretension to rank as a naval power, and fully preoccupied with her efforts to secure supremacy throughout the Italian peninsula, it was not until this task had been accomplished that it was brought home to the Roman people how irksomely their compact with the Carthaginians restricted them.

Although separated from the mainland by the Straits of Messina (Messana), Sicily was obviously an extension of Roman territory. As matters stood, Hiero II of Syracuse reigned over no more than a sliver of the island; the balance of the terrain was regarded by the Carthaginians as rightfully their own.

The vital issue between Rome and Carthage was precipitated when a band of mercenaries captured Messana by treachery, violently ejected the inhabitants, and made free with their property. Under the cognomen of Mamertines they held the key to Sicily, and in concert with certain mutinous Campanians who had seized Rhegium, [3] controlled the passage of the Straits.

Hiero was determined to destroy the nest of freebooters and mutineers in Messana, and to this end organized a force far superior to anything the Mamertines could put into the field. In their hour of peril the lawless occupants of Messana were sharply divided. One faction was strongly in favor of calling on the Carthaginians for aid; a party of equal strength preferred to seek the backing of Rome, confident that reluctance to see the Carthaginians establish themselves firmly in Sicily would persuade the Senate to overlook the freebooters' earlier defiance of it. The request for aid was duly forwarded, and with it Rome was brought face to face with the most momentous decision in her whole history. To accede to the petition would inevitably lead to war with the

---

[2] The treaty of 509 B.C., renewed in 348 B.C., and the even more restrictive compact of 306 B.C.

[3] The present-day port of Reggio.

Carthaginians. Yet were the opportunity let slip, the whole of
the richly productive island would undoubtedly fall under
the sovereignty of Carthage in perpetuity. Since alliances
are rarely founded upon anything but expedience, in the
upshot the Senate voted that the Mamertines should be afforded every assistance. Command of the army to be sent
across the Straits was entrusted to the Consul Appius Claudius Caudex.[4]

Meanwhile, command of the Carthaginian forces in Sicily
and of their Mamertine supporters had been entrusted to the
experienced North African leader Hanno. Nonetheless, by
passing the Straits under cover of the night, Appius Claudius
contrived to inflict so crushing a defeat on Hanno that the
discomfited Carthaginian was only too glad to escape with
his life. As a salutary reminder of what defiance of Roman
power brought in its train, Appius Claudius then proceeded
to plunder the countryside right up to the gates of Syracuse.

Having deliberately staked their claim to Sicily, the Senate confronted the inevitability of a lengthy war with Carthage with reasonable fortitude. It is highly questionable,
however, if any of the "potent grave and reverend signiors"
envisaged a conflict whose first phase was destined to last
for three-and-twenty years—from 264 to 241 B.C.

From the outset it was quite clear to the Roman authorities that the final defeat of Carthage could only be ensured
by vanquishing her on the element she had made peculiarly her own. Yet primarily the Romans were a pastoral
people, with an extremely limited seaboard to foster a community practiced—as were their rivals—in all the seagoing
skills, attributes they had hitherto tended to discount. However, since naval warfare appeared to be ineludible, as a
nation of hardheaded realists they set about the task of mastering its technique as speedily as possible.

At the outset of the campaign in Sicily, of course, the
Romans were fighting on their familiar *terra firma*. Thus
when the Carthaginians threw a considerable force into the
coastal town of Agrigentum, under the command of Hannibal,[5] the Consul M. Valerius Maximus, having won over
Hiero of Syracuse, was able to blockade the stronghold and
cut off the inflow of supplies and reinforcements. Sent to the

4 Son of the venerated Censor.

5 He was the son of Gisco, one of Carthage's most distinguished
military commanders.

succor of the beleaguered city, Hanno was decisively defeated, and a sortie by the garrison was as summarily repelled; Hannibal escaped by night through the hostile lines, leaving Agrigentum to the Romans' none too tender mercy.

With Agrigentum, Messana, and Syracuse in their hands, the Romans steadily drove their adversaries back on their western strongholds. It was obvious, however, that the expulsion of the enemy from Sicily would still leave the issue undetermined; that the conflict would simply be transferred from dry land to salt water. With ample supplies of admirable timber readily at hand, Rome thereupon set about the hasty construction of a battle fleet, the manpower for which could be amplified by calling on the Lucanians and other allies whose people included a number of experienced seafarers.

To all intents and purposes, the ship's company was divided into those whose task was to "work" the vessel and those whose business it was to "fight" it. Since the latter component was made up of the typical Legionary, the aim was to stage something as nearly resembling a land battle as circumstances would permit. This entailed grappling an enemy vessel and then "boarding and entering" it to fight out the issue hand-to-hand, in the time-honored way.

To this end the Romans devised an exceedingly ingenious boarding ramp, termed the *corvus,* which could be lowered in an instant, a heavy spike in the fore-end thudding into the enemy vessel to pinion it. Once in position, the Legionaries could swarm across it, close with their antagonists, and fight out the issue in the manner to which they were thoroughly accustomed. In short, close combat was substituted for the tactical handling of the vessels themselves, a technique of which the Romans were yet to achieve mastery.

Rome's first essay in naval warfare, in 260 B.C., could scarcely have been more discouraging. Putting to sea with seventeen ships and leaving the rest of the fleet to follow, the Consul Gnaeus Cornelius Scipio was surprised off Lipara and captured, with the whole of his squadron, by the Carthaginians. His colleague, however, the Plebeian commander C. Duilius, evened the score by gaining a decisive victory over Hannibal's fleet of one hundred thirty vessels, off the promontory of Mylae, to the northeast of Messana. Carthage had been beaten on her own particular element, with the loss of fifty of her ships, thirty-one of which had been captured by boarding parties.

In the following years only the stubborn, indomitable spirit of Hamilcar Barca—with his base in Panormus—served to stiffen his countrymen's morale and maintain the fighting spirit of the troops garrisoning the few strongholds on the western coast of Sicily which still remained in Carthaginian possession. The severe measures taken by Rome with the helpless Greek States, however, tended to impair her hold on Sicily, although Scipio the Elder's victory over Hanno and his consequent capture of Aleria, in Corsica, served to deprive Carthage of an essential source of ship's timber.

For eight years the war dragged on indecisively, with Rome holding the slightly more favorable balance of advantage. In 256 B.C., even with Rome's resources as strained as those of her fretful allies, the Senate determined to carry the fight to North Africa itself, where the enemy's want of a proper fortress system should favor a bold offensive. War for a limited objective—Sicily—had been expanded into a campaign for the total overthrow of a rival with whom it had become altogether too dangerous to palter.

An expeditionary force of 40,000 picked troops and 100,-000 seafarers embarked on 330 vessels, under the command of the Consuls M. Atilius Regulus and L. Lanlius Volso. Off Economus, midway between Gela and Agrigentum, their armament encountered an armada of 350 ships manned by 150,000 troops and seamen, led by Hanno and Hamilcar. The Romans were proceeding in wedge formation, in what amounted to a hollow triangle, while the Punic fleet advanced in an extended line of four divisions, with its left thrown forward at an obtuse angle to hug the Sicilian coast, and its right deployed to outflank the hostile array as it passed abeam.

Tactically, the Romans found themselves at serious disadvantage from the very outset. Their wedge, designed to split the Punic line, was itself broken by the feigned withdrawal of the hostile center and its own overexuberant advance; while the Punic right swooped on their antagonists' rear guard, and their left on the third Roman division, which hastened to throw off the transports it had been assigned to guard. But although the Romans might be outmaneuvered and outsailed, they were anything but outmatched. By their ingenious employment of the *corvus* and their sheer fighting quality, they were able to defeat the enemy center and relieve their own hard-pressed rear. Their own loss of twenty-four vessels was more than balanced by the capture or destruction of ninety-four belonging to the enemy.

What arouses the greatest astonishment about this encounter is the fact that the Carthaginians, with their far greater skill in sea-fighing, should have adopted a formation which put a premium on the whole engagement's degenerating into an inchoate *mêlée*. For "the surer of himself an Admiral is, the finer the tactical development of his fleet, the better his Captains, the more reluctant must he necessarily be to enter into a *mêlée* with equal forces, in which all these advantages will be thrown away, chance reign supreme, and his fleet placed on terms of equality with an assemblage of ships which have never before acted together." [6] It was because the *mêlée* presented the Romans with the opportunity to engage in the particular type of fighting in which they excelled that what should have been their defeat was turned into outstanding victory.

After a necessary delay for repairs, the elated victors headed for the coast of Africa, where the troops were disembarked to set up an entranched camp at Clupea. Since Carthage, like Britain in the seventeenth and eighteenth centuries, put all her trust for defense not in fortified strongholds but in her floating "wooden walls," the fruitful land lay wide open before them. Yet it was at this juncture that the Senate, with the ineradicable but fatal itch of the civilian executive to interfere in matters military, took it upon themselves to recall Manlius and the greater part of the fleet and the army, leaving Regulus to attempt completion of Carthage's conquest with a mere 40 ships, 500 Horse and 15,000 Foot. Had the lone Consul set about his task with real celerity, there is every likelihood that it could have been accomplished. Capturing Tunis, it was not until the next spring that he appeared before Carthage, a great city that by now had been reduced to the direst straits. With the Roman enemy at the gate, the Numidians had taken advantage of the general confusion to overrun and pillage all the countryside accessible to them. In the city itself famine and epidemic disease were exacting an increasingly heavy toll. In desperation, the Council sent an embassy to the Proconsul to learn on what terms he would be prepared to make peace. Elated by what appeared to be easily won success, Regulus demanded that the Carthaginians dismantle the whole of their fleet, cede all Sicily, with Sardinia, and meet all the expenses of the war. This was to seek altogether too great an advantage of abjection. Public indignation demanded the scornful rejection of so arrogant a proposal. In a pinch Numidian Horse and Greek mercenaries could be hired, while the civic force, although no more than partially trained in arms, declared their readiness to fight to the death in defense of their hearths and the altars of their gods. All

[6] Captain A. T. Mahan, *The Influence of Sea Power Upon History*.

that was required was a commander with the needful military skill to lead them, and fortunately he was to hand in the person of the Lacedaemonian soldier of fortune Xanthippus.

Appointed Commander-in-Chief, Xanthippus boldly took the field at the head of a motley throng of mercenaries and citizen-soldiery, supported by a large body of war elephants. In the ensuing encounter the Romans committed the cardinal error of underestimating the ability of the opposing General and the fighting quality of his followers. The outcome was a resounding defeat for Roman arms, with Regulus himself taken captive and not more than a couple of hundred of his men succeeding in making good their retreat to Clupea.

This was unmitigated calamity, but the Senate hastened to do their utmost to repair it. The Consuls for the year 255 B.C. were ordered to put to sea and bring off the garrison and fugitives from Clupea. In this task they were successful, thereafter putting out for Sicily. But off Camarina they were caught by a sudden tempest; almost the whole fleet was wrecked, and the coast of Sicily from Camarina to Pachynus was strewn with fragments of ships and the bodies of men.

Indomitably, the Romans set to work to make good their losses. Fresh troops were recruited and put under intensive training; keels were laid down for two hundred and twenty new vessels; and in the incredibly short space of three months they were all ready for sea.

For the time being operations in North Africa were suspended. There was ample work still to do in Sicily, where Cornelius Scipio surprised the rich and populous Panormus,[7] a stroke which gave the Romans a new base and endowed them with virtually unchallenged control of the north coast of the island. In 253 B.C., however, the Roman fleet while sailing in unfamiliar waters off the coast of Africa was again caught in a violent storm, losing over one hundred and fifty vessels. In consequence, naval activities were reduced to convoy duties and sporadic patrols off the coast. In military operations there was something of a lull until Hasdrubal, the son-in-law of Hamilcar, reinforced the Carthaginian forces in Lilybaeum with 30,000 men and 140 war elephants, moving on to challenge L. Caecilius Metellus before the walls of Panormus.

Siege operations were abruptly terminated when, in a shattering sortie, Metellus achieved a brilliant victory, putting the Carthaginians and their array of war-elephants com-

7 The modern Palermo.

pletely to rout. "One hundred and twenty elephants were captured; and the Carthaginian army, whose strength depended upon these animals, was obliged once more to shut itself up in its fortresses." [8] Since the important island of Lipara was already in Roman possession and the coastal haven of Eryx soon fell into their hands, their enemies now retained nothing but the ports of Drepana and Lilybaeum. Under the circumstances Carthage, for the second time, offered peace.

Rome, however, was too confident of her ascendancy to propose anything like acceptable terms. So operations were resumed with the siege of the Carthaginian forces in Lilybaeum. But despite the best efforts of the besiegers supplies and reinforcements continued to be thrown in to the beleaguered garrison, while those investing the town were the constant prey of raiding parties of Carthaginian Horse. A Roman attempt to create a diversion by seizing the other enemy stronghold of Drepanum by a *coup de main* proved a costly failure. This setback was followed by the Carthaginians' utter destruction of a fleet of Roman transports off Sicily's southern coast.

Rome was wellnigh exhausted. The strain on her material resources had been exceeded only by that imposed on her manpower. The damage she had suffered to her trade and agriculture was enormous. Between 252 and 247 B.C. her burgess roll fell by a sixth; taxation had risen as her coinage had progressively become debased. Yet all along both the Government and the people "fully realized that victory was only possible if Carthage could be defeated at sea," [9] a bleakly discouraging prospect to a people whose naval policy, fundamentally, was to avoid having one.

All in all, however, Carthage was in little better state than Rome. Drained by her losses, divided in her councils, her people groaning and mutinous under their burden of taxation, she failed to take advantage of her success at sea by vigorous action on the land.

Then once again the Romans aroused themselves to a supreme effort. Voluntary contributions and a compulsory State loan found the necessary funds to create an entirely new fleet of two hundred vessels, manned by 60,000 men, and in 241 B.C. it put to sea under the command of the Patrician Consul G. Lutatius Catulus.

---

[8] Mommsen, *op. cit.* The Romans constructed huge rafts to ferry the captured elephants across to the mainland.

[9] Mommsen, *op. cit.*

Intelligence that this formidable armada had occupied the harbors of Drepana and Lilybaeum impelled the Carthaginian authorities to send Hanno, at the head of a hastily equipped force of two hundred fifty sail and accompanying transports, to the relief of these vital Sicilian outposts. Despite a high wind and a running sea favorable to superior pilotage, the Carthaginians, in their heavily overladen craft, found themselves outsailed and outmaneuvered near the little island of Aegusa. "The last great effort of the Roman patriots had brought fruit; it brought victory, and with victory peace." [10]

By the terms of the compact concluded between the rivals Carthage was to pay an indemnity of 3,200 Euboic talents, return all prisoners without ransom, and surrender Sicily with its adjacent islands. For the time being her maritime predominance had vanished, and with its loss went her control of Mediterranean commerce, while her own land was to be plagued by a revolt of the mercenaries in her pay which called for all Hamilcar Barca's ruthless energy for its suppression. Rome had gained her first province, was shortly to acquire Sardinia and Corsica, and was clearly mistress of her own seas. Yet it was abundantly evident that "the new Roman navalism was the handmaid of Roman soldiering; and the character of the naval war, with its disasters, was not such as to turn the Romans into sailors or to inspire in them more than a gloomy determination not to be beaten by the sea." [11]

With Carthage apparently quiescent, Rome was free to turn her attention to consolidating her sway over her new possessions at the foot of the Italian peninsula. In Sicily Hiero II was endowed with a show of independence which lay entirely at Rome's indulgence. Messana, by virtue of its importance to Roman shipping, was transformed into a federated State; other communities were granted autonomy on payment of a tithe of their produce, although a heavy proportion of the land passed into the possession of the victors and a few favored Sicilians. In Corsica and Sardinia stern measures had to be taken to deal with the sporadic resistance movements by which these islands continued to be pestered.

On the mainland the Ligurians continued to be a thorn in the flesh of the authorities for some considerable time; Car-

10 Mommsen, *op. cit.*
11 F. E. Adcock, *The Roman Art of War Under the Republic.*

thaginian agents were as active to stir up trouble in Liguria as in the islands. The Adriatic had become a Roman sea, but complaints of the piracy practiced by Illyrian freebooters on Roman trade led to an open breach and a resort to arms. In the ensuing conflict Illyria was speedily reduced to submission. Her land was made tributary and restrictions were placed on the movements of her armed ships, penalties at which her Greek kinsmen of Macedon looked on unmoved. In due course the Greek States of Corcyra, Epidamnus, and Apollonia came under consular authority, and Demetrius of Pharos was rewarded for his timely aid in the recent conflict by the award of certain territories in Dalmatia. Conquest—pacification—confederation: however stumblingly, the Alexandrian concept of *Homonoia* had become the *leitmotif* of Roman policy.

With her relationship established with the Greek territories bordering the Adriatic, Rome next turned her energies to the extension of her natural boundaries to the north, where the Alps formed the obvious geographical frontier. But the plain of the Po and the mountain passes were still in Celtic hands. Forty-five years had elapsed since the last Gallic war, for during the Pyrrhic and Punic conflicts the Gauls, somewhat surprisingly, had kept the peace. But a new and far less complacent generation had arisen, in conspiratorial communication with the Transalpine Celts, and ripe for insurrection.

Sporadic outbreaks in 238 and 237 B.C. culminated in a widespread uprising in 236 B.C. which brought a powerful barbarian force before Rome's northern outpost of Ariminum. But where pollarchy prevails competent warfare is out of the question. Disputed authority and dissension in the Celtic ranks led to a speedy settlement on the moderate terms imposed by Rome. A far more serious uprising was provoked by an agrarian law, sponsored by the Plebeian Consul G. Flaminius, which threatened to swamp Celtic-held territories with the surplus population of Rome and its immediate environs. In 225 B.C. some 50,000 warriors on foot, supported by another 20,000 on horseback, advanced by way of the Apennines directly on the capital. Of the two consular armies currently serving with the Eagles one was in Sardinia and the other at Ariminum, where it could easily be bypassed. Both, however, were given orders to repair in all haste to Etruria, the point of immediate danger. Pending the arrival of the army of Sardinia, Etruscan and Sabine militia sought to block the route by which the invaders must advance, while the Umbrian levies were in position to fall on their flank; a reserve of 50,000 was hastily mustered for the defense of Rome itself.

Plundering as they went, the Gauls dealt harshly with such of the militia as sought to engage them, and it was not until the Legions from Sardinia were in position to challenge them that their destructive progress was abruptly halted. Near Telamon, at the mouth of the river Ombrone, in a victory as decisive as any achieved by Roman arms, 40,000 of the invaders perished on the field, while 10,000 captives went to swell the galley row-benches and the labor gangs on the estates of the Patricians and their clients.

Under the leadership of Flaminius, the victory of Telamon was followed by the systematic if somewhat pedestrian conquest of Cisalpine Gaul. With colonies established, in 218 B.C., at Placentia, Cremona, and Mutina, Rome had secured her flank and extended her boundary to the Alps.

Rome's preoccupation with her internal problems had by no means gone unremarked in a resurgent Carthage. To compensate for surrendered Sicily, Hamilcar Barca was encouraged to penetrate and colonize southeast Spain, where he founded a new Carthage—Cartagena. In 229 B.C. Hamilcar died, and the reins of leadership were taken over by his son-in-law Hasdrubal, who negotiated a settlement with the Romans which laid down that while the Carthaginians should exercise control south of the river Ebro, that part of Spain to the north of it should be regarded as a Roman sphere of influence. South of the stream stood the independent Greek city of Saguntum,[12] whose continued alliance with Rome was allowed for in the compact.

In 221 B.C. Hasdrubal was assassinated, the victim of a private vengeance. He was succeeded as a national leader by Hannibal, the son of Hamilcar Barca and the heir to his military genius and his lifelong determination to be avenged on Rome.

The prelude to a renewal of strife between the age-old rivals was Hannibal's siege of Saguntum, whose neutrality he violated on the plea that Rome had already transgressed it by her interference in local politics. Culpably neglected in its hour of peril, the city fell after eight months' close investment; and Hannibal had the satisfaction of knowing that, having secured his rear and a line of communications with the homeland, he could forge ahead with his plans for the overthrow of the hereditary enemy, whose strength, as

[12] The modern Sagunto.

he was shrewd enough to realize, had gained immeasurably from Italy's consolidation.

Hannibal's plans envisaged a descent on Rome itself, not by sea but from a *point d'appui* in Cisalpine Gaul, from which he could maintain overland contact with his Spanish base. Guides, supplies, "intelligence" sources, and even recruits were almost certain to be found among the restless and inflammable Gauls; while Philip V of Macedon, long irritated by the trend of Roman policy, might be persuaded actively to support the invader and even to beguile the peninsula's Graeco-Italian settlers into harrying the Romans from the southeast.

With Spain secured by 2,500 Horse, 12,000 Foot and 29 war-elephants, in the early days of May, 218 B.C., Hannibal started on his toilsome passage of the Pyrenees and the Alps, at the head of 102,000 Horse and Foot and 37 of the mammoth beasts that served as his principal "shock troops." The transit of the Pyrenees alone cost him 20,000 men, while it was needful to leave Hanno behind with a force of 10,000 to secure the lines of communication. Moreover, since at the moment Philip of Macedon was in arms against the Spartans and the Aeolians, he could not be looked to for support. It was possible, therefore, that Rome, with her current command of the sea, might launch a sudden attack on Carthage itself. However, as another commander was to point out many centuries later, "war is an option of risks," and Hannibal was determined to drive ahead.

The first clash came when the Carthaginians, moving down the left bank of the river Ticinus, suddenly gained touch with a Roman force mustered in some haste by Scipio the Elder. Surprise was mutual; but in the vigorous onfall that ensued the Roman Legions were routed; the Horse, outflanked and taken in rear by the Numidian cavalry, were put to flight, bearing in their midst their wounded Consul, whose life had been saved by the exertions of his son, the future Scipio Africanus.

With inferior numbers and a weak cavalry element, the Consul fell back until he could re-marshal his men under the shelter of Placentia's stout walls. Playing for time, which should bring him reinforcements, Scipio decided to cross the Trebbia and take up a strong position on a spur of the Apennines, a feat he succeeded in accomplishing although harried by enemy cavalry, which only drew off to plunder the Romans' recent camping site.

Meanwhile, the Senate had recalled the Consul Sempronius Longus and his troops from Sicily, where the only success scored by the Carthaginians had been their capture of the off-lying Liparian islands.

Effecting a junction with the elder Scipio, the rashly ambitious Sempronius permitted himself to be lured into a battleground of Hannibal's choosing. The Roman Horse were speedily overcome and the Numidians then drove hard at the Legions' flanks. At the same time another enemy force emerged from concealment to fall on the Romans in the rear. Held in front, outflanked, and with their rear under surprise assault, only the admirable discipline of the hard core of Legionaries enabled them to cut their way clear. Out of the 40,000 Roman troops engaged, not more than 10,000 survived to withdraw hurriedly to Placentia; their unfortunate comrades were killed in the fight, drowned in the Trebia, or trampled to death on the battlefield itself by the trumpeting war-elephants.

The Consuls elected for the year 217 B.C. were Gnaeus Servilius and Gaius Flaminius. Servilius with his army at Ariminum, and Flaminius at Arretium, guarded the two highways leading from the plain of the Po to Rome. Hannibal, seeking to surprise Flaminius, moved by way of Genoa to Faesulae, but his attempts to lure the Roman out of his camp were without success, the example of Sempronius being far too fresh in his successor's mind. Hannibal thereupon moved right round the Roman camp and positioned himself between Flaminius and the capital. Still Flaminius did not move, and it was not until the Carthaginian had marched south to reach the vicinity of Lake Trasimene that he learned that the Consul had broken camp and was following him.

Once more the Roman weakness in scouting led to their being ambushed. Flaminius himself was slain, and a mere 6,000 men contrived to cut their way clear, leaving 15,000 fallen and as many to be rounded up as captives.

The road to Rome lay temptingly wide open. But Hannibal was fully aware that the capital was strongly garrisoned and could speedily raise additional forces. It would be impossible to capture the city except by close investment, and the Carthaginian was without the necessary siege engines needful for the task.

In Rome itself the gravity of the situation in the field led to the appointment as Dictator of the experienced but cautious Quintus Fabius Maximus. Deliberately avoiding anything in the nature of a major engagement, it was the fixed design of "the Laggard"—as the impatient Romans dubbed him—gradually but steadily to wear down his opponent's strength. Whenever Hannibal moved, Fabius followed, harassing his foragers, cutting off stragglers, nipping off a stray patrol, but never permitting himself to be drawn into full-scale battle.[13]

With the spring of 216 B.C. Fabius's term as Dictator expired. In his place G. Terentius Varro and L. Aemilius Paulus were appointed Consuls. Of the two, Varro was far more inclined than his colleague to pursue a vigorous, aggressive policy.

Hannibal had spent the winter at Geronium; the district having been stripped bare of grain and forage, spring found him under the necessity of moving elsewhere. At Cannae, on the river Aufidus, the Romans were known to have accumulated a great store of foodstuffs and forage, garnered from the fruitful plains of Apulia. Hard put to subsist his motley following, Hannibal marched swiftly around the flank of the Roman forces confronting him, hastened to Cannae, and captured it by a *coup de main*. By this shrewd stroke he cut off his enemies from their supplies and secured them for his own use.

Hard on the Carthaginians' heels, the Roman forces marched to Canusium, within striking distance of the enemy host at Cannae. At this juncture the Romans had under command 7,200 Horse and 80,000 Foot; Hannibal's forces totaled 10,000 cavalry and 40,000 infantry.

The day after the arrival of the Romans at Canusium it was Varro's turn to take over command, and he was feverishly eager to display his skill and valor. Marching out of camp, he offered battle, and Hannibal closed with him, employing no more than his cavalry and 8,000 light infantry in a day-long action which, as the Carthaginians intended, left Varro in possession of the field and under the delusive conviction that he had won a signal victory.

With Aemilius in command, on the day following, a third of the troops were sent across the Aufidus to protect a small bivouac set up by the Roman foragers to ward off interference by the enemy Horse.

With Varro again in command, the bulk of the force was transferred across the stream and drawn up facing eastwards, with the foragers' bivouac on the extreme right flank; one division of 10,000 men was left in the main Roman camp, with orders to capture the enemy's cantonment during the course of the forthcoming battle and to intercept any attempt to retreat.

---

[13] The *Dictator*'s cautious policy passed into military terminology and became known as pursuing Fabian tactics.

As the opponents confronted each other, the Roman Horse was drawn up on the flanks with the Foot, in unusually deep files, between them and the Roman Legions on the right instead of in their usual position in the center. The allied Foot were on their left. Hannibal's dispositions took the form of a crescent, with the strongest cavalry force placed on the left wing, with the design of cutting off the Romans from both their camps. He had deliberately kept his center thinly manned in the hope that, in the event of a setback, some of the Legionaries—as at the Trebia—would attempt to break free and escape across the stream, a contingency for which he had made every preparation.

After some preliminary skirmishing, the heavy cavalry on the Carthaginian left charged home, crushing the Roman Horse in fierce hand-to-hand fighting, which speedily involved the Legions of the right. At the outset, the Numidian cavalry on the Roman left attempted no more than a holding attack, keeping their opponents occupied until their comrades, having destroyed the Roman right wing, swept round to take their antagonists in rear. This was the signal for the Numidians to bring maximum pressure to bear, with the result that the Roman Horse were quickly killed, wounded, or put to flight, with the Carthaginian light cavalry in hot pursuit.

In the center, under the desperate forward surge of the Legions, what had been a salient in the Carthaginian ranks was featly transformed into a re-entrant, into which the Romans crowded precipitately, shouting their cry of victory. Their exultant clamor was indeed all too premature. While both centers were locked in ruthless hand-to-hand fighting, the Carthaginian wings wheeled inward to fall on the Roman flanks, while the heavy cavalry crashed into the Legions' rear. What had been a battle swiftly degenerated into a massacre.

Flight was impossible and no quarter was given. Never, perhaps, was an army of such size annihilated on the field of battle so completely, and with so little loss to its antagonist, as was the Roman army at Cannae. Hannibal had lost not quite 6,000 men, and two-thirds of that loss fell upon the Celts who sustained the first shock of the Legions. On the other hand, of the 76,000 Romans who had taken their places in the line of battle, 70,000 covered the field. . . . The garrison also of the Roman camp, 10,000 strong, were for the most part made prisoners of war, only a few thousand men, partly of these troops, partly of the line, escaped to Canusium.[14]

Rarely has craft and flexibility of maneuver achieved a greater triumph over stout fighting quality hampered by rigidity.

Hannibal had won an overwhelming victory, but it was a success he was quite unable to exploit. He was in command of an admirable army of maneuver whose very qualities rendered it the least likely instrument for the successful conduct of siege operations; and not a single one of the fortified Latin cities revolted, all held firm to Rome. In the capital itself, whatever misgivings might be felt privately, public confidence was unshaken; everyday business was pursued as usual, and men even sold each other plots of the land occupied by the enemy.

Yet no one better than Hannibal realized, however grudgingly, that until the Eternal City was in his hands, his victories led nowhere. Urged to march on the capital with all speed, he hesitated and procrastinated so fatally that his cavalry commander, Mahabal, was driven to open protest. "Of a truth the gods have not bestowed all things upon the same person," he exclaimed. "You know how to conquer, Hannibal; but you do not know how to make use of your victory."

But Hannibal knew his army, its capabilities and its limitations. Cavalry—his strongest arm—could not conduct a successful siege. Rather, "the whole strength of Carthage was to be employed in extending the war to new areas to produce the encirclement of Italy, by thrusting the Romans out of Spain, by regaining Sardinia, and, above all, by re-establishing themselves in Sicily." [15] It was a design in which Philip V of Macedon might well be persuaded to collaborate.

Cannae perfectly illustrated the truth that victory in a single battle does not necessarily win a war. Rome was surprised and bewildered but in no way deterred from its solid determination to continue the struggle. Thus while Hannibal and his opponents waged an indeterminate conflict in Italy, while Publius and Gnaeus Scipio sought to pin down Hasdrubal in Spain, and while the Consul Marcellus successfully pressed the siege of Syracuse, the Senate were searching frantically for a leader with the necessary genius for war

---

[14] Mommsen, *op. cit.* Almost at the same time the Legion sent to Gaul fell into an ambush and was virtually wiped out.

[15] Professor Hallward in *The Cambridge Ancient History*, Vol. VIII.

that would bring such success to Roman arms as would leave her unassailable. In default of any trustworthy commander of riper years their choice fell at last on Publius Cornelius Scipio the Younger, whom posterity was to salute under the name of Scipio Africanus.

Born in 235 B.C., he had fought with distinction at the Trebia and also at Cannae, two reverses whose lessons he had been one of the few properly to assimilate. And he was firmly resolved to better the instruction. From the day he was appointed to supreme control his record is one of almost unbroken success. At the outset, command of the sea enabled him to seize New Carthage by a *coup de main* and thus establish himself on his enemies' flank and attack them in the rear, as well as threaten their maritime line of communications. His next move was to drive Hasdrubal out of Spain into Gaul, whence he crossed into Italy. He next engaged Mago and Hasdrubal the Younger (son of Gisgo), compelling the former to seek refuge in the Balearic Islands and driving the latter back across the water to his base in Mauretania.[16] The domination of Spain by Carthage was at an end, and by 206 B.C. the whole country had made submission to Rome. With the defeat of Hasdrubal the Elder on the river Metaurus and the conclusion of peace with Philip V of Macedon, Hannibal was isolated in the "toe" of Italy, the initiative had passed into the hands of the Romans, and the struggle had entered upon its terminal phase.

Scipio "was more than ever revolving in his mind how to begin the war with Carthage," [17] with Spain as the springboard which would enable him to carry the fight into the heart of the enemy territory. With this end in view he was at considerable pains to win over Massinissa, son of Gala, King of Numidia, with the aim of augmenting his cavalry with some of the excellent Numidian Horse. His embassy to Syphax, King of the Massaesylians, however, failed to wean that Monarch from his allegiance to Carthage.

In the spring of 204 B.C. Scipio safely transported an expeditionary force of 25,000 Roman troops across the Mediterranean to land them at Cape Ferina, near Utica. There he was joined by Massinissa and a useful body of Numidian cavalry. In the interim, Hasdrubal, son of Gisgo, had been equally busy raising a force of 6,000 Horse, 20,000 Foot, and 140 war-elephants, while Syphax was engaged in mustering a large body of cavalry.

[16] Morocco.
[17] Polybius, *The History*.

Scipio's first need was to secure his base, and to this end he laid siege to Utica. The approach of Hasdrubal and Syphax, however, persuaded the Roman leader to raise the siege and feign to enter into negotiations with his enemies, with the aim of winning time thoroughly to acquaint himself with the disposition of their forces and the general layout of their respective camps. It was an exercise in guile which, however doubtful its abstract morality, enabled him to launch simultaneous night assaults on both encampments, which were fired and were soon blazing fiercely, while the attackers, making the most of the element of surprise, struck down their sleep-fuddled enemies before they could snatch up a weapon with which to defend themselves. In all, some 40,000 men were slain or perished in the flames and 5,000 were captured, together with a great haul of Numidian horses and six war-elephants. Though Hasdrubal and Syphax themselves contrived to escape, their combined armies were virtually annihilated.

Scipio lost no time in following up this initial blow with an attack on the force hastily got together by Hasdrubal and Syphax, an encounter in which the former was overwhelmed and the latter taken prisoner. Massinissa was reinstated in his heritage, which gained for Rome a valuable cavalry recruiting-ground that Carthage had hitherto regarded as exclusively her own. In an atmosphere of general panic, both Hannibal and Mago were recalled to Africa, the latter dying of a wound during the return passage across the Mediterranean. At long last the Italian soil was free of the invader's footprint.

By late June of 203 B.C. Hannibal found himself at the head of an army of something under 20,000, which he hoped to augment with such mercenary cavalry as could be hired. Concentrated at Hadrumetum,[18] he was given the foreboding news that Massinissa had joined Scipio at the head of 4,000 Horse and 6,000 Foot. But Hannibal's return had so encouraged the patriot party in Carthage that not only were tentative peace negotiations with Scipio broken off, but his envoys were seized and imprisoned.

Infuriated by this treacherous breach of the customary usages of war, early in 202 B.C. Scipio struck his camp at Tunis and marched inland, heading for Hannibal's concentration at Zama, which lay five days' march southwest of Carthage, burning and ravaging the country as he went, to cut off

18 Susa.

the source of supplies on which Carthage so largely depended.

Hannibal's realization that his army was infinitely inferior to his opponent's was reflected in the order of battle he adopted. With a patchwork force which ranged from Balearic slingers to Moorish light infantry, from native Carthaginians to Macedonian hirelings, he drew up his troops in three parallel lines, with the third, or reserve, line, held some two hundred yards in the rear of the other two, and with no less than eighty war-elephants deployed in extended order along his front. With only 2,000 cavalry to guard his wings, there was no hope of turning the enemy's flanks; the only thing to do was to break the Roman front—a stroke in which it was anticipated that the war-elephants would play a leading part.

Scipio maintained the normal battle formation with one significant deviation; instead of drawing up his *maniples* in three lines checkerwise so that the second line covered the intervals in the first, the men in the second line were marshalled immediately behind those of the first, thus deliberately creating lanes down which the enemy's war-elephants could pass. The light troops (*velites*) were posted in these lanes with orders to harass the elephants as they plunged down them.

Not only was this disposition completely successful, but the elephants making their way to the side, disordered also the Carthaginian cavalry on the wings, so that Scipio's cavalry—which, moreover, was by the arrival of Massinissa's troops rendered far superior to that of the enemy—had little trouble in dispersing them, and were soon engaged in full pursuit.

The struggle of the infantry was more severe. The conflict lasted long between the first divisions on both sides; at length in the extremely bloody hand-to-hand encounter both parties fell into confusion, and were obliged to seek a support in the second divisions. The Romans found that support; but the Carthaginian militia showed itself so unsteady and wavering, that the mercenaries believed themselves betrayed and a combat arose between them and the Carthaginian civic force. But Hannibal now hastily withdrew what remained of the first two lines to the flanks, and pushed forward his choicest troops along the whole line. Scipio, on the other hand, gathered together in the center as many of the first line as were still able to fight, and made the second and third divisions close up on the right and left of the first. Once more on the same spot began a still more fearful conflict; Hannibal's old soldiers never wavered in spite of the superior numbers of the enemy, till the cavalry of the Romans and of Massinissa, returning from the pursuit of the beaten cavalry of the enemy, surrounded them on all sides; this not only terminated the struggle, but annihilated the Phoenician army. The same soldiers, who fourteen years before had given way at Cannae, had retaliated on their conquerors at Zama. With a handful of men Hannibal arrived, a fugitive, at Hadrumetum.[19]

There were many who anticipated that Scipio's victory would be followed by the prompt beleaguerment of Carthage. But the city was supremely well fortified, and its reduction would have demanded much time and energy at the very moment when Philip V of Macedon, in alliance with Antiochus of Syria, was again threatening war. A halt to operations in Africa was essential, and an uneasy and precarious peace was concluded by the terms of which Carthage agreed to forfeit a war indemnity of ten thousand talents of silver, to hand over all war vessels and elephants, to concur in the reinstatement of Massinissa in his former kingdom, and to refrain from embarking on any warlike operations without the consent of Rome.

Hannibal had accepted defeat with dignity and restraint; Rome had shown farsighted magnanimity, since it was the essence of her philosophy to regard victory as a posterior harmonizer of conflict. Yet as Polybius realistically commented, the fact could not be burked that "to the Carthaginians it was a struggle for their own lives and the sovereignty of Libya; to the Romans for universal dominion and supremacy"—to that ultimate condition of world control which Zama had brought a very appreciable step nearer.

[19] Mommsen, *op. cit.*

PART II

❧ ❦ ❧

Arma Virumque Cano

"Right is only in question
between equals in power;
while the strong do what
they can, and the weak
suffer what they must."

—Thucydides

Chapter IV

❧ ❦ ❧

SERVANTS OF THE EAGLES

"For empire and greatness it importeth
most that a nation do profess arms as
their principal honor, study and occupation."

—Francis Bacon

Nothing could better support the validity of Clausewitz's
dictum that "war is the pursuit of policy by other means" than
the history of Rome. "There is a lot of law in the point of

a sword," and the prime instrument of Roman policy was the Roman army.

From the very earliest days of the people's militia [1] the belief had ever been encouraged that service with the armed forces, far from being an onerous duty, was in itself an inestimable privilege and the only road that led to civic honors. After the Allia defeat of 390 B.C. and the formation of a regular standing army, service in the ranks was eagerly sought by the scions of substantial families among the Patricians' clients, wherein "the poorest rank of soldier possessed above forty pounds sterling, a very high qualification at a time when money was so scarce that an ounce of silver was equivalent to seventy pounds weight of brass." [2] For many years, admittance to Rome's native Legions was strictly confined to freemen, Roman citizens; and in all levies "preference was given to the climates of the north over those of the south; the race of men born to the exercise of arms was sought for in the country rather than in cities; and it was very reasonably presumed that the hardy occupations of smiths, carpenters and huntsmen would supply more vigor and resolution than the sedentary trades which are employed in the service of luxury." [3] Vegetius ably sums up this matter of choice in his comment that "the soldiery to whom the defense of the country is consigned and in whose hands is the fortune of war, should, if possible, be of reputable families and unexceptionable in their manners. Such sentiments as one may find in such men will make good soldiers. A sense of honor, by preventing them from behaving improperly, will go far in making them victorious." In the Legions' proud ranks there was no room for the starvation recruit, driven to seek service to fill his belly, for the rootless nondescript, or for the individual whom society in general had contemptuously rejected.

In assaying the most desirable qualities in the would-be soldier, in an age when the weapons system made small technical demands on the individual's intelligence, Vegetius shrewdly commented, "No one can doubt that the peasants are most fit to carry arms, for they from their infancy have been exposed to all kinds of weather and have been brought up to the hardest labor. They are able to endure the most intense heat of the sun, are unacquainted with the use of

[1] The Roman militia was organized on similar lines to the Anglo-Saxon *fyrd*.

[2] Footnote in Edward Gibbon's *The Decline and Fall of the Roman Empire*, based on a record by Dionysius.

[3] Gibbon, *op. cit.*

baths, and are strangers to the other luxuries of life. They are simple, content with little, inured to fatigue, and prepared in some measure for a military life by their continual employment in their farm work, in handling the spade, digging trenches, and carrying burdens." [4]

Recruits for the heavy infantry of the Legions were not accepted under a height of five feet ten inches, and the age for enlistment was preferably under twenty-one, when "instruction of every kind is more quickly absorbed and more lastingly imprinted on the mind. Besides this, the indispensable military exercises of running and leaping must be acquired before the limbs are too much stiffened by age." [5] Swimming was also taught since it was recognized that "it is sometimes impossible to pass rivers on bridges, and the flying and pursuing army are often obliged to swim over them." [6]

According to Sallust, something comparable to cadet training often preceded the recruit's enlistment in the regular forces. For "the Roman youth, as soon as they were of an age to carry arms, were trained in the strictest manner in their camps to all the fatigues and exercises of war. For it is certainly better," he adds, "that a soldier perfectly disciplined, should, through a desire for emulation, repine at his not being yet arrived at a proper age for action than have the mortification of knowing it is past." [7]

On his acceptance into the service an oath was administered to the recruit with every circumstance of solemnity. He vowed never to desert his Standard, "to submit his own will to the commands of his leaders," and "to be prepared to sacrifice his life to his country's cause." [8]

With a shrewd appreciation of the value of symbols, the veteran Legionary no less than the raw recruit was encouraged to regard the emblem borne by his particular formation as epitomizing the *esprit de corps* by which he and all his comrades were so intensely animated. The golden Eagle

---

[4] Flavius Vegetius Renatus, *De Re Militari*. Even with the more complicated weapons of the late eighteenth century, what all nations sought by way of recruits were "respectable, docile country lads, brought up by careful, thrifty parents in a decent cottage home." Hon. Sir John Fortescue, *History of the British Army*.

[5] Vegetius, *op. cit.*

[6] Sallust (Gaius Sallustius Crispus, 83–35 B.C.), *Historiarum Libre Quinque*.

[7] *Ibid.*

[8] It was only with the re-establishment of dynasties that the recruit took an oath of personal loyalty to the Emperor.

(*Aquila*), borne at the head of the Legion by the *aquilifer,* "was the object of their fondest devotion; nor was it esteemed less impious than it was ignominious to abandon that sacred Ensign in the hour of danger." [9] Lesser *signa* distinguished the Cohorts (battalions) and *maniples*. In general, they were crowned with the representation of an open hand encircled with a wreath—the symbol of fidelity. Men of exceptional reliability were selected as *signiferi* to bear these standards, since the tactical deployment of the troops was largely controlled by their movement.

From the very outset the aim of the recruit's training was to ensure a superb condition of physical fitness. "The first thing to be taught," Vegetius insisted, "was the military step, which can only be acquired by constant practice of quick and collective marching. Nor is anything of more consequence either on the march or in the line than that they should keep their ranks with the greatest exactness. For troops who march in an irregular and disorderly manner are always in great danger of being defeated." [10] They also add, it may be subjoined, appreciably to their own fatigue. With the Legion it was the invariable practice to "march with the common step twenty miles in five summer hours." [11] This was a march pace that could be maintained day after day, in virtually any variety of terrain or climate, with very few men prepared to risk the rasping comments of the drillmaster and the jeers of their comrades by falling out along the route.

So as to ensure that they would "charge the enemy with vigor," recruits were exercised in running, acquiring a fleetness of foot which enabled them "to occupy on occasion an advantageous post with greater expedition, and balk the enemy in their designs upon the same." [12] It also accelerated the speed with which a reconnaissance could be conducted and ensured the upkeep of a lively pursuit in the event of the enemy turning tail.

There was no remission from constant training, either for the raw recruit or war-hardened Legionary.

Military exercises were the important and unremitted object of their discipline. The recruits and young soldiers were constantly trained both in the morning and in

9 Gibbon, *op. cit.*
10 Vegetius, *op. cit.*
11 *Ibid.*
12 *Ibid.*

the evening; nor was age or knowledge allowed to excuse the veterans from the daily repetition of what they had completely learnt. Large sheds were erected in the winter quarters of the troops, that their useful labors might not receive any interruption from the most tempestuous weather; and it was carefully observed, that the arms destined to this imitation of war should be of *double* the weight which was required in real action.[13]

This employment of double-weight weapons was always insisted upon when the troops were scheduled for exercise at the post—in effect, a device not unlike the dummy stuffed with straw and suspended from a gallows, employed in the present-day bayonet exercise. To get the best out of this particular form of training, having paraded with

round bucklers woven with willow withies, twice as heavy as those used on real service, and wooden swords double the weight of the common ones . . . every soldier fixed a post firmly in the ground about the height of six feet. Against this, as against a real enemy, the recruit was exercised with the above-mentioned arms, as with the common shield and sword, sometimes aiming at the [dummy] head or face, sometimes at the sides, at others endeavoring to strike at the thighs or legs. He was instructed in what manner to advance and retire, and, in short, how to take every advantage of his adversary; but above all was particularly cautioned not to lay himself open to his antagonist while aiming his stroke at him. They were likewise taught not to cut, but to thrust with their swords. For the Romans not only made a jest of those who fought with the edge of that weapon but always found them an easy conquest. A stroke with the edges, though made with ever so much force, seldom kills, as the vital parts of the body are defended both by the bones and armor. A stab, on the contrary, although it penetrates but two inches, is generally fatal. Besides, in the attitude of striking it is impossible to avoid exposing the right arm and side; but on the other hand, the body is covered while a thrust is given, and the adversary receives the point before he perceives the sword. This was the method of fighting principally used by the Romans; and their reason for exercising recruits with arms of such a weight at first

13 Gibbon, *op. cit.*

was, that when they came to carry the common ones, which were so much lighter, the difference might enable them to act with greater security and alacrity in time of action.[14]

If the trainee had the good fortune to undergo instruction on the parade ground known as the Field of Mars in Rome itself, the work session was invariably followed by a refreshing swim in the nearby river Tiber.

Once the recruit had passed satisfactorily through his probationary period of training, he was given his military mark, which endowed him with full status as a Legionary. "This mark was imprinted on the hands of the soldiers, either with a hot iron, or in some other manner, and was indelible." [15] With this somewhat painful ceremony performed, the recruit's name was engraved on his shield, and he took his place in the ranks as a full-fledged Legionary.

As a duly authorized member of his formation, the new Legionary was fitted out with a long, sleeveless leather *tunica,* woolen or leather breeches coming just below the knee, and a pair of stout hobnailed sandals. The *tunica* was reinforced with iron bands across the shoulders and about the chest and waist, while an apron of metal strips hung from the waist in front. A crested metal helmet gave protection to his head and body, while his legs below the knee were encased in metal greaves, that on the right leg being of stouter make than that on the other limb, since his right side was more exposed than his left, which was shielded by a concave oblong buckler four feet in length and two and a half in breadth, framed on light wood, covered in bull's hide, and strongly barded with plates of brass. The convex form was adopted as more likely to deflect an opponent's sword blows. In addition to a pair of relatively light throwing javelins, he was furnished with a heavy *pilum,* six feet in length and tipped with a triangular, eighteen-inch steel point. Hanging from a shoulder belt over the right hip was a *gladius,* the stabbing sword, with a two-edged pointed blade two feet in length and four inches in width, lacking anything in the nature of a cross-hilt or bowl-guard, but with short, thick quillons and terminating in a pommel and tang end. The weapon was worn on the right side of the body so that it could be drawn without getting tangled up with the buckler. A dagger (*pugio*) was suspended from the waist-belt.

[14] Vegetius, *op. cit.*
[15] Polybius, *op. cit.* Cf. Vegetius.

Subsequent to Rome's conquest of Spain, the Legions were furnished with weapons of Iberian manufacture, the Spanish sword-cutlers having earned an extremely high reputation for the excellent quality of the work turned out by their forges.

On the line of march, few "footsloggers" can have been more heavily burdened with equipment and assorted gear than was the Roman Legionary. For in addition to his protective armor and weapons and several spare *pila*, he was weighed down with field rations for at least three days, a mess kit, cooking spit, gallipot, drinking cup, a basketwork valise of spare clothing, a water gourd, a section of shelter tent, and either a spade, saw, pickax or sickle, sometimes with the addition of a load of wood to serve as fuel. To facilitate the transportation of these *sarcinae*, as many as could be made to fit were trussed up into a neat pack. It was a prodigious load, but his training had accustomed him to cope with practice weights of up to sixty pounds. So Virgil was not indulging in fulsome adulation when he wrote:

> The Roman soldiers, bred in war's alarms,
> Bending with unjust loads and heavy arms,
> Cheerful their toilsome marches undergo,
> And pitch their sudden camp before the foe.

The heavy burden carried by the individual soldier was deliberately legislated in order to reduce the accompanying first-line transport to a minimum. Pack animals and light two-wheel carts were very well able to keep pace with the marching columns, carrying such necessities in the way of tools, forges, and rations as the countryside would be unlikely to provide. For, true to the Ciceronian principle that "war should be made to support war," the Roman forces invariably laid the resources of the territories in which they operated under requisition, falling back on their mobile supplies only in moments of emergency.

The Legionary's diet was nourishing enough if scarcely Lucullan, although Vegetius insisted that there should be at his disposal "corn, wine, vinegar, and even salt, in plenty at all times." Not a particularly voracious flesh-eater, if the occasion demanded it the Roman soldier was well content to consume his meat ration in the form of *offula* (sandwiches). Vegetable stew flavored with garlic, porridge, and bread played a big part in his diet, and he was only too grimly acquainted with the wholesome but uninspiring properties of the *bucellum*, or ration biscuit. The bread ration was even made a servant of discipline, a minor punishment being temporarily to put the delinquent on the less appetizing barley bread instead of the normal wheaten variety. Frugal yet remarkably hardy, few troops can have occasioned less anxiety over their subsistence than the men who marched behind the Roman Eagles.

On campaign, the day's march invariably started at an early hour, since arrival at the appointed halting place needed to be in sufficiently good season to allow ample time for the elaborate process of pitching camp. For no matter how short a stay had been legislated for at any given spot, as elaborate a cantonment was constructed as if the troops were destined to inhabit it indefinitely. This was as much a matter of discipline as of precaution.

Great care was taken in selecting a site for the camp, which was never pitched on a location liable to flooding, or on a slope where it could be secretly approached on the reverse incline of the hillcrest by an enemy. Visual range on all sides was as much a *sine qua non* as was access to wood for fuel, forage, and clear running water. For as Vegetius sagely insisted, "Water must be wholesome and not from marshes or fouled places; bad water is a kind of poison and the cause of epidemic distemper." He also added the wise counsel, "If an army is to continue in the camp for any considerable time, attention must be had to the sanitation of the place."

Once a campsite had been selected, the first task was for "the pioneers to level the ground, and remove every impediment that might interrupt its perfect regularity. Its form was an exact quadrangle; and we might calculate that a square of about seven hundred yards was sufficient for the encampment of twenty thousand Romans." [16] About this area the Legionaries dug a ditch nine feet broad and seven feet deep. With the soil taken from this trench they then erected a wall, or breastwork, three to four feet in height, surmounted by strong palisades which the troops carried with them from camp to camp.

Four "gates" were left in the wall, about forty feet in width, and these were protected by elbow-shaped, curved and transverse earthen ramparts, which compelled any would-be entrant to approach with his unprotected right side facing the sentries, standing with their *pila* poised.

An open space two hundred feet in width was left clear

16 Gibbon, *op. cit.*

between the palisaded wall and the carefully aligned "streets" of shelter tents, to ensure security and rapid communication. The *Porta Praetoria,* or front "gate," was joined to the *Decumene,* or rear "gate," by a roadway fifty feet wide, a thoroughfare leading to the place appointed for punishment or the bruiting abroad of announcements of general interest. About two-thirds of the distance from front to rear, this *via praetoria* [17] was intersected by another roadway at right angles to it, the *via principales,* which joined the two side "gates."

"In the midst of the camp, the *Praetorium,* or General's quarters, rose above the others," fronting the *Porta Praetoria;* this command post, although not in its mathematical center, was the veritable hub of the encampment.

In the event of its being necessary to pitch camp under observation of the enemy, only a third of the force available was put to digging the ditch and erecting the defences; the balance of the troops stood guard over their laboring comrades.

Once the wall and ditch had been completed, the Legionaries' small shelter tents—of which each man bore a component—could be set up in orderly "lines." Each shelter accommodated one *contubernium* (squad) of eight men, two of each formation being away in turn on guard duty. The remainder, their long march and the strenuous day's toil over, lost little time in rolling themselves in their *sagulae,* [18] and with their packs for pillows, relapsing thankfully into slumber. Only a few of the more hardened gamblers stayed awake long enough to indulge in an elementary form of dicing. Ordinarily, the Roman soldier had few forms of distraction, although when in permanent quarters he was known as an enthusiastic patron of cockfighting, [19] on which he wagered heavily.

A Roman camp, being a place where the auspices were taken, was in that degree a *templum* also, encompassing as it did a definite area of consecrated ground. The *cardo* and *decumanus,* cross-lines of a temple, constituted the two main "streets" of the camp area, meeting at its heart where, hard by the *Praetorium,* was situated the *auguraculum,* where the Eagles and other regimental emblems were laid up under guard. There, too, was the altar where the Com-

[17] Literally, the Avenue of the Generals.

[18] The *sagulum* was a voluminous cloak which could be rolled up and slung from the right shoulder to the left hip.

[19] The historian Pomponius Mela solemnly affirmed that Rome started to decline only after cockfighting had lost its universal appeal!

mander worshiped and made sacrifice for the victory and
well-being of his men.

Tools as much as weapons are implements of war, a fact
perfectly realized by the Roman Legionary, "to whom the
use of the spade and pickax were no less familiar than that
of the sword and *pilum*. Thus whenever the trumpet gave
the signal for departure, the camp was almost instantly
broken up, and the troops fell in to their ranks without delay or confusion." [20]

Singularly enough, although as early as 685 B.C. Tyrtacus
had encouraged his men to sing on the line of march, and in
479 B.C. the Greek *hoplites* had been aided in keeping step
by the crisp melodies rendered by a band of flute players,
the Romans made no organized use of military music to
lighten the way on their route. Not that the Legion was entirely lacking in musical instruments, possessing as it did
trumpets, cornets, and *buccinae*. But the trumpet was confined to sounding the charge and the retreat;

> the cornets were used only to regulate the motions of
> the Eagles; the trumpets served when the soldiers were
> ordered out to any work without the Eagles; but in
> time of action the cornets and trumpets sounded to-
> gether. The *classicum*, which was a particular sound of
> the *buccina*, or horn, was reserved for the Commander-
> in-Chief and was used in the presence of the General
> or at the execution of a soldier, as a mark of his au-
> thority. The ordinary guards and outposts were always
> relieved by the sound of trumpet, which also directed
> the movements of the soldiers on working parties and
> on field days. The cornets sounded whenever the Eagles
> or Standards were to be struck or planted. These rules
> were punctually observed in all exercises and reviews,
> so that the soldiers might be ready to obey them in ac-
> tion without hesitation.[21]

But of the drum and cymbals, long since familiar to all
Eastern armies, the Romans made no use whatever.

From the time of its original adoption, the makeup of
the Legion and its deployment in battle formation underwent virtually no change. The 6,000 men of which it was

20 Vegetius, *op. cit.*
21 *Ibid.*

composed were still divided into ten Cohorts, the first of which exceeded the others both in the number and quality of its soldiers, as men of some family and education were selected to serve in it. This Cohort had the care of the Eagle and the Standard [22] of the whole Legion. Consisting of 1,105 heavy infantry, it was known as the Millarian Cohort, and proudly took its place on the right of the front line or *principes*.[23] The second Cohort consisted of 555 heavy infantry, who took their place in the front line of *principes*, being known as the Quingentarian Cohort. On the left of this formation were drawn up the third, fourth, and fifth Cohorts, all of a strength of 555, to complete the first line of *principes*. Behind them were aligned the sixth, seventh, eighth, ninth, and tenth Cohorts of the *hastati*, of similar 555 strength per unit. Behind them again were ranged the *ferrentari* and *velites*, light troops disposed—at least at the outset of an engagement—in seven Cohorts of varying strength. The fourth line was made up of the veteran *triarii*, to act as a general reserve.

With the replacement of a national militia, called up only in times of emergency, by a standing regular army, all Legionaries enlisted for a definite period—at the outset, for one year. In due course the twelve months' engagement was extended to one of eight years, and then to one of twenty years, at the option of the Legionary. Indeed, in the ranks of the *triarii* would be found many *evocati*, veterans who had earned distinction and who had volunteered for a further tour of duty after completing twenty years of unblemished service. Among the privileges enjoyed by the *evocati* was a higher scale of pay, the right to a mount on the line of march, and exemption from all camp "fatigues." The pay of the ordinary rank and file was approximately that of the skilled town workman.[24] Out of this wage the Legionary bought his uniform and contributed towards the cost of his subsistence, including the outlay on the annual regimental banquet! He was also entitled to a prescribed share in any

---

[22] *Vexilia*, rectangular cloth banners hanging from a cross-piece surmounting the staff. Vegetius, *op. cit.*

[23] The numbers of the Millarian Cohort were swollen by the fact that it carried on its muster rolls the names of all the Legion's clerical staff.

[24] Wage rates started at the modest sum of approximately sixpence (seven cents) a day, but by the reign of Domitian, (A.D. 81–96) they had risen to an annual stipend of 1,200 sesterces with, of course, a share in the war booty. The sesterce was worth approximately twopence.

war booty accumulated, and the sale of prisoners of war into bondage, while a system of bonuses and pensions included land grants for those conspicuous for outstanding gallantry and long-sustained exemplary service. Each Legion maintained a savings bank, in which at least half the man's share of war booty was credited. As with all modern armies, decorations were awarded for outstanding bravery in battle or for other meritorious service "beyond the line of duty." The most cherished of these was the *corona civica* (civic crown), bestowed upon the Legionary who had saved a comrade's life in combat. In addition, a Legionary could be rewarded with extra pay, promotion, and the *dona militaria* in the form of brooches (*fibulae*), disc-shaped metal decorations for the breastplate (*phalerae*), neck chains, and armlets.

The Legions furnished by Rome's Latin allies were organized on similar lines to those raised from among the purely Roman citizenry; and although they gave a remarkably good account of themselves on innumerable occasions, it is questionable if they ever attained quite the dynamism, the stern pride, the *élan,* and the stubborn fighting quality of the Legions of purely Roman origin.

The hard-bitten *Impeditus* of the Legions undoubtedly constituted the backbone of Rome's formidable army, and it was said of the Legionaries by one who had seen them on parade as well as having fought against them *à outrance,* that so magnificent was their discipline that "the effusion of blood was the only circumstance which distinguished a field of battle from a field of exercise." [25]

But save in very exceptional circumstances, infantry alone cannot sustain the whole burden of a campaign. So in addition to the Legions, Rome recruited a considerable body of cavalry, as well as *auxilia,* from Cretan and Numidian archers (*sagitarii*) to slingers from the Balearic Islands, a supplementary force which tended to expand as Rome's military commitments increased.

Balearic *fustibulii* had fought in the armies of Philip and Alexander of Macedon and with the Carthaginians. They carried two slings, one for short and one for long range, and constant training had endowed them with extraordinary accuracy of aim. From their earliest days these islanders were exhorted by their elders deliberately to select a target and then take careful aim at it—and it was an empty belly

[25] Josephus, *De Bellum Judaico.*

for anyone who missed! For "the children were not allowed to have their food by their mothers till they had first struck it with their sling." In the opening stages of a battle the slingers often rendered valuable service in "softening up" the enemy prior to the main assault.

In the early days the Legions had cavalry forces integrally assigned to them. This body of Horse "was divided into ten troops or squadrons; the first, as the companion of the first Cohort, consisted of a hundred and thirty-two men; whilst each of the other nine amounted only to sixty-six. The entire establishment formed a regiment . . . of seven hundred and twenty-six Horse, naturally connected with its respective Legion, but occasionally separated to act in the line, and to compose a part of the wings of the army." [26]

Equipped with metal helmet, cuirass, shield, sword, *pila*, and a heavy *hasta*, or thrusting spear, the cavalry needed to be well mounted. So far as the Italian native breeds were concerned, the best horseflesh came from the southern end of the peninsula, particularly from Apulia and Tarentum. Another source of supply was Spain. During the Carthaginian occupation of the country two thousand Libyan horsemen had formed part of the permanent garrison. Since Libyans never rode their mares, the two thousand stallions on which these troops were mounted were utilized for crossing with the local breeds, with very beneficial effect. From the hybrid which resulted the Romans acquired many of their remounts, once the custody of Spain had passed into their hands. Other useful equine importations came from Thessaly and Cappadocia.

The temporary alliance between Scipio Africanus and Massinissa also afforded an opportunity to cross the horses of southern Italy with North African Barbs, which must have added considerably to the fire and stamina of the native breed if not to their stature, which was about that of a modern polo pony. Since in the course of their empire-building campaigns the Romans constantly encountered barbarian hordes highly skilled in the use of missile weapons, they found it necessary to add appreciably to the powers of resistance of the cavalryman's body-armor. Every endeavor was made, therefore, to raise a stock of bigger and better horses, as being the only way in which the cavalry steed could be relied upon to carry a heavier weight and still retain its mobility. It was the perennial problem of protection

[26] Gibbon, *op. cit.* Cf. Vegetius and Polybius.

versus speed, and it would be idle to pretend that the Romans found a really satisfactory answer to it.[27]

The Legions were supported by special troop units such as the corps of engineers and artificers. Not only were these ancillaries responsible for the siting and layout of camps, temporary or permanent, under the *architectus, mensor* (surveyor), and *hydraularius* (water engineer), but the construction of the magnificent roads the Romans drove through every captured territory was also their responsibility. Siege works, bridges, shipbuilding and repair, the upkeep of equipment, armor, weapons, "artillery," and transport—all came under the purview of the *Praefectus Fabrum,* or Senior Engineer Officer.

Although inclined to be impatient of the tedium inseparable from siege operations, the Roman Army set about their conduct with its usual capability. A great number of siege engines were employed in any walled city's beleaguerment; the Legionaries worked under the supervision of the Engineer Corps to batter the walls with such artillery as was in operation prior to the invention of gunpowder.

Of these pieces the *ballista* was the equivalent of the howitzer, projecting stones and baulks of wood weighing from one hundred to one hundred and thirty pounds. "These machines," Procopius [28] recorded, "have the general shape of a bow; but in the middle there is a hollow piece of horn loosely fixed to the bow, and lying over a straight iron stock. When wishing to let fly at the enemy, you pull back the short strong cord which joins the arms of the bow, and place in the horns a bolt . . . Men standing at each side of the *ballista* draw back the cord with little devices [winches]; when they let it go, the horn rushes forward and discharges the missile." The "barrel," a grooved track, was sharply inclined and shot the projectile into the air on a forty-five-degree-angled curve. The favorite materials for fashioning the cord were twisted gut, women's hair plaited, or the sinews from a bull's neck. A crew of from five to ten men operated the weapon, and the utmost range they could obtain was approximately one thousand yards. Alternative missiles for the machine took the form of iron-pointed beams

---

[27] Horseshoes from the time of Nero (A.D. 54–68) have survived, and since they are no more than four inches lengthwise and across, the animal that was shod with them cannot have been of anything but light build.

[28] Procopius, *Historiae.*

or poles, twelve feet long, capable of piercing four rows of *plutei,* shields or screens on heavy standing frames and covered with thick wickerwork or hides. The *ballistae* were mounted on carriages drawn by mules; the number assigned to each Legion rose, over the years, from ten to fifty-five.

What corresponded to a medium howitzer was the *onager,*[29] a mortar firing stones up to one hundred and sixty pounds in weight to a distance of over two thousand feet. In some respects it resembled a small *ballista,* save that it had but one arm, a lever pulled to a horizontal position by a windlass, which was released to fly back to the vertical position with maximum violence.

A lighter weapon was the catapult, a flat-trajectory field-piece, projecting heavy arrows, darts, bolts, or javelins almost horizontally. The arms of the catapult were straight lengths of timber and its elasticity, or power of recoil, was produced by the torsion of a stout cable twisted to the greatest possible tension. The two slim timber beams were inserted in the two large cables and the ends, like a bow, were connected together by a strong cord. The carriage was then pushed forward until the claws of the trigger were over the bowspring. The middle of the cord was then drawn back in the carriage by a windlass and held in place by a hook when it had reached the rear of the nearly horizontal track, which was grooved to hold the long, sliding carriage, on the back of which was the trigger. A block was then thrust under the heavy rear end of the trigger and the claws held down in this fashion on the cord. The missile was then laid on the grooved upper surface of the carriage, with its end resting on the cord between the claws of the trigger. The block was then withdrawn and the trigger fell of its own weight. Thereupon, the missile was abruptly released, with considerable power propelling it. Served by four men, the weapon's approximate range was one thousand yards.

For the assault of a walled town the Romans frequently employed movable towers (*turres ambulatoriae*) built on rollers and shifted by means of levers. Some were as much as forty feet square at the base and thirty feet square at the top; the tallest specimen, one hundred and eighty feet in height, having ten stories (*tabulata*) all connected by stairs. Ramps could be let down from the upper stories to come to rest on the enemy walls. Across these the assault troops would pour, under the protective fire of archers and slingers perched in the highest story of all. In the tower's base was housed

---

29 Literally, "the wild ass."

a battering ram (*aries*), a huge beam with a heavy iron or bronze head resembling a ram, sixty to a hundred feet in length, suspended horizontally by ropes or chains. Swung back and forth endwise by a team of muscular men, its impact was so powerful that no wall could long withstand it, despite the bags of straw or wool let down by the defenders to deaden the force of the blows.

Another aid in tearing down the enemy defenses was the *falx muralis,* a single or double iron wall-hook projecting from the end of a long beam, suspended from upright supports, and designed to tear down the walls in which it became entangled. The ram was sometimes housed in a stoutly built, movable shed known as a *testudo arietaria,* with a sloping roof strong enough to withstand the heavy stones hurled down on it by the defenders.

In many instances the besiegers would construct an *agger,* a vast embankment or causeway of earth, timber and stones, revetted with logs. Built out at right angles to the enemy walls, from the rear it sloped up to a height almost equal to that of the fortification against which it was raised. Begun out of range of the besieged garrison's fire, as it crept nearer to the walls the men at work on its construction were shielded by the erection of *vineae,* stout sheltering sheds behind which the work could proceed unharried. As the ramp approached the fortifications, these *vineae* were replaced by even more stoutly constructed *musculi,* with roofs thick enough to stand up to the impact of the strongest missiles.

With the *agger* completed to a width of fifty feet, a *maniple* of the Legion would rush the defenses—which had been kept under continual fire by the slingers and archers—using scaling ladders if necessary to get them over the sector of town wall to which the *agger* led.

In many respects a condition of siege is an admission of military failure. Those besieged have lost the invaluable asset of mobility; the forces of investment, having failed in the field to inflict decisive defeat on their opponents, have lost the power of maneuver. Like all well-trained, aggressive-minded troops, the Romans resented the necessity for conducting siege operations, but once committed to them, they set about their prosecution with their customary efficiency.

Rome's debt to Greek culture and influences was perhaps at its greatest when it came to the arts of healing. It was claimed by Greek historians that Achilles had been instructed in the practice of the surgeon's craft by Chiron himself, and that two sons of Aesculapius had served with the Greek armed forces. Medical men who had accompanied Alexander the Great to India had mastered the technique of rhinoplasty according to the ancient method described by Susruta as early as the sixth century B.C.[30] An operation of the utmost delicacy, it brought about a degree of expertise in the handling of surgical cases from which the fighting man was undoubtedly the principal beneficiary. By the time of the Punic Wars, Greek medical practitioners were in great demand in Rome itself, and a considerable number were attracted to the armed forces.

With the Legions, the team of one surgeon and one *medicus* per hundred men was supplemented by from six to eight *deputatii* and a score of *capsarii*,[31] or bearers, all with a good grounding in first aid, whose duty it was to seek out, tend, and remove the wounded. Provided with a horse equipped with a sidesaddle to transport the injured, the *capsarus* carried a water flask slung over his shoulder and was girded about the loins with a broad belt from which was suspended a pouchful of bandages. The zeal of these bearers was further stimulated by the reward of a *bezant*[32] for every dangerously wounded man they contrived to bring safely off the field of battle.

To the medical corps must also be attributed the excellent sanitary arrangements characteristic of a Roman garrison or field camp. It was the medicos who sited the "necessaries" and made arrangements for their regular filling in; the medicos who ensured that water for drinking and cooking purposes was always drawn *up*stream from the locations assigned for bathing parties or for watering the horses, mules, and oxen. It was the medicos who kept an alert eye on the cookhouses and the personal cleanliness of the men themselves, and it was to their skill and vigilant supervision that the standard of hygiene maintained by the Roman Army was centuries ahead of that supported by the forces of any of its contemporaries save those of Greece itself.

In garrison the troops were served by a number of sutlers, who sold them extra food and small luxuries and such supplies as were not official issue. They were also prepared to

[30] Mastery of this art was essential to the Indian surgeon, since amputation of the nose was commonly decreed as the punishment for adultery and many other offenses.

[31] Named from the *capsa,* or bandage bag, with which they were equipped.

[32] The equivalent, in contemporary spending value, of approximately twenty-five shillings, or three dollars and fifty cents.

purchase booty and prisoners from the Legionaries, paying cash on the spot. By regulation, they could only erect their booths outside the confines of the camp, even when accompanying the troops on active service—an ordinance much resented, since on one occasion at least the sutlers had been caught by an enemy raiding party and massacred to a man.

Officers' grooms and servants were invariably slaves.[33] They were known as *calones* and were under military discipline. Other *calones* fulfilled the functions of packmasters, wagoners, and mule-skinners.

At various times the Romans employed large and ferocious dogs in close combat, not infrequently protected about the head and shoulders by armor. They were particularly effective against barbarian hordes whose nether limbs, like their throats, were unprotected and extremely vulnerable to canine assault.

The Roman Army's chain of command, sound and well balanced in its lower echelons, was often weakest where it should have been strongest—at the top. Legion Commanders —normally men in their late thirties or early forties, with a minimum property rating of 400,000 *sesterces*—had all to achieve appointment to the Senate and then to work their way up through various military *or civil* posts before, as Consuls or *Legatii*, they could be considered for command. The fact that an individual could attain sufficient seniority in the Senate to qualify for field command, on a maximum of civil service and a minimum of soldiering experience, put a premium on generalship of a dangerously amateur quality. Furthermore, when two Legions took the field together, the practice of their respective leaders assuming command on alternate days led inevitably to vacillation and infirmity of purpose, to divided councils and lack of impetus and consistent planning. It is true that, many centuries later, the first Duke of Marlborough and Prince Eugene of Savoy survived the pitfalls of dual command with outstanding success. But it is rarely that two men of military genius have been able to see eye-to-eye to such a degree as "the little Abbé" and "Corporal John." For the most part the Napoleonic dictum "Let *one* man command. *One* bad general is better than two good ones," is not to be gainsaid. It is

---

[33] Domestic slaves were members, if lesser units, of the family to which they belonged. Prædial slaves, such as war captives and convicts, "had neither rights nor mercy." It was they who manned the galleys' rowing benches.

indeed highly significant that in moments of acute crisis even the Senate was driven to recognize this immutable fact by the appointment, however temporary, of a military Dictator with overriding powers.

The *Legatii* were nominated to serve under the Consuls as what would nowadays be termed Lieutenant Generals. They were of Senatorial rank, and men who had held a *curule* magistracy, i.e., been Quaestors in Rome. The most senior could act for the Consul (*propraetore*) or be assigned the command of a detached force. Recruiting duties, command of a reserve camp, even the construction of a fleet of transports, were all tasks that might come the way of the *Legatii* if a Consul were in overall command.

Under the *Legatii* were six military Tribunes; one of them, the deputy commander of the Legion, was normally of high birth and destined for a subsequent career in politics. "The other five Tribunes were of equestrian rank and described as *Tribuni angusticlavii*. Most of them were men in their thirties or upwards whose previous experience had been mainly as municipal magistrates." [34]

The office of Quaestor corresponded in its military incarnation to the Quartermaster General of a modern fighting force. Such an individual was responsible for the bulk purchase of supplies, provisions, clothing, arms, equipment, and means of shelter for the troops. In addition, he undertook the guardianship of all booty and prisoners-of-war, subsequently supervising their sale. It was his task to see to the pay of the troops, and he exercised general administrative authority over all units, regular or auxiliary. On the other hand, a Quaestor might be assigned to the Military Governorship of a province, over which he would rule in the name of the Senate.

In command of the cavalry and of the auxiliaries were officers known as Prefects. Some were Romans, some chiefs of the countries furnishing the contingents. Like all Officers, they were distinguished from their men by a cuirass made of gilded bronze and molded to fit the torso's contours. There was also a *Praefectus castrorum*, whose duty was to locate, survey, and subsequently police the camp occupied by the Legions. The senior long-service professional Officer of the Legion, he was a former Chief Centurion and normally a man of thirty years' service or more. [35]

The backbone of the corps was formed by the Centurions,

[34] Graham Webster, *The Roman Army*.
[35] *Ibid.*

sixty to a Legion, who fulfilled positions of command rang-
ing from the equivalent of Platoon Officer to a rank com-
mensurate with that of Lieutenant Colonel. Thus the Centurions of the first Cohort were senior in rank to their
opposite in numbers in the second Cohort; they, in turn,
were senior to those of the third, and so on down through
the ten Cohorts. The senior Centurion of the first Cohort,
known as the *Primipilus*, occupied a post of very considerable
power and responsibility, and often it was not attained until
the veteran was in his fifties. A man who had reached this
elevated position enjoyed the unreserved confidence of the
Legion Commander and invariably participated in all councils of war. Polybius said of them as a class that they "were
not so much bold and adventurous as men with a faculty
for command, steady and rather of a deep-rooted spirit, not
prone prematurely to attack or start battle, but men who, in
face of superior numbers or overwhelming pressure, would
endure and die in defense of their post."

Every Centurion carried in his wicker knapsack, not a
Marshal's baton, but the insignia of his office—a stave of vine,
myrtle, or laurel, with which he was at liberty to administer corporal punishment to any delinquent caught *in
flagrante delicto*. For discipline in the Legions was exemplary, a deserter, for example, being soundly flogged before
being sold into slavery; while the greatest of all military
crimes was for a man to surrender while still in possession
of his arms. If nothing else, this strictness had the effect of
imbuing the populace with the salutary belief that "de-
gradation from the rank of a soldier and dignity of a citizen
was the most ignominious stigma which could be affixed upon
one who had demeaned himself." [36]

Similar in rank and responsibility to the Centurion were
the Decurions, serving either with the cavalry or the auxiliaries. Each Centurion and Decurion was assisted by a
subordinate known as an *optio*, since he was appointed at the
discretion of the individual he served.

A junior officer in each Century, known as the *Tesserarius*,
was available to take command of small pickets and
fatigue parties and the like; while certain specialist officers
were known as *Immunes*, since the nature of their duties
relieved them from participation in any "fatigues."

---

[36] J. Lempriere, *Classical Dictionary*. Decimation was sometimes employed as an extreme form of punishment when a whole unit had
failed to live up to the high standard demanded of it. Appius
Claudius resorted to it in 280 B.C. after the reverse suffered by
Roman arms at Heraclea.

The *Corniculorius* occupied a position equivalent to that of the present-day Adjutant, and was assisted by an *Actuarius,* chiefly concerned with accounts. For the rest, the Command Staff included the *Librarii* and a *Cerarius*,[37] clerks who, among other things, operated the compulsory savings bank into which half a Legionary's donative, or bonus, was always paid. They also acted as treasurers of the soldier's burial club.

Attached to the Legion were certain *Beneficiarii,* strongly suspected of owing their position to the favor of the Tribunes: the *Contubernales,* or volunteer aides-de-camp; *cohors praetoria,* who served as the Commander's bodyguard and combined these duties with those of military police; and ten *Speculatores,* the forerunners of the modern Intelligence Staff. The *Speculatores* were also responsible for counterintelligence and that particular form of propaganda to which Gibbon refers when he writes of the Roman device of "scattering libels amongst the enemy." In addition, they were concerned with military signaling and the transmission of messages by a variety of means, from beacons to the Legionary's burnished shield, which was employed to flash reports in much the same manner as the latter-day heliograph.[38]

But from a Staff point of view, it was not until the time of Gaius Julius Caesar that "the military art had progressed sufficiently so that the military mind was able to differentiate between 'intelligence' and operational functions. This was a significant development in the evolution of the Staff, and consequently carried Staff functioning beyond the Staff system of Alexander," [39] which for so long had served the Romans as a model.

In general, there was a progressive tendency for the more youthful among the Patrician class to seek service with the cavalry. For all that, the Patricians played a small but essential part in the Legions' composition, forming as they did the hard core of the officer element. In addition, there were a number of *Tribuni militum* who were also of gentle birth. A *Tribunus militum* would often be given command of a detached group of Legionaries, assigned to garrison a small outpost or to carry out a minor mission away from the parent formation. But when the Legion fought as a whole, the leadership of its tactical units reverted to the Centurions.

[37] Literally, a writer on wax tablets.

[38] It is recorded that with Rome's occupation of ancient Britain, given clear weather a message could be flashed from Hadrian's Wall to the capital in thirty hours.

[39] Lieutenant-Colonel J. D. Hittle, *The Military Staff.*

The Roman Army was primarily an infantry force, a body of foot soldiers to whom the other branches of the Service were unquestionably held to be subservient. And it was not until the battle of Adrianople in A.D. 378 that the horseman came into his own as the *primus inter pares* of the battle-field.

In 264 B.C. a Carthaginian Admiral had informed the Romans that "they might wash their hands in the sea only by his leave." [40]

The peculiar maritime demands of the Punic Wars brought it home to the Romans that sea power was something they must attain if victory over Carthage were to be rendered possible. For all that, the tendency persisted to try and conquer the sea from the land, rather than the land from the sea; the ocean was still regarded as a barrier rather than a means to ensuring timely strategic movement. Yet as Mahan points out, it was the fact that Rome had been strong in the seas between the homeland and Spain which made all the difference in the rate at which his brother could reinforce Hannibal in Italy. Indeed, at the outset of the conflict, it was as much Rome's instinctive reluctance to embark on a maritime venture as it was Hannibal's unlooked-for drive into upper Italy that delayed the prosecution of the war before the gates of the enemy's capital.

At all times the Romans regarded their army as the senior service. Even so, as early as 338 B.C. the authorities had sanctioned the appointment of two officials, *Duoviri Navales*—each of them to command a squadron of ten small warships, probably with the aim of putting down the pirates that preyed on Roman commerce in the Tyrrhene Sea. It will be recalled, however, that in Rome's quarrel with Tarentum the Tarentines had made short work of a good half of the Roman vessels, and that when the Army's appearance before the defiant city had brought Pyrrhus into the quarrel, the Senate had concluded a treaty with Carthage by which it was enabled to make use of Punic sea power rather than create any of its own.

In 267 B.C. a measure was introduced to appoint four Quaestors [41] of the fleet, of whom

the first was stationed at Ostia, the port of Rome; the second, stationed at Cales, then the capital of Ro-

[40] Cassius Dio, XI, 43.
[41] *Quaestores classici.*

man Campania, had to superintend the ports of Campania and Magna Graecia; the third, stationed at Ariminium, superintended the ports on the other side of the Apennines. The district assigned to the fourth is not known. These new standing officials were intended to exercise not individual, but a conjoint, guardianship of the coasts, and to form a war marine for their protection. The objects of the Roman Senate—to recover their independence by sea, to cut off the maritime communications of Tarentum, to close the Adriatic against fleets coming from Epirus, and to emancipate themselves from Carthaginian supremacy—were very obvious.[42]

And having achieved that emancipation as the outcome of the Second Punic War, Rome philosophically, if unenthusiastically, accepted the fact that only domination of the western Mediterranean would enable her to maintain the position she had won.

Suzerainty over the bulk of Sicily and possession of some of the island's most useful ports had the effect of stimulating Rome's interest in both her mercantile and her fighting marine, although she relied heavily on those of her allies and dependents who boasted a considerable maritime element among their populations for the seafarers to man her vessels.

The galley, introduced by the Cretans and Greeks *circa* 1300 B.C.,[43] was the type of vessel common alike to the Aegean and the tideless Mediterranean. By the time the Romans began to take a serious interest in maritime affairs, the galley was utilized almost exclusively as a vessel of war. It differed from the "round ship" of commerce in its greater length and relative narrowness of beam. Although it did possess a sail, the galley relied for its propulsion mainly on the men sweating at the row-benches. These oarsmen were always predial slaves—war captives or convicts—and since life on the row-benches was short, the demand for replacements was unending and ever on the increase. *Biremes* demanded double the number of men required for a galley propelled by a single bank of sweeps to larboard and starboard. The introduction of outriggers permitted the employment of more and more oarsmen in *triremes*; although it is to be borne in mind that in all the multiple-

42 Mommsen, *op. cit.*

43 A Greek vase of this period, picturing the earliest type of galley, is still in existence.

reme classes, up to *quinquereme*, the galleys were identified by the number of men pulling on each oar.[44]

The Romans relied less upon maneuvering to ram or shear away the opponent's oar-bank than upon closing, grappling the enemy with the *corvus*, and then "boarding and entering" to determine the issue in close combat. Their preference, therefore, was for the more capacious *quinquereme*, capable of carrying the maximum number of fighting men. A Roman fleet of *quinqueremes* could brush aside the resistance of lighter craft, and in battle with its peers the fighting quality of the Roman Legionaries was the decisive factor. As the opposing vessels closed, the opponents "engaged with all kinds of missile weapons, with stones, arrows, darts, or shot from the *Onagri, Ballistae* or *Scorpiones. . . .* Turrets were also erected on the largest ships, to enable them to annoy the enemy and destroy them more easily, as from the top of a rampart. Arrows covered with tow and a composition of incendiary oil, sulphur and bitumen were also shot from the *Ballistae* into the enemy ships and fixing in their sides paid with wax, pitch and rosin, instantly set them in a flame." [45] It was a softening-up which led straight into the grapple and the decisive hand-to-hand tussle.

The recommended battle formation was "not in a direct line, as an enemy is drawn up on land, but in the form of a half-moon: thus the wings will be advanced, and the center hollow; and if the enemy attempt to force the center, they will by this disposition find themselves entirely surrounded. The ships of the greatest force and the best troops are for this reason to be posted on the wings." [46]

At best, however, even the *quinquereme* was of limited holding capacity, and with crowded row-benches and anything up to a Cohort of marines crammed aboard, there was little room for stores and water for a long voyage. Vessels kept the seas only for brief periods, hugging the shore so as to be ready to run for shelter in the event of one of those violent storms suddenly blowing up in the manner peculiar to this particular latitude.

Although principally dependent on its oarage, the Roman galley was rigged with a mainmast and sometimes a foremast, with a single sail to each. It was also furnished with the embryo of a bowsprit in the form of an *artemon*, a small

[44] Thus a *quinquereme* did not imply a craft with five banks of oars, but a vessel with five men pulling on each sweep.

[45] Vegetius, *op. cit.*

[46] *Ibid.*

sloping mast over the bows. The sails were furled by a complicated system of brails, or cords passing through rings.
But it was upon their oar-benches that the leaders relied
in action.

"Naval strategy has for its end to found, support, and increase, as well in peace as in war, the sea power of a
country"; [47] and although somewhat laggard in its recognition of this fundamental fact, when comprehension of its
profound validity did strike home to the Romans, they took
in hand—however reluctantly—all the measures necessary
for its implementation.

"We cannot find in Roman military history anything to
match the far-ranging movements of Alexander the Great,
which seemed to mock distance and terrain . . . but within
the natural ambits of its needs the Roman art of war was in
the main well served by the mobility and endurance of its
soldiers." [48]

War, to Rome, was in no sense a glorious adventure; it was
a necessary evil in which the obvious necessity obscured the
underlying evil. What had to be done was tackled with resolution, tenacity, and a cool, stoic courage that victory failed
unduly to elate, or defeat disproportionately to depress. The
system whereby the Senate controlled policy to the extent
of directing the actual conduct of operations in the field—
as at Cannae, when the impetuous Varro was deliberately
encouraged to seek an encounter—had nothing whatever to
recommend it. It cannot too often be affirmed that "the
politician has nothing in his gift but disaster so soon as
he leaves his own business of creating or obviating wars, and
endeavors to conduct them." [49] Fortunately for his fellow
countrymen, the fighting ability of the Roman soldier was
on sufficiently high a level to retrieve the blunders to which
he was committed all too often by the well-intentioned
but uninstructed intervention of the politico amateur strate-
gist.

The Roman Army had its defects, of course. It demanded
considerable time for deployment from the line of march to
battle formation, and it was particularly weak on reconnaissance, which meant that it was always in danger of
being surprised and could frequently be jockeyed into fighting

[47] Bigot de Morogues.

[48] Adcock, *op. cit.*

[49] General Sir Ian Hamilton, *A Staff Officer's Scrap Book*, Vol. I.

on ground of the enemy's choosing. But the Legions benefited enormously from a corporate spirit which overrode all
personal ambition, conciliated all sense of grievance, disregarded all petty legalism, and welded all ranks into a corporate sense of purpose. They were warriors who believed
that the man who was afraid of death, feared life; and they
bore themselves accordingly.

With such paladins as her executive instrument, with
Carthage brought to submission, Spain overawed, and Italy
held in thrall, it is little wonder that Rome should turn her
eyes speculatively to the East. What Alexander the Macedonian had once accomplished could surely be achieved
again!

Chapter V

AFTERMATH OF VICTORY

"It hath been written that from no victory
shall the ass's kick be missing."

—Dionysius the Younger

Victory and defeat are the obverse and reverse of the
same coin; and which state is the more difficult for a nation
to adjust itself to, is extremely hard to determine. The
entail of defeat is spiritual and physical exhaustion, em-
bittered by a sense of bewildered but resentful humiliation,
which invariably leads to a witch-hunt for scapegoats before
it resolves itself into a sullen determination to reverse the
verdict "next time." Victory, on the other hand, never seems
to bring the fulfillment expected of it, either for the nation
as a whole or for the individual, since in both cases expectation has been pitched far too high. Once the shouting
has died away and the initial sense of infinite relief has
ebbed, the casting up of accounts breeds a growing sense
of having been cheated in some obscure way. The refulgent
hopes of the wartime orators have not been realized; the pos-

sible redemption of their cozening pledges seems as remote
as do the stars in their courses. On a very different plane
the victors' feeling of frustration is no less acute and exasperated than that experienced by the vanquished. It was all
going to be so glorious and uplifting; it has all turned out
so "flat, stale, and unprofitable."

So it was with the Rome of 201 B.C. With the peace concluded in that year "closes the heroic period of Roman history, the period of vigorous effort and strong national life,
of energy in the government, devotion in the people, of
manners still uncorrupted and institutions still unimpaired." [1]
It was not that Rome's odyssey of conquest had in any sense
come to an end. In the absence of any contemporary acceptance of the concept of the balance of power, domination
was the only course to pursue, a domination that was in-
divisible. Warned by the failure of Hellas to present a
united front to the world, owing to its stratification into a
hodgepodge of jealous, bickering little city-states, Rome was
determined to preserve and at the same time to expand a
unity that was based upon the incorporation and assimilation
of kindred and even alien elements, over whom the domination of the Eternal City should never for a moment be in
question.

But first of all it was necessary for Rome to deal with the
immediate aftermath of victory, the discontents it had begotten, and the domestic readjustments which the drastically
altered makeup of its society so clearly demanded. Nor were
the social problems few or easily resolved. The sturdy yeoman
class, which had supplied so many stalwarts to the Legions,
was in grave danger of decay, its demise foreshadowed by the
growing monopoly of land ownership enjoyed by a new and
ostentatiously thriving plutocracy. Made up in part by hard-
faced land speculators, and in part by government contractors
who quite shamelessly had profiteered out of carnage, these
Plebeian *arrivistes* had not only competed successfully for
state grants of real estate, but had bought up the vineyards,
the olive groves, the arable, the pastures, and the messuages
of cultivators too thriftless or too debt-ridden to compete
against the stream of foreign imports selling at prices with
which they found it impossible economically to compete. [2]
As for the dispossessed themselves, the best they could
hope for was menial employment on the farms of the

---

[1] How and Leigh, *op. cit.*

[2] Both Carthage and Sicily, for example, were the source of grain
imports that undersold the homegrown variety.

diminishing ruck of unpauperized clients, or work as serfs alongside the helots toiling on the bloated properties of the *nouveaux riches*.

Everywhere slave labor had replaced the wage earners, who flocked to Rome in their myriads, impoverished, idle, discontented, and only deterred by bribes and doles from combining openly with others of like kidney to seek redress for the parlous state into which they had sunk.

Casualties had wiped out nearly a fourth of the burgess population, the traditional source of the Legions' very best recruits, and suitable replacements to fill the yawning gaps in the ranks were hard to find. Even the shrunken Legions themselves needed vigorous pulling together. Inevitably, the survivors of the recent conflict looked for some relaxation of the exacting daily round now that the strain of war had ended, and the reaction to that perdurable strain had begun to make itself felt—a more easy and self-indulgent camp life, rendered possible even for the humblest Legionary by the sale of his war booty, had done much to weaken the moral fiber and sap the standard of discipline, so that the Centurions and the drillmasters were confronted with an uphill task when they set about their restoration.

In short, her victory in arms had "left Rome face to face with grave problems of policy. A wise statesmanship had to consider the proper government of the provinces and the modification in her municipal constitution entailed by empire; the unification of Italy; the reorganization of the Army, and the restoration of rural economy and sound finance." [3]

Perhaps of all the tasks confronting the Senate, that of reorganizing the Army was the one calling for most immediate attention. For

the war waged by Hannibal had interrupted Rome in the extension of her dominion to the Alps, or to the boundary of Italy, as was now the Roman phrase, and in her organization and colonizing of the Celtic territories. It was self-evident that the task would now be resumed at the point where it had been broken off, and the Celts were well aware of this. Thus in the very year of the conclusion of the peace with Carthage hostilities had recommenced in the territory of the Boii who were the most immediately exposed to danger; and a first success obtained by them over the hastily assembled Roman levy, coupled with the persuasions

[3] How and Leigh, *op. cit.*

of a Carthaginian Officer, Hamilcar, who had been left behind from the expedition of Mago in northern Italy, produced in the following year (200 B.C.) a general insurrection spreading beyond the two tribes immediately threatened, the Boii and Insurbes. The Ligurians were driven to arms by the nearer approach of danger, and even the youth of the Cenomani on this occasion listened less to the voice of their cautious chiefs than to the urgent appeal of their kinsmen who were in peril.[4]

Guerrilla warfare with the freebooting mountaineers was destined to drag on for over twenty years before the border could be regarded as anything like tranquilized. The foundation, in 177 B.C., of the burgess colony of Luna (Spezia) helped to a certain degree in checking the barbarians' raids, at the same time creating a useful port of embarkation for the West, while Samnium was repeopled with tribesmen loyal to Rome. The foundation of Aquileia, the last Latin colony in Italy, brought into being to command the eastern passes and serve as a control point for the northern Adriatic, involved a running conflict with the Istrians, while the reduction of the predatory Dalmatians was not completed until 156 B.C., two years before the successful defense of Massilia (Marseilles) registered the first unqualified Roman victory in Transalpine Gaul.

Compared with these exhausting demands on her armed forces, Rome could afford to dismiss the sporadic outbreaks of rebellious violence in Corsica and Sardinia as of relatively minor importance.

Rome had never forgotten, or forgiven, Philip V of Macedon for having sided with Hannibal at the time of the Second Punic War, although his support for the Carthaginian had taken no tangible form.

Despite the distraction of Alpine guerrilla warfare the Senate's design for expansion to the East remained unshaken, and war was declared on Philip under the pretext that he had injured Rome's allies, the Athenians, and the Kings of Egypt and Pergamum.[5] The Macedonian had added to his offense by utilizing his greatly strengthened fleet to seize the islands and towns on the coast of the Aegean which

---

4 Mommsen, *op. cit.*
5 On the Asiatic shores of the Aegean.

were under the protection of the King of Egypt, at this juncture a minor—an enterprise in which Philip had been joined by Antiochus, King of Syria.

It is conceivable that the Senate would have been prepared to tolerate a self-contained Macedonian State as a friendly neighbor. But "it was impossible that they could permit it to acquire the best part of Asiatic Greece and the important Cyrene, to crush the neutral commercial States, and thereby to double its power. Further, the fall of Egypt and the humiliation, and perhaps the subjugation, of Rhodes could not but inflict deep wounds on the trade of Sicily and Italy." [6] Harassed on her northern frontiers and war-weary as she might be, once more Rome stoically girded her loins for conflict.

Few men can have had so poor a sense of timing as Philip of Macedon. The moment to strike effectively at Rome had clearly arisen in 212 B.C. With Hannibal master of Tarentum, there was every encouragement for the Greek Monarch to send his Macedonian phalanx to the Carthaginian's support. But Philip had shillyshallied, the golden moment had passed, and "opportunity is not a harlot to beg the favors of the hesitant."

When, ten years later, the Senate dispatched an army into Greece under the Consul Publius Sulpicius Galba, not only had Philip to confront the might of Rome, but also to contend with Rome's *socii*,[7] the Aetolians, who were joined in due course by the opportunist Boeotians and Achaeans.

Ironically enough, for a State that was predominantly a land power, Rome's first blow was delivered by her fleet. Under Gaius Claudius Cento, an armada of 100 decked and 80 light open craft bore in on Chalcis in Euboea, Philip's principal Grecian stronghold, the depot for his stores and magazines and the pool of his war captives. Caught by surprise, "the undefended walls were scaled; and the garrison was put to death; the prisoners were liberated, and the stores were burnt; unfortunately there was a want of troops to hold the important position. On receiving news of this invasion, Philip immediately, in vehement indignation, started from Demetrias in Thessaly for Chalcis, and when he found no trace of the enemy there save the scene of ruin, he went on to Athens to retaliate. But his attempt to surprise the city was a failure, and even the assault was in

---

6 Mommsen, *op. cit.*

7 A term wide enough to cover anything from willing allies to coadjutors very little removed from hired mercenaries.

vain." [8] In this manner the Macedonian threat to Athens was nullified, whereafter winter conditions called a halt to major operations.

For his opening move in the ensuing spring campaign Sulpicius planned a three-pronged attack—by the Dardanian *socii* from the north, by the Aetolians and certain other auxiliaries from the south, and by the Legions in the center —supported by the allied fleet to the east. This converging movement was designed to break through the defiles of the Apsus range and confront Philip on the open plains of Macedon. But contemporary methods of intercommunication were far too imperfect to permit of the needful nicety of timing in what, in any case, would have been an operation of the extremest delicacy. In the event, the venture developed in so piecemeal a fashion as to prove a costly failure, which drove back the Romans, scattered the *socii*, and left Philip master of the field.

Encouraged to take the offensive, in the spring of 198 B.C. the Macedonian Monarch found himself confronted by a new Roman commander in T. Quinctius Flamininus. A mere thirty years of age, normally of strong Hellenic sympathies, he was a skilled diplomat who only just missed qualifying as that worst of abominations, a political soldier. In effect, "he belonged to the younger generation, who began to lay aside the patriotism as well as the habits of their forefathers and, though not unmindful of the fatherland, were still more mindful of themselves and of Hellenism." [9]

Having failed to reduce his opponent to an accommodating frame of mind by diplomacy, Flamininus had no alternative but to bring him to battle. The question was, how best to ensure that victory which ambition as much as patriotism demanded should be his. "Helped out of his perplexity by some chiefs among the Epirots, they conducted a Roman corps of 4,000 infantry and 300 cavalry by mountain paths to the heights above the Macedonian camp; and, when the Consul attacked the enemy's army in front, the advance of that Roman division, unexpectedly descending from the mountains commanding the position, decided the battle. Philip lost his camp and entrenchments and nearly 2,000 men, and hastily retreated to the pass of Tempe, the gate of Macedonia proper." [10]

Philip still possessed a force of 26,000, and with this

body of troops he moved forward by way of Larissa to the vicinity of the Roman camp.

Here the advanced guards met, but after a skirmish of reconnoitering parties, both Generals, embarrassed by the difficult ground and anxious to secure supplies, moved by parallel lines on Scotussa, separated by a range of hills and groping about through the mist and rain of autumn, in ignorance of each other's movements. On the third day, a casual encounter in dark and dirty weather, between the Macedonian reserve, posted to secure the flanking heights, and a scouting party of Flamininus, brought on a general engagement. The Romans were getting the worst of the skirmish, till their supports reinforced the attack, when the tables were turned again by the advent of the Macedonian cavalry and light infantry. Their victorious charge was only stemmed by the gallantry of the Aetolian Horse, inferior as skirmishers to the Numidian alone, who gave the Consul time to draw out his whole force for action. Then Philip yielded, against his better judgment, to the desire of his troops. With the right wing of the phalanx he hastily climbed the hill, formed on the ridge, received his retreating troops on the right, and charging at once in dense deep column, with the weight of the phalanx on the sloping ground, drove in and shattered the Roman left. But the rapid advance had dislocated his line [formation]. Flamininus, passing to his right, hurled his *maniples,* with the elephants in front, upon the unformed Macedonian left, disordered by haste and the uneven ground. The battle was decided by the brilliant stroke of a nameless Tribune, who, disengaging some companies from the victorious right, fell with disastrous effect upon Philip's defenseless rear.[11]

It was the old, old story of rigidity versus pliability of maneuver. Once the inflexible phalanx had been broken up or even badly dented, it had no alternative battle formation on which to fall back, and in the ensuing *mêlée* it was easy prey for the Legionaries' busy, thrusting swords. The action of Cynoscephalae utterly discredited the outdated phalanx formation, reliance on which had brought Philip of Macedon to such desperate straits that he had no option but to sue for peace.

Disregarding the inordinate claims for recompense ad-

11 How and Leigh, *op. cit.*

vanced by the Aetolians, the grasping Boeotians, and other greedy associates in the recent conflict, in 196 B.C. Flamininus concluded a pact by whose terms Philip surrendered his foreign possessions, his fighting marine, the province of Orestis, reduced his army, and paid an indemnity of one thousand talents. As a power, Macedon virtually ceased to exist, although Rome refrained from annexing it on the understanding that its foreign policy would be under the control of the Senate.

The Aetolians and the members of the Achaean League [12] might grumble that their respective rewards fell far short of expectation and mutter that Greece had only changed masters. But the status quo was restored in Rhodes and Pergamum, Thessaly neutralized, and the Spartan coast relieved from interference. With whatever mental reservations, the freedom of Hellas had been officially affirmed; but, "rent by faction, corrupt in morals, decayed in population, permeated by socialism, the Greek States with their petty politics, were overshadowed by the power and proximity of Rome," [13] to whom, however, their direct annexation appeared as yet to be a supererogation. Her commercial and political interests seemed to be secured by a conglomerate of theoretically free and precautiously friendly powers, acting as checks on one another and serving as useful buffers against potential enemies. Wars had been waged for far smaller gains than these.

Throughout the conflict with Philip of Macedon diplomacy had succeeded in averting any intervention on the part of Antiochus III, Monarch of that Kingdom of Syria which had been brought into being with the breakup of the ancient Empire of the Seleucids. Sovereign of a corrupt court and a people of shallow culture and Oriental laxity, Antiochus still held on precariously to his possessions of Caria, Phrygia, and Lydia, despite the increasing pressure of the barbarians along his borders. Successful in his war with the Egyptian, Ptolemy Philopator, he secured Palestine and Coele-Syria, dowering therewith his daughter Cleopatra on her betrothal to the adolescent Ptolemy V (Epiphanes).

In 197 B.C. the ceded territories and even the free States of the Aegean coast had come under threat from a powerful

---

[12] The Achaean League was formed by the citizens of Patrae, Dyme, and Pharoe; the Aetolian League by the inhabitants of the territory bounded by Epirus, Acarnania, and Locris.

[13] How and Leigh, *op. cit.*

Syrian fleet and army. By 196 B.C., despite the stout resistance put up by Rhodes, Antiochus had occupied Ephesus, whence he crossed into Europe to restore and fortify Lysimachia, on the far side of the Hellespont, ignoring alike the protests of Rome and the stereotyped warning addressed to him by Flamininus—the policy of appeasement, as always, only serving to encourage the aggressor. A gesture of singularly offensive defiance was the reception given to Hannibal on his arrival in Ephesus, where he was welcomed with every circumstance of honor. It was an affront to which Rome's feeble reply was the withdrawal of her garrisons from Greek soil, a craven move which fostered the arrogance of the Syrian while at the same time arousing the fermenting disaffection of the Greeks, where the open partisanship of the perennially disgruntled Aetolians encouraged Antiochus to proclaim himself the liberator of Hellas.

In the autumn of 192 B.C. Antiochus took the field at the head of a small force of Syrians, designed to serve as the nucleus of a Graeco-Asiatic host that would include, it was confidently hoped, the forces at Philip of Macedon's command as well as those of the Achaean League and others of the dissident city-states.

But Philip preferred a benevolent conqueror to a shifty ally; Epirus thought it wiser to sit on the fence, while on second thoughts the Achaean League wisely preferred to adhere to Rome. Save for the effervescent Aetolians and the pigheaded Boeotians, response to "the Liberator's" call to arms was scarcely enthusiastic. The inertia of Rome, however, encouraged Antiochus and his motley following to secure a base at Chalcis, in Euboea, and indulge in rather empty demonstrations against Larissa, in Thessaly. Furthermore, at Hannibal's suggestion, a combined land and sea force was assigned to him for the purpose of kindling a third Punic War in Carthage, supported by a campaign in Italy itself. At the same time emissaries were sent to Spain to encourage the local insurrectionary movement, which again had assumed formidable proportions.

It was not until the spring of 191 B.C. that Rome took the problem of dealing with Antiochus seriously in hand. Having provided for the safety of the homeland and the adjacent islands, the Senate set about the doubling of the fleet and the reinforcement of the vanguard of Roman troops already in Epirus to a total of 40,000, inclusive of allies and auxiliaries. Among the last-named was a strong force of Numidian cavalry and a number of Libyan war-elephants sent by the loyal Massinissa. The whole force was under the command of the Consul Manius Acilius Glabrio, who was assisted by two Tribunes, Lucius Valerius Flaccus and the rumbustious Marcus Porcius Cato.

Roman preparations were pushed forward with such exemplary dispatch that, with some help from the Macedonian troops, Thessaly was speedily cleared of all trace of the enemy, the whole army thereafter concentrating at Larissa.

In face of these expeditious activities, Antiochus resolved to entrench himself at Thermopylae,[14] there to await the arrival of those numerous reinforcements his lieutenants had been sent back to Syria to organize. The army under immediate command, "decimated by sickness and desertion in its dissolute winter quarters," was supplemented by a mere 4,000 Aetolians, of whom no more than half obeyed their commander's order to occupy and hold the mountain path by which, in earlier days, Xerxes had succeeded in overwhelming the Spartans.

The other 2,000 Aetolians threw themselves in the neighboring town of Heraclea, where they took no other part in the ensuing battle than that of attempting during its progress to surprise and plunder the Roman camp. Even the Aetolians posted on the heights discharged their duty of watching with remissness and reluctance; their post on the Callidromus allowed itself to be surprised by Cato, and the Asiatic phalanx, which the Consul had meanwhile assailed in front and dispersed, when the Romans, hastening down the mountains, fell on its flank. As Antiochus had made no provision for any eventuality and had not even thought of retreat, his army was destroyed partly on the field of battle, partly during its flight; with difficulty a small band reached Demetrias, and the King escaped to Chalcis with five hundred men. He embarked in haste for Ephesus; Europe was lost to him all but his possessions in Thrace, and even the fortresses could be no longer defended.[15]

The allied fleet, which had already severed the Syrian's line of communication, now took up the offensive, and with the defeat near Chios of Antiochus's lieutenant Polyxenidas,

---

[14] Where, in the Graeco-Persian War of 480 B.C., for three whole days a handful of Spartans repelled the attacks of an overwhelming Persian host; one only of the gallant defenders surviving to retail the story.

[15] Mommsen, *op. cit.*

such straws in the wind as the declaration of fidelity to Rome on the part of the small States of Smyrna, Samos, and Chios gave a broad enough hint of the general trend of neutral opinion.

Antiochus, however, had at last bestirred himself to raise a great host in his own territory, while strengthening his fleet at Ephesus and dispatching Hannibal to raise a new navy in Phoenicia.

In March of 190 B.C. the incompetent Livius Cornelius Scipio, by pressure of family influence, was endowed with the consular command of the Roman forces; his own exceedingly modest military talents being buttressed by the presence at his elbow of the brilliant Scipio Africanus.

Since the majority of war-begotten alliances are little more than enmities temporarily disguised, the Aetolians had by this stage in affairs been given ample time in which to regurgitate a long-cherished sense of grievance against Antiochus. Their sullen acceptance of a six months' armistice therefore left Scipio Africanus free to push on to the Hellespont by way of the long and arduous land route, thrown open to him by Philip. In the interim the fumbling Livius, recalled at the outcome of the defeat of the allied Rhodian squadron at Samos, had been succeeded by L. Aemilius Regillus. With Polyxenidas mewed up in the harbor of Ephesus, the new Consul's principal tasks were to make every preparation to facilitate the crossing of the Hellespont, while keeping a watchful eye on the naval armament in Ephesus and taking every precaution to prevent its juncture with the fleet belatedly organized by Hannibal. This auxiliary armada was eventually met and defeated by the well-handled Rhodian squadron, off Aspendus, in Pamphylia.

This success was followed up by the Roman Admiral Eudamus's triumph over Polyxenidas, who was swept from the seas with a loss of forty of his ships, a stunning blow which gravely shook the confidence of the mercenaries in Syrian pay. Antiochus, who had signally failed to harass Scipio's difficult march through Thrace, hastily evacuated his position guarding the Hellespont, sacrificing his stores and permitting his opponents to land on the Asiatic side of the waterway unopposed.

Irresolution was crowned by rashness when, at Magnesia in the late autumn of 190 B.C., Antiochus flung his unintegrated, unwieldy levies at a Roman force barely half the strength of the 80,000 opponents—including 12,000 Horse— by whom it was confronted. Led by Gnaeus Domitius in the absence of Scipio, who was prostrated on a bed of sickness, the Legions made ready to deal with the Syrian's

immense mass of troops, formed in two divisions. In the first were placed the mass of the light troops, the peltasts, bowmen, slingers, the mounted archers of the Mysians, Dahae, and Elymaeans, the Arabs on their dromedaries, and the scythe-chariots. In the second division the heavy cavalry (the Cataphraclae, a sort of cuirassiers) were stationed on the flanks; next to these, in the intermediate division, the Gallic and Cappadocian infantry; and in the very center the phalanx armed after the Macedonian fashion, 16,000 strong, the flower of the army, which, however, had not room in the narrow space and had to be drawn up in double files 32 deep. In the space between the two divisions were placed 54 elephants, distributed among the companies of the phalanx and of the heavy cavalry.[16]

The Roman left was flanked by a river, and therefore called for the minimum of squadrons for its protection. The bulk of the Horse, together with the light troops, were concentrated on the right, under the orders of Eumenes of Pergamum. With so motley a throng to deal with, it was only necessary to create a condition of confusion for the battle to go in favor of the controlled and disciplined. To this end Eumenes threw out his right-wing skirmishers to loose a hail of missiles at the chariot teams, breaking their line and turning back the scared and infuriated animals on the camels, who broke and stumbled rearward, spreading panic and disorder. A charge by the whole righthand brigade of Horse drove in the confused and panicky left wing, bearing on the left flank of the central column and forcing it to halt and endeavor to form square. Heedless of what was going forward elsewhere on the field, Antiochus had pressed impetuously towards the Roman main camp. Stripped of its supports, the phalanx found itself assailed both front and rear, decimated by a hail of missiles, and under ever-increasing pressure. Even so, it withdrew in reasonably good order until utterly disrupted by the frightened, trumpeting elephants tearing through its ranks. It was only as he retired from his unsuccessful attempt on the Roman camp that Antiochus became aware of the disaster brought about by his imbecile failure to control his forces, which by this time

16 Mommsen, *op. cit.* Cf. Polybius.

had got completely out of hand; the slaughter inflicted on them was only aggravated by their desperate but futile effort to defend their camp.

With Antiochus's incontinent flight, the whole barbarian military façade collapsed. Asia Minor obviously could not compete with the organized might of Rome, and the peace solicited was concluded by the ten members of a commission led by Gnaeus Manlius Volso, maintained, like the army of occupation, at Antiochus's expense. Mulcted of an indemnity of fifteen thousand talents, his belligerent rights were severely delimited and he was forced to surrender all his possessions west of Mount Taurus and the Halys river, while Cappadocia assumed an independence he was in no position to challenge, and his Armenian satrapies became minor principalities. In the interests of Rome, Pergamum became a useful buffer between Syria and Macedon.

But if Rome instituted no new provinces, various protectorates were created to reward those—including Eumenes, the victor of Magnesia—whose service in the recent war called for recognition and reward. It was characteristic of the deterioration in personal integrity begotten of the rise of the Roman plutocracy that, "Volso occupied his troops and served his own pockets . . . by crushing the Asiatic Celts and levying contributions all round. His action illustrates the dangerous powers of the imperium exercised at a distance from control by annually changing officers," [17] animated by the determination to pile up wealth by any means, so long as opportunity offered.

The Greeks, being as difficult to please as pampered children, were vociferous in their demands for recompense out of all proportion to the services they had rendered, and in general remained fractiously opposed to the stern limits set to Hellenic nationalism. As inconsequent as they were powerless, they entirely failed to grasp the fact that the only way in which to ensure internal peace and prosperity was gracefully to accept a foreign supremacy which at least was benevolent in intention. It was, indeed, to be a considerable time before the conglomerate of jealous, spiteful midget States ceased to nag and fulminate, to abandon their irresponsible parody of freedom and accept the principle of equilibrium as the destiny marked out for them. Of them all, only the island of Rhodes seemed reasonably content with the award of the mainland province of Lycia and most of adjacent Caria, in return for maintaining control of the

[17] Mommsen, *op. cit.*

neighboring waters in the interest of Rome. On the Adriatic the chain of posts under Roman suzerainty was completed by the acquisition of Cephallenia and Zacynthus, with supervision of the foreign relations of the captured territories.

There were squabbles, conspiracies, and spasmodic shows of insurrection; but, secure in her principle of *Divide et imperia*, Rome could afford to permit these fitful April tempests to blow themselves out.

In one particular, however, the long arm of Rome reached out in vain. After the debacle of Magnesia, Hannibal had taken refuge at the Court of Prusias, King of Bithynia, from whom the Senate demanded the exile's surrender. Realizing that little mercy awaited him at the hands of a people he had so often and so successfully defied, and scorning the indignity of surrender, the proud, unbending Carthaginian chose to end his life with a dose of poison from the finger ring from which he would never be parted.

Not inappropriately, perhaps, the same period (184-182 B.C.) also witnessed the death in self-imposed exile of Hannibal's lifelong foe and worthiest opponent, Scipio Africanus. Long out of favor with the Senate, in which he had so often been the butt of Cato's implacable enmity, and accused of unwarrantable lenity in his treatment of the defeated Antiochus, Scipio had deliberately withdrawn from public life, despite his continued favor with the crowd, to eke out existence on his estate at Liternum, in Campania. His legacy to Rome was his daughter Cornelia, the mother of Tiberius and Gaius Graccus, "the Gracci."

With the expulsion of the Carthaginians, Rome had assumed suzerainty over both northern, or Hither, Spain— the northeastern territory which included the present-day Aragon and Catalonia—and Further Spain, which embraced Andalusia, Murcia, and Valencia. In this latter area the Greek and Punic towns—Emporiae, Saguntum, New Carthage, Malaca, and Gades—adhered to Rome,[18] although these centers penetrated no further than the coastal fringe. Many of the more cultured and wealthy of the indigenous Turdetani responded with some readiness to Roman innovations and ideas; but the west, north, and center of the land were still in the hands of a proud and hardy race of highlander guerrilleros, prone to plunder and apt for war-

[18] For similar self-protective reasons Massilia clung closely to her Roman suzerain.

fare although entirely lacking in orthodox military organization. As successors to the Carthaginians, the Romans were determined to define and consolidate their Iberian frontiers and round off their possessions by the reduction of Celtiberia—the two Castiles—while at the same time repelling the incursions of the Portuguese tribes and the inhabitants of the unconquered north.

Distance and the prolongation of those guerrilla campaigns of which the Iberian tribesmen never seemed to weary, while presaging the consolidation of a standing, long-service professional Roman army, constituted a heavy additional drain on the country's resources, already under considerable pressure in other fields. Moreover, "the frequent prorogation and the independence of the commands reacted on the character of the officers," while "the uncertain nature of the warfare, the scantiness of the booty, and the unsatisfied greed of the ever-changing officers, helped to give a stamp of treachery, avarice and violence to the Spanish struggle; and here, too, the system of annual reliefs was especially ruinous." [19]

Although outbreaks of insurrection were sporadic, it was necessary to garrison Spain permanently, with no less than four strong Legions—at least 40,000 men. Thus

the old Roman custom of sending troops only where the exigencies of war at the moment required them, and of not keeping the man called to serve, except in very serious and important wars, under arms for more than a year, was found incompatible with the retention of the turbulent and remote Spanish provinces beyond the sea; it was absolutely impossible to withdraw the troops from these, and very dangerous even to relieve them extensively. The Roman burgesses began to perceive that dominion over a foreign people is an annoyance not only to the vanquished but the victor, and began to murmur loudly regarding the odious war-service of Spain. While the Generals, with good reason, refused to allow the relief of the existing corps as a whole, the men mutinied and threatened that, if they were not allowed their discharge, they would take it of their own accord. [20]

It was only with the introduction of long-service contracts,

[19] How and Leigh, *op. cit.*
[20] Mommsen, *op. cit.*

and the growing professionalism which came to characterize the time-serving soldier, that discontent gradually subsided and the Legionary, like any other sworn man at arms, acquired the veteran's complete indifference to his environment, as long as the day-to-day amenities to which he is accustomed are uninterruptedly available.

The transition of the Legionary from the original concept of the "embattled farmer" called, like Cincinnatus, from the plough to temporary service in a national militia, was gradual, but it was an inevitable part of the price of empire. In his place, the professional man-at-arms came slowly but inevasibly into being: a man who looked to war booty and the cumulative rewards of long and faithful service to compensate him for his years of separation from homeland and family. To such a man, the leader who could best ensure him such rewards was the individual to whom he gave his fealty—even before that which he owed the State. It was an outlook that was destined to influence most profoundly the development of events in the not-so-distant future. In the meantime Spain was molding him into the form that one day he would make peculiarly his own.

The wars themselves, which the Romans waged in Spain, were but of subordinate importance. They began with the very departure of Scipio (206 B.C.) and continued as long as the war with Hannibal lasted. After the peace with Carthage, there was a cessation of arms in the peninsula; but only for a short time. In 197 B.C. a general insurrection broke out in both provinces; the Commander of the Further Province was hard pressed; the Commander of Hither Spain was completely defeated, and was himself slain. It was necessary to take up the war in earnest, and although in the meantime the able Praetor, Quintus Minucius, had mastered the first danger, the Senate resolved in 195 B.C. to send the Consul Marcus Cato in person to Spain. On landing at Emporia he actually found the whole of Hither Spain overrun by the insurgents; with difficulty that seaport and one or two strongholds in the interior were still held for Rome. A pitched battle took place between the insurgents and the consular army, in which, after an obstinate conflict, man against man, the Roman military skill at length decided the day with its last reserve. The whole of Hither Spain thereupon sent in its submission. So little, however, was this submission meant in earnest, that on a rumor of the Consul having returned to Rome, the insurrection immediately recommenced. But the rumor was false; and after Cato had rapidly reduced the communities which had revolted for the second time and sold them *en masse* into slavery, he decreed a general disarming of the Spaniards in the Hither Province, and issued orders to all the towns of the natives from the Pyrenees to the Guadalquivir to pull down their walls on one and the same day. No one knew how far the command extended; and there was no time to come to any understanding; most of the communities complied; and of the few that were refractory not many ventured, when the Roman army soon appeared before their walls, to await its assault.

These energetic measures were certainly not without permanent effect. Nevertheless the Romans had almost every year to reduce to subjection some mountain valley or mountain stronghold in the "peaceful province," and the constant incursions of the Lusitanians into the Further Province terminated occasionally in the severe defeat of the Romans. In 191, for instance, a Roman army was obliged, after heavy loss, to abandon its camp, and to return by forced marches into the more tranquil districts. It was not until the victory gained by the Praetor Lucius Aemilius Paulus in 189 B.C., and a second still more considerable success achieved by the brave Praetor Gaius Calpurnius beyond the Tagus over the Lusitanians in 185 B.C., that quiet for some time prevailed. In Further Spain the hitherto almost nominal rule of the Romans over the Celtiberian tribes was converted into something more real by Quintus Fulvius Flaccus, who after a great victory over them in 181 B.C. compelled at least the adjacent cantons to submission; and especially by his successor, Tiberius Graccus, who achieved results of a permanent character not only by his arms, by which he reduced three hundred Spanish townships, but still more by his adroitness in adapting himself to the views and habits of the simple but haughty nation. He induced Celtiberians of note to take service in the Roman army, and so created a class of dependents; he assigned land to the roving tribes, and collected them in towns . . . and so imposed a serious check on their freebooter habits; he regulated the relations of the several tribes to the Romans by just and wise treaties, and so stopped, as far as possible, the springs of future rebellion . . . although the Celtiberians still from time to time winced under the yoke.[21]

To no one can downgrading come more ungratefully than to an anointed Sovereign. Instead of bringing Philip of Macedon the rewards even a somewhat lethargic ally might reasonably anticipate, the outcome of the war of 200-196 B.C. against Antiochus had denuded him of his earlier conquests in Thessaly, Aetolia, and Thrace and left him surrounded by hostile neighbors, while subjecting him to constant Roman surveillance and reproof. With characteristic native guile, he employed the cloak of submission to obscure his resolve to renew the struggle for untrammelled sovereignty by every available means. Nursing his revenue, encouraging the expansion of his population, cultivating potentially useful neighbors, strengthening his frontiers, he worked steadily but unobtrusively to prepare for the day when Macedon once again should challenge the might of Rome.

The gage was nearly thrown down in 183 B.C., but in the outcome rupture was averted by the intervention of Philip's son Demetrius. A hostage for Macedon's good behavior and installed in the Eternal City itself, Demetrius, like so many who undergo psychological naturalization, had become more Roman than the Romans. It followed that the thought of a breach between his native land and the country which had become his spiritual home was not to be entertained, and it was with the utmost readiness that he cooperated with Flamininus and the Senate in their endeavor to form a strong and reliable Roman party in Macedon.

But Demetrius had failed to reckon with the innate hostility of Perseus, offspring of the Monarch and a concubine, but nonetheless the King's eldest son and heir presumptive to the throne. Gaining his father's ear, Perseus managed to persuade him that Demetrius was conspiring against the life of his elder brother. Thoroughly deluded, Philip consented to the younger man's recall from Rome, and when forged documents were produced to him purporting to prove Demetrius's guilty intentions, the unhappy King gave orders that his son should be put to death—a fiat that Perseus took care to see carried into execution with the minimum of delay.

The judicial murder of the hapless Demetrius in 181 B.C. was almost immediately followed by the aging King's

[21] Mommsen, *op. cit.* Cf. Polybius.

discovery that he had been tricked. But before he could take the necessary steps formally to disinherit the son who had been guilty of fratricide, he was overcome by a mortal sickness. Perseus, informed of his father's irretrievable decline, kept the intelligence to himself and thus secured mastery of the Kingdom before the news of Philip's death (in 179 B.C.) had been given general circulation.

When Perseus ascended the throne he found at his disposal the fruits of six-and-twenty years' careful husbanding. His treasury was full, his magazines bulging; with allied detachments and a certain number of mercenaries, he could muster an army of over 40,000 trained men; a force strong enough confidently to challenge a Rome whose commitments in Spain and on her Alpine borders already constituted a heavy drain on her military resources. The one thing for which he had not made due allowance was the fact that he was far better at planning than at carrying his designs into execution. Liberally anointed with self-approbation as he might be, the moment of action invariably found resolution and dynamic action replaced by indecision and a fatal infirmity of purpose. In the scroll of history there are two types of individual—those who make a show and those who make a difference. It was written in the destiny of Perseus that he should fall into the lesser category.

Greece, ever turbulent and dissatisfied, was ripe for insurrection; Perseus's matrimonial connections with Syria and Bithynia held out some hope of useful alliances, although there was less to be looked for from the bibulous Dalmatian Genthius, Prince of Scodra. Moreover, the support of Carthage was uncertain in the extreme. Perhaps even more important, nothing had been done to improve the tactical flexibility of the phalanx, while there was a notable insufficiency of strongholds to act as rallying points.

In any case, the stir and undertow of belligerence was by no means lost on the watchful Eumenes of Pergamum, who in 172 B.C. persuaded the Senate, despite Perseus's parade of virtuous remonstrance, unostentatiously to prepare for war.

At the close of the year Perseus's denunciation of the treaty of Cynocephalae, and his demand for recognition on terms of equality with Rome, rendered conflict inevitable; although for a brief period the Macedonian permitted himself to be hoodwinked by a pretense of negotiation, meanwhile Rome hurried forward her preparations while sedulously setting her propaganda agencies to work to undermine such popularity as Perseus enjoyed in the East.

With war declared and his potential allies—Rhodes, Syria, Bithynia, and Byzantium—either hastening to affirm their neutrality or openly siding with Rome, Perseus took to the mountains, where the sharpening of his sword seemed to consume an unconscionable amount of time. Meanwhile, P. Licinius Crassus had landed in Greece at the head of a force of close on 50,000 Roman and allied troops, while a powerful fleet under C. Lucretius operated from its base at Chalcis.

Posting an ample reserve in Illyria, Crassus advanced undisturbed to Larissa, thus putting himself in a position to isolate the Macedonian and gain touch with the fleet and such Greeks as had rallied to the Eagles, less out of love for Rome than from a waspish dislike of Perseus and his overweening pretensions.

Unfortunately, Licinius Crassus was less successful in demonstrating his military skill in the field than in extolling it to the Senate, and as the outcome of a decisive reverse when Perseus loosed his cavalry at him at Callicinus, he was forced to retire behind the Peneius. But instead of following up his success with the greatest possible energy, Perseus feebly sued for peace, which was, very understandably, refused with some asperity.

Another indecisive encounter at Phalanna was followed on both sides by a series of moves to secure positions of advantage, which served to demonstrate only too eloquently that nepotism and corruption in the appointment of military leaders, matched as it was by the brutality, libertinage, avarice, and slovenly indiscipline of the troops, had reduced the Army to as low an ebb as it had ever reached.[22] In the circumstances it is scarcely any wonder that "the wretched Roman commander knew not how or where to attack; while the army marched to and fro in Thessaly without accomplishing anything of importance. Perseus might have assumed the offensive; he saw that the Romans were badly led and dilatory; the news had passed like wildfire through Greece, that the Greek army had been brilliantly victorious in the first engagement; a second victory might lead to a general rising of the patriot party, [23] and, by com-

---

[22] So low had the general standard of the Army fallen that furloughs and discharges could be bought, while all ranks devoted more attention to plunder than to inflicting defeat on the enemy.

[23] Actually the Epirots were the only community to change sides.

mencing guerrilla warfare, might produce incalculable results." [24] But Perseus was wedded to the deadly fallacious
belief that wars can be won without seizing the initiative
and retaining it at all hazards.

By 168 B.C. it was clear that, with the Army relapsed
into inactivity and the fleet reduced to virtual impotence
by desertion and disease, drastic steps would have to be
taken lest Rome should suffer a humiliating setback. Gal-
vanized into realization of what was so desperately needed,
the Senate appointed L. Aemilius Paulus, son of the stalwart
who had fallen at Cannae, to take over the command. A
veteran in his sixties, "a man of the old nobility, but of
humble means, and therefore not so successful in the
Comitia as on the battlefield, where he had remarkably distinguished himself in Spain and still more in Liguria," Paulus had experienced the singular honor of being elected
Consul for a second period. In all respects he was precisely
the man to restore the troops' discipline and morale and
inspire them with that faith, alike in their leadership and
in their own fighting quality, which is the sure precursor of
victory.

Under the stimulation of this born leader of men, the
Illyrian freebooters were speedily swept from the seas, while
the Praetor Anicius inflicted condign defeat on the tosspot
Genthius and made himself master of the Dalmatian's
capital in thirty days. Outflanked by a move which turned
the line of the Elpius, Perseus fell back to Pydna. Here, in
June of 168 B.C., a skirmish of watering parties brought
on the crucial conflict which was to decide the fate of
Greece and confer on Rome the supremacy of the known
world.

With both sides wrought up to battle,

the gray-headed Roman General, passing through the
ranks in person, without helmet or shield, carefully
arranged his men. Scarce were they in position when
the formidable phalanx assailed them; the General himself, who had witnessed many a hard fight afterwards
acknowledged that he had trembled. The Roman vanguard dispersed; a Paeliginian cohort was overthrown
and almost annihilated; the Legions themselves hurriedly retreated till they reached a hill close by the
Roman camp. Here the fortune of the day changed.
The uneven ground and the hurried pursuit had dis-

24 Mommsen, *op. cit.*

ordered the ranks of the phalanx; the Romans in single
cohorts entered at every gap, and attacked it on the
flanks and in rear; the Macedonian cavalry which alone
could have rendered aid, looked calmly on, and soon fled
in a body, the King among the foremost. And thus
the fate of Macedonia was decided within an hour.[25]

Over 3,000 phalangites fell to the thirsty Roman swords;
in all, 20,000 Macedonians bestrewed the battlefield, while
11,000 were taken captive. A mere fifteen days after Paulus
had assumed command, the conflict had been brought decisively to an end. In the process, the phalanx as a worthwhile battle-formation had finally been discredited; the pro-
teanism and durability of the *maniple* had been established
past further argument.

Perseus, forsaken by all but a handful of his followers,
was ruthlessly hunted down, to fall at last, together with
his store of treasure, into the victors' hands to adorn the
triumph that was so rightly the veteran Consul's due.

Fortunately for Greece, the terms of settlement were in
the generous hands of Aemilius Paulus. Reluctant to strain
the overloaded fabric of the State and anxious to maintain
the structure and spirit of the Republic, Macedon was declared free, although regal rule was abolished and her armed
forces reduced to a few frontier guards. Illyria was dis-
membered, its territory divided into three "free" states,
paying tribute, and its fleet confiscated. Epirus was dealt
with far more harshly—seventy of its towns were sacked
and 150,000 of its nationals enslaved. Rhodes's ill-timed
affectation of Hellenism had cost her her invaluable possessions on the mainland, to the serious detriment of her commerce. Despite Eumenes's timely warning, Pergamus's preference for benevolent neutrality rather than active support
was penalized with quite unwarrantable severity. By 168
B.C. Rome's protectorate over Egypt had received universal
recognition; nothing remained but to organize and tran-
quilize the dominions that had come under the Roman sway.
From time to time it was necessary to deal firmly with such
sporadic outbreaks of rebellion as that of the Pretender
Andriscus of Macedon, and that of the Achaean League,
the last-named leading to the sack of Corinth and the reduction of Thebes and Chalcis to the status of mere villages. Widespread terrorism and attempted reprisal instigated
by the self-styled "patriot" parties led to the removal of a

[25] Mommsen, *op. cit.*

thousand hostages, including the historian Polybius, to
Rome, where, all things considered, they could at least congratulate themselves on being well out of the factional turmoil raging throughout the rebarbative lands of Hellas.

As the reign of terror passed and the tools of Rome
vanished one by one from the stage of politics, some
measure of peace returned to Hellas. But deeper sores remained; social democracy, the fruit of wild theory and
wilder revolutions, was rampant in thought and act.
Public and private bankruptcy, brigandage, depopulation,
marked the ruin of the country. There was war between
rich and poor, faction and faction, city and city. Marriage was neglected, property insecure. . . .

But the rapidity of her ruin saved Greece from the extremities of war and the furies of faction. The regime
of fussy confederacies, of political hysterics, of social
disorganization and ceaseless Roman commissions had
ended. There was at least a chance of peace, security
and progress. No doubt Rome had sown rebellion and
reaped discord, but the true cause of the ruin of
Greece is to be found in her political vices. By their
narrow patriotism and incapacity for combination, by
their lack of tolerance and their quarrelsome intrigues,
her leaders pulled down destruction on their own
heads.[26]

One of democracy's most serious defects is that on occasion it places in the lead political charlatans who will
encompass the ruin of a people in a matter of weeks, and in
Greece such men abounded.

There is nothing against which a defeated nation has to
be more on guard than the unrebuked encroachments of
one of the principal victor's lesser allies, aflame to reap a
reward out of all proportion to its deserts. In the Second
Punic War the support given to Roman arms by Massinissa
had proved of considerable value. But the Senate's design to
maintain an equable balance of power between Numidia
and a reborn Carthage had been thrown completely out of
gear by the rapid enlargement and consolidation of Massinissa's domains, which had come to engirdle Carthage on
every side, from the borders of Mauretania to the sands of
Cyrene. With his capital at Cirta, a bulging treasury, and

[26] How and Leigh, *op. cit.*

a formidable army, the Numidian Sovereign had transformed a nomadic population of Libyan and Punic peoples into a vigorous nation—rival to a Carthaginian neighbor whose astonishing postwar recovery was the constant target of Cato's denunciation in the Senate. Sent on a mission to Carthage in 175 B.C., on his return to the capital he never ceased to inveigh against a Power in whose miraculous resurgence he perceived a renewed and even more formidable threat to Rome's dominance throughout the world. Time after time he ended his peroration in the Senate with the demand, *"Censeo delendam esse Carthaginem!"*—"Carthage must be destroyed!"

Pride, commercial jealousy, and nervous dread had not far to seek for a *casus belli*. Certain Punic partisans of Numidia had been banished from Carthage, and Massinissa's demand for their reinstatement, although supported by Rome, had been refused. The vain, obese Hasdrubal, however, was no Hannibal, and the defeat he suffered at the Numidian's hands was followed by the cold-eyed slaughter of his surrendered troops. Having watched her rivals obligingly cut each other's throats, Rome herself moved into action. Loftily affirming that a treaty had been ignored, her stipulation for disarmament neglected, and an ally wantonly attacked, she ostentatiously pushed forward her preparations to take the field. It was in vain that the Punic emissaries made absolute submission, rendered up three hundred hostages, and affirmed their readiness to obey "such further commands as should be imposed by the Consuls." The army sailed, and on its arrival at Utica the "further commands" were issued one by one. In response arms were delivered, ships surrendered, the walls of Carthage stripped. Then came the final mandate—to destroy the proud city itself and settle its inhabitants ten miles from the sea on which its prosperity had so long depended.

In a fury of despair, the Carthaginians repudiated their earlier submission and prepared to defend their beloved city to the last man. "Day and night all, without distinction of age and sex, were occupied in constructing machines and forging arms; the public buildings were torn down to procure timber and metal; women cut off their hair to furnish the strings indispensable for the catapults; in an incredibly short time the walls and the men were once more armed." [27]

In 147 B.C. the conduct of the siege was confided to Publius Scipio Aemilianus, son of I. Aemilius Paulus and adopted grandson of the hero of Zama. Thorough rather

27 Mommsen, *op. cit.*

than brilliant, Scipio speedily realized that not the least potent of a besieger's weapons is the specter of starvation, and with 700,000 souls mewed up within the narrow compass of the city walls, the obvious step was to cut off the supplies introduced into the beleaguered stronghold by the Numidian deserter Bithyas and the swarm of merchant seamen whose fat profits more than compensated for the risks incurred in running the blockade. Setting grimly to work, Scipio constructed a mole ninety-six feet broad to close the mouth of the harbor. His next move was to attack the outer quay, defended by a hastily erected rampart. At the first attempt the assault was thrown back with desperate courage. But a lodgement was at length effected and the blockade completed.

Yet it was not until the spring of 146 B.C. that Scipio deemed the city's defenders so reduced by pestilence and want as to justify an assault in strength. At the given word, the outer harbor was set aflame and abandoned, and unperceived in the smoke and tumult the Legionaries scaled the city wall and burst into the marketplace. In prolonged and bloody street fighting, they forced their way from house to house and street to street, sparing none that crossed their path. For seven days the conflict raged far and wide, until 50,000 men and women, herded into the Byrsa [28] of the Old Town, were left with no option but to surrender.

The Roman deserters alone, nine hundred in number, and the General Hasdrubal with his wife and his two children had thrown themselves into the temple of the God of Healing; for them—as for soldiers who had deserted their posts, and for the murderers of Roman prisoners—there were no terms. But when, yielding to famine, the most resolute of them set fire to the temple, Hasdrubal could not endure to face death; alone he ran forth to the victor and falling on his knees pleaded for his life. It was granted; but, when his wife who, with her children, was amongst the rest on the roof of the temple, saw him at the feet of Scipio her proud heart swelled at this disgrace brought on her beloved perishing home, and, with bitter words bidding her husband be careful to save his life, she plunged first her sons and then herself into the flames. [29]

By Rome's explicit instruction, Carthage was razed to the ground, its site ploughed up, and all visible evidence that

[28] Citadel.
[29] Mommsen, *op. cit.*

it had ever existed deliberately obliterated. "Where the industrious Phoenicians had bustled and trafficked for five hundred years, Roman slaves would henceforth pasture the herds of their distant masters."

Loaded with booty but heavy with the presentiment that retribution would follow on such wanton destruction, Scipio returned in triumph to the official *supplicatio* that awaited him. Of his vast haul of captives only Hasdrubal, "pot-bellied, strutting, an incapable coward, glutton and tyrant," as Polybius contemptuously termed him, was granted easy terms of restricted liberty. The rest died in chains on the row-benches or in slavery.

In Spain—"a rough land but a fit nursery for men"— where Rome's policy had been virtually hand-to-mouth, warlike operations had broken out again in 154 B.C. after a period of relative quiet the occupying authorities had turned to singularly small advantage. One Consul, Q. Fulvius Nobilor, suffered defeat near Numantia, in the country of the Celtiberians; another was very roughly handled by the Lusitanians in the south. For ten years the popular leader Viriathus waged his "fiery war" against the Legions and their local supporters, demonstrating that genius for guerrilla fighting by which the Spaniard has always been characterized. Legion after Legion vanished in the defiles of the mountains, whose heights were crowned with captured trophies of Roman arms. At last, in 146 B.C., the Senate, freed from preoccupation with war in Greece and North Africa, despatched Scipio's brother, Q. Fabius Maximus, with two Legions to the Further Province, supported by G. Laelius in Hither Spain. Little progress was made, however, until treachery stepped in to accomplish what straightforward conflict had failed to achieve. Viriathus was stabbed to death as he slumbered; his successor proving unequal to the task he had taken up, peace with Lusitania was concluded by 137 B.C.

In the Hither province only two strongholds, Termantia and Numantia, obstinately held out; the latter, strong in position and further advantaged by the incapacity of C. Hostilius Mancinus and the other Roman leaders, successfully bade defiance to its besiegers for twelve solid years. In the end a sortie in force reduced the egregious Mancinus to sue for terms for his army's capitulation. At length, in 134 B.C., Scipio Aemilianus, the conqueror of Carthage and Rome's only general, was elected Consul for the second time and assigned to the command in Spain. Strengthening the wearied and disgruntled Legions with fresh blood and supporting them with allied troops, he settled down to deal with defiant Numantia once and for all. Contemptuous of the fighting quality of his troops, Scipio proceeded to wage a war of mattock and spade. The river Douro was blocked by a boom and a double line of circumvallation was drawn around the doomed city, which was more than five miles in length.

Starved into submission, it was only in the last extremity that, in 133 B.C., the garrison surrendered "as brave men to the mercy of the brave."

All resistance was now broken, for the able and generous Decimus Brutus had already settled Lusitania, founded Valentia, and crushed the Gallacci, thus completing the subjugation of Spain. Guerrilla fighting and brigandage, of course, were virtually indistinguishable, but the land at last was freed from the appalling blight of national war.

In the general reorganization of the territory, the temperate policy recommended by Tiberius Graccus was generally adopted, and the country's growing prosperity was greatly facilitated when Q. Metellus Baliaricus succeeded in suppressing piracy in the waters between Spain and the Balearic Islands.

Rome's shortsightedness in curbing that sea power of Rhodes she had formerly found so useful, now proved a rod she had put in pickle for herself. For there had never been a continuing Roman thalassocracy, no abiding effort to police the seas, and piracy continued with only spasmodic attempts at its suppression throughout that *mare nostrum* which was anything but a *mare clausum* to the freebooters who roamed it at their will. It was this reluctance to accept full responsibility for the maritime dominance of Mediterranean waters that persuaded Rome to regard her conquest in North Africa not so much as vanquished territory, to be occupied and administered as a mere appanage of the homeland, but rather as tributary domain, rendering a moderate *stipendum*, with the capital city of Utica as a useful center of Roman trade and with the defense of its frontiers left to Numidia—another client State—which bordered it on three sides.

Even so, Rome's victories in Hellas, Spain, and North Africa had committed her to a world policy from which there was no return. Reversion to the old circumscribed agrarian ways and limited commitments was no longer possible. The only alternative was to strive for that "Harmony in Unity" which increasing acquaintance with the political philosophy of Alexander's heyday served to impress as the most justifiable aim a great nation could pursue.

Chapter VI

A HOUSE DIVIDED

"Democracy is the very worst form of government in the world—except every other form of government."

—Sir Winston Churchill

Victory in 201 B.C., which brought the Second Punic War to an end, had been followed by a social upheaval of no small magnitude. But conditions then were as nothing compared with the chaotic and unhappy state of the country after the quelling of ebullient Hellas, the extirpation of Carthage in the Third Punic War, and the imposition of a veneer of tractability on the more accessible parts of Spain.

The fundamental cause of unrest was the radical change which had overtaken the ownership and working of the land. Originally, the Roman territory had been a terrain of small-holders, worked by the owner and his family, with a few larger estates, comparatively modest in extent, whose proprietor commonly managed his property through a paid steward and a sufficiency of serfs, who were maintained in tolerable health and comfort on the principle that a good workman was a piece of property whose upkeep it would be folly to neglect. As both Plato and Aristotle insisted, serfdom was "a necessary condition of universal soldier-ship, of unfettered political activity, and of literary and artistic cultivation." In other words, culture can only be acquired by those who are given the leisure to nurture it; the toil of the many ensured that a few were possessed of the wit and education to legislate for all.

But the old days, when it was unlawful for any citizen to hold more than 500 *jugera* [1] of land or keep more than 100 head of cattle and 500 sheep on common pasture

[1] Two *jugera* equalled approximately an acre and a quarter.

118

had long since gone by the board. With the progressive emergence of the capitalist-speculator intent on the accumulation of wealth without compensatory distribution of wages, free labor in its most honorable form was ousted by slave labor, which not only condemned the wage earner to idleness but tended also to destroy a healthy spirit of competition, while lowering the justifiable esteem in which manual labor in any form had hitherto been held. With more and more speculators and war-profiteers acquiring large land holdings, the more wily and unscrupulous of the old breed of freemen slid into comfortable berths as agents, overseers, and go-betweens—political dependents and bribery-manipulators who swamped the *Comitia Centuriata* and corrupted the far-reaching legislation for which this "voice of the people" had so long been responsible.

With the enormous inrush of war captives,[2] more and more of the dwindling number of agricultural wage earners were thrown out of work as their tasks were taken over by slave labor, to become dependent for their existence on doles and the distribution of a modicum of free food. Drifting into the capital, they made up a shiftless, ever-increasing element of menacing unrest.

In any case agriculture had seriously lost ground throughout the homeland. Corn could be imported from Sicily, from Numidia, and even from Egypt at far lower cost than it could be grown in Italy, whose soil was little suited to the production of grain crops. When Cato was asked what was the most profitable use for slaves on the land, his reply was, "To supervise good grazing." What next? "Tolerable grazing." What next? "Bad grazing." What next? "Corn growing." And pasture is far more economical in the employment of labor than arable; one herdsman or shepherd will account for many more acres than an equivalent number of agricultural laborers can render profitable.

Also to be taken into consideration were the claims to recompense, in bounties and land grants, of a very considerable number of discharged soldiers—men who were not inclined to forgo what they considered to be their due reward for services rendered for want of a little agitation on their own behalf. Yet so much of the most suitable land for

---

[2] To give some idea of the extent of this slave population: the whole of the Bruttian people had been sold into bondage as punishment for their fidelity to Hannibal, 150,000 Epirots had been sold by Aemilius Paulus, and 50,000 Carthaginians by Scipio. Since these hauls included members of both sexes, the slave population automatically increased by the ordinary process of reproduction.

the purpose had passed from the hands of the administration into the possession of rapacious speculators and *nouveaux riches*—on terms that would have sustained remarkably little inquiry—that the claims of the veterans could not be met with anything like the expected generosity. Another class of the unsatisfied and discontented was added to that of the unjustly dispossessed.

To hold in bondage large numbers of men who had not only been born to freedom but had been trained as soldiers, was as dangerous for the State as for the individual slave-owners. Nor was their contemporary treatment such as to encourage resigned acceptance of the lot which had befallen them. They were turned out on the hills, no better sheltered than the herds they tended, undernourished and unclad; in far too many instances no slightest effort was made to provide them even with the common necessities of life. When a body of these wretched men begged their master to provide them with a little warm clothing against the inclemency of the winter climate, he cynically retorted, "What, are there no travelers with clothes on?" [3]

With desperate men, such a hint was more than sufficient to destroy any lingering respect they might have had for any law save the law of self-preservation. The shepherd slaves speedily turned themselves into a savage *banditti* for whom the highway became the natural source of supply to satisfy their wants. With the countryside swarming with men who went unrestrained by their masters and unpunished by those representatives of the law who made no serious effort to track them down and bring them to justice, for the traveler to take the road without a heavily armed escort was for him to invite spoliation.

Occasionally, when too many substantial families had been forced to flee their country homes and seek refuge in the towns, public agitation spurred the authorities to grudging action. Thus in 185 B.C. a Praetor had been sent to root out misrule in Apulia, where seven thousand slaves had been condemned for brigandage and many others rounded up and incarcerated in large prison enclosures (*ergastula*), where they might be under temporary restraint but where they could also rehearse their wrongs and plot schemes of vengeance for the future.

In tyranny and cynical materialism the *nouveaux riches* landowners of Sicily were even more culpable than their counterparts on the mainland. And it was their brutalized

<hr>

[3] Strabo.

attitude towards their slaves which, in precipitating a ghastly servile insurrection, revealed the debased and degenerate state into which much of Roman society had fallen.

The trouble started in the city of Enna, the center of a prosperous pastoral district and the home of Damophilus, one of the wealthiest of the local landowners. Famous for the number of his slave herdsmen, he was equally notorious for his cruel treatment of them—a depravity in which he was only surpassed by his wife, Megallis, whose conduct towards her female helots viciously extended the bounds of sadistic inhumanity. At length the bitter draught overflowed, and four hundred of his bondsmen met secretly at Enna to take counsels of vengeance against Damophilus.

At Enna there lived another rich proprietor named Antigenes, and among his slaves was a Syrian, known by the Greek name of Ennus. "This man was a kind of wizard, who pretended to have revelations of the future, and practiced a mode of breathing fire, which passed for supernatural power. At length he gave out that his Syrian gods had declared to him that he should be king hereafter; and to the confederate slaves of Damophilus, Ennus seemed in truth a prophet and a king sent to deliver them. They prayed him to become their leader, he accepted their offer; and the whole body entered the city of Enna, with Ennus at their head, breathing fire." [4]

With a few rags of skins about their nakedness, armed with reap hooks, spits, and stakes pointed and hardened in the fire, they swarmed through the streets, bursting into the houses and massacring all who came their way, without regard to age or sex. More and more slaves from the surrounding estates crowded in to join Ennus and his earlier followers, and every man's foes were those of his own household. Damophilus was dragged from his home and put to lingering death with every circumstance of barbarity. Megallis, handed over to the female slaves, was first tortured and then cast down the crag on which the city stood.

As it seemed, the wildest dreams of Ennus had been fulfilled. Assuming the diadem, he took the royal name of Antiochus, endowing all his followers with the nationality of Syrians. The *ergastula* were broken open and their occupants swarmed out to swell the ranks, until the self-appointed monarch found himself the leader of 10,000 exultant but

---

[4] Florus explains that he produced this effect by concealing "a nut in his mouth which he had filled with brimstone and fire, and, breathing gently, sent forth flame together with his words." Lucius Annæus Florus, *Epitome of Roman History*.

desperate men. In the prevailing state of misrule, the efforts of Achaeus, the Greek slave who had been appointed Generalissimo, to organize an army were more successful than his halfhearted attempts to moderate excesses and preserve some kind of order.

A few days after the massacre at Enna, Cleon, a Cilician slave, fomented a similar insurrection near Agrigentum and soon found himself at the head of several thousand men; he disappointed Roman hopes that the two leaders would quarrel over their respective claims to primacy by openly acknowledging the sovereign authority of "King Antiochus."

At the time of the insurrection's outbreak Sicily's Praetor was absent from his post. With his successor's arrival, a mere 8,000 men were all that could be got together to confront a rabid horde of erstwhile bondsmen which had swollen to well over 20,000. Outnumbered and with no more than a hastily improvised force under command, the Praetor was utterly defeated, and the tide of insurrection speedily engulfed the whole island.

Rome was thrown into a state of bewildered consternation, a quickening alarm which stirrings of rebellion in other parts of the republic did nothing to allay. But the Praetors holding office throughout the provinces were on the alert, and all attempts on the part of the bondsmen to stage armed uprisings were ruthlessly put down. In Rome itself 150 slaves, proved to have been organizing an outbreak, were summarily put to death.

In Sicily the insurrection had assumed such dangerous proportions that C. Fulvius Flaccus, a colleague of Scipio in the year 147 B.C., was sent to crush it. For a twelvemonth he wrestled with the problem in vain, and was replaced by L. Calpurnius Piso. The best the newcomer could achieve was to gain possession of Messana. His siege of the naturally defensive stronghold of Enna, however, met with nothing but frustration. He was succeeded in his turn by P. Rupilius—another comrade-in-arms of Scipio—who opened his campaign by laying siege to the rebels' other fastness of Tauromenium. The beleaguered garrison's resistance was so desperate that no assault was capable of breaking through the defenses, while even aching want failed to reduce their stubborn will to fight on. Reduced to the direst straits for want of food, "they devoured the children, the women, and at length began to prey upon each other." Even then the place was taken only by treachery, but fall it did, with all the survivors of the garrison being put to torture and then hurled down a precipice to their death.

Rupilius then advanced on the last bastion of resistance at Enna.

The fate of the insurgents was inevitable. Cleon of Agrigentum chose a soldier's death, and sallying forth with all who breathed the same spirit as himself, he died fighting valiantly. Of the end of Achaeus we are not informed. Ennus, with a bodyguard of six hundred men, fled to the neighboring hills, but despairing of escape, the greater part of the wretched men slew one another. The mock king himself was taken in a cave, together with his cook, baker, bathing-man, and jester. He showed a pusillanimity far unlike the desperate courage of the rest and died, eaten by vermin, in a dungeon at Morgantium.

Thus was crushed for a time this perilous insurrection, the result of the slave system established by Roman conquest. The well-being of Sicily had now been so seriously impaired that extraordinary measures were deemed necessary for restoring order. The Sibylline books were consulted. The oracular page ordered the propitiation of "Ceres the most ancient," and a solemn deputation of priests proceeded to the august temple of the goddess in the city of Enna. This circumstance, seemingly unimportant, becomes significant, when it is considered that the war originated in the neglect of agricultural labors.[5]

Ten commissioners were entrusted with the task of drawing up laws for the better regulation of the rural districts, the code formerly established by Cicero at Syracuse being taken as the basis for their legislation. A scale of tithes was arrived at, their collection being left to Roman contractors, while a reformed judicial system was devised to deal with complaints, from whatever source. Belated as these measures might have been, there can be no question but that the general condition of the Sicilian landowners and those who toiled for them was considerably improved by the new system, and agriculture again flourished in Sicily as it had done in former times.

But if the fires of insurrection had been damped down, future events were only too starkly to demonstrate that in no sense had they been extinguished.

[5] Florus, *op. cit.* Cf. Mommsen and Liddell.

The servile rebellion of 134-131 B.C. was only symptomatic of a far graver and more debilitating malaise of which Rome had become the unconscious victim. Over the years the Eternal City and all it stood for had undergone such tremendous internal changes, while at the same time so stupendously extending its external responsibilities, that the old traditional gubernatorial system was quite unable to cope with the many and vexed problems with which it constantly found itself confronted. The machinery of administration equal to controlling the destinies of a small, self-contained City-State was quite inadequate for the governance of a great empire.

For in structure the administration had remained virtually unaltered. Of the two Consuls, the rule still applied that one must be a Patrician and the other a Plebeian. The same was true of the two Censors, originally appointed—in 443 B.C.—with the intention of taking out of the hands of the Military Tribunes some of the more important functions hitherto reserved for the ex-consular members of that body, such as nominating members of the Senate and organizing the census of all claiming the status of Roman citizen. Originally the office of Censor had been confined to the Patriciate, but after 400 B.C. Plebeians had qualified for the post in the same way as they had become eligible for the military tribunate. The administration of justice remained in the hands of those officials known as Praetors, while the control of markets and festivals, together with certain other policing responsibilities, were still confided to two *Curule Aediles,* who however were no longer required to be of Patrician birth. For the young man ambitious to learn the business of government and advance his career in the public service, a tour of duty in the office of Quaestor—the lowest rung in the ladder of public life—was a prerequisite to nomination for the Senate. To preside over the details of finance or those of some provincial administration, to tackle the question of the Eternal City's water supply, to delve into port regulations with regard to the discharge of incoming grain ships—these and similar tasks offered a rough and ready tuition in the craft of getting things done more or less in accord with the rules laid down.

Outwardly, therefore, the system worked out for the governance of the Republic appeared to have undergone little change. Impetuous youth was still held in check by a preponderance of men of mature years in the higher councils of the State; there was still a minimum age limit, for example, for appointment to the dignity of Consul, although on occasion it had been waived in times of war when the current holders of the office had proved sadly wanting in the necessary faculty of generalship.[6] But on the surface, at least, there was little sign of radical change.

Yet in correspondence with the advance of the Plebeian and the decay of the Patrician families, a silent revolution had been wrought in most parts of the constitution. The assembly of the *Curies,* through which all free men were entitled to express their will by means of their votes, had become little more than a mere form; their influence on events was entirely nugatory. Election to the Senate was still theoretically open to any citizen who had qualified by service in the unpaid junior posts, had won the suffrages of his fellow citizens, and reached the age of forty-seven. But since no office was remunerated, and the grant to cover the expenses of such *scribae* (clerks) as it might be necessary to employ was entirely at the discretion of the newcomer's fellow Senators, the way was clearly opened for political pressure to be brought to bear on any novice of limited pecuniary resources. Again, the allowance made to the *Aediles* to provide the expenses for the public games, spectacles of ever-increasing costliness, had been withdrawn. Thus the choice of men for this office was limited to individuals of the new moneyed class who could afford to court public favor by their munificence. In short, the regimen of the Patrician had largely passed away, to be superseded by that of the plutocrat. At the same time the tenacious retention of outmoded forms, pedantic legalisms, and moribund but long-accepted ritual stultified much of the fresh thinking which growing contact with Hellenic culture might otherwise have stimulated. Where Hellenism did penetrate, its most noticeable effect was to encourage an emasculating self-indulgence and sybarite love of luxury, which in extreme instances bordered closely on effeminacy. The androgynous and even the avowedly perverted escaped the reprobation that in any robustly healthy society would instinctively have been meted out to them.

Having set out on the path of conquest and expansion, the forward policy hitherto so vigorously pursued seemed to have fallen into abeyance. Erstwhile friends and allies were either neglected or ignored and the regulation of overseas dependencies was handled with weakness and indecision. Pergamum produced a pretender to the Throne whose de-

---

[6] Scipio Africanus the Younger, for example, was appointed Consul in his thirty-eighth year so that he might assume command in the Third Punic War.

fiance went uncorrected for so long that its eventual deflation cost far more than if the situation had been dealt with promptly. Had Rome sufficiently rebuked the adolescent posturing of the young King Mithridates VI of Pontus,[7] the future would have been spared a deal of costly strife. A usurper was cravenly recognized in that Syria which in times past had never dared to question the fiat of Rome. The Senate meekly reversed its own decision which had denied Cyprus to Egypt, while the threatening growth in the might of Parthia under the alien Scythian dynasty of the Arsacidae was myopically ignored.

But perhaps Rome's most culpable neglect was her failure to clear the Mediterranean of the pirates who swarmed on its waters. Infesting the trade routes, levying tribute from the coastal towns, driving a brisk trade in kidnapped slaves, the corsairs established their headquarters in Crete and the secret inlets of Cilicia without the slightest fear of suffering disturbance.

Always prone to gibe at the uncompromising fact that the maintenance of an overseas empire demands the upkeep of a numerous, active, and well-ordered fighting marine, Rome had so grossly neglected her minuscule navy that it was not unknown for the Quaestors of the Fleet to cower inactive in their harbors while the freebooters pillaged the mercantile shipping just outside them. It is true that the seas in the vicinity of the Balearic Islands were very largely free from the activities of the corsairs, and some effort was made to expel them from Dalmatian and Ligurian waters. But in the Aegean and the East the pirates were the masters. Such was the inevitable penalty paid for Rome's shortsighted discouragement of Rhodian sea power. The foundations of empire rest on "production, with the necessity of exchanging products; shipping, whereby the exchange is carried on, and colonies, which facilitate and enlarge the operations of shipping, and tend to protect it by multiplying points of safety" [8] —these, and the necessary naval force to afford the country's maritime commerce the needful protection. Rome had the means of production, her mercantile marine was numerous and well-found, and she possessed the overseas markets in which to dispose of her products. It was her lack of a fullfledged fighting marine which so materially delayed her progress along the path of empire.

To the more percipient amongst her leading men, it was

7 Otherwise known as Cappadocia-by-the-Sea.
8 Mahan, *op. cit.*

clear that if Rome were to prosper, reorganization and fresh inspiration were urgently needed to revitalize and redirect her destiny. Indeed, change was already in the making. But instead of taking the form of the normal competition of parties for the reins of power, of government and opposition with rival policies for the electorate to choose between, it bogged down in a class struggle between *optimates* and *populares*—between the champions of tradition and the old time-tested, ordered way of life, and those as concerned to pull down and destroy as ostensibly they were eager to build anew. It was a state of affairs which, in the prevailing circumstances, was virtually inescapable.

"Where the wealthy classes devote themselves mainly to material interests, where there is no strong middle class, no intelligent industrial population, no permanent and powerful organ of the public will, the politicians have it all their own way, party becomes faction, and popular government is a mere delusion." [9] For generation after generation the Senate had owed the maintenance of its power to its incorruptibility and the useful service it had performed, which had won it the acquiescence of the people in its rule. But these conditions no longer pertained. Identified with a clique that represented anything but the best in the community, the Senate had lost its moral authority; those in lesser positions of trust became restive and critical; the ordinary ruck of the people turned either mutinous or cynically indifferent; while the opposition of the younger men of the Patrician *Equites* [10] and the proconsulate [11] élite confronted it with new dangers.

Yet nothing could have been more starkly apparent than the need (1) to restore the basis of the social and military system by reviving agriculture and returning the yeomanry to the land; (2) to provide for the employment or relief of the poor in the capital and ensure its incorruptible policing; (3) to enfranchise the Italian allies and develop local government within their territory; (4) to consolidate the provinces by conscientious, upright rule and gradual Romanization; (5) to reorganize the army and navy on a thoroughly professional basis; and lastly, (6) to establish a stable, defensible frontier, a systematic budget, and improved communications throughout all the territories under Roman sway.

[9] How and Leigh, *op. cit.*

[10] Deriving from such well-dowered Patrician families as still flourished, they furnished the body of Horse in the Army of the City.

[11] Men who, for one reason or another, had been continued in their Consular functions, and were thus additional to the normal Consular establishment.

Of them all, the most pressing problem was that of the revival of agriculture, which would again encourage the increase of the sterling smallholder class of the community, and of a free, wage-earning peasantry. It was their championship of this particular cause which brought Tiberius Graccus and his brother Gaius to prominence on the stage of national affairs.

The Gracci were the sons of a distinguished Plebeian and the grandsons of the General who had raised a slave-legion during the course of the Punic Wars. The father, T. Sempronius, a Roman of the old school, had served with distinction both as a soldier and a diplomatist, his marriage to Cornelia, a daughter of Scipio Africanus, the conqueror of Zama, having greatly advantaged his career. Educated by Greek tutors and subjected to the humanistic philosophy of the Scipionic school of thought, his sons were determined that the vague, dilettante theories of their preceptors should be translated into vigorous action. Of the two, Tiberius, despite the bravura he had displayed in his nineteenth year at the storming of Carthage, was the more temperate and sedate; Gaius, the more impetuous and exuberantly loquacious.

At the time of Tiberius's election as Tribune of the People in 134 B.C., "the fearful consequences of the previous misgovernment, the political, military, economic and moral decay of the burgesses were naked and open to the eyes of all." [12] From the outset his resolve was to make agricultural reform his prime objective. It was a design in which he knew support would be forthcoming from the prominent Jurist Publius Mucius Scaevola, the *Pontifex Maximus* Publius Crassus Mucianus, and from his father-in-law, the ex-Consul and ex-Censor Appius Claudius, one of the most respected members of the Senate.

Immediately after entering office, therefore, Graccus proposed the enactment of an agrarian law which in a general sense was largely a renewal of the Licinio-Sextian law of 387 B.C.

Under it all the State lands which were occupied and enjoyed by the possessors without remuneration—those that were let on lease, such as the territory of Capua, were not affected by the law—were to be resumed on behalf of the State; but with the restriction, that each occupier should reserve himself 500 *jugera* and for each son 250 (so as not, however, to exceed 1000 *jugera* in

12 Mommsen, *op. cit.*

all) in permanent and guaranteed possession, or should be entitled to claim compensation in land to that extent. Indemnification was to be granted for any improvements executed by the former holders, such as buildings and plantations. The domain-land thus resumed was to be broken up into lots of 30 *jugera*; and these were to be distributed partly to burgesses, partly to Italian allies, not as their own free property, but as inalienable heritable leaseholds, whose holders bound themselves to use the land for agriculture and to pay a moderate rent to the State. A collegium of three men who were to be regarded as ordinary and standing magistrates of the State and were to be annually elected by the Assembly of the people, were to be entrusted with the work of resumption and distribution; to which was afterwards added the important and difficult function of legally settling what was domain land and what was private property. The distribution was accordingly designed to go on continuously, and to embrace the whole class that should be in need of it.[13]

Special provision was made to deal with the Italian domains, which were very extensive and difficult of adjustment, and measures were to be taken to furnish a definite sum annually from the public chest for the purchase of Italian lands for distribution.

At the outset Graccus's proposals were greeted with more astonishment than indignation. Men who, in return for a nominal rental, had been in possession of landed property for generations refused to believe that the occupation of it could be disturbed. Moreover, they urged, although the suggested measure pretended to apply only to State lands, it did in fact seek to interfere with the rights of private property; for these lands were held on formally sanctioned lease, had been made matters of purchase and sale, moneys were secured on them for the benefit of widows and orphans, family tombs and mausoleums had been erected on them; if this law were passed, no man's land could be called his own.

In effect, to right one category of wrongs Graccus was quite prepared to create another. But by this time he was no longer in charge of his proposal, it had taken charge of him; he had aroused the "vile usurping crowd," and the mob's hero who does not go on from one extravagance to

[13] Mommsen, *op. cit.* Cf. Appian.

another soon finds himself the mob's victim. Driven by the tempest he himself had stirred up, Graccus rushed headlong into a storm of opposition, not only from the patriciate and plutocracy, but also from those moderates who feared revolution more than they favored reform—a caucus subsequently reinforced by the spokesmen of the exasperated Italians.

There were crowded meetings, eloquently harangued by the impassioned Tribune; the rural voters, on whom he depended, poured into the city. The Senate, the organ of the landowners, resorted to obstruction. M. Octavius, a friend and colleague of Graccus, interposed his veto, to which Tiberius, equally constitutionally, replied by placing his seal on the Treasury and blocking every executive act. He did more. Eager to avail himself of the presence of the country voters and the momentary consternation of the landlords, he declined to wait for the slow pressure of time and opinion, and pushed his proposal while the iron was still hot. The bill, once more moved, was again vetoed in spite of personal appeals to Octavius. Finally, after a fruitless negotiation with the Senate and repeated efforts to appease his colleague, he asked the people to declare that a Tribune who acted against the popular will, *ipso facto* forfeited his office. Octavius was deposed and dragged away.[14]

Octavius resisted, and in the tumult which ensued, one of his slaves lost an eye, while others of his entourage suffered injury. Appeal had been made to the crowd, with the inevitable result that violence had taken the place of reason.

"These acts of Tiberius Graccus are commonly said to have been the beginning of revolution in Rome; and the guilt of it is accordingly laid at his door." [15] Certainly it can hardly be ranked as anything but a *coup d'état*. "A magistrate could only resign; he could not be deposed. In an apology he felt bound to offer later, Tiberius descanted on the right of the people to control their magistrate; it was a mere sophistry. Government becomes impossible if the people can cancel their mandate for every passing whim. To defy the right of intercession cut the ground from his own feet." [16]

14 How and Leigh, *op. cit.*
15 A. H. Beesly, *The Gracci, Marius and Sulla.*
16 How and Leigh, *op. cit.*

By this time, however, such considerations as legality and abstract questions of right and wrong had been obliterated by popular clamor. A successor to Octavius was duly appointed and the Graccian law carried by a single vote of the people, bellowing their approval. Three commissioners were thereupon elected to execute its provisions—Tiberius himself, his father-in-law, and his brother Gaius, a stripling of twenty then serving under Scipio in Spain. Graccus was attended home by a jubilant crowd, which hailed him as the founder not of a family or a city but of the whole Italian race. The Senate meanwhile mildly avenged itself by docking the newly-appointed commissioners' allowances!

In a matter of weeks Tiberius Graccus had arisen to the summit of power, unable to stir an inch abroad without an adoring crowd trooping at his heels—a form of protection he reinforced by habitually carrying a dagger concealed beneath his gown. Buoyed up, however, with the self-confidence begotten of popular favor, he went on to formulate measures which touched the members of the Senate at their tenderest point.

The recently defunct Attalus Philometor, last of the line of Eumenes and last sovereign of Pergamum, had bequeathed his kingdom, with all his lands and treasure, to the Roman people. In the ordinary way the Senate would at once have assumed the disposition of this handsome bequest. But Graccus gave notice that it was his intention to propose a bill whereby the moneys should be distributed to those who were to receive allotments of public land, in order to assist them in purchasing stock, in erecting farm buildings, and the like. He added, in tones of open menace, that he would bring the subject of Pergamum's future government before the people without permitting the Senate to interfere.

This was nothing less than revolution, and Graccus sought to curry favor, bolster up his position and induce the burgesses unconstitutionally to confer on him the office which protected him, by propounding further popular measures— for extending the right of appeal, for abolishing the exclusive privilege of Senators to act as civil jurymen, for shortening the period of compulsory military service, and even for the admission of the Italian allies to Roman citizenship.

When Graccus next appeared in the Senate House, a colleague ironically inquired if the envoy of the late King of Pergamum had brought him a purple robe and diadem! More directly, a veteran Senator and ex-Consul, Titus Annius,

taxed the Tribune with violating the constitution. Touchy as
are all those intoxicated by the plaudits of the multitude,
Graccus promptly indicted his opponent for treason against
the majesty of the people. Annius duly presented himself for
judgment, and before Graccus could launch on his denunciation, icily commented, " 'I suppose, if one of your brother
Tribunes offers to protect me, you will fly into a passion and
depose him also.' Graccus saw the effect produced and broke
up the assembly." [17]

At this juncture, some of Graccus's more responsible well-
wishers became alarmed at the prospect of a law which had
made the *triumviri* absolute judges, without appeal, on disputed questions with regard to landed property. Many allotments of public land had been granted whose titles had been
lost; and everyone holding grants under such conditions saw
his property at the mercy of irresponsible adjudication.

Careful examination of Graccus's proposed measures had
not only revealed their undoubted merits, but exposed their
indubitable flaws. His appeal to mob passion to ensure their
unqualified adoption laid him open to the charge that if at
first he had risked himself in order to save the commonwealth, he was now obliged to put the commonwealth at
stake to secure his own safety. This could only be ensured by
offering himself for re-election at the approaching Assembly
of the Tribes.

When the day came, however, harvest work occupied the
bulk of the country voters; of those who did appear, many,
with typical fickleness and irresponsibility, had grown cold
towards the candidate, while the mass of those who resided
in the city were either the clients or dependents of the
dwindled Patriciate or swollen democracy.

When the day of the election came, the Prerogative
Tribe gave its vote for Graccus; so also did the next.
But it was objected that the same man could not be
chosen in two successive years; and after a hot debate
the Assembly was adjourned till next day.[18]

It wanted yet some hours of nightfall. Graccus came
forth into the Forum, clad in black, and leading his
young son by the hand. In anticipation of his untimely
end, he committed his precious charge to his fellow
citizens. All hearts were touched. The people surrounded

[17] Appian, *op. cit*. Cf. Beesly.
[18] Liddell, *op. cit*.

him with eager gesticulations, and escorted him home, bidding him be of good cheer for the morrow.[19]

The father's affection and the statesman's bitter dismay at finding the dearest object of his life about to be snatched from him by violence need not have been tinged with one particle of personal fear. A man of tried bravery, like Graccus, might guard his own life indeed, but only as he regarded it as indispensable to a great cause. That evening he told his partisans he would give them a sign next day if he should think it necessary to use force. It has been presumed that this proves he was meditating treason.[20]

At least it implics that he was prepared to meet force with counterforce; how far that can be held to approximate treason must be a matter of individual opinion.

In the event, the Assembly met the following morning upon the Capitol, the area in front of the temple of Jupiter being filled for the most part by adherents of Graccus, among whom the Tribune himself was conspicuous. The Senate mustered hard by in the temple of Faith. Proceedings opened with a demand from Nasica, one of the reformer's bitterest opponents, that Scaevola, the presiding Consul, should stop the reelection, but the lawyer-politician declined.

Upon this, Fulvius Flaccus hurried from the Senate, informed Graccus of the purport of Nasica's speech, and warned him that his death had been resolved upon by his enemies.

Then the friends of Graccus girded up their gowns and armed themselves with staves, for the purpose of repelling force by force. In the midst of the uproar Graccus raised his hand to his head. Immediately his enemies cried that he was asking for a Crown. Exaggerated reports were carried into the Senate House, and Nasica exclaimed, "The Consul is betraying the republic! Those who would save their country follow me!" So saying, he drew the skirt of his gown over his head, after the manner used by the *Pontifex Maximus* in solemn acts of worship. A number of Senators followed, and the people respectfully made way. But the nobles and their partisans broke up the benches that had been set out for the Assembly, and began an assault on the

19 Appian, *op. cit.*
20 Beesly, *op. cit.*

adherents of Graccus, who fled in disorder. Graccus abandoned all thoughts of resistance; he left his gown in the hands of a friend who sought to detain him, and made towards the temple of Jupiter. But the priests had closed the doors; and in his haste he stumbled over a bench and fell. As he was rising one of his own colleagues struck him on the head with a stool; another claimed the honor of repeating the blow; and before the statues of the old Kings at the portico of the temple the Tribune lay dead. Many of his adherents were slain with him; many were forced over the wall at the edge of the Tarpeian Rock, and were killed by their fall. No fewer than three hundred lost their lives in the fray.[21]

When Scipio, encamped before Numantia, was brought the intelligence of his kinsman's end, that stern political realist exclaimed, in the words of Homer, "So perish all and everyone who dares such deeds as he."

In the capital itself, "Gaius Graccus had just returned from Spain, and asked leave to bury his brother's corpse. This was refused. The triumphant party ordered the bodies of Tiberius and his friends to be thrown into the Tiber before morning. Thus flowed the first blood that was shed in civil strife at Rome." [22]

The intentions animating Tiberius Graccus had been of the best; the headstrong, impatient methods he employed in trying to put them into execution could scarcely have been more inept. By turning the Tribal Assembly against the Senate and seeking to submit Rome to mob rule, he set in motion a movement whose fruition would have rendered the continued operation of the republican system of governance impossible. The course on which he was bent led inescapably to revolution, and revolutions are apt to create more problems than they solve. Yet it was clear that a struggle had commenced between the oligarchy and those who resented and opposed it—a struggle that was to last till the autocratic Sulla for a time restored the Senate to sovereignty, only for it to be wrested from them again by a dictator yet more potent than Sulla. For the moment, however, an uneasy truce supervened, with both sides taking stock of their op-

21 Appian, *op. cit.* Cf. Plutarch and Beesly.
22 Appian, *op. cit.*

ponents' potentialities. As yet, the *Comitia* had neither the morale nor the organization to qualify it as a genuine organ of popular government; and since, subsequent to the death of Graccus, the Senate had the wisdom to follow the path of moderation, their opponents were denied legitimate grounds for complaint.

An Agrarian Commission cautiously set about the redistribution of land, and although there were many left dissatisfied, the fact remains that a census taken at this time revealed that some 80,000 citizens had returned to work the soil and were thus registered as men able to bear arms.

In place of Tiberius Graccus the choice of the electors fell on P. Licinius Crassus, blood brother of the Consul Scaevola, who had been adopted into the family of the Crassi. His daughter had lately been married to young Gaius Graccus, and he now became the acknowledged leader of the party.

It was at this juncture that Scipio Aemilianus returned from his successful campaign for the reduction of Numantia, a hardfought struggle in the course of which he had been greatly impressed by the soldierly qualities of a youthful subordinate from Arpinum, of humble birth and rude manners, who was known to his comrades-in-arms as Marius. It was a name with which a far wider circle of his fellow countrymen was destined to become fatefully acquainted.

Scipio's official *supplicatio* was not enhanced by the spoils of victory and a long train of captives, for the Numantians had buried themselves and their treasure beneath the ruins of their city. But with his personal prestige and powerful connections, his presence in the capital at this particular moment might well be pregnant with far-reaching consequences, and many eyes turned to him with expectation. It might be thought that his approval of the death of Graccus sufficiently indicated what part he intended to adopt. But it was possible for him to condemn the conduct of the individual without disapproving of his purpose. The men of Rome, like those of Rome's dependencies, had fought under his banners; the cause of the time-expired soldiery, their claim to land holdings on which to raise another generation to serve the Eagles sword in hand, was bound to be one he cherished warmly.

But whatever doubt might pertain as to Scipio's ultimate aim, he speedily made it clear that he had no intention of pandering to the *mobile vulgus*.

One of the partisans of Ti. Graccus, by name C.

Papirius Carbo, a man of ready wit, but in character turbulent, reckless and unprincipled, hoped to raise himself to importance by means of the rabble. He was a Tribune for the year 131 B.C., when he carried a law for introducing the ballot into the legislative assemblies of the People. He also brought forward another bill, for making it legal to reelect a Tribune to a second year. Scipio and Laelius opposed the measure, and the former spoke so warmly against it that it was rejected by the Tribes, although young G. Graccus came forward to speak in its favor. It was then that Carbo publicly demanded of Scipio what he thought of the death of Graccus. "That he was rightly put to death," Scipio promptly replied. At these words an angry shout was raised. Scipio turned sternly from the quarter from which it came—"Peace," he said, "ye stepsons of Italy: remember who it was who brought you in chains to Rome!" [23]

Scipio's waning popularity with *hoi polloi* was speedily demonstrated when the rival claims of the conquerer of Numantia and P. Licinius Crassus for command of the troops assigned for the suppression of a rebellion in Pergamum [24] were put to the vote. Out of thirty-five Tribes only two cast their votes in favor of Scipio. In the same year popular feeling was reflected in the election, for the first time, of two members of the Plebeian order to the Censorship, the most august magistracy of the State.

The plutocratic landowners had endeavored to baffle the working of the new agrarian law by adopting an attitude of passive resistance. To counter this policy Carbo and his colleagues issued a proclamation, calling for information against all who had failed to register themselves as holders of public land. The call was only too eagerly complied with, and the *triumvirs* were soon overwhelmed with the names of defaulters.

Portions of the public land had often been alienated by grant or sale, not only to Romans, but to Italians. The holders were now, in consequence of Carbo's proclamation, suddenly called upon to produce their title deeds,

[23] Liddell, *op. cit.* Cf. Appian.

[24] The revolt in Pergamum was suppressed eventually by P. Perpenna and M. Aquillus, the latter of whom settled the Roman Province of Asia in 129 B.C.

which in many cases were missing; so that a vast number of these holders were liable to be stripped of lands which were undoubtedly their own. Further, in cases where persons held property, partly public and partly private, there were no documents to show which part was public and which private. The commissioners acted in the most arbitrary way, and exasperated a vast number of persons through all Italy; and thus a new popular party was called forth, which exercised a most important influence on the events of the next fifty years. In Carbo's rash haste to win the Roman countrymen he recked not with the hostility of Latins and Italians; and those who had lately worshipped Graccus now rose like one man to oppose those who pretended to represent Graccus.[25]

These new opponents of the Agrarian law perceived no virtue in cooperating with the unpopular pluto-patrician oligarchy. The bulk of them being agrestic ex-servicemen, they instinctively turned to Scipio, who had always manifested sympathy with them, to champion their cause. Reluctant as any soldier might be to mire himself with party politics, it was an appeal that Scipio could not find it in himself to ignore or reject. He began by moving that a decree should be issued withdrawing from the *triumvirs* the judicial power with which they had been invested by Graccus and transferring the jurisdiction to the Consuls. The decree was authorized, and C. Sempronius Tuditanus was entrusted with the task of dealing with matters far beyond the ken of a man considerably more interested in literature and art than in affairs of business. Perhaps fortunately for Tuditanus, news came of an outbreak of unrest on the Illyrian frontier, and this served as an admirable excuse for his hurried departure to join the Army, "confident that he could better cope with barbarous enemies than the more barbarous complexities of the law."

When it was realized that the Consul to whom the jurisdiction had been transferred from the Senate had himself found an excuse to flee, discontent became widespread, while many voices were heard to accuse Scipio of having sacrificed Roman interests to the Italians. Reports were even bruited abroad that he intended to repeal the Sempronian law by force and let loose the Italian soldiery on the people of Rome.

[25] Liddell, *op. cit.*

Scipio felt that it was necessary to explain his motives, and announced his purpose of delivering speeches, one day in the Senate and the day after in the Forum. The first only of these purposes was fulfilled. By his speech in the Senate he pledged himself to maintain the rights of the Latins and Italians against the *triumvirs,* and prevent the unjust resumption of the lands that had been granted to them. The Senate loudly applauded; and Scipio was escorted home by the mass of the Senators, with a jubilant crowd of Italians. Many thought this the most glorious day of his life. He retired to rest early, in good health. In the morning he was found dead in his bed. By his side lay the tablets on which he had been noting down the heads of the oration which he had intended to make next day.[26]

The death of Scipio struck consternation in the heart of his followers and those who had put their faith in his advocacy of their cause. Nor were there wanting those to declare that he had been murdered. For a time suspicion was attached to Gaius Gracchus, to his sister Sempronia, and even to his mother Cornelia, although Cicero was firmly of opinion that the guilt rested squarely on the shifty Carbo. Since the matter was not susceptible of proof, it was not further pursued.

Thus died the best General Rome could boast in a time of generally mediocre military talent, a man of generosity and public spirit, warmly esteemed by his friends and respected for his integrity even by those with whom he was in total disagreement. Aged no more than fifty-five, "he might have lived some years to moderate the fury of party strife, to awe the factions, and to support just claims. His death at this moment was probably the greatest loss the Republic could have suffered." [27]

In most storms there comes a lull, while Nature gathers her forces to renew the disturbance. Human tensions often show a similar tendency temporarily to relax; a delusive calm prevails which all too often proves no more than the prolegomenon of further turmoil. So it was with the Rome of

[26] Liddell, *op. cit.* Cf. Appian, Florus, and Marcus Velleius Paterculus, *Historiae Romanae.*

[27] *Ibid. op. cit.* Cf. Cicero's *Dialogues,* and the eloquent tribute to Scipio by Mommsen.

128 B.C. The turbulent Carbo had momentarily vanished from the scene; Gaius Graccus was silently marshaling his strength; Fulvius Flaccus was content to let the agrarian law he had sponsored entangle itself in the resistance it encountered in the Senate, thankfully departing the mephitic world of politics to take up a military command in Gaul.

But the storm clouds were only just over the horizon. In 126 B.C. a law sponsored by the Tribune M. Junius Pennus brought about the expulsion of non-citizens from Rome, a measure designed to prevent an influx of Italians from usurping votes or intimidating opinion. This was followed by the revolt of Fregellae, the hitherto loyal and prosperous Latin dependency commanding the passage of the Liris. Captured by treachery, Fregellae was ruthlessly dismantled, and in its place the Roman colony of Fabrateria was founded on confiscated lands. "With its fall collapsed whatever other agitation may have existed, but the fate of Fregellae sank deep into the Italian heart, as its revolt was the forerunner of a more terrible rebellion." [28]

Gaius Graccus, who in 126 B.C. had gone on service to Sardinia, on his return to Rome two years later announced his candidacy for the tribunate. He had served with the Army for twelve years instead of the obligatory ten; his work as Quaestor in Sardinia had been performed with diligence and honesty; attempts to discredit him by linking him with the outbreak in Fregellae were too far-fetched to gain worthwhile credence. Despite organized opposition, therefore, in 124 B.C. he was elected Tribune amidst scenes of popular enthusiasm which did nothing to render him more acceptable to the reigning oligarchy of plutocrats and reactionary members of the patriciate. Sincere, an ardent orator, and with all the single-minded enthusiasm of the idealist who would fit everyone into his pattern of perfection regardless of the resistant minority, he embraced his dead brother's cause entirely undaunted by the fate his elder had suffered.

In the program Gaius championed it is sometimes difficult to differentiate between reform and revenge, since its untrammeled adoption would inevitably have involved the reduction of the Senate to impotence by dividing and neutralizing the strength of the upper classes, a process leading almost inescapably to government by a single autocrat.

Foremost among the measures Gaius urged was his bill for renewing and even extending the agrarian law earlier sponsored by his elder brother. This was coupled with a measure

[28] How and Leigh, *op. cit.*

for founding new Roman colonies overseas. Further, it was proposed to furnish corn at low cost to anyone possessing the Roman franchise. Arrangements for the public distribution of corn during periods of scarcity had long been one of the politicians' favorite devices for ensuring popularity. But it was now proposed, even in normal times, to establish the right by law. Thus Latins and Italians, denied the status of Roman citizenship, would be endowed with a dubious privilege of supplying their "betters'" needs by the sweat of their brows.

Furthermore, corruption in the magistracy was no longer to be subject to the lax jurisdiction of the Senate, but was to be handed over to a body of three hundred citizens, to be chosen annually from those enjoying possession of the "Equestrian" rate of property.[29] By this the "Equestrian" order, as a political body, entirely distinct from a mere military class, was accorded positive recognition. Another measure which was designed to fetter the power and patronage of the Senate dealt with the assignment of the consular provinces. "Hitherto the Senate had refrained from determining these provinces till after the elections, and they thus had a ready way of marking displeasure by allotting unprofitable governments to Consuls they disliked. But Graccus now proposed that the two consular provinces should be fixed before the elections, and that the new Consuls, immediately upon their election, should settle between themselves what province each was to administer, either by lot or by agreement." [30] Senatorial power was to be further curtailed by the removal of responsibility for roads and public works from the Censors and the Senate to the Tribunes.

The support of the city mob having been won by the *Lex Frumentaria,* which ensured them full bellies with or without a compensating return in toil, an even wider appeal for popularity was launched with the proposal to shorten the legal term of liability for military service, hitherto fixed as operative between the ages of seventeen and forty-five. Since Rome was in one of those moods in which it refused to recognize that a nation which is not kept perpetually on its toes stands every chance of being beaten to its knees, the measure found acceptance. Fortunately for Rome's future

[29] The constitution of juries formed the principal ground for political controversy for the ensuing half century.

[30] Beesly, *op. cit.* Cf. Appian. Graccus had his way in this, and his provision persisted as long as the Republic lasted.

destiny, modifications of the traditional ruling did not prove permanent. [31]

So far Gaius's "energy, eloquence and honesty had carried him through. With bitter invectives he lashed the corruption of Senators and diplomatists, and the cruelty of the magistrates to the allies and subjects . . . He secured his own reelection for 122 B.C. with M. Flaccus, the Consul of 125 B.C., as colleague, and the election of C. Fannius as Consul. So far he had been able to combine various interests in an attack on an unpopular body and win support for his own schemes. The hardest question of all remained. The plan of regeneration and reform demanded the incorporation of Italy in Rome. Forgetting Fregellae, he dreamed himself strong enough to propose a measure whose details are unknown, but which perhaps offered the full franchise to the Latins, and to the Italians, the *Jus Latinum*. The bill, if carried, would swamp the electorate, assist agrarian reform, strengthen his party, but it was also just and reasonable. Yet, in spite of his appeals to patriotism and prophecies of peril, of all his startling stories of Roman tyranny, of magistrates flogged for a dirty bath or a peasant murdered for a harmless jest, the meaner instincts of the mob applauded the arguments of Fannius, and refused to be crowded out of their places at the games or share their cherished doles." The Roman mob was determined to be exclusive even in its enjoyment of the vicious palliative of *panem et circenses*.

More devoted to his projects than politically astute, Gaius had unconsciously played into his opponents' hands. With considerable parade of conscious rectitude, the Senate rushed to the rescue of the people, whose champion, they vehemently averred, was whittling away the value of the very gifts he had made them.

It was a significant reflection of giddy, ever-veering popular favor that with the Tribunician elections neither Gaius nor his unflagging supporter Flaccus was returned to office, although reelection had now become legal. Then in 121 B.C. Opimius, another ruthless opponent of Gaius, became Consul, and it was patent that the opposition to the reformer was steadily mounting. Then news arrived from the new colony of Junonia—founded on the site of Carthage, where Gaius had been one of the commissioners entrusted

[31] For a time it was ordained that six years' continuous service entitled the man to his discharge, while twenty years in the infantry and ten in the cavalry exempted the veteran from all liability to further soldiering.

with the distribution of the land—that the settlement had been "planted on the ground cursed by Scipio; that the wrath of the gods had been shown by the fact that wolves had torn down the boundary posts. The Senate met, and the Tribunes at their request called a meeting of the Tribes upon the Capitol, to rescind the law for colonizing Carthage. The place was ominous, for there Tiberius Graccus had been slain." [32]

On the appointed morning the impetuous Flaccus was the first on the scene, at the head of a large crowd armed with daggers. Gaius followed, supported by a considerable suite.

Flaccus spoke vehemently to the Tribes, while Graccus stood aloof in the portico of the temple in which Opimius was offering sacrifice. Here he was encountered by Antyllius, a retainer of the Consul, who insolently pushed his way through the crowd, crying, "Make way for honest men!" Graccus cast an angry look upon the man, who presently fell pierced by many wounds. A cry of murder was raised, and the crowd fled in alarm to the Forum. Graccus retired to his house, regretting the imprudence of his followers. Meantime the body of the slain man was paraded before the eyes of the terrified people. The Senate issued a decree, by which Graccus was proclaimed a public enemy and Opimius invested with dictorial power. The Consul took station during the night in the Temple of Castor, by the side of the Forum, summoning the Senate to attend, armed, at a special sitting early next morning, and sent round to the Knights [Equites], desiring them also to come armed to the Forum. Each man was to bring two armed slaves. With this force he occupied the Capitol at daybreak, and prepared to execute the will of the Senate.

Graccus was irresolute; but Flaccus summoned to his house all who were ready to resist Senatorial authority. Here he armed them with the Celtic weapons which he had brought home from his Gallic campaigns, and kept up their courage by deep potations of wine. Early in the morning he occupied a strong position on the Aventine, where he was joined by Graccus, who sighed over the necessity of using force.

When the Senate met, the popular leaders were summoned to attend in their places and explain the proceed-

[32] Liddell, *op. cit.* Cf. Paterculus.

ings of the previous day. They answered by proclaiming liberty to all the slaves who should join them. Nothing could more clearly show the desperate aspect which the struggle had assumed. Yet before blood flowed, Graccus insisted on trying negotiation, and Q. Flaccus, a handsome youth of eighteen, son of the ex-Tribune, was sent. But the Consul was resolved to use his dictatorial power; and the only answer he returned was that the leaders must appear before the Senate and explain their conduct; and when young Quintus came back with a fresh message, Opimius arrested him. He now set a price on the heads of Graccus and Fulvius Flaccus, and ordered an immediate attack on the Aventine.[33]

For their leader the Senate chose not Opimius but the Spanish conqueror, D. Junius Brutus, who opened his assault on the objective under cover of a shower of arrows from a body of Cretan bowmen.

Little or no resistance was offered. Flaccus fled with his eldest son. Graccus retired into the Temple of Diana, where he was hardly prevented from putting an end to his own life by two faithful friends, the Knights Pomponius and Laetorius. Urged by them to flee, he threw himself on his knees and prayed the goddess to punish the unworthy people of Rome by everlasting slavery. All three then took their way down to the *Porta Trigemina,* hotly pursued. Pomponius, made a stand in the gateway to cover his friend's escape across the Sublician Bridge, and fell pierced with many wounds. Laetorius showed no less devotion by gallantly turning at bay upon the bridge until he knew that Graccus was safely over, when he sprang into the river and perished. Graccus with a single slave reached the grove of Furina, and here both were found dead. The faithful slave had slain his master and then killed himself upon the body. One Septimuleius brought in the head of Graccus, and was rewarded by the fierce Opimius with its weight in gold.[34]

Flaccus and his eldest son went into hiding, but the whereabouts of their retreat was betrayed and they were

[33] Liddell, *op. cit.* Cf. Florus, Appian, Paterculus.

[34] Characteristically, Septimuleius had first filled the skull with lead to add to the weight! Liddell, *op. cit.* and the authorities previously listed.

dragged into the open and butchered. With great condescension, Opimius permitted the younger son to choose the manner in which he would be dispatched. Great numbers of Graccus's followers were thrown into prison and subsequently put to death without trial; "the stream of Tiber flowed thick with their corpses"; while the inconstant herd plundered their houses without a hand being raised to stay them. The son of Gaius Graccus was never heard of again; save for Sempronia, the widow of Scipio, not one of the race remained.

The Gracci had perished because they had failed to realize that however well-intentioned, in the too impulsive exploitation of human misery and injustice there comes a point of diminishing returns; that revolution is no substitute for the steady processes of evolution. Nonetheless, the fires of revolt that they had kindled were only awaiting the hour, *and the man,* to burst forth once more in devouring flame.

There is nothing more calculated to divert attention from internal disorder than the incidence of external war. Thus from 120 B.C. to 104 B.C. Rome was too heavily engaged in conflict beyond her boundaries for unrest on the home front to occupy more than a tithe of the authorities' attention. The ineffective indictment of Opimius and the suicide of the shifty Carbo were no more than sensations of the hour. With warfare lowering on the horizon, such domestic issues as the Italian franchise, transmarine colonization, and the Romanization of the provinces went into abeyance, although the purchase, mortgage, and seizure of land continued unabated—all under the unwinking gaze of the avaricious M. Aemilius Scaurus, who in 115 B.C. had reached the consulate. In 119 B.C., however, the Senate's design to ensure popular favor had been vigorously opposed by G. Marius,[35] whose outstanding qualities as a soldier had won him the support of the influential family of the Metelli and brought him election to the tribunate. Little as they may have realized it at the moment, events were shaping that were to render the name of Marius only too grimly familiar to them all.

As early as 123 B.C. it had been necessary to organize an expedition to subdue the restless Balearic Islands, and in 119 B.C. an uprising by the Dalmatians had called for the organization of another force for its suppression. Far more serious was the reanimation of the war in the southern parts of

[35] At this time he was thirty-eight years of age.

Gaul. The successful defense of Massilia by Fulvius Flaccus had earned him an official *supplicatio* in 123 B.C., and his successor, C. Sextius, had succeeded in founding the colony of Aquae Sextiae.[36] These conquests brought the Romans in contact with the Allobrogians, between the Rhone and the Isère, and these people, combining with Bituitus and his Arvernians, rose in arms and threw themselves on the troops commanded by the Consul Q. Fabius. A desperate battle was fought out near the river Isère, in which the Consul, with 30,000 men, completely routed a horde of 200,000 Gauls, of whom no less than 120,000 fell in the encounter and the pursuit that followed. Soundly defeated in the field, the Gauls had no alternative but to sue for peace, and the dominion of Rome was firmly established in that angle of Gaul which lies between the Alps and the Pyrenees.[37] Indeed, the whole northern coast of the Mediterranean, from Syria to the Pillars of Hercules, now owned to the sovereignty of Rome.

A very different state of affairs, however, prevailed in Africa. Numidia, so valuable as a source of cheap grain for Rome, had come by now under the rule of Massinissa's two grandsons, Adherbal and Hiempsal. But by their side stood their bastard sibling, Jugurtha, a strong active man, who had shared with Marius much of the military distinction won in the campaign of 134 B.C. and whose appetite for power paid little heed to ordinary scruples. Considerably older than his two blood relations, he was an adventurer only too ready to lend ear to the counsel of certain renegade Romans that he should purchase the Senate's support and seize the Numidian Crown. "At Rome," they assured him, "all things might be had for money." [38]

It is possible that had the Princes submitted passively, Jugurtha might have rested content with a divided sovereignty. But Hiempsal exhibited so firm a spirit of independence that there was no course left open to the power-hungry aspirant to the Throne but to arrange for the younger man's assassination. Thoroughly alarmed, Adherbal flew to arms, only to discover that although the people might be with him, his military chiefs were not. The young Prince was compelled to take refuge in the Roman Province of

---

[36] In later centuries, under the name of Aix, it attracted many visitors on the score of its medicinal hot springs.

[37] Known to the Romans as "the Province," it is still named Provence.

[38] Sallust (Gaius Sallustius Crispus), *Jugurtha*.

Libya, whence he took ship to Rome to plead his cause in person.

At the outset general feeling in the Senate inclined in his favor. But such was the state of corruption into which that body had fallen that few of its members were of sufficient probity to reject the bribes distributed among them by Jugurtha's gold-laden emissaries, and it was finally decided to dispatch a commission of ten to Numidia to superintend the division of the country between Adherbal and his un-scrupulous rival. When it was announced that the mission was to be headed by the predatory Opimius, any lurking suspicion that the fulfillment of its task might be character-ized by fair dealing was instantly dismissed. In the outcome the eastern half of the kingdom—the original patrimony of Massinissa, and mostly arid desert—was assigned to Adher-bal. The western and far richer area, which had formerly been subject to Syphax, was allotted to Jugurtha.

Bribery and corruption appeared to have serenely tri-umphed until the Tribune-elect, C. Memius boldly exposed the intrigue in the Forum, whereupon all those whom Jugurtha had not thought it worth while suborning, with an unwonted display of rectitude denounced the bargain so re-cently struck and demanded that the Numidian should be brought to heel by force.

With war declared, the command was first bestowed on one of the Consuls-elect for the ensuing year (111 B.C.), L. Calpurnius Bestia. The Romans' initial forward movement was arrested with such singular lack of reason, however, that suspicion could scarcely be suppressed that Bestia had been bribed to stay his hand. It was thereupon decreed that Jugurtha should be brought to Rome under a safe conduct in order that he might give evidence on the charge that there had been corrupt dealings. Proceedings when the Numidian appeared before the Senate rendered it clear past any perad-venture that the Tribunician vote had been bought with African gold. Thus, despite the vehement protest of the peo-ple, Jugurtha was permitted to return whence he had come. A commission of three, headed by Scaurus, was appointed to inquire into the conduct of all who had been concerned in the Numidian's affairs, while the command in North Africa was assigned (109 B.C.) to the Consul Q. Metellus. His second-in-command was that protégé of the Metelli family, Gaius Marius, now approaching his middle years, and allied to the oligarchy despite his humble origins through his marriage to Julia, the sister of the Patrician G. Julius Caesar.

At the outset of his campaign Metellus allowed himself to be surprised on the line of march. But in the ensuing battle Jugurtha suffered sanguinary defeat; his many dead included no less than forty war-elephants. But the Romans' attack on the fortress of Zama proved a costly failure. Jugurtha could doubtless have prosecuted a guerrilla war almost indefinitely, but he saw far greater advantage in coming to terms with his opponent. Metellus was prepared to treat only if the conditions included the Numidian's own surrender. To this Jugurtha refused to consent, and operations were resumed.

Meanwhile the conduct of Marius began to excite distrust in the mind of the General. When he named the rude soldier his lieutenant, he expected doubtless that the offer of serving under a Metellus would be honor sufficient. But the military talents of Marius had become manifest, and he had become a favorite with the soldiery. "If he had had half the army," he used to say, "he would soon make an end to the war." He gave out that he meant to offer himself for the consulship, and requested leave of absence as soon as he could be spared.[39]

The next year's campaign had opened before Marius obtained permission to repair to Rome. Entirely unscrupulous, as ready to hector—or bribe—a politician as he was to playact his way into the good graces of the man in the ranks, once he had arrived in the capital he made no pretense of disguising his aim. "Make me Consul, and you shall have Jugurtha, dead or alive, at Rome," was his vaunt; and on this pledge he was elected by an overwhelming majority, the people being only too delighted to elevate to the chief magistracy one of their own kind who also happened to be, at least in popular estimation, the finest soldier in the country's service.

It was not without irony that, with Marius still absent, the second campaign of Metellus was so successful that the stronghold of Cirta was brought to surrender and Jugurtha was forced to seek refuge with Bocchus, King of Mauretania, whose daughter he had married. Persuaded to support his son-in-law in arms, Bocchus, with his own and the Numidian's forces under command, advanced on Cirta.

Marius meanwhile had been anything but idle. Haranguing any audience that would give him hearing, he expressed the

39 Sallust, *op. cit.* Cf. Beesly.

utmost scorn for all Senatorial commanders, "men of old pedigree, but ignorant of war; who never saw an army till they became Generals, and then set about studying Greek books of tactics. *He* was a New Man; *he* had no images to show; *he* knew no Greek; *he* had no skill in setting out banquets; *he* did not esteem a cook a better man than an honest farm-bailiff: but he had images of his own—spears, trappings, standards, prizes won by valor, and scars upon his breast." [40]

It was demagogy of the most blatant, and like all appeals to envy and class hatred, it won the frantic plaudits of the crowd. It is little wonder, therefore, that Metellus received instructions to hand over command to his erstwhile lieutenant.

Although he had boasted of needing only half the army of Metellus, Marius busied himself in mustering a far more powerful force, numerically, than his predecessor had ever commanded, even creating the precedent of enlisting men without the customary property qualification, the better to swell the ranks. In a great bustle, he set off for Africa with his infantry, leaving the cavalry to follow under the command of his Quaestor, L. Cornelius Sulla,[41] the thirty-one-year-old scion of a distinguished family whose fallen fortunes he was determined to repair. It was his first campaign, and under Marius's tutelage he learned much of the art of generalship—and many other things!

The task that Marius had undertaken with such overweening confidence proved anything but easy to execute. His first success was the capture of the oasis-stronghold of Capsa, after a march of incredible difficulty and strain. Having thus cleared eastern Numidia, the victor entered on a long and difficult expedition to Molochath. Having by a lucky chance captured one of Jugurtha's treasure-holds, Marius found his position too advanced, and determined on a difficult retreat fraught with considerable danger. With Bocchus joining forces with Jugurtha, the Romans found themselves enveloped, and in successive pitched battles they fought their way free, with the second occasion affording Sulla a brilliant opportunity to demonstrate his inborn aptitude for war.

From winter quarters at Cirta negotiations were privily resumed with Bocchus, without whose surreptitious aid the conflict threatened to be interminable. For the necessary con-

[40] Sallust, *op. cit.*
[41] By some translators the name is rendered as Sylla.

sideration the Moor was quite prepared to betray his Numidian kinsman and ally; the bargain was sealed, and Jugurtha was entrapped and borne off to Rome in chains to grace the public triumph of his captor.

If the credit for Jugurtha's capture belonged largely to Sulla's cool and subtle diplomacy, the people lauded Marius as the conqueror and their own particular hero. Thus was bred a rivalry, the consequences of which were gravely to affect the future destiny of Rome. For the moment it seemed to matter little that much loss in lives and treasure had been incurred for remarkably scant result. As the price of betrayal, Bocchus was assigned the western half of Numidia, with the remainder of the territory being bestowed on Gauda, a grandson of Massinissa. No new province was formed, no vast indemnity exacted.

But if the military results of the enterprise were no more than paltry, the political outcome was striking. Corruption and incapacity had played right into the hands of the *populaires*. A reasonably successful Patrician commander, by vote of the Tribes, had been superseded by a son of the people. The ground of opposition had shifted from home to foreign policy, and the military power had come irreversibly to the forefront. And Marius personified the might of the army *and* of the people. It is little wonder, therefore, that on January first, 104 B.C., "Rome's only General" should have entered upon his second consulate with every circumstance of popular acclaim.

Chapter VII

CREATION OF A PRECEDENT

"The same purposes, otherwise conceived,
the same problems, otherwise approached."
—G. H. Young, *Last Essays*

Jugurtha had constituted a definite challenge to Roman sovereignty and prestige in the Mediterranean, but a far greater menace had been piling up beyond the Alps and the

Pyrenees. Cimbrians and Teutones had massed in the north-east and had been joined by the smaller tribes of the Ambrones, Tugeni, and Tigurini, until their members totaled over 300,000 with an even greater swarm of their women and children tagging at their heels.

Intent on settling in lands far more fruitful and enticing than the harsh, inclement territories on which they had turned their backs, "nothing could resist their impetuosity; all who came in their way were trodden down, or driven before them like cattle. Many respectable armies and Generals employed by the Romans to guard the Transalpine Gaul were shamefully routed; and the feeble resistance they made to the first efforts of the barbarians was the chief thing that drew them towards Rome. For, having beaten all they met, and loaded themselves with plunder, they determined to settle nowhere till they had destroyed Rome and laid waste all Italy." [1]

In 105 B.C. at Aurosio, in the vicinity of the river Rhône, one Roman army was so shatteringly defeated that 80,000 rank and file and 40,000 men belonging to the supply services were slain; a mere ten survivors contrived to get clear of the shambles. As the "Cimbrian panic" reached its height and it became more and more difficult to raise men to fill the yawning gaps in the ranks, public indignation with a corrupt and feeble administration was coupled with the demand that the supreme military command should be vested in the people's popular idol, Marius.

Marius had already spent over two years in the far-reaching reorganization of Rome's armed forces, seeking to extirpate all lingering traces of the erstwhile militia system in favor of a thoroughly professional standing force based upon a paid volunteer rank and file enlisted for a definite term of years, and supplemented by contingents from Italy and abroad. More cavalry was legislated for—Italian, Thracian, and Numidian—and stronger bodies of light-armed Foot from Liguria and the Balearics. New methods of training had been adopted, derived from the masters of the gladiatorial schools, the whole aim being to cultivate to the utmost the dynamism of the skilled individual swordsman. Company Ensigns were abolished, although the cohort, with its six sections of 100, had its battalion Colors, and the Legion, 6,000 strong, still marched behind the revered and dearly cherished Eagle. The heavy pack and other impedimenta were now slung on the end of poles, carried over the shoulder and universally known

---

[1] Plutarch, *op. cit.* Cf. Livy and Appian.

as "Marius's mules." [2] Since recruits not of peasant stock
were liberally enrolled, the forces were speedily transformed
into a body of men who had no future save in the army—a
fundamental change not without its latent dangers. If the
reorganization had been undertaken out of military necessity, which called for a professional soldier class because
conditions demanded the creation of just such a class, con-
versely it brought into being a remarkably handy tool for
any aspiring autocrat to have at his disposal, once he had
won its confidence and trust. And that was a task to which
Marius had devoted himself with guileful assiduity. Un-
couth, virtually illiterate, but

> surpassing his equals in prudence and foresight, and
> contesting it with the common soldiers in abstemious-
> ness and labor, he entirely gained their affections; for it
> is no small consolation to anyone who is obliged to work,
> to see another voluntarily take a share in his labor,
> since it seems to take off the constraint. There was
> not, indeed, a more agreeable spectacle for a Roman
> soldier, than that of his General eating the same dry
> bread which he ate, or lying on an ordinary bed, or
> assisting his men in drawing a trench or throwing up a
> bulwark; for the soldier does not so much admire those
> officers who let him share in their honor or their money,
> as those who will partake with him in labor and dan-
> ger; and he is more attached to one who will assist him
> in his work, than to one who will indulge him in idle-
> ness. [3]

As an ex-ranker, all this, of course, was a familiar line of
reasoning with Marius, and he exploited his knowledge to
the very fullest advantage.

Elected Consul for the fourth time in succession, in defiance of all precedent, Marius left Rome in some haste on
learning that the Cimbrians, having been repulsed by the
Celtiberians, had recrossed the Pyrenees. By this time the
Teutons had entered Gaul from the northeast, and the combined hordes were fast mustering on the frontier of the
Gallic Province (Provence).

In the summer of 102 B.C. Marius pitched his camp in a
strong, well-provisioned position at the junction of the Isère
and the Rhône, specifically chosen on the score that it

[2] Plutarch's *Lives*. (*Gaius Marius*).
[3] *Ibid*.

barred both the highways into Italy, the route over the Little
St. Bernard, and the road along the coast. At the outset
Marius was content to stand on the defensive, encouraging
the barbarians to expend their strength in fruitless assaults
on his field-works. "At last they drew off in the direction of
the south, in order to march into Italy by the road along the
coast. They were six days marching past the Roman camp
in enormous crowds, with numberless heavily laden carts.
The Romans from their entrenchments jeered at them as
they passed, asking if they had no commands for their
wives. When the procession had gone by, Marius followed
with his force. In this way they traveled until they came to
Aquae Sextiae;[4] from here it was only a little way to the
Alps, and Marius was compelled to consider the question of
a decisive battle." [5]

A scuffle between hostile watering parties brought on a
general action, during the course of which the Ambroni
horde, in crossing the stream, fell into such hopeless disorder that they fled back to their camp and the protection to
be found in a barricade of wagons. "Here the fight was renewed after a strange fashion, for the wives of the Ambrones,
armed with swords and hatchets, rushed with wild cries to
meet them as they fled, forcing them back towards their
enemy; and those who saw that all was lost, fell into a frenzy
and threw themselves into the midst of the combat, letting
themselves be cut and hacked to pieces." [6]

But the contest was by no means ended. Three days later
the barbarians were once more full of fight, and assembled
in loose array for another assault on the Roman position.
Marius thereupon drew up his men on the hillside in strict
order of battle, waiting quietly until their enemy came within range of their throwing spears. The *pila* loosed, they drew
their swords and closed resolutely with their foes. Under the
heat of the southern sun the struggle swayed back and forth
until the barbarians, exhausted by their impetuous, unruly
onfall, began to give way. As they sought desperately to reorganize their disarray, a reserve of three thousand Romans
sprang from their ambush and fell on their rear. Caught between two avenging scythe-blades, the barbarians were cut
to ribbons, the survivors of the sanguinary *mêlée* fleeing

---

[4] Now Aix-en-Provence.
[5] Sallust, *op. cit.*
[6] *Ibid.*

in the utmost confusion. By contemporary reckoning,[7] close
on one hundred thousand of the savage invaders were either
slain or taken captive.

Aquae Sextiae was an outstanding success for Roman
arms, but there was little breathing space for Marius and
his Legions, for other hordes of the Cimbrians had swarmed
through the Alpine passes to rout Q. Lutatius Catulus on the
Adige. Retreating along the southern bank of the Po, the
Romans surrendered the country north of the river to the
barbarians' plundering hands. The road to the capital lay
wide open and almost without barrier. But the invaders were
too busy with their spoil to seize the opportunity so freely
offered to them.

Lingering in Rome only long enough to ensure his election
as Consul for the fifth time, Marius hastened north to join
Catulus. In the hectic rush and bustle of departure there was
not even time for a visit to his wife's sister, Aurelia, to congratulate her on the birth of her son, Gaius Julius Caesar.[8]
Even had his leisure been unlimited, it is doubtful if he
would have found opportunity to inquire as to the well-
being of another infant with whose future his nephew was
to be so indissolubly associated—the five-year-old Gnaeus
Pompeius.

By the spring of 101 B.C. the Romans had again crossed
to the northern bank of the Po and were in close touch
with the Cimbrians, who were still hopefully awaiting the
arrival of those Teutonic allies whose whitened bones now
served as fencing for the Massiliots' vineyards. With the intelligence of the fate that had befallen their allies, the
Cimbrians braced themselves to carry on the war with their
own resources, demanding of Marius that he fix a day and
an hour for the battle.

The clash came on the last day but one of July. For this
occasion the Cimbrian warriors were drawn up in a hollow
square which report put at over thirty furlongs in length and
breadth. Fifteen thousand of their Horse "issued forth in
great splendor. Their helmets represented the heads and open
jaws of strange and frightful wild beasts; on these were fixed
high plumes, which made the men appear taller. Their breast-
plates were of polished iron and their shields were white and
glittering. Each man had two-edged darts to fight with at a

[7] *Vide* Plutarch.

[8] There is some question whether Caesar was born in 102 B.C. or
100 B.C., but majority opinion favors the earlier year.

distance, and when they came hand-to-hand they used broad and heavy swords." [9]

Despite his employment of the tactical device of an ambush at Aquae Sextiae, in principle Marius was faithful to the strategy of inner lines, to which the battle practice of the Roman soldier was so peculiarly adapted. At Vercellae he abode by it steadfastly, and he was also careful to align his 50,000 troops so that the sun shone into the enemies' eyes and the dust cloud stirred up by the myriad trampling hooves blew back into their faces. The engagement opened with a relatively successful attempt on the part of the Cimbrian Horse to lure the Roman Cavalry away from their supporting Foot. But the ruse availed them nothing. The decision lay with the infantry. Desperately determined to retrieve their tarnished reputation, the troops which had constituted Catulus's command, fighting under the immediate eye of Sulla, held firmly in the center, with Marius's steady veterans in close support on either flank.

Thrown into tangled disarray by the hail of *pila* beating in on them, the Cimbrian formations faltered, uncertain of their next move and already panting and exhausted with the torrid summer heat. The Romans, on the other hand, "were so strengthened by labor and exercise, that not one of them was observed to sweat or be out of breath, notwithstanding the suffocating heat and the violence of the encounter." Advancing with a resolution that in itself was intimidating, the men of the Legions clove their way through the disordered enemy ranks, dealing out death and destruction with every thrust of their sword-arms.

The greatest and best parts of the enemy's troops were cut to pieces on the spot. The Romans drove back the fugitives to their camp, where they found the most shocking spectacle. The women, standing in mourning by their carts and carriages, killed those that fled; some their husbands, some their brothers, others their fathers. They strangled their little children with their own hands, and threw them under the wheels and horses' feet. Last of all, they killed themselves. They tell of one that was seen slung from the top of a wagon, with a child hanging at each heel. The men, for want of trees, tied themselves by the neck, some to the horns of oxen, others to their legs, and then pricked them on, that by the starting of the beasts they might be strangled or torn to

[9] Plutarch, *op. cit.*

pieces. But though they were so industrious to destroy themselves, above sixty thousand were taken prisoners, and the killed were said to be twice that number.[10]

There can be little doubt that the brunt of the fighting had been borne by Catulus's troops of the center, with Sulla as the most prominent of the subordinate leaders, and their commander was not slow to advance his men's claim to special recognition. It was a pretension Marius was far too wily publicly to asperse. He was quite content privily to encourage his own obedient sycophants to bruit abroad their own particular version of events, with the result that "the whole honor of the day was ascribed to Marius, on account of his former victory and present authority; nay, such was the applause of the populace, that they called him *the third founder of Rome,* as having rescued her from a danger no less dreadful than that from the Gauls." [11] Still seeking to have it both ways, "Marius contented himself with a single 'triumph,' which he shared with Catulus; but the rivalry of the Generals became a political antagonism between the popular and Senatorial champions"—a harbinger of that bitter social strife that was presently to rend the populace in twain.

The menace of barbarian invasion had been so overpowering as almost to shut out thought of events elsewhere. Yet the reprehensibly casual administration of the law of bondage, which had retained in conditions of servitude large numbers of individuals legally entitled to their liberty, had led in 105 B.C. to another servile rising in Sicily. Near Agrigentum the defeat of a body of Roman troops that had sought to quell a localised insurrection led to a movement of rebellion, headed by "Salvius the Soothsayer," which speedily became widespread. With Salvius, at the head of 20,000 followers, laying siege to the city of Murgantia in the east, another body of well-armed insurrectionaries, under the leadership of a Cilician slave named Athenio, brought the strongly fortified port of Lilybaeum under close investment. Finding his objective impregnable, Athenio drew off his followers and marched to join forces with Salvius, who had assumed the name of Tryphon and set up the seat of his sovereignty at the fortress of Triacola. Assuming regal status, Tryphon appointed a Senate and walked abroad in the

[10] Plutarch, *op. cit.*
[11] *Ibid.*

robes (*toga praetexta*) of a Roman magistrate, closely attended by a bodyguard of lictors.

At the outset, the Romans could make no headway whatsoever against this flood tide of rebellion. In 101 B.C., however, the Roman forces came under the command of M. Aquillius, the colleague of Marius during his fifth consulship; his assumption of the appointment followed closely on Tryphon's death and Athenio's succession as the rebels' leader.

Aquillius lost little time in bringing the revolted slaves to action, in an encounter in which the Roman leader was severely wounded in a hand-to-hand fight with Athenio, who nonetheless fell to his opponent's sword. With Athenio's death, the heart seemed to go out of the rebellion, with the insurgents dwindling away until all that was left was a band of about a thousand desperate men, under the leadership of a certain Satyrus.

With no hope of holding out indefinitely against the superior force that could be brought against them, this remnant eventually surrendered, and were sent to Rome to serve as gladiators. But "being brought out into the arena to fight with wild beasts, rather than make sport for the conquerors they slew one another at the foot of the altars which stood there; and Satyrus, being left alone, fell on his own sword." [12]

In a few months the last embers of rebellion had been stamped out, and a draconic code of laws was drawn up to ensure that the spirit of revolt should know no recrudescence. But "the misery caused in Sicily by this long war, which ended in 100 B.C., may be estimated by the fact that, whereas Sicily usually supplied Rome with corn, it was now desolated by famine, and its towns had to be supplied with grain from Rome." [13]

"The mother of the Gracci cast the dust of her murdered sons into the air, and out of it was born Marius." [14] Unquestionably from the days of the Gracci onwards the authority of the old nobility, concentrated in the Patriciate, had been steadily on the wane. And since it is far easier to emasculate an aristocracy than curb the power of a plutocracy, the struggle under Marius's sixth consulship was rather

[12] Liddell, *op. cit.*
[13] Beesly, *op. cit.*
[14] Honoré Gabriel Riqueti, Comte de Mirabeau.

between the radical extremists and the wealthy parvenus than between *optimates* and *populares*. Nonetheless, the continued appointment of Marius was in itself a triumph for the man-in-the-street; for although by craft and shameless tergiversation he sought to beguile his opponents in the Senate, he assiduously "courted the people, and endeavored to ingratiate himself with the meanest of them by such servile condescensions as were not only unsuitable to his dignity, but even contrary to his disposition, assuming an air of gentleness and complaisance for which nature never meant him." [15]

Perhaps the individual who most discerningly penetrated the Consul's specious mask of dissimulation was his erstwhile military superior, Metellus, whose Numidian laurels Marius had so brazenly arrogated to himself. For Metellus was "naturally an enemy to those who endeavored to gain the populace by evil arts, and directed all their measures to please them. Marius, therefore, was very desirous to get him out of the way. For this purpose he associated with Servilius Glaucia and Appuleius Saturninus, two of the most daring and turbulent men in Rome, who had the indigent and seditious part of the people at their command. By their assistance he got several laws enacted; and having planted many of his soldiers in the Assemblies, his faction prevailed, and Metellus was overborne." [16] In his place the election of Valerius Flaccus was carefully engineered, and Flaccus, as far as Marius was concerned, "was rather his servant than his colleague."

With this support Marius succeeded in forcing through measures which conferred the status of Roman citizens on a thousand allied Camerinum warriors, as well as on three citizens in every colony which enjoyed the Latin franchise, a boon greatly coveted by the soldiery whose fidelity he was determined to retain. Another measure, aimed at solidifying the support of the troops, brazenly deprived the inhabitants of the transalpine provinces of their land holdings, to reward the victors of Aquae Sextiae and Vercellae. [17]

The nobles resented these concessions, and even the commons regarded them with uneasiness and distrust. They sought to interrupt the proceedings on the occur-

[15] Plutarch, *op. cit.*

[16] Plutarch. Cf. Appian.

[17] Saturninus also brought in a measure to alter the Appuleian law governing the price of grain, blatantly seeking popular favor by lowering the cost from 6½ *asses* and *modius* (the price fixed by Graccus) to the derisory sum of 5/6 of an *as* for the same quantity.

rence of rain and thunder. "Be still," cried Saturninus, "or it will presently hail!" His adherents armed themselves with stones. Tumults arose in the Forum; the Senators and their partisans among the populace were driven away by the fury of the veterans, and Saturninus carried his rogation with open violence. Marius kept warily aloof, and affected great horror at the illegal disturbance. He excited the nobles underhand to protest against the execution of a law carried in a manner so irregular, which the Tribunes insisted on their accepting under specified penalties. As soon, however, as they had committed themselves, Marius withdrew his countenance from them, and left them the choice of submitting with dishonor, or enduring the punishment of refusal. The Senators, entrapped and cowed, took the oath required, till it came the turn of Metellus; but the haughtiest of the nobles, though urged and entreated by his friends to yield to necessity, disdained to swerve from the principles he had avowed. Saturninus demanded that he should be outlawed, and fire and water forbidden him. His friends were numerous and strong enough to have defended him with arms, but he forbade them draw their swords, and went proudly into banishment.[18]

As far as Marius and Saturninus were concerned,

their object seemed to be attained; but even now to those who saw more clearly the enterprise could not appear other than a failure. The cause of the failure lay mainly in the awkward alliance between a politically incapable General and a street-demagogue, able but recklessly violent, and filled with passion rather than with the aims of a statesman. They had agreed excellently, so long as the question related to their plans alone. But when the plans came to be executed, it was very soon apparent that the celebrated General was in politics a mere incapable; that his ambition was that of the farmer who would cope with and, if possible, surpass the aristocrats in titles, and not that of the statesman who desires to govern because he feels within him the power to do so.[19]

It was Marius's cardinal flaw that while he strove publicly to dissociate himself from the questionable practices

[18] Appian, *op. cit.* Cf. Sallust.
[19] Mommsen, *op. cit.*

of his familiars, at the same time he sought diligently to profit by them. Matters came to a head with the consular elections.

The orator Antonius had been chosen for one; for the second place C. Memmius was illegally opposed by Glaucia, who, as *Praetor* of the year, was ineligible. Memmius was publicly murdered by bravos, and the next day there was an appeal to arms. On the one side stood the rustics and veterans, whipped up from the country, with whose aid Saturninus and Glaucia seized the Capitol, at the same time opening the prisons and summoning the slaves. On the other were the *Optimates* with their clients, and the *Equites* of the eighteen centuries, with their armed slaves. The Senate summoned Marius to interfere and empowered the magistrates to use force. Reluctantly he prepared to attack his friends. They had gone too far, and the Consul must either stamp out riot or proclaim revolution. The Senate turned out *en masse;* the tottering Scaurus, the aged Scaevola, donned their disused armor. The city was guarded within and without. There was a battle in the Forum, the first fought in Rome; the rebels were driven to the Capitol, and when Marius cut off the water, finally surrendered. Hoping to save them, he placed them in the *Curia Hostilia,* but when the young nobles stormed the roof and pelted the prisoners to death, he was forced to let them perish.[20]

Among many others who fell on that momentous day was the feckless, power-hungry Saturninus.

The explosion into violence at least had the effect of putting the underlying cause of it into something like proper perspective. It was not so much that the measures sponsored by Marius and his associates were inadmissible in themselves, as that they presaged unqualified military dictatorship, with the Senate reduced to impotence and the tribunate beguiled into rendering absolutism its ductile support. But those who resorted to open homicide and the attempted use of *force majeure* could scarcely pretend to that integrity which is essential to the exercise of power. For "in the massacre had fallen four officers of the Roman people, with other men of note; and with them fell the power and credit of Marius. The cause of the disaster lay partly in the vacillation and incompetence of Marius, who could neither control nor sup-

20 How and Leigh, *op. cit.*

port his associates; partly in the reckless and riotous conduct of Saturninus and Glaucia, which alarmed the wealthier classes and consolidated the opposition. Men were ready to support a strong and upright man in cleansing the administration, but not to sacrifice material interests to military rowdyism and mob rule." [21]

As the *Equites* moved into closer accord with the members of the Senate, Metellus returned in triumph, a protesting Tribune being done to death by the fickle crowd, which was now only too eager to identify itself with the winning side. As for the victor of Aquae Sextiae and Vercellae, so consistently was he shunned that he temporarily withdrew to the east, where the Romans might certainly have found occasion for energetic interference, and where he hoped that conflicts and battles would occur and that the people would once more need his experienced arm. But this also miscarried, and he returned and opened his house; but his halls stood empty.[22]

Not the least regretful outcome of the recent clash was the deep feeling of exasperation it aroused against the *Populares*. Retribution was exacted against them by the repeal of the Appuleian corn laws; and when the Tribune Titius, a paltry ape of Saturninus, attempted to revive the Agrarian Bill in 99 B.C., not only was it annulled on religious pretexts, but the Tribune and other democrats were zealously convicted by the Equestrian Courts, whose increase in judicial power had long been a cause of complaint on the part of the Senate. But the fact that the slave uprising in Sicily was still a matter of painful memory to those now in authority, had the effect of binding the Senate and the Equestrian Order closer together, while in no sense inclining them to lenity in their attitude towards the proletarian element in the population. Furthermore, in unreflective reaction to the efforts of Saturninus to bring the Italians to closer and more equitable association with Rome, certain laws against aliens were re-enacted for the purpose of preventing irregular voting and the exertion of undue influence by Italians in the *Comitia*. The *Lex Licinia Mucia* created violent resentment among Rome's allies by prohibiting noncitizens from claiming or exercising the franchise, by inquiring into the status of resident aliens, and by ordaining the expulsion of those who usurped the right. Useful as such a measure might be for the restocking of the associated peoples'

---

21 How and Leigh, *op. cit.*
22 Appian, *op. cit.* Cf. Beesly and Mommsen.

depopulated townships, the legislation seemed to express extraordinary ingratitude for the allies' patriotic exertions in the Cimbric campaigns, since it reduced the man who had fought and bled for Rome to the status of a stranger within its gates and one liable to punishment if he transgressed against the rules that held him to be an alien.

The general atmosphere of suspicion, dissension, and unrest was by no means ameliorated by the measures brought forward by the well-intentioned but politically maladroit Tribune for the year 91 B.C., Livius Drusus. His proposals included a *Lex Frumentaria* to increase the doles handed out to the indigent—designed to cover the expense involved by depreciation of the coinage, which could only have had the effect of inflating prices. This measure was to be accompanied by an Agrarian Law which was virtually a paraphrase of the project to establish colonies on the public lands of Italy and Sicily. Then, in a bid to win the support of the Senate for legislation which patently favored the *publicani*, Drusus submitted a *Lex Iudiciaria*, postulating an agreement between the Senate and the *Equites*, by which the number of the former was to be doubled by the addition of three hundred members to be selected from among the Knights, and from whom were to be chosen the judges for the Equestrian Court. Since this was no more than a specious compromise, it failed to satisfy either the Senators or the *Equites*, although the partisans and opponents of the proposals were soon arguing the issues furiously.

Not content to have stirred up debatable matters which had long been bitterly controversial, Drusus blindly plunged on to seek legislation that would confer the untrammeled franchise on the Italians, a measure unpopular with all parties in Rome. Immediately the cry went up that the Tribune was inciting the allies to revolt, and so great was public indignation that it was clear that the proponent of the obnoxious legislation went in danger of his life. "For some time he had avoided public places, and received those who came to transact business with him in a covered walk behind his house. One evening, as he was dismissing his visitors, he cried out that he was stabbed, and fell to the ground. A leather-cutter's knife was found planted in his loins. He expired soon after, mournfully saying that it would be long before the Republic would have a servant as disinterested as himself" [23]—the apologia of all would-be reformers who fail to relate their ideology to reality.

[23] Liddell, *op. cit.* For the various stories as to the manner of Drusus's death, see *The History of Rome* by Wilhelm Ihne-Imme.

The excitement produced by this last disappointment of their hopes was great throughout the towns of Italy. It was greater still when a Tribune named Varius, a native of Sucro in Spain, who had become a Roman citizen, introduced a law which declared that all who had favored Italian claims had been guilty of high treason against the People of Rome. Under this law the veteran Scaurus and the leading Senators were at once impeached. Some sought safety in exile. . . . There was no evidence against Scaurus but the word of the accuser, and the wary statesman contented himself with saying in defense, "Q. Varius, the Spaniard, says that M. Scaurus, the Chief of the Senate, has endeavored to excite the allies to rebellion. Scaurus denies the fact. Choose ye, *Quirites,* which ye will believe!" He was acquitted, and so disappears from the stage a man who for more than twenty years had been the virtual chief of Rome.[24]

The award of Roman citizenship and the rights of the franchise was a form of recognition the allies demanded as their right in return for their unfailing support of the Republic in times of war, when their troops had fought side by side with the Legions and with equal valor and pertinacity. With Drusus's advocacy of their cause their expectations had risen to such heights that the death of their champion and the consequent collapse of their hopes engendered a mood of bitter rancor which needed little provocation to explode into violence.

In the event, the outbreak of civil strife was precipitated by an act of entirely unpremeditated outrage. Servilius, the Proconsul stationed in the Picenian territory, was given the intelligence that the citizens of Asculum were actively organizing insurrection. Proceeding to that city with a small retinue and finding the people assembling for some quite innocuous festal purpose, without pausing to make inquiry he stormed at them so unrestrainedly that they set upon him and slew him. Blood once spilled, the passions of the mob were aroused so violently that all Romans dwelling in the city were gloatingly put to the sword, without regard to age or sex.

The news of the massacre at Asculum spread like wildfire. A general league was formed of Rome's erstwhile dependents

---

[24] Appian, *op. cit.* Cf. Beesly, Liddell, Mommsen.

—Picentians, Marsians, Pelignians, Marrucinians, and Vestinians, the Samnites, the Apulians, and the Lucanians—and a formal statement of their claims was drawn up and dispatched to Rome (90 B.C.). "They had," so they justifiably emphasized, "long done faithful service to the Republic; they had furnished two-thirds of her armies; they had conquered the world for her, yet they were still treated like mere aliens." The Senate frigidly replied that "no embassies could be received till reparation had been made for the late acts of violence." [25]

The steps taken by the eight allied people starkly foretold the course the impending struggle was bound to pursue. Rome's adoption of the Alexandrian concept of conquest as a precursor of assimilation had not been carried to its logical conclusion: "Unity in Concord"—*Homonoia*—can only exist between equals. With her failure to give this fundamental consideration full and proper recognition, the situation hardened appreciably.

It was no longer a question of whether or not the Italians should become citizens of Rome, but the far graver issue of whether or not Rome should continue to predominate in the Italian confederation.

The Italian League's first act of open defiance was to declare Corfinium, a strong city in the Pelignian Apennines, the capital of the confederation.[26] Two Consuls were to be the chief Officers of the League, each to have six *Praetors* under his command, while a Senate was to be elected for the conduct of public business. Even in the act of defying the Eternal City, Rome's outdated mechanism of administration was painstakingly reproduced!

The outbreak of the social war undoubtedly took the Roman Senate by surprise, as it found it entirely unready to cope with the situation. At the very outset Campania, the favored land of the Roman nobles and plutocracy, was overrun. At the head of the Legions the two Consuls of the year, Rutilius Lupus and L. Julius Caesar,[27] met with nothing but frustration. Caesar signally failed to relieve the beleaguered Roman stronghold of Acerrae, while the attempt of Rutilius Lupus to crush the Marsians, concentrated

[25] Appian, *op. cit.*

[26] It was to be renamed Italica.

[27] Husband of Aurelia and father of the youthful Gaius Julius Caesar.

near the river Liris, met with humiliating defeat; the Consul himself was slain during the course of the encounter. The command of a supporting column had been assigned to Marius, who, although grown plethoric and physically unwieldy with his advancing years, was only too eager to reestablish himself in popular favor by a display of his military talents. On the Liris, however, he had been too widely separated from Rutilius Lupus to come to his colleague's timely support, and was only apprised of the Consul's defeat by the number of dead bodies that kept floating down the stream.

But if he could not get the better of them, Marius at least knew how to keep his enemies at bay. His handling of the hostile Pompaedius Silo, for example, was typical of the astuteness of a man whose immediate aim was to gain time. Challenged by his opponent, "If you are the great General you are reported to be, then come out and fight," the veteran's retort had been, "If *you* are the great General you would fain be thought, then *make* me come out and fight!" [28]

It was an anxious time for Aurelia, the wife of L. Julius Caesar and fond mother of a son not yet in his teens, in whose ancestry there had been an intermittent recurrence of the blight of epilepsy. But the boy seemed quite undisturbed by the prevailing atmosphere of tension and alarm, lending himself obediently to the instruction of his tutor, Antonius Gnipho, and occupying his leisure with the composition of a tragedy on the story of Oedipus and a poem in honor of Hercules. The child is father to the man, so the juvenile Caesar was scarcely one to be perturbed by "bloody excursions and alarms."

Notwithstanding the best efforts of Marius and the two Consuls for 89 B.C.—Gn. Pompeius Strabo [29] and L. Porcius Cato—the unpromising trend of operations in the field and the threat of additional uprisings in Gaul and in Spain persuaded the Roman Senate to authorize a law [30] for granting the franchise to those of the erstwhile allies who had taken no open part in the Social War.

The effect of this timely concession immediately appeared; a division of opinion was created in many of the insurgent communities. But in others it excited a

---

28 Plutarch, *op. cit.* Cf. Appian.

29 The father of Pompey the Great.

30 Termed the Julian Law after L. Julius Caesar, who had been entrusted with the task of drafting it.

still more vigorous determination. Thus while the Senate prudently disarmed the wavering or lukewarm, they made strenuous exertions to crush those who should continue the war. A portion of the Italian League, the Samnites above all, showed no inclination to accept favors from Rome; the deadly hostility of ancient times revealed itself in the fact that they scrupled not to send an embassy to solicit the aid of Mithridates (King of Pontus). Desperate resolution could not have been more strongly shown than by calling in an Asiatic Monarch to share in the spoils of Italy. The same desperation appears in a proclamation offering freedom to all slaves who should enlist in the Italian army.[31]

But Rome's offer of enfranchisement struck at the very root of the uprising, offering the moderates a chance to return to their allegiance and sowing rancorous discord between them and the separatists who stood for the outright severance of all former ties. The situation swung further in Rome's favor with her extension of the franchise to include Cisalpine Gaul, thus expanding the Italian municipal system to the river Po.

The new departure, although leaving the obdurate Samnites and certain other determined separatists still in arms, nonetheless had the effect of forestalling the consolidation of the revolt, cutting the insurgents' supplies, and bringing an invaluable influx of recruits to the Roman Eagles. The turning point in the struggle came with the resounding defeat of a rebel army seeking to relieve the beleaguered insurgent stronghold of Asculum, and the capture of the city itself. With the surrender of the independents' "capital" of Corfinium, the organized resistance of the northern confederacies virtually collapsed.

In the south, Sulla—already named by his troops the *Imperator*—crowned a succession of victories by his capture of the League's new center of Bovianum. The Samnites still obstinately held out and much desultory fighting continued in the central provinces, but the back of the rebellion had been broken. To all intents and purposes the Social War, as such, was at an end. As in all civil strife, the country's prosperity had been among the first casualties. There was a demoralizing dearth of money, which served painfully to exacerbate the cleavage between rich and poor. "The chronic cry of anarchic socialism, *'Novae tabulae,'* the canceling of

[31] Liddell, *op. cit.*

debts, was raised"; [32] and the enforcement of the laws governing debtor and creditor could no longer be ensured. Something over 300,000 casualties denied the land its necessary labor, while so deplorably lowering the Legions' standards that they were prepared to enlist slaves. The demoralization of the troops was so acute, indeed, their mood so insubordinate, that when a Roman Admiral was done to death by his mutinous marines, Sulla dared go no further than to warn the offenders to purge their offence by valor in battle.

However, the fact remained that by the time the major task of subjugation had been completed, the whole of Italy had become Roman up to the Po. Instead of a series of more or less autonomous States, connected with the Eternal City in various degrees of dependence, there had arisen a number of urban communities of Roman citizens, with an approximately similar type of organization, and with few and trifling differences of status and privilege. Local self-government was built up on the Roman pattern, on the same fundamental code of laws. "The central authority would interfere in cases of difference between localities or of military necessity, as the central jurisdiction took cognizance of treason, conspiracy, and crimes of special gravity." [33] Nonetheless, "once the new citizens were equalized with the old —for in the first laws, in fear of swamping the *Comitia,* they were restricted to eight of the thirty-five tribes—the absurdity of the Comitial system became glaring. Only those near Rome could be serious voters; except on special occasions, the bulk of the Italians abstained, and showed a total indifference to urban politics." [34] Enfranchisement, in removing a sense of inferiority, had conferred the obligation of choice; and men dread choice almost as much as they fear death. Nonetheless the fact remained that Rome had moved an appreciable step nearer the ideal of "Unity in Concord." But the inclusion of the Italians in the Roman franchise furnished the *populares* with an excuse for resentment and agitation which only awaited unscrupulous manipulation to expand into a cause that would again set the whole land aflame.

Had there been no King Mithridates of Pontus, it is unlikely that Rome would have been afflicted with civil war— the presence of Sulla in the capital would have denied any

32 How and Leigh, *op. cit.*
33 *Ibid.*
34 *Ibid.*

movement for civil rebellion the opportunity to take active form. But Rome's preoccupation with the Social War had not only presented Mithridates with the chance to extend his power at the expense of his neighbors, but had also tempted him to encroach on the Roman province of Asia, the erstwhile kingdom of Pergamum, and gain control of Delos, the chief mart of Roman trade in the Archipelago. In the province of Asia itself the tyrant's orders to slaughter all those of Italian stock was enthusiastically carried out, a single day witnessing the massacre of no less than eighty thousand hapless victims of the barbarian's blood-lust.

This was an affront to her sovereignty that Rome simply could not afford to ignore; and in 88 B.C. the Senate determined to organize an expedition to reclaim the province of Asia and deal with Mithridates as he deserved. The question immediately arose, To whom should the command be entrusted?

The obvious choice was Sulla, whose activities in the Social War had rendered those contributed by Marius almost painfully inconspicuous. But Marius had long regarded rupture with the East (which he had done his utmost clandestinely to foment) as a heaven-sent opportunity to reinvest himself in that military glory to which time had given a tarnish that more recent events had signally failed to refurbish. Even with Sulla nominated Consul-elect and with his military appointment a foregone conclusion, Marius was determined at any cost to secure the command for himself.

Looking round for an ally to further his cause in the Senate —as had Saturninus in earlier days—Marius found a ready tool in the Tribune P. Sulpicius. As fanatical as the defunct Drusus, greedy of gain, animated by a bitter enmity against Sulla's consular colleague, Q. Pompeius Rufus, and endowed with a facility for inflammatory mob-oratory that made him the darling of those who thought only with their ears, Sulpicius was just the sort of pliable and venal creature to suit his patron's abiding purpose.

In general, there was no inclination among the people of Rome to see Sulla superseded. But if the Italian element could exercise a weight in the *Comitia* proportionate to its numbers, Marius, ever a favorite with the Italian countrymen, would be certain for the assignment. Sulpicius, therefore, boldly came forward with a sweeping measure of reform, by which the new Italian citizens and freedmen were to be distributed evenly through all the Tribes, and in this manner be placed on a level with the old citizens. Thus in every Tribe the new citizens, with the freedmen, would form a majority—a majority whose votes would be at the disposal of Marius.

It was scarcely to be expected that this radical innovation would be anything but resented by the old citizens, and as the day for the casting of votes drew nigh, their mounting fury found expression in innumerable scuffles with the would-be interlopers, in which stones and staves figured prominently.

The Consuls endeavored to postpone the day of conflict by proclaiming an *institium* or general holiday, the effect of which was to suspend all public business. But the Tribune determined to proceed to a vote, just as if the Consuls had issued no proclamation, and ordered a body of three thousand young men to attend him, with concealed daggers, in the Forum: they were to strike when he commanded, not sparing even the Consuls, if need be. On the appointed day the Tribune arose, and, declaring the public holiday illegal, he demanded of the Consuls that they recall their proclamation and suffer business to go on. A loud outcry arose from the old citizens, upon which, at a sign from the Tribune, his adherents drew their daggers. Their opponents fled. Pompeius Rufus escaped only by hiding himself; his son, who was married to Sulla's daughter, was ruthlessly murdered. Sulla fled into the house of Marius, which faced the Forum, whence he was obliged to return and declare the *institium* at an end. The law then passed without opposition; and, as a matter of course, the command in the Mithridatic war was transferred to Marius.[35]

Sulla went straight from the Forum to the encampment where the troops he had led so successfully were all concentrated, and where the news that he was to be superseded was already in circulation, to the soldiery's astounded indignation.

Sulla was faced with the inescapability of making a decision that would determine his whole future, and very probably that of the State. To yield to Marius would ensure the end of his own career and might well help to inflict irremediable damage on the country at large. Convinced that an immediate confrontation with his lifelong rival constituted the lesser of two evils, and confident of the personal loyalty of his troops if not of some of his wavering subordinate Officers

[35] Appian, *op. cit.* Cf. Plutarch, Florus, Livy.

—Sulla set out for Rome at the head of the six Legions under his command.

In the capital all was consternation. The Senate, more out of fear of Marius than distrust of Sulla, sent to demand of the latter why he was in arms against his country. "To set her at liberty," was Sulla's uncompromising answer. "The Praetors then went out, invested with all the insignia of their office, to command him to desist; but the soldiers broke their *fasces* and stripped them of their robes. Sulla meantime continued to advance, and was joined by his colleague, Q. Pompeius Rufus, so that henceforth all his acts ran in the joint name of the two Consuls of the year" [36]—a nice concession to legality which was probably not without effect on the reactions of the more legalistically minded.

Sulla's prompt and resolute action caught Marius and his minion, Sulpicius, on the wrong foot, and before any concerted counteraction could be taken an advance guard of the Legions had seized the Esquiline Gate and the adjoining sectors of the wall, despite the hail of stones and tiles hurled down on them from the rooftops. In the meantime Marius had contrived to muster a motley throng of armed men in the marketplace near the Esquiline Gate, and at this point Roman soldiers first met their fellow countrymen in open strife within the walls of their capital.

At the first rush the Legionaries were beaten back, but Sulla, seizing an Eagle, threw himself into the thick of the fray, and the situation steadily veered in his favor. Meanwhile, another of the Legions attacked Marius and his forces in the rear, driving him to retreat on the Capitol, whence he took the desperate step of issuing a proclamation offering liberty to all slaves who joined his banner. This irresponsible act, however, only revealed his weakness, while at the same time serving to alienate many of those who otherwise might have supported him. With the rabble dispersed and their more reputable followers in palsied disarray, Marius, Sulpicius, and a handful of their more immediate supporters took refuge in flight. Sulpicius was betrayed by one of his own slaves and immediately put to death, whereafter Sulla enfranchised the betrayer for his loyalty to the State and then had him cast from the Tarpeian Rock for his treachery to his master. The enactments for which Sulpicius had been responsible were abrogated *in toto*; counterrevolution was established upon the ruins of vaulting tribunician ambition.

[36] Appian, *op. cit.* Cf. Livy.

For all that, elections for the consulate, while returning a firm but independent supporter of the Senate in Gn. Octavius, also elevated to power L. Cornelius Cinna, well known as a partisan of Marius. At the moment, however, Cinna was determined to pursue whatever course held out the greater promise of advantage to himself.

With a price on his head, Marius had separated from the majority of the partisans who had aided his escape and furtively made his way to Ostia, where, with a characteristic sense of self-protection, he had earlier arranged for a vessel to stand by lest he be driven to flight. His aim was to reach North Africa, where it should be possible to organize the armed support that would return him to power. Caught in a heavy gale, and in sore want of provisions, Marius and his few remaining companions put ashore near Circeii, where the fugitives soon learned that the search for the ex-Consul was being actively pursued in every region bordering on the coast. Another attempt to escape by sea was foiled when the crew of the vessel in which Marius had hoped to take passage refused to risk the consequences of aiding him in his flight. With his pursuers hard on his heels, Marius was driven to seek concealment in the desolate swamp that fringed the mouth of the river Liris. But even this dismal retreat afforded no safe refuge. Run down by a party of soldiers,

> they hauled him out naked and covered with dirt, and carried him to Minturnae, where they delivered him to the magistrates; for proclamation had been made that he should be put to death wherever he was found. . . . No citizen would undertake this office; but a horseman, either a Gaul or a Cimbrian, went up to him sword in hand with an intent to dispatch him. The chamber in which he lay was somewhat gloomy, and a light glanced from the eyes of Marius which darted on the face of the assassin; while at the same time he heard a solemn voice saying, "Dost thou dare to kill Marius?" Upon this the assassin threw down his sword and fled, crying, "I cannot kill Marius!" The people of Minturnae were struck with astonishment—pity and remorse ensued— "Let him go," they said, "let the exile go and await his destiny in some other region!" [37]

[37] Appian, *op. cit.* Cf. Beesly.

Thus, the beneficiary of superstition and the sense of awe he had managed to create, Marius was sped on his way in a vessel that set him ashore at Carthage, where he learned that his son had already repaired to the Court of Hiempsal, King of Numidia, to seek support for his father's cause.

With Sulla diligently prosecuting the war against Mithridates in the East, affairs in Rome had again reached a point of crisis. For with Sulla no longer available to oppose him, Cinna—who had sworn to sustain his reforms—brazenly announced his intention of restoring the laws of Sulpicius, embodying the full and final emancipation of the Italians. But Cinna had grossly misjudged the prevailing climate of opinion, as he had placed far too much reliance on the support of Pompeius Strabo and the troops he commanded; for that wily opportunist carefully remained inactive in remote Picenum. The Patricians, when Cinna summoned the Assembly of the Tribes to muster in the Forum, took up the challenge, and Gn. Octavius appeared at the head of an armed force to disperse the large crowd of country voters who had flocked in determined to stand up for what they interpreted as their rights. In the clash that followed, the *publicani* suffered heavy casualties before fleeing in disorder with Cinna at their head. Deprived of the consulship and outlawed, Cinna repaired to Campania, "where he declaimed to the new citizens on the persecution to which he was exposed for his devotion to their interests."

It was not long before Cinna succeeded in collecting an armed following, including the experienced soldier Q. Sertorious. Nor did he scruple to unite himself with the Samnites and Lucanians, the avowed enemies of the current administration, while the Campanians discovered more zeal for the defense of their putative rights than they had ever evinced in the struggle to obtain them. The Senate issued proclamations which were no more than a waste of good parchment, and then precipitately rescinded the limitations on the Italian franchise imposed by Sulla. It was at this juncture that Marius landed on the coast of Etruria at the head of a few personal followers and an armed force made up of five hundred fugitive slaves, a rag, tag, and bobtail speedily expanded by large numbers of discontented serfs entirely indifferent to the political issues in dispute but thirsting for vengeance and plunder. Thus while Cinna advanced on the capital from the east, Marius was steadily approaching it from the west. Other forces were on the move under Sertorius and the sinister C. Papirius Carbo; and thus Rome found herself encircled by four armies of her own rebel-

lious citizens, backed by the resources put at their disposal by
the Samnites.

To resist these accumulating dangers the Senate hastily
recalled the half-forgotten veteran Metellus, bidding him
make peace with the Samnites on any terms. But the terms
they attempted to exact were so inordinate [38] as to be inadmissible, and the General hastened to Rome, leaving his
subordinate Plautius, however, to check any Samnite advance.
But Plautius was speedily overpowered, and the rebellious
Romans found themselves reinforced by the whole strength
of the Samnite confederacy. There could be no peace for
Italy, they proclaimed, "until the forest shall be demolished
in which the Roman wolves had made themselves a den."

Treason was already at work within the city, and Marius
was barely prevented from effecting his entrance by way of a
gate on the side of the Janiculum, being repulsed only at
the cost of a sharp engagement. In their extremity the Senate
sent a message to the vacillating Pompeius Strabo at Picenum,
bidding him march to the defense of the capital. But he was
still undecided as to which line to pursue, and extremely
doubtful as to the subordination of the troops under his
command.

The divided sympathies, mutual suspicion and latent
treachery which characterized the cantonment at Picenum
were starkly revealed in an incident in which the youthful
Pompey, serving under his father, played the leading part.
As a junior officer, "one Lucius Terentius was his comrade,
and they slept in the same tent. This Terentius, gained by
Cinna's money, undertook to assassinate Pompey, while
others set fire to the General's tent. Pompey got information
of this when he was at supper, and it did not put him in
the least confusion. He drank more freely, and caressed
Terentius more than usual, but when they were to have gone
to rest, he stole out of the tent and went and planted a
guard about his father. This done, he waited quietly for the
event. Terentius, as soon as he thought Pompey was asleep,
drew his sword and stabbed the coverlets of the bed in many
places, imagining that he was in it." [39] The fate meted out
to the would-be assassin, caught in the act, was as exemplary
as it was swift.

The ambivalence prevailing throughout the camp broke

---

[38] Not only did they demand untrammelled admission to the franchise, but insisted on compensation for their losses, and the surrender
without return or reciprocity of their fugitive slaves.

[39] Plutarch, *op. cit.*

into open discord when Strabo finally resolved to obey the Senate's command and march to the capital's support. With the order to take the road, mutiny broke out among certain elements in the ranks by whom Strabo was disliked as much as he was distrusted. An attempt on his life was only frustrated by the devotion of Pompey, who threw himself on the ground declaring that "the mutineers must pass over his body before they reached the object of their fury." [40] Since the youthful officer had already won the devotion and respect of the majority of the men in the ranks, his spirited defiance of a rebellious minority served effectively to curb the rising tide of insubordination.

But what arms had failed to achieve, famine and pestilence insidiously accomplished. The population of the city were swept off in ever-mounting number, and the contagion swiftly spread to the besiegers' camps beyond the walls. When Strabo himself fell a victim to the malaise, [41] the Senate's powers of resistance were paralyzed. A deputation was sent to Cinna to offer terms of accommodation. When these were refused, a second embassy was charged only to solicit an amnesty.

Cinna received the plenipotentiaries seated in a chair of State, with the insignia of the consular office he claimed to bear prominently displayed. By his side stood Marius, grimy, squalid, and unshorn, garbed in the black rags of an outlaw. Only the restoration of Cinna to his consulship, and of Marius to his quondam dignities and privileges, served to spare Rome's delivery to the Samnites for complete destruction. Even so, the victorious Generals were under promise to their rank and file to surrender their capture to rapine and pillage, with which irresponsible slaughter went hand in hand; among the many slain was the harmless, if ineffective, Consul, Octavius. His head was severed from his body and carried to Cinna, by whose order it was publicly exposed, suspended before the *rostra* in the Forum. Thus the pattern was set for bestial atrocities that multiplied apace as the savage factional strife took on new fury and the thirst for vengeance or plunder was succeeded by a ghoulish delight in the horrors which accompanied it; and the populace "debauched and degraded, learned to gloat upon the blood of its victims." [42]

"Wrong was punished by wrong. The noble lords and their

[40] Plutarch, *op. cit.*

[41] Some accounts attribute his death to the hand of an assassin, others maintain that he was struck down by lightning.

[42] Mommsen, *op. cit.*

friends had killed the people in the Forum. They were killed in turn by the soldiers of Marius. Fifty Senators perished, not those who were especially guilty, but those who were most particularly marked as Patrician leaders. With them fell a thousand *Equites,* commoners of fortune, who had thrown in their lot with the aristocracy." [43] Antonius the orator, P. Crassus, and two of the kinsmen of the stripling Julius Caesar were among the many massacred, which included a number of adherents of the absent Sulla. It was the very heyday of those with private wrongs to avenge or debts to cancel, and offered unquestionable proof that "a multitude is ever found to be what its leaders and counsellors are." [44] Even had they so desired, neither Cinna nor Marius were in a position to "ride in the whirlwind and direct the storm." The ghastly hurricane they had raised could only be endured until it blew itself out.

From time to time news reached the capital of Sulla's progress in the East, where Mithridates's earlier success had been halted by the reduction of the formidable stronghold of Piraeus and the complete overthrow of the Pontic army at Chaeronea. The intelligence of Sulla's victories was of scant comfort for the two men who held Rome in uneasy thrall. Cinna remained sole Consul until the Calends of January, 86 B.C., when Cinna for the second time, and Marius for the seventh, assumed the *fasces.*

Characteristically, Marius signalized the first day of his authority by ordering that the Senator Sext. Licinius should be hurled from the Tarpeian Rock, a matter of private vengeance which made no pretense to legality.

But the tyrant was not destined for long to pursue his depraved and vengeful course. Worn down by his earlier exertions, bloated and debauched by his more recent indulgence in wine-bibbing and riotous living, he sank rapidly under the effect of an inflammatory fever, and thirteen days after he had seen his cherished expectations realized by the seventh tenure of his high office, he died—hated by his enemies, feared even by those who professed themselves his friends. For even those who had given him their support had been brought to realize that men such as Marius do not establish a dictatorship in order to guard a revolution, but foment a revolution in order to establish a dictatorship.

A good enough soldier, with a gift for leadership which quickly won the confidence of those who followed him, Mar-

[43] James Anthony Froude, *Caesar.*
[44] A dictum of Scipio Africanus, as recorded by Polybius.

ius was hopelessly at sea in the subtle chicaneries of politics; and like many a man before and after him, he revealed his limitations because his vanity always spurred him to go beyond them. But the thing most to be deplored about the career of a man such as Marius was that it created a precedent whereby any aspiring politico-military adventurer was encouraged to aim for supreme power without the slightest regard as to his ability to wield it wisely and for the public good.

Moreover, the career of Marius bore striking witness to the fact that usurped power corrupts even more absolutely than power legitimately conferred.

Chapter VIII

THE RISE OF POMPEY

"There are few of us who are strong enough to make circumstances serve us."

—W. Somerset Maugham

With the death of Marius, his place by the side of Cinna was taken temporarily by L. Valerius Flaccus, and the reign of terror came to an end, more as the outcome of exhaustion than as the result of a new spirit of reconciliation. At the cost of a grisly toll in bloodshed, a certain number of slaves had won their freedom, a highly questionable law for the relief of debtors had been enacted, and some fine bargains had been secured at the auctions for the disposal of the property of the dead. Finally, the laws of Sulla had been repealed *in toto*, their author deposed and outlawed, and the insignificant Flaccus nominated to take over command of the army in the East—where Sulla was coping magnificently with a task that Flaccus at least had the intelligence to realize was quite beyond his competence.

Sulla's scornful disregard of the pinchbeck administration

of which Cinna was the figurehead was betokened by his complete want of attention for anything that emanated from it.

He was a second Coriolanus, a proud, imperious aristocrat, contemptuous, above all men living, of popular rights; but he was the first soldier of his age. For his eastern campaign he took with him at most 30,000 men. He had no fleet. Had the corsair squadrons of Mithridates been on the alert, they might have destroyed him on his passage. Events at Rome left him almost immediately without support from Italy. He was impeached, he was summoned back. His troops were forbidden to obey him, and a democratic commander [Flaccus] was sent out to supersede him. The army stood by their favorite commander. Sulla disregarded his orders from home. He found men and money as he could. He supported himself out of the countries which he occupied, without resources save in his own skill and in the fidelity and excellence of his Legions. He defeated Mithridates, he drove him back out of Greece and pursued him into Asia. The interests of his party demanded his presence in Rome; the interests of the State required that he should not leave his work in the East unfinished; and he stood to it through four hard years till he brought Mithridates to sue for peace upon his knees. He had not the means to complete the conquest or completely to avenge the massacre with which the Prince of Pontus had commenced the war. He left Mithridates still in possession of his hereditary kingdom; but he left him bound, so far as treaties could bind so ambitious a spirit, to remain thenceforward within his own frontiers. He recovered Greece and the Islands, and Roman provinces in Asia Minor. He extorted an indemnity of five millions. He raised a fleet in Egypt, with which he drove the pirates out of the Archipelago back into their own waters. He restored the shattered prestige of Roman authority, and he won for himself a reputation which later cruelties might stain, but could not efface.[1]

They were stirring times in which to be growing into manhood, especially for a youth like Julius Caesar who, even in early adolescence, had been noted for his possession of "an old head on young shoulders," and a remarkably cool brain. In appearance he was "a tall, slight, handsome youth, with

1 Froude, *op. cit.* Cf. Plutarch.

dark piercing eyes,[2] a sallow complexion, large nose, lips full, features refined and intellectual, neck sinewy and thick, beyond what might have been expected from the generally slender figure. He was particular about his appearance, used to bathe frequently, and attended carefully to his hair. His dress was arranged with studied negligence, and he had a loose mode of fastening the girdle so peculiar as to catch the eye." [3]

At this formative period of his life it was of considerable significance that it had been to Marius, during the brief period of his seventh consulship, that Caesar owed his first official appointment, that of *Flamen dialis*.[4] Of equal consequence was the constant companionship of the younger Marius, the lad his uncle had adopted, and his association with the two Ciceros, Marcus and his brother Quintus, who had been sent to Rome for their education. To self-proclaimed progressives such as these, the Marian principles of liberal humanism were, of course, not to be questioned, although to a mind as acute as Caesar's it must have seemed more than a little anomalous that the theoretical rule of the *populares,* which Cinna was said to represent, in actual fact worked out to the absolutism of a single individual. Even at little more than adolescence, it was not overlooked by the observant Caesar that the inevitable outcome of anarchy is despotism.

Not that he harbored any misgivings with regard to Cinna. On the contrary. For with the sudden death of his father at Pisa in 84 B.C., the younger man broke off the wealthy match his sire had arranged for him, to woo and wed Cornelia, the daughter of the all-powerful Cinna himself, a marriage which associated him even more closely with the popular party the dictator still ostensibly represented.

In marked contrast to the contemporary Caesar, the slightly older Pompey [5] presented a far more flamboyant figure to the world. "In his youth he had a very engaging countenance, which spoke for him before he opened his lips. Yet that grace of aspect was not unattended with dignity, and amidst his youthful bloom there was a venerable and princely air. His hair naturally curled a little; which, together with the

[2] *"Nigris vegetisque oculis,"* Suetonius.

[3] Froude, *op. cit.*

[4] Priest of Jupiter, an appointment analogous to that of the boy-bishops of the Middle Ages, and possessing little religious responsibility or significance.

[5] If 102 B.C. is accepted as the year of Caesar's birth, Pompey was not quite six years his senior.

shining moisture and quick turn of his eye, produced a
stronger likeness of Alexander the Great than that which appeared in the statues of that Prince. So that some seriously
gave him the name of Alexander, and he did not refuse it:
others applied it to him by way of ridicule." [6] In effect, an
attractive young man, endowed with that particular sort of
comeliness which turns women's heads without turning men's
stomachs, and one whose vanity was so naïve as to con-
stitute a pardonable foible rather than a vertiginous offense.
Concerned to correct, or at least to live down, the common
belief that his father, despite his ability as a soldier, had
yielded to an insatiable avarice, Pompey diligently sought "by
his application to martial exercises, his eloquent and per-
suasive address, his strict honor and fidelity, and the easi-
ness of access to him on all occasions," [7] to create an image of
himself that would ensure his popularity with all with whom
he came into contact—from a potential political supporter to
the famous courtesan Flora, who "took a pleasure in her old
age, in speaking of the acquaintance she had with Pompey." [8]

Admittedly, Caesar was no prudish anchorite where the
opposite sex was concerned; indeed, it came to be written of
him by one chronicler that "above all things he valued his
victories over women." [9] But with Caesar—save perhaps
in one instance—his amours were things apart; whereas it
came to be said of Pompey that "though he took his measures with so much care and precaution in this respect, he
could not escape the censure of his enemies, who accused
him of acquaintance with married women, and said he often
neglected or gave up points essential to the public, to gratify
his mistresses." [10]

Like his younger contemporary, Pompey had contracted
an early marriage, his bride being Antistia, daughter of the
Praetor Antistius. Since there was more than sufficient reason to suppose that Cinna would associate the son with the
opposition he had experienced at the hands of the father,
Pompey and his bride withdrew discreetly to the former's
estate in the Picene, as much for prudence's sake as on the
score of "an old attachment which the cities in that district
had for his family." In times of uncertainty there is a cer-

6 Plutarch, op. cit.
7 Ibid.
8 Ibid.
9 Mommsen, op. cit.
10 Plutarch, op. cit.

tain comforting reassurance in resort to a familiar environment.

If, for the nonce, Pompey restrained his innate tendency to catch the public eye, Caesar, although closer to the center of things, as yet made no attempt to draw its attention to himself. It is probable, however, that he had a truly percipient gaze lighted upon them both; even at this early juncture in affairs it would have rested longer on the cool, self-contained, unobtrusive Caesar than upon the far more sparkling and colorful Pompey.

For three numbed years Cinna exercised a control that went virtually unchallenged. Sulla was at a safe distance from the center of power, and his hands were full. Of his supporters, those who had escaped slaughter had sought safety in flight. The Senate was no more than a ductile cypherage. The moderates passively assented in things as they were, since they feared that any overt move to better them would only end by rendering them infinitely worse. The majority of the provinces—Sicily, Sardinia, Spain, Africa, even Gaul—seemed quiescent, while the democrats and new burgesses were so obsessed with the novel toy of equality as to be oblivious of the fact that they had been almost entirely deprived of their liberty. Yet Cinna and his immediate followers, lording it in unchallenged authority, governed merely from day to day, without thought for consolidating their position. "Their total lack of political plans, of any effort to reorganize the Government upon democratic lines, is the final proof that the democratic party, so called, had no genuine program and could provide no real alternative to Senatorial misrule." [11] Even the mutiny of the troops sent with Flaccus on his assignment to supersede Sulla, and their incontinent slaughter of their contemptible Generalissimo, occasioned no more than a temporary jolt to their complacency. In their bemused condition of false security, they even neglected to organize a proper army and fleet, or take any steps for the defense of the ports.

At last, early in 84 B.C., came the startling news that Sulla, having successfully completed operations in the field, was on his way back to Rome at the head of his victorious Legions. Even to the most obtusely self-satisfied, the writing on the wall spelled out that the day of reckoning was close at hand. The successful General's imminent return was astutely heralded by his proclaimed intention to recognize

[11] How and Leigh, *op. cit.*

the equalization of the suffrage and to confine his vengeance to the revolutionary leaders.

In considerable trepidation, the Senate sought to effect a compromise. Sulla was, of course, to disband his army and come to Rome, if necessary under a safe conduct. In the meantime all levies were to be suspended. But Cinna and the notorious Marian, Papirius Carbo, dismissed the Senate's proposals as no more than whistling to a scorpion in the hope of persuading it to dance. Hastily, Cinna sought to gather together some sort of array that would stand and face the conqueror of Mithridates. The temper of such troops as he contrived to muster was starkly revealed when a rumor flew around the camp that Cinna had made a pretext to lure Pompey to his tent and had there put him to death. "Upon this, numbers who hated Cinna, and could no longer bear his cruelties, attacked his quarters. He fled for his life; and being overtaken by one of the inferior officers, who pursued him with a drawn sword, he fell upon his knees and offered him his ring which was of no small value. The Officer answered with great ferocity, 'I am not come to sign a contract, but to punish an impious and lawless tyrant,' and then killed him on the spot." [12]

With Cinna's death Carbo, blocking every attempt of the Senate to elect a successor, took over sole control as the surviving Consul. By specious asseverations to the effect that the peoples' recently won rights were in jeopardy, he contrived to get together a force of new citizens which at one moment totaled close on 100,000, although as little more than an armed mob, it had nothing like the fighting quality of a trained and disciplined army. It was clear that with Italy apparently of one mind, many of the more obdurate members of the Senate—now almost denuded of its traditional oligarchs—in default of a settlement on terms of their own devising, were prepared to recommend a resort to arms. For all that, none of the Marianites were elected Consuls for 83 B.C. Nor did Carbo insist on continuing in the office; those selected were the feeble "moderate" L. Cornelius Scipio and the uncompromising C. Norbanus, more accomplished as a rabble-rouser, however, than as a leader of troops.

When Sulla landed at Brundusium at the head of his five seasoned Legions, it seemed, at least on the surface, that he was confronted by a united Italy. But Sulla was a veteran of

[12] Plutarch, *op. cit.*

the political arena as well as of the field of Mars. To disarm
suspicion, conciliate the moderates, propitiate the Italians,
and attract the waverers, "he proclaimed an amnesty to all
who should abandon the democrats, guaranteed the rights of
the new citizens, promised to observe the strictest discipline,
and swore his troops on oath to treat the Italians as
burgesses of Rome." [13] As for the veterans who looked
upon him as their own particular idol, they were men whose
erstwhile civic feeling had been swallowed up in an inalienable *esprit de corps,* men who knew only one loyalty, to a
leader who held that cowardice and indiscipline were the
only vices which called for condemnation.

It was a new development, a new phenomenon, this unqualified loyalty to an individual rather than to the State,
and one which in no sense went unremarked by Caesar
and by Pompey.

Pompey, indeed, was speedily to make acquaintance with
this remarkable change in the psychology of the Roman
fighting man, and at first hand. With Sulla's arrival in the
homeland and his speedy advance into Campania, it had
become urgently necessary for Pompey to decide with which
party to identify himself, and almost inevitably he chose
to throw in his lot with Sulla. Appreciative of the fact that a
somewhat unexpected adherent who presents himself at the
head of a useful fighting force is far more welcome—and
personally much safer!—than one who comes emptyhanded,
Pompey had been at pains to recruit a sizeable body of
troops. "Thus Pompey at the age of twenty-three, without a
commission from any superior authority, erected himself into
a General";[14] and in that capacity was given an early chance
to show his metal. Three of Carbo's supporters "came
against him all at once, not in front, or in one body, but
they hemmed him in with their three armies, in hopes to
demolish him entirely. Pompey, far from being terrified, assembled all his forces and charged the army of Brutus at the
head of his cavalry. The Gaulish Horse on the enemy's side
sustained the first shock; but Pompey attacked the foremost
of them,[15] who was a man of prodigious strength, and
brought him down with a push of his spear. The rest immediately fled, and threw the infantry into such disorder that the whole was soon put to flight. This produced so

13 How and Leigh, *op. cit.* Cf. Appian and Orosius, *Historiarum
adversus Paganos Libri.*

14 Plutarch, *op. cit.*

15 L. Brutus Damasippus.

great a quarrel among the three Generals, that they parted and took separate routes."[16]

For Pompey, the test of battle had more than sufficiently demonstrated his personal valor as well as his daring as a leader; and since success in battle is the first thing that troops demand of their General, their personal devotion to the young Patrician under whom they had agreed to serve was thus early assured.

Sulla had not yet been informed of these transactions, but upon the first news of Pompey's being engaged with so many adversaries, he dreaded the consequence, and marched with all expedition to his assistance. Pompey, having intelligence of his approach, ordered his Officers to see that the troops were armed and drawn up in such a manner as to make the handsomest and most gallant appearance before the Commander-in-Chief: for he expected great honors from him, and he obtained greater. Sulla no sooner saw Pompey advancing to meet him with an army in excellent condition, both as to age and size of the men, and the spirits which success had given them, than he alighted; and upon being saluted of course by Pompey as *Imperator,* he returned the salutatation with the same title: though no one imagined that he would have honored a young man, not yet admitted into the Senate, with a title for which he was contending with the Scipios and the Marii.[17]

Perhaps "he was only playing on the youth's vanity; for Pompeius, who was for his courage and good looks the darling of the soldiers and the women, was very vain, and flattery was a potion which it seems to have been one of Sulla's cynical maxims to administer in strong doses." [18]

Sincere or otherwise, the treatment unquestionably worked, and Pompey remained among the most faithful of those who had hitched their wagons to Sulla's particular star, and many of them were men of outstanding courage and integrity with wide experience both of politics and war. Metellus Pius [19] joined him from Liguria; young M. Licinius Crassus, who had escaped when his father and elder brother had been slaughtered in the Marian massacre, hastened to him from exile in Spain. L. Philippus, who was dispatched to recover

---

[16] Plutarch, *op. cit.*
[17] Beesly, *op. cit.*
[18] *Ibid.*
[19] Son of the Metellus so shamefully treated by Marius.

Sardinia, M. Licinius Lucullus, and several other men of note made offer of their services; with the endorsement of their presence under his banner, Sulla pushed on through Apulia. At Mount Tifata, a spur of the Apennines near Capua, the Consul Norbanus sought to bar Sulla's path, but being soundly thrashed for his temerity, he took refuge in flight to Capua.

But while Sulla and Metellus, cantoned in Campania, busied themselves with preparations for their march on Rome, in the capital itself the self-elected Consuls, Carbo and Marius the Younger, sought successfully to raise levies for the defense of the party they represented. Large bodies of men were recruited in Etruria and Cisalpine Gaul, especially from the Marian veterans. The Lucanians and the ever-rumbustical Samnites promised energetic support, and the future proved them as good as their word. The violent, blood-crazed Carbo, taking adroit advantage of the wave of war hysteria, engineered the outlawry of Sulla and his partisans by decree of the people; with that the conflict entered upon a new and deadlier stage which gave no hope of compromise or quarter. All things considered, it was scarcely a timely juncture at which to detach so experienced a soldier as Sertorius to uphold Marian interests in Spain.

With the opening of the campaign of 82 B.C., Sulla, moving upon Rome, found himself opposed by Marius, while in Picenum Metellus was confronted by Carbo, who from his base at Ariminum kept his grip upon Gaul and Etruria. Pompey, when assigned to go north to Metellus's support, demurred, in an unwonted parade of modesty, that "it was not right to take the command from a man who was his superior both in age and character; but if Metellus should desire his assistance in the conduct of the war, it was at his service." When it was pointed out that it was not intended that Pompey should supersede his elder but do his best to render him all the support in his power, he obligingly took his way northward, where he contented himself with threatening Etruria from Spoletium.[20]

It was at Sacriportus, near Signia, that Sulla came up with Marius as the latter retired on Praeneste, driving him back headlong on that formidable stronghold, whose stout walls became henceforward the center about which the struggle raged. This crucial action uncovered Rome, which was evac-

[20] Beesly, *op. cit.*

uated by the Praetor L. Brutus Damasippus, but not before he had avenged himself by massacring the remaining *optimates*—including the aged Scaevola—and such of their clients as he could run to earth. "The Senate had been assembled as if to dispatch business in the *Curia Hostilia*, and there Carbo's cousin, and the father-in-law of Pompeius, were assassinated; the wife of the latter killing herself on hearing the news. The corpses of those killed were thrown into the Tiber." [21] It was a butchery in which Marius the Younger had readily connived. Of no man could it be more truly said, "Like father, like son."

Leaving Q. Lucretius Ofella to blockade Marius, Sulla hastened to occupy Rome, utilizing his short stay to seize the government and turn its legal machinery against his opponents. From Rome Sulla passed on to Etruria to organize combined operations against Carbo.

Carbo, who had succeeded in bringing Metellus to a halt, beat a hasty retreat, on learning of his colleague's defeat at Sacriportus, leaving Norbanus to hold the valley of the Po. "Metellus immediately resumed the offensive. He defeated in person one division of Carbo, five of whose cohorts deserted in the battle. His lieutenant, Pompeius, defeated Censorinus at Sena and sacked the town. Pompeius is also said to have crossed the Po and taken Mediolanum (Milan), where his soldiers massacred the local Senate. Metellus, meanwhile, had gone by sea along the east coast north of Ariminum, and had thus cut Carbo's communications with the Po. This drove Carbo from his position, and he marched into Etruria." [22]

Pompey, who had already harried Carbo on his line of march, pressed on with Crassus through Umbria, while Sulla approached the theater of operations from Rome direct. Contact between Sulla and Carbo was made near Clusium, and in a cavalry fight hard by the Clanis, two hundred and seventy of Carbo's Spanish Horse went over to his opponent, while victory graced Sulla's banners in another encounter at Saturnia, on the Albegna. He was less fortunate in a second clash near Clusium, where Carbo was sufficiently successful to risk detaching a flying column for the relief of Praeneste. This force, however, was met and routed by Pompey and Crassus, upon which Carbo, abandoning all hope, made good his flight to Africa. Norbanus, after roughly handling Lucullus, was decisively defeated by Metellus, and

21 How and Leigh, *op. cit.* Cf. Mommsen.
22 Liddell, *op. cit.*

with this last reverse the Marian cause in the north rapidly disintegrated. Norbanus also sought safety in a hurried departure for Rhodes.

In the south, on the other hand, Praeneste still doggedly held out, while a body of Samnites and Lucanians, seventy thousand strong, were on the march for the relief of beleagured Marius. But the vanguard of Sulla's troops was approaching under Pompey, and Sulla himself was on the move, heading south. With a sudden and ill-considered change of plan, the Marian leaders, Pontius of Telesia and Lamponius, determined to march at once on Rome and by a sudden rush on the "wolf's lair" force Sulla to abandon his attempt to relieve the capital—held by a pitifully small garrison—before he could be reinforced. Success might secure everything; even failure would not avert revenge.

Strategically, however, the move was exceedingly rash, since it involved the likely chance of being caught and crushed between the forces of Sulla and Metellus. But the possession of Rome was worth almost any risk, and with Sulla concentrated elsewhere, Marius would be set free to harry the enemy's rear or, if necessary, guard his colleagues' line of retreat. With sudden resolve, Pontius and Lamponius broke camp and set out hotfoot for the capital. Being informed of the move, Sulla immediately gave the order to take the road, marching on a highway parallel to that followed by his opponents. It was a race for life and death—the life or death of Rome.

Marching by the Latin highway, the Marians reached the environs of the capital well ahead of their opponents.

The band of volunteers which sallied from the city, mostly youths of quality, was scattered like chaff before the immense superiority of force. The only hope of safety rested on Sulla. The appearance of his foremost horsemen under Balbus in the course of the morning revived the sinking courage of the citizens; about midday he appeared in person with his main force and immediately drew up his ranks for battle at the temple of the Erycine Aphrodite before the Colline Gate (not far from *Porta Pia.*). His Officers adjured him not to send the troops, exhausted by the forced march, at once into action; but Sulla took into consideration what the night might bring to Rome, and late as it was in the afternoon, ordered the attack. The battle was obstinately contested and bloody. The left wing of Sulla, which he led in person, fell back as far as the city wall, so that it became necessary to close the city gates; stragglers even brought in accounts to Ofello that the battle was lost. But the right wing under Marcus Crassus overthrew the enemy and pursued him as far as Antemnae; this somewhat relieved the left wing also, and an hour after sunset it in turn began to gain ground. The fight continued the whole night and even on the following morning; and it was only the defection [23] of a division of three thousand men, who immediately turned their arms against their former comrades, that put an end to the struggle. Rome was saved.[24]

For those who had opposed him, Sulla was entirely without mercy. The Samnites were virtually exterminated; "the prisoners, even the deserters, were butchered by masses in cold blood within earshot of the appalled Senators, sitting in the temple of Bellona to hear the victor's harangue. He bade them attend to his discourse, the noise they heard, he said, came from a few malefactors whom he was chastising.

"Praeneste fell; Marius died by his own hand; the garrison and its Officers, with the majority of the citizens, were put to the sword. As the remaining strongholds were gradually reduced, the doom of destruction went out against Samnites and Etruscans." [25] Whatever else might befall, Sulla was determined that the cancer of ochlocracy should be ruthlessly excised from the body-politic.

As a wan and trembling condition of peace descended on the mainland Sardinia surrendered, fighting gradually died away in Spain, and Gaul made submission. In the East, however, Mithridates was again aggressively astir, temporarily driving the Roman garrisons from Cappadocia. Although momentarily restrained by Sulla's intervention, it was clear that the King of Pontus was by no means reconciled to the indefinite acceptance of the Roman dictat.

At the approach of Pompey at the head of six Legions and a fleet of one hundred and twenty ships, the Marian leader in Sicily, Marcus Perpenna, hastily evacuated the island and went into exile. Having executed the Marian representatives, including Carbo, captured at Cossyra (Pantelleria) Pompey

[23] However unendearing in some of his characteristics, it is clear that Sulla could attract the fighting man to his banner. Five Cohorts deserted to him at Sacriportus, five more from Carbo. A whole Legion went over to Pompey, as Sulla's representative, and six thousand men changed sides in Sulla's favor at Faventia, followed shortly after by a whole Lucanian Legion.

[24] Mommsen, *op. cit.*

[25] How and Leigh, *op. cit.*

passed over to Africa to deal with Cn. Domitius Ahenobarbus.

"Domitius advanced to meet him, and put his troops in order of battle. There happened to be a channel between them, craggy and difficult to pass. In the morning it began, moreover, to rain, and the wind blew violently, insomuch that Domitius, not imagining there would be any action that day, ordered his army to retire. But Pompey looked upon this as his opportunity, and he passed the defile with the utmost expedition. The enemy stood upon their defense, but it was in a disorderly and tumultuous manner, and the resistance they made was neither general nor uniform. Besides the wind and the rain beat in their faces. The storm incommoded the Romans too, for they could not well distinguish each other. Nay, Pompey himself was in danger of being killed by a soldier, who asked him the word [26] and received not a speedy answer. At length, however, he routed the enemy with great slaughter, not above three thousand escaping out of twenty thousand.

"The soldiers then saluted Pompey *Imperator*, but he said he would not accept that title while the enemy's camp stood untouched; therefore, if they chose to confer such an honor on him, they must first make themselves masters of the entrenchments.

"At that instant they advanced with great fury against them. Pompey fought without his helmet, for fear of just such an accident as he had just escaped. The camp was taken and Domitius slain; in consequence of which most of the cities immediately submitted and the rest were taken by assault." [27]

This exploit exhibited Pompey at his most characteristic. By instinct he was a military opportunist, in the sense that no conditions were so severe as to deter him from trying to seize the initiative and with it the element of surprise, a flair he cultivated even to the point of rashness. Thereafter, his ability to exploit his personal popularity to turn initial success into solid victory was a clear indication of his faculty of leadership.

With Domitius accounted for and his followers slain or scattered, in 81 B.C. he drove out the usurper, Hiarbas of Numidia, restored Hiempsal II, and re-established the authority of the Senate. All this was accomplished in forty days. It is comprehensible, therefore, that on his return to

[26] I.e., the password for that day.
[27] Plutarch, *op. cit.*

Rome his troops should mutter indignantly when Sulla sought to deny their hero an official "triumph," which in any case by the terms of accepted regulations he was too young and unqualified to be accorded. But Sulla was supple enough to know when the strict letter of the law defeats the purpose for which it was framed. So for the first time, one who ranked as a mere Equestrian was granted an official *supplicatio*, and in addition was, somewhat ironically, awarded the title of *Magnus*. L. Licinius Murena was accorded a similar indulgence in recognition of his activities against Mithridates.

Sulla's proscription of those he deemed enemies of the State—scarcely to be distinguished from those who had incurred his personal enmity!—ranged far and wide. Determined to pulverize the demagogic party and extirpate its leaders, "his was a dangerous, not a vindictive or irritable temperament; he set no value on human life, yet for his time and race could show comparative moderation." [28]

It was undoubtedly due to this undertow of clemency that Julius Caesar, son-in-law of the still execrated Cinna and erstwhile companion of the younger Marius, was spared the punishment which his quondam associations might well have brought down upon him. Since he had taken no active part in the recent struggle, all that was demanded of him was that he should put away his wife, Cornelia, as Pompey at Sulla's behest had obediently parted from his wife in favor of the dictator's stepdaughter Aemilia. Quite firmly, but quite calmly, Caesar refused to comply with this injunction, persisting in his rejection of it when his disobedience cost him his personal property and his well-remunerated post as *Flamen dialis*. Thereafter, he deemed it wiser temporarily to give Rome a wide berth, retiring in some haste—and a singularly ineffective disguise—into the mountains of Samnium. "Here he was pursued and captured by the Sullan bloodhounds, who were everywhere; and the story ran that he bribed his captor to set him free with a gift of two talents. In due course, he ventured back to Rome, where his friends were bringing influence to bear on Sulla on his behalf." [29] Although one of the dictator's staunchest supporters, Cicero was too young to have much say in the affair. But it was a different matter with distinguished Patricians such as Aurelius Cotta and Mamercus Aemilius, to say nothing of the College of Vestal

28 How and Leigh, *op. cit.*
29 W. Warde Fowler, *Julius Caesar.*

Virgins, whose championship of the erstwhile *Flamen dialis* must at least have been disinterested. "These may have done something; but it is due to Sulla, who had sympathy for everything truly noble, to suppose him struck with powerful admiration for the audacity of the young Patrician, standing out in such severe solitude among so many examples of timid concession; and to this magnanimous feeling in the Dictator much of the indulgence which he showed may have been really due." [30] Outwardly, however, Sulla was not particularly forthcoming, but in the end he yielded with the somewhat ungracious comment, "I grant you this boon; but I charge you to look after this youth who wears his belt so loosely!" [31]

Caesar did not stay long in Rome to risk arousing Sulla's displeasure a second time. He was now old enough to serve his first campaign, a duty still obligatory on all young men of his generation. In 81 B.C. he sailed for Asia Minor, with anticipations of plenty of work ahead. Mithridates was still harassing Roman outposts and rumbling like a volcano about to erupt; the Asiatic coasts swarmed with the pirates of Cilicia, as brazenly active as they were incredibly naïve, as Caesar was speedily to discover. For it was off the island of Pharmacussa that the vessel in which he was making his passage was run aboard and fell into the possession of a band of these selfsame corsairs.

Caesar being brought captive to their lair,

they asked him only twenty talents for his ransom. He laughed at their demand, as the consequence of their not knowing him, and promised them fifty talents. To raise the money he dispatched his people to different cities, and in the meantime remained with only one friend and two attendants among these Cilicians, who considered murder as a trifle. Caesar, however, held them in great contempt, and used to send, whenever he went to sleep, to order them to keep silence. Thus he lived among them thirty-eight days as if they had been his guards rather than his keepers. Perfectly fearless and secure, he joined in their diversions, and took his exercises among them. He wrote poems and orations, and rehearsed them to these pirates; and when they expressed no admiration, he called them dunces and barbarians. Nay, he often threatened to crucify them. They were

30 Thomas de Quincey, *Introduction to Caesar's Commentaries.*
31 Warde Fowler, *op. cit.*

delighted with these freedoms, which they imputed to his frank and mordant vein. But as soon as the money was brought from Miletus [32] and Caesar recovered his liberty, he manned some vessels in the port of Miletus in order to attack these corsairs. He found them still lying at anchor by the island, took most of them, together with the money, and imprisoned them in Pergamum. After which, he applied to Junius, who commanded then in Asia, because to him, as Praetor, it belonged to punish them. Junius having an eye upon the money, which was a considerable sum, demurred about the matter; Caesar, perceiving his intention, returned to Pergamum, and crucified all the prisoners, as he had often threatened to do at Pharmacussa, when they took him to be in jest.[33]

Obviously, there was no going back on the fate he had foretold for the culprits. But at least Caesar was imbued with sufficient humanity to have them strangled before they were nailed to their respective crosses, sparing them the agony of a lingering death. Should the occasion demand, he could be quite ruthless, but cruelty for cruelty's own sake was in no sense native to him.

With this episode rounded off to his satisfaction, Caesar proceeded to Rhodes for a course of study under the famed rhetorician Apollonius. If mouthing sonorities from a rostrum was part of the price demanded for political advancement, then command of oratory was just one more trick that must be mastered and put to use.

Recalled to military duty, Caesar saw active service at the siege and capture of Mytilene, the last island stronghold to hold out in the running war with Mithridates. It was in this brief campaign that the youthful *optio* was awarded the "civic crown," for saving the life of a fellow-soldier, by his General, Manucius Thermus.

Not long after, Caesar joined the Marine contingent in the fleet commanded by Servilius Isauricus. It was during this period that the young Officer gained that experience of maritime warfare, its possibilities and its limitations, that was to stand him in such remarkably good stead in the years to come.

If it were necessary for Caesar to make his way in the

---

[32] Possibly Melos, one of the Cyclades.
[33] Plutarch, *Lives* (*Gaius Julius Caesar*).

teeth of considerable prejudice, both the conditions and general atmosphere under the regimen reestablished by Sulla, could scarcely have been more favorable for the advancement of a career such as Pompey envisaged for himself.

Sulla was perfectly clear as to what he intended to do, and no one was allowed to stand in his way. Under his control the legal fiction of the consulship was reinstituted. Yet when Lucretius Ofella, "presuming on his services at Praeneste, entered the Forum as a candidate, though he had not yet filled the praetorship, Sulla at once ordered one of his guard to cut down Ofella. And to prevent any show of independence in the Centuries, he made use of a terrible apologue. 'A husbandman,' he said, 'was troubled with vermin. Twice he shook his tunic; but they continued to annoy him, and the third time he burnt it. Let those who have twice been conquered by arms, beware of fire the third time!' " [34] Yet "making every allowance for vengeful passions, the solid part of Sulla's bloody work remains due to deep conviction of political necessity." [35] Constant oscillation from unenlightened autocracy to the perversities of demagogic dictatorship parading as "the will of the people" had thrown reputable governance into the discard. The corruption of the Senate and its failure to retain popular respect had only been matched by the *Comitia*'s inability to realize that government in the interest of a single class is the very negation of government for the benefit of the people as a whole.

Thus Sulla set about the regeneration and reinvigoration of the Senate by expanding it through the election of three hundred men of "equestrian" fortune, whom, in the first instance, he took it upon himself personally to nominate.[36] The *Equites*—a Gracchan innovation, but which had speedily recruited the most venal entrepreneurs or outright representatives of the plutocracy—were as a middle order abolished, with the best of them finding accommodation in the Senate. A higher standard was demanded of those appointed to the magistracy; the aedileship, an office long possible only to the rich, ceased to be an essential step in a career devoted to service to the State.

Abuse of power by the *Comitia* was circumscribed by curtailment of the legislative functions of the Tribes; the interference of the Assembly in executive and judicial business was

[34] Appian, *op. cit.*

[35] How and Leigh, *op. cit.*

[36] The numbers of the Senate were doubled, from three hundred to six hundred.

severely restricted. "But a more searching reform was really needed to prevent parliamentary intrigues, capricious decrees, and votes snatched by chance or violence from the fluctuating majorities of this ignorant and unwieldy mass." [37] Since the Romans transformed but rarely abolished an office or an institution, "the tribunate, the especial weapon of Graccus and the democracy, was reduced from the strongest force in the State to its position in the war-period, as the instrument of the Senate in controlling recalcitrant officials and managing the popular assembly. Its unconfined powers of veto, indictment, arrest and legislation, exercised as they had lately been, led straight to anarchy or monarchy, according as they fell into the hands of an all-powerful individual or were exercised by different holders for conflicting purposes." [38] And in neither, as Sulla believed, lay Rome's path towards national health and prosperity.

The Romanization of all the territories over which the Eternal City exercised dominion, with a well-defined separation between civil and military authority, was the aim from which Sulla never departed—an objective supported by the extended and equalized franchise and furthered by a vast scheme of colonization by ex-Legionaries, which domiciled 120,000 veterans in Etruria alone, with settlements almost as numerous in Latium and Campania.

Sulla was determined to construct something stable erected on a firm foundation, even if he had nothing but old bricks with which to build it. If what he managed to accomplish constituted one more precedent for the empire, offered one more proof that, however manipulated, the traditional constitution had become unworkable, that in the failure of the Senate the only resource was the single man, doubtless the implication was no more lost on Julius Caesar than it was overlooked by Pompey.

In 80 B.C. Sulla elected to fill the consulship in company with Metellus Pius. But in the year following, in obedience to his own law which prohibited re-election to the office within ten years, he declined to accept the proffered offer of the *curule* chair. Claudius Pulcher and Servilius Isauricus were the men who assumed the consular robes, but everyone was perfectly well aware as to where the real power resided.

To all outward appearances, Rome and Italy had settled down to make the best of conditions as they found them, with Sulla enabled to take his voluptuous leisure at his Puteolan villa on the Bay of Naples, with fishing as the less indulgent alternative to the compilation of his Memoirs. Almost conterminously with the Dictator's withdrawal from public life, however, "the Romans, although delivered from slaughter and tyranny, began gradually to feed the flame of new seditions. Quintus Catulus and Aemilius Lepidus were chosen Consuls, the former of the Sullan faction and the latter of the opposite party. They hated each other bitterly and began to quarrel immediately, from which it was plain that fresh troubles were imminent." [39]

With the Dictator's death in 78 B.C., "Lepidus declared himself the chief of the popular party, and promised to rescind the acts of Sulla. To prevent a renewal of civil war, the Senate bound him and Catulus alike by oath not to have recourse to arms. Lepidus, however, having left the city as if for his province of Transalpine Gaul, went no further than Etruria; and here, at the end of his consular year, pretending that his oath no longer bound him, he engaged in active preparations for war. The Senate summoned him to Rome, for the purpose of holding the *Comitia*. He obeyed, but it was at the head of an army. Catulus took post before the Mulvian Bridge, with Pompey as his lieutenant." [40] To call promptly on Pompey's services was nothing more than elementary prudence, since it was truly said of Catulus that "he was more able to direct the civil government than the operations of war." [41]

Pompey's response to the call on his services was immediate. "He did not deliberate which side he should take. He joined the honest party, and was declared General against Lepidus, who by this time had reduced a great part of Italy, and was master of Cisalpine Gaul, where Brutus acted for him with a considerable force.

When Pompey took the field, he easily made his way in other parts, but he lay a long time before Mutina, which was defended by Brutus.[42] Meanwhile Lepidus advanced by hasty marches to Rome, and sitting down before it, demanded a second consulship. The inhabitants were greatly alarmed at his numbers; but their fears were dissipated by a letter from Pompey,

[39] Appian, *op. cit.*

[40] Liddell, *op. cit.*

[41] Plutarch, *op. cit.*

[42] M. Junius Brutus the father of that Brutus who, together with Cassius, was to assassinate Julius Caesar.

in which he assured them he had terminated the war without striking a blow. For Brutus, whether he betrayed his army, or they betrayed him, surrendered himself to Pompey, and having a party of Horse given him as an escort, retired to a little town upon the Po. Pompey, however, sent Germinius the next day to dispatch him, which brought no small stain upon his character [43]

but was only too characteristic of the lawless, amoral condition into which the Republic had degenerated. "Lepidus was defeated, and, soon giving up the struggle, sailed shortly afterwards to Sardinia, where he died of a wasting disease. His army was frittered away little by little and dissolved; the greater part of those who remained under arms being taken up by Perpenna to Sertorious in Spain." [44]

Sertorious, indeed, was the only Marian leader of note on whom the departed demagogue's followers could rally. "War with Sertorious, which had been going on for eight years, was not an easy war to the Romans since it was waged not merely against Spaniards, but against other Romans. Sertorious had been chosen Governor of Spain while he was cooperating with Carbo against Sulla; and after taking the city of Suessa during the armistice, he fled and assumed his Governorship. He had an army from Italy itself, and he raised another from the Celtiberians, and drove out of Spain the former Praetors, who, in order to favor Sulla, refused to surrender the government to him. He had also fought stubbornly against Metellus, who had been sent against him by Sulla. Having acquired a reputation for bravery, he enrolled a Council of three hundred members from the friends who were with him, and called it the Roman Senate in derision of the real one. After Sulla died, and Lepidus later, he obtained another army of Italians which Perpenna, a lieutenant of Lepidus, brought to him; and it was supposed he intended to march against Italy itself. He would have done so had not the Senate become alarmed and sent another army and General into Spain in addition to the former ones. This General was Pompey.

"Pompey courageously crossed the Alps, not with the expenditure of labor of Hannibal, but by opening another passage around the sources of the Rhône and the Eridanus. . . . Directly Pompey arrived in Spain, Sertorious cut in

[43] Plutarch, *op. cit.*

[44] Appian, *op. cit.*

pieces a whole Legion of his army, which had been sent out foraging, together with its animals and servants." [45]

Wanting in proper "intelligence," and victims as much of the Romans' traditional weakness in reconnaissance as of Pompey's youthful inability unerringly to distinguish between shrewd military opportunism and unwarranted rashness, there was some excuse for Sertorious's contemptuous comment that "if the old woman Metellus had not come up, he should want no other weapon than a rod and a ferula to chastise the boy with." That Sertorious had some warrant for his disdain is witnessed by the fact that he was able to plunder and destroy the Roman town of Lauro without Pompey's being able to raise a finger to prevent him. "Pompey thought he had blocked up the enemy, and spoke of it in high terms, when suddenly he found himself surrounded, and being afraid to move, had the mortification to see the city laid in ashes in his presence." [46]

But if Pompey's inaugural campaign had been bleakly inauspicious, better fortune had crowned Metellus's campaign against Hirtuleius, one of Sertorious's most trusted lieutenants, whose defeat near Italica [47] drove his beaten army back into Lusitania. Yet even with the junction of Pompey's army with the forces under Metellus, Sertorious and his followers could not be brought to book; it was scarcely encouraging for the Senate to learn that his cooperation had been solicited by envoys from Mithridates, who was obviously bracing himself for a vigorous renewal of the war against his old antagonists.

At the end of 75 B.C. Pompey wrote an urgent letter to the Senate, in which he protested that "after having exposed me, in spite of my youth,[48] to a most cruel war, you have, so far as in you lay, destroyed me and a faithful army by starvation. . . . I have exhausted my personal resources, even my expectations, and in the meantime for three years you have barely given me the means of meeting a year's expenses." [49] In arid, meagerly productive Spain, "making war support war" was not a course that could long be pursued by either side. As Pompey was at pains to point out, "Hither Spain, so far as it is not in the possession of the enemy, either we or Sertorious have devastated to the point of ruin, except

[45] Appian, *op. cit.*

[46] Plutarch, *op. cit.*

[47] Not far from Seville.

[48] At the time of writing, Pompey was twenty-eight.

[49] Sallust.

for the coast towns, so that it is actually an expense and a burden to us." [50]

What the faulty Roman "intelligence" had failed to reveal either to Metellus or Pompey was the fact that conditions in the enemy camp were none too satisfactory either. Many of Sertorious's troops had deserted, and this so enraged him that he was betrayed into acts of great severity, not excluding decimation with one unit which had given particular offense. Moreover, he had still further exasperated the Romans among his followers by forming his bodyguard exclusively of Spaniards. Furthermore, his immoderate indulgence in wine and his lascivious way of life were rapidly undermining his constitution and dulling his undoubted military talent.

In due course, even the Spaniards began to fall away from him, and then treachery stepped in to hasten the ruin that was fast overtaking him. In 72 B.C., invited by Perpenna to a banquet at Osca, the General, having drunk freely as had become his custom, was an easy prey for the daggers of his assassins.

But when Perpenna had wrought this shameful deed, he found that the name of Sertorious was still powerful among the Spaniards. Many of them, the Lusitanians above all, now that their great leader was no more, forgot his faults and deserted the standard of Perpenna; when that officer endeavored to lead the remnant of the army against Pompey, his men dispersed and he was taken prisoner. When brought before Pompey, he endeavored to gain favor by handing to him letters which had been interchanged by Sertorious with some of the chief men in Rome. But Pompey, with prudent magnanimity, threw the letters into the fire and ordered Perpenna to be put to death. In the course of a year the last relics of the Marian party in Spain were extinguished. [51]

But the sour conclusion was not to be evaded that Rome had triumphed less by virtue of her own arms than through the chronic disunity of her enemies.

Indeed for all its delusive façade of peace and prosperity, there was something rotten in the state of Rome and her dominions.

If it had chanced about the time when Caesar returned from Asia (i.e., at the end of 74 B.C.), that curiosity

50 Sallust.
51 Liddell, *op. cit.* Cf. Mommsen.

had prompted an intelligent Jew or Parthian to travel through the Roman Empire from east to west, and to record his observations, his book must have been singularly depressing to the patriotic Roman reader. The undertaking would have been a bold one; the traveler in constant insecurity. In Asia Minor he would find a gigantic war just breaking out. He would learn as he passed through the interior that the great King of Pontus [Mithridates] had blockaded Chalcedon, and that a beaten Roman General [M. Aurelius Cotta] was with difficulty holding out within its walls. He would wonder that Tigranes of Armenia did not lend a hand to his natural ally of Pontus, and help to sweep the vanquished Romans once and for ever out of Asia. . . . Taking ship at some port in the Asiatic Province, and witnessing perhaps the arrival of troops for the newly appointed General, Lucullus, he would wonder at their apparent inadequacy, and mark the total inability of the harassed and impoverished provincials to make up the deficiency of preparation. In his voyage to Italy, he would be told thrilling sailors' tales of the pirates; of capture and slavery, of ransom and ruin. Even off the port of Brundusium he would still be in danger; he would hear of Roman fleets unable to leave the port except under cover of night, and of attacks made in broad daylight on the rich cities of the western coast.

He might reasonably prefer a journey through Italy to further risk of capture by the masters of the sea, and would be warned against visiting Sicily by stories of the insecurity of all life and property under the government of the infamous Verres. Nor would such stories be needed to convince him that the Romans were their own worst enemies; for in Italy itself he would see signs enough of cruelty and misgovernment. He would find the roads occupied by bands of armed slaves of powerful physique and formidable mien, fresh from victories over Roman Legions, and expecting the speedy downfall of the tyrant city.[52]

For with L. Licinius Lucullus launched on his campaign in Asia and Pompey pinned down in Spain, Crassus had found himself confronted by yet another servile revolt, which had swiftly assumed formidable proportions. The insurrection had originated with a band of gladiators who had escaped

[52] Warde Fowler, *op. cit.*

from their training school at Capua and taken refuge on Mount Vesuvius. Under the leadership of the Thracian, Spartacus, and the two Gauls, Crixus and Oenomaus, they had dispersed a militia force sent to blockade their stronghold, evaded the Praetor Varinius, and retired into Lucania, ever the welcoming habitat of lawlessness and brigandage. With the unreliable militia of Varinus ignominiously defeated, Spartacus had experienced no difficulty in attracting to his side the herdsmen-slaves of southern Italy. With ever-increasing numbers, the open country had speedily fallen under the insurgents' sway along with a number of towns, which had been stormed and sacked. In the following year (72 B.C.), although a rebel detachment under Crixus had been cut to pieces near Mount Garganus, Spartacus himself had defeated both Consuls and the Proconsul of Cisalpine Gaul. It was the rebel leader's aim to force a passage over the Alps and secure for his followers a return to their homes in Thrace and Gaul. "But his undisciplined *banditti*, unworthy of their farsighted leader, could not bear to leave Italy unplundered, and while they roamed about the country, gave M. Crassus time to collect a force of eight Legions. By wholesome severity he taught his raw troops to face the rebels, and driving Spartacus before him, blockaded him in the extreme corner of Bruttium. In the hope of rekindling the servile war in Sicily, Spartacus bribed the pirates, who then were masters of the Sicilian waters, to transport his troops across the straits. The faithless corsairs broke their word," [53] and Spartacus found himself under the necessity of piercing the long line of circumvallation by which Crassus had hemmed him in so closely.

But when the Romans in the city heard of the siege, they thought it would be disgraceful if this war against gladiators should be prolonged. Believing also that the work still to be done against Spartacus was great and severe, they ordered up the army of Pompey, which had just arrived from Spain, as a reinforcement.

On account of this vote, Crassus tried in every way to come to an engagement with Spartacus so that Pompey might not reap the glory of the war. Spartacus himself, thinking to anticipate Pompey, invited Crassus to come to terms with him. When his proposals were rejected with scorn, he resolved to risk a battle, and as his cavalry had arrived he made a dash with his whole army through the lines of the besieging force and pushed on to Brun-

[53] How and Leigh, *op. cit.*

dusium, with Crassus in pursuit. When Spartacus learned that Lucullus had just arrived in Brundusium from his victory over Mithridates, he despaired of everything and brought his forces, which were even then very numerous, to close quarters with Crassus. The battle was long and bloody, as might have been expected with so many thousands of desperate men. Spartacus was wounded in the thigh with a spear and sank upon his knee, holding his shield in front of him and contending in this way against his assailants until he and the great mass of those was thrown into confusion and butchered in crowds. So great was the slaughter, it was impossible to count them. The Roman loss was about one thousand. The body of Spartacus was not found. A large number of his men fled from the battlefield to the mountains, and Crassus followed them thither. They divided themselves into four parts, and continued to fight until all perished except six thousand, who were captured and crucified along the whole road from Capua to Rome.[54]

The chief burden of the "Gladiators' War" had unquestionably fallen upon Crassus, although Pompey appeared on the scene in time to cut to pieces a band of five thousand helot fugitives and to join in the hunt, roundup, and crucifixion of the scattered parties of insurgents. With characteristic egotism, Pompey thereupon claimed for himself the honors and rewards of victory as the leader who had ended the servile rebellion as well as the Spanish war. Writing to the Senate, he unblushingly averred that " 'Crassus had beaten the gladiators in a pitched battle, but that it was *he* who had cut up the war by its roots.' The Romans took pleasure in speaking of this, one among another, on account of their regard for Pompey, which was such, that no part of the success in Spain, against Sertorious, was ascribed by a man of them, either in jest or earnest, to any but Pompey.

"Yet these honors and this high veneration for the man, were mixed with some fears and jealousies that he would not disband his army, but, treading in the steps of Sulla, raise himself by the sword to sovereign power, as Sulla had done. Hence the number of those who went out of fear to meet him, and congratulate him on his return, was equal to that of those who went out of love."[55]

Since the bulk of the work of suppressing the Spartacus uprising had undoubtedly fallen on the shoulders of Crassus,

[54] Appian, *op. cit.*

[55] Plutarch, *op. cit.*

"there arose a contention for honors between himself and Pompey. Crassus did not dismiss his army, for Pompey did not dismiss his. Both were candidates for the consulship. Crassus had been Praetor as the law of Sulla required. Pompey had been neither Praetor nor Quaestor, and was only thirty-four years old; but he had promised the Tribunes of the People that much of their former power should be restored." [56] It was a *volte face* which embodied about as blatant an attempt to secure public support as any power-hungry aspirant for office has ever attempted, for an agitation had long been in the making for the restoration of the full powers of the tribunate. Already, by a law of the "moderate," C. Aurelius Cotta, acceptance of the post of Tribune had ceased to be a disqualification, as under Sulla, for higher office. Yet notwithstanding the zealous efforts of Julius Caesar and certain other "moderates," the Tribunes remained without independence, committed without reserve to the service of the Senate. The opposition also demanded a searching reform of the governing corporation, together with the replacement of the venal and easily influenced Senatorial jurors by members of the Equestrian Order, and the revival of the censorship —suppressed by Sulla—the better to purge corruption in the Senate itself. Pompey, officer of the Senate and partisan of Sulla as he undoubtedly had been, could only hope to gain the objectives on which his heart was set by open force or playing on the sympathies of *hoi polloi* in general and the "moderates" in particular. For the nonce, he was prepared to try peaceful persuasion rather than the sword. If it came to it, it would call for little effort to strap on his scabbard—and his army was still embodied and within easy marching distance of the capital.

A jealous and suspicious Senate might have been prepared to grant to his youth and victories the illegal "triumph" Pompey demanded, and even the *curule* chair. On the other hand, no body of men could have been more reluctant to endorse his supremacy by awarding lands to his veterans or nominating him for the coveted command in the East. Yet Crassus, the cautious financier, was not inclined to risk his fortune in an unequal contest with his popular rival on behalf of the Senate. In the event, "the democratic leaders adroitly turned the discontent of the Generals to their own ends. Pompey and Crassus, smothering their jealousies for a time, jointly agreed to adopt the democratic program, and in return were promised the consulship. Pompey was also to re-

56 Appian, *op. cit.*

ceive a 'triumph' and allotments of land for his soldiers; Crassus, the inferior partner in the alliance, had to content himself with a simple 'ovation.'

"Pompey and Crassus were elected Consuls for the ensuing year of 70 B.C. without opposition, and at once began the task of reversing the ordinances of Sulla. The Tribunes received again their old prerogatives, in particular the right of initiating legislative proposals. Once more the Censors revised the list of the Senate, and justified their appointment by erasing no less than sixty-four names from the roll. The Senators, whose corrupt perversion of justice had been branded by Cicero in his orations against that prince of pillagers, C. Verres, the scourge of the Sicilians, were not, however, entirely excluded from the jury box." [57] A compromise was effected under which the juries in criminal cases were composed of three panels, one of Senators, one of Knights of the Equestrian Order, and one of *Tribuni ararii*. [58]

In all this surge of reform and reorganization it is almost certain that Julius Caesar played a more significant part than was strictly compatible with his relative youth, his lowly standing as no more than a military Tribune, and his modest place in the social and political hierarchy. At this stage in his career Cicero undoubtedly supported the new policy,

and Cicero was intimate with Caesar, and politically at one with him. The man who, with the approval of the Consuls, proposed and carried the bill for reconstructing the tribunals, was one of Caesar's uncles, L. Aurelius Cotta. Caesar had most likely already come to know Crassus through the medium of money transactions, and as the ablest of rising democrats, may have been called by him into consultation. But whether or not Caesar was behind the scenes, the actors certainly played their parts in a way which he must have approved. They pulled down the Sullan constitution and gave the shattered Marian party another chance. They declined the absolutism that was open to them and preferred to let the old constitution have a new lease on life. They even disbanded their forces before the year was out, and at the close of it retired into private life without securing to themselves fresh provinces and armies. Thus they

[57] How and Leigh, *op. cit.*

[58] The *tribuni ararii* were originally responsible for the payment of the troops, but the term had come to refer to private men of reasonable substance, of much the same standing as the Equestrian Order.

seemed to be leaving free space for younger aspirants for power, whether at home or in the provinces.[59]

For Crassus the relinquishment of office meant little more than the exchange of his official robes for the plain, unadorned toga of an ordinary citizen. But for Pompey the opening for drama, the opportunity to make an impression, was on no account to be missed. "It was the custom for a Roman Knight, when he had served the time ordered by law, to lead his horse into the Forum before the two magistrates called Censors, and after having given an account of the Generals and other officers under whom he had made his campaigns, and of his own actions in them, to demand his discharge. On these occasions they received proper marks of honor or disgrace, according to their behavior.

Gellius and Lentulus were then Censors, and had taken their seats in a manner that became their dignity, to review the whole Equestrian Order, when Pompey was seen at a distance with all the badges of his office, leading his horse by the bridle. As soon as he was near enough to be observed by the Censor, he ordered his lictors to make an opening, and advanced with his horse in hand, to the front of the tribunal. The people were struck with admiration, and a profound silence took place; at the same time a joy, mingled with reverence, was visible on the countenances of the Censors. The senior Censor then addressed him as follows: "Pompey the Great, I demand of you, whether you have served all the campaigns required by law?" He answered with a loud voice, "I have served them all; and all under myself, as General." The people were so charmed with this answer that there was no end to their acclamations. At last the Censors rose up and conducted Pompey to his house, to indulge the multitude, who followed him with the loudest plaudits.[60]

Such was the manner in which the two men respectively, and in each case very characteristically, signified their temporary withdrawal from public life. "Had they done otherwise than they did, Caesar might never have risen to power; the task of solving the great problems of the age might have fallen to men of hardly more than average ability, and

59 Warde Fowler, op. cit.
60 Plutarch, op. cit.

wanting in the breadth and generosity of view that was altogether indispensable. As we now see it, these two men seemed to have been already marked out by destiny to make Caesar's path easier for him." [61]

It is, of course, always helpful to have someone else blunder over the handling of a problem for which oneself will some day be called upon to find the right solution.

Chapter IX

PROGRESS OF A POPULAR IDOL

"But wild ambition loves to slide, not stand,
And Fortune's ice prefers to Virtue's land."

—Dryden

A man whose popular acclaim is based largely upon his prowess as a military leader is apt to suffer progressive public neglect when preservation of the public weal is no longer dependent upon his sword. Of all human emotions, gratitude, especially for the warrior, has the shortest memory. Moreover, "should the soldier be desirous to preserve the rank in the Forum which he had in the field, he who cannot distinguish himself in the field, thinks it intolerable to give place in the administration too. When, therefore, the latter has got the man who shone in camps into the assemblies at home, and finds him attempting to maintain the same pre-eminence there, of course he endeavors to humble him." [1]

With an army at his back, or even with the *curule* chair to lend him its political authority, Pompey was a visible power in the land. Without either, he was just another rusting scabbard, although "he took pleasure in having a number of retainers about him, because he thought it gave him an air of

61 Warde Fowler, *op. cit.*
1 Plutarch, *op. cit.*

greatness and majesty," [2] and minimized to a certain degree his relegation to military and political inactivity.

Yet the call on Rome's martial leadership and military resources showed no sign whatever of abatement. In the East as well as in the West, Rome's hegemony was under constant and mounting peril. In the Balkan peninsula it demanded all the energies of M. Lucullus to contain the raids of the barbarian tribes, who were not finally brought to interim submission until 73 B.C. Ineffectual opposition had spurred Mithridates of Pontus and his son-in-law coadjutor, Tigranes of Armenia, to a fresh departure into aggression. But far more immediately perilous were the audaciously predatory activities of the corsairs who roamed at will over a Mediterranean they sailed virtually unchallenged.

The power of the pirates had its foundation in Cilicia. Their progress was the more dangerous because at first it was taken little notice of. In the Mithridatic war they assumed new confidence and courage on account of some services they had rendered the King. After this, while the Romans were engaged in civil wars at the very gates of their capital, the sea was left unguarded, and the pirates by degrees attempted higher things; they not only attacked ships, but also islands and maritime towns. Many persons distinguished for their wealth, their birth, and their capacity embarked with them and assisted in their depredations, as if their employment had been worthy of the ambition of men of honor. They had in various places arsenals, ports, and watchtowers, all strongly fortified. Their fleets were not only extremely well manned, supplied with skillful pilots, and fitted for their business by their lightness and celerity, but there was a parade of vanity about them more mortifying than their strength, with gilded sterns, purple canopies, and plated oars, as if they took pride and triumphed in their villainy. Music resounded and drunken revels indulged on every coast. Here Generals were made captive; there the cities the pirates had captured were paying their ransom, all to the great disgrace of the Roman power. The number of their galleys amounted to a thousand, and the cities they were master of, to four hundred. . . . They not only insulted the Romans at sea, but infested the great roads and plundered the villas near the coast. [3]

2 Plutarch, *op. cit.*
3 *Ibid.*

Temples were despoiled;[4] women were outraged or, if of sufficiently wealthy family, held to swingeing ransom. Nor were the corsairs respecters of rank or office, the two Praetors Sextilius and Bellinus being seized and held, together with their lictors and train of attendants.

Occasional efforts were made to cope with the menace, but they were never thoroughly followed through. In three sporadic campaigns (78–76 B.C.) Publius Severus had inflicted condign defeat on a pirate fleet off Patara, destroyed a number of their strongholds in Lycia, Pamphylia, and Cilicia, and gone on to cross the Taurus and capture the mountain fast-nesses of the Isaurians. But although his efforts won for the victorious General the honorific title of Isauricus, they did little more than briefly diminish the scope of the corsairs' activities. Binding up their hurts, they betook themselves to their erstwhile haunts in Crete "and laughed at the empty triumph of their conqueror."

In 74 B.C. the Admiral M. Antonius temporarily drove the pirates from the coasts of Italy, only to suffer humiliating defeat at the hands of the Cretans off Cydonia. In 68 B.C. Metellus was dispatched with a strong army to bring the Cretans to heel, but it demanded two hard-fought campaigns for him to reduce the islanders' principal cities and thus qual-ify for the title of Creticus. Meanwhile, the corsairs, having shifted their bases, scoured the waters of the Mediterranean unhindered. "They formed now a piratical State, with a pe-culiar *esprit de corps,* with a solid and very respectable or-ganization, with a home of their own, and the germs of a symmachy, and doubtless also with definite political designs. The pirates called themselves Cilicians; in fact, their vessels were the rendezvous of desperadoes and adventurers from all countries, the ruined men of all nations, the hunted refu-gees of all vanquished parties, everyone that was wretched and daring."[5] And once more their power extended un-challenged over these narrow seas, so that the Romans found their trade and navigation entirely crippled. A Roman fleet was burnt in the roads of Ostia itself, and the essential corn ships from Egypt, Carthage, and even Sicily, dared no longer put to sea. Famine and riot stared the rulers of the Republic implacably in the face.

At length, in 67 B.C., the Tribune Gabinius, an intimate friend of Pompey, brought in a bill in the Assembly of the

---

[4] From one temple at Samothrace treasure to the value of one thousand talents (£240,000; $672,000) was borne away.

[5] Mommsen, *op. cit.*

Plebs to endow the still popular idol with virtually unlimited power to clear the seas of the pirates infesting them.

> The decree gave him the empire of the sea, as far as the Pillars of Hercules, and of the land for four hundred furlongs from the coasts. There were few parts of the Roman Empire that this commission did not take in; and the most considerable of the barbarous nations, and the most powerful Kings, were moreover comprehended in it. Besides this, he was empowered to choose out of the Senators fifteen lieutenants to act under him, in such districts, and with such authority, as he should appoint. He was to take from the Quaestors and other public receivers, what money he pleased, and equip a fleet of two hundred sail. The numbers of nautical forces of mariners and rowers were left entirely to his discretion.[6]

Although supported by the people in general, there was understandable reluctance in the Senate to endow any man with such tremendous, wide-ranging powers. "They, therefore, all, except Caesar, opposed the measure passing into law. Caesar was in favor of it, not out of regard for Pompey, but to insinuate himself in the good graces of the people, which he had long been courting."[7] It was a deliberate move to ensure popularity with the ordinary folk of the Tribes, and embarked upon with the cold-blooded detachment of the born tactician. The day well might come when he would seek the assent of the people for some contemplated venture of his own. In that hour his earlier deference to their wishes would be remembered in his favor!

The issue was at the same time so vital and so explosively controversial that

> Senate or no Senate, it was decided that Gabinius's proposition should be submitted to the Assembly, and the aristocrats were driven to their old remedy of bribing other members of the College of Tribunes to interfere. The renegades were thus secured, and when the voting day came Trebillius, who was one of them, put in a veto; the other, Roscius, said that the power intended for Pompey was too considerable to be trusted to a single person, and proposed two commanders instead of one. The mob was packed so thick that the

6 Plutarch, *op. cit.*
7 Froude, *op. cit.*

housetops were covered. A yell rose from tens of thousands of throats so piercing that it is said a crow flying over the Forum dropped dead at the sound of it. The old Patrician Catulus tried to speak, but the people would not hear him. The vote passed by acclamation, and Pompey was for three years Sovereign of the Roman world.[8]

There can be no question that Pompey justified all the hopes reposed in him and turned to the best account the unstinted means placed at his disposal, and "as the price of provisions fell immediately, the people were greatly pleased, and it gave them occasion to say, 'The very name of Pompey terminated the war.'" [9] Dividing his command into thirteen areas under his deputies, he moved with his main forces from west to east. Convergent drives hustled his quarry from one lurking place to another. "By stationing his fleet in all quarters, he enclosed the pirates as it were in a net, took great numbers of them and brought them into harbor. Such of their vessels as had dispersed and made off in time, or could escape the general chase, retired to Cilicia, like so many bees into a hive. Against these Pompey proposed to go himself with sixty of his best galleys; but first he resolved to clear the Tuscan sea and the coasts of Africa, Sardinia, Corsica, and Sicily, of all piratical adventurers; which he effected in forty days." [10] With the western Mediterranean swept clear, the corn ships from Africa, Sardinia, and Sicily were again at liberty to ply between their home ports and the havens on the Italian mainland.

After a short stay in Rome, Pompey set out again to complete his mission. Utilizing Brundusium as his base, he set to work to hunt down such of those corsairs as were still afloat or had taken refuge in one or another of their strongholds. The popular hero's brief sojourn in Rome had been, of course, a veritable triumph. "As soon as the people were informed of his approach, they went in crowds to receive him, in the same manner they had done a few weeks before, to conduct him on his way. Their extraordinary joy was owing to the speed with which he had executed his commission, so far beyond all expectation, and to the supernatural plenty which reigned in the markets.

8 Froude, *op. cit.*

9 Plutarch, *op. cit.*

10 *Ibid.*

Still, however, there remained a great number, and indeed the most powerful part of these corsairs, who sent their families, treasures and all useless hands, into the castles and fortified towns upon Mount Taurus. Then they manned their ships, and waited for Pompey, at Coracesium in Cilicia. A battle ensued and the pirates were defeated; after which they retired into the fort. But they had not long been besieged before they capitulated and surrendered themselves, together with the cities and islands which they had conquered and fortified, and which by their works, as well as situation, were almost impregnable. Thus the war was finished, and the whole force of the pirates destroyed, within three months at the farthest.[11]

Of the pirate fleet, 1,300 craft were burnt or sunk, 72 taken in action, and 306 surrendered. One hundred and twenty towns and strongholds had been stormed and destroyed, 10,000 pirates killed, and 20,000 taken captive. With many of the prisoners liberated and returned to restore and cultivate the ruined, desolate slopes of Cilicia, and others settled in the underpopulated district of Dyma in Achaia, Crete—long mutinously in arms—surrendered at discretion. The Roman people who had been saved from hunger, the merchants whose commerce had been rescued from decay, the soldiery enriched by the spoils of war—all lauded the name of the man who had accomplished in so short a space of time what had vainly been desired for seventeen years.

Unquestionably, Pompey's suppression of the sea rovers was a brilliant piece of work, which shone all the more brightly in comparison with the utter failure of Lucullus to hold his own against the rampant Mithridates. "Lucullus, the hope of the aristocracy, was lying helpless within the Roman frontier, with a disorganized and mutinous army. His victories were forgotten. He was regarded as the personification of every fault which had made the rule of the Senate hateful. Pompey, the people's General, after a splendid success, had come home with clean hands; Lucullus had sacrificed his country to his avarice." [12] Moreover, on political grounds Cicero thought that Pompey ought to be recognized by the moderate party he intended to form as the only way in which to save the constitution.

Caesar, too, had been fascinated by the speed and pro-

11 Plutarch, *op. cit.* Cf. Mommsen.
12 Froude, *op. cit.*

fessional competence with which Pompey had set about his task. Indeed, at this particular period Caesar was in more genuine sympathy with the hero of the hour than at any other time in their joint lives, widely as their paths had diverged hitherto, and different as had been their respective experience in the public service. For subsequent to his spell of soldiering in the East, Caesar's activities had been almost exclusively civilian, despite his appointment as a Military Tribune. An appearance in the Courts for the prosecution of Cornelius Dolabella, son of the Consul of that name, charged with extortion and abuse of power during his command in Macedonia, had displayed a sound but uninspiring turn for oratory, and a brain that few cogent points eluded. But in days wherein nothing flourished more vigorously than booming rhodomontade, plain straightforward oratory was not enough to enable him to scale the heights of lapidary debate.

Promoted to Praetor Caesar had been appointed to Spain

but was detained in the city by his creditors, as he owed much more than he could pay, by reason of his political expenses. He was reported as saying that he needed 25,000,000 sesterces [13] in order to have nothing at all. However, he arranged with those who were detaining him as best he could and proceeded to Spain. Here he neglected the transaction of public business, the administration of justice, and all matters of that kind, because he considered them of no use to his purpose; but he raised an army and attacked the independent Spanish tribes one by one until he had made the whole country tributary to the Romans. He also sent much money to the public treasury at Rome,[14]

being rewarded with official recognition for his efforts. He then proceeded to expend the balance of his tour of duty in mastering those details of jurisprudence, administration, and supply involved in the smooth running of a provincial governorship.

On the death of his wife Cornelia, Caesar had wed Pompeia, a cousin of Pompey, and inevitably with the conclusion of his Quaestorship and his return to Rome, this new relationship threw the two men more into each other's company. Like all true Romans, they were both awake to

[13] About £250,000, or $700,000.
[14] Appian, *op. cit.*

the danger and scandal of the existent maladministration, and both were inspired with a sincere desire to remedy the many glaring errors and bring some sort of order out of the prevailing state of chaos. But home affairs stand ever at the mercy of foreign policy, and to concentrate on brooming the domestic hearth when the roof is blazing can never be anything but a supererogation.

While Pompey had been preoccupied in dealing with the Mediterranean corsairs, events in the East had again reached a point of crisis. War with Mithridates and his supporters had been dragging on, with greater or lesser intensity, since 120 B.C. Brought to an uneasy pause in 84 B.C., it had broken out again in that same year, only to be halted when Sulla had peremptorily ordered Murena, the overimpetuous Roman commander on the spot, to come to a composition with the King of Pontus, if anything like reasonable terms could be agreed. With Rome still to conquer and all Italy yet to bring under his sway, Sulla had been of no mind to do anything but discourage the activities of an enemy in his rear.

It had been the death of Nicomedes of Bithynia in 75 B.C. that had aroused Mithridates from his temporary lapse into tranquillity. Dying without heir, Nicomedes had bequeathed his Kingdom to the Roman people. But Mithridates had promptly conjured up a pretended son of the late King, and to support his claims had marched into Bithynia at the head of a formidable force made up of 16,000 Horse and 120,000 Foot, well trained after the Roman fashion and supported by a substantial fleet. In face of this overwhelming armament, the whole country submitted without a blow (74 B.C.)

The Consuls for the year had been M. Aurelius Cotta and L. Licinius Lucullus, and to the latter the task of curbing Mithridates had been entrusted. His force of five Legions—2,500 Horse and 30,000 Foot—had, however, included two bodies of troops from Fimbria, of extremely doubtful quality.

Nonetheless, at the outset the course of events had gone consistently in Lucullus's favor, and throughout 73 and 72 B.C. he had continued his successful penetration of the Kingdom of Pontus. The siege of Cyzicus, where the besiegers had in their turn become the besieged, saw the annihilation, in little more than a twelvemonth, of the vast muster which Mithridates had assembled and trained with such anxious care. With some warrant, Lucullus had sent letters wreathed in laurel recounting his success.

In 71 B.C. Lucullus had continued his advance, with Mithridates fleeing to the refuge of his son-in-law, Tigranes of Armenia, the capture of the King of Pontus being frustrated by the fact that "the Roman horsemen stopped to collect a quantity of gold which had fallen from a mule in the King's suite." [15]

Since Tigranes had refused to surrender his father-in-law to the Roman commander's demand, Lucullus had pushed on with his advance into Armenia until the country's second capital, Artaxata, north of Mount Ararat, had emerged from the mist as the Romans' next objective. During the course of a bitter, discouraging winter, however, Lucullus had been confronted with a precisely similar situation to that which had halted Alexander the Great's war-weary troops on the banks of the Sutlej. The rank and file had refused point-blank to carry on any further. Unpardonable as such indiscipline might have been, it had not entirely lacked excuse. The Legions from Fimbria, for example, had been away from their homes for the best part of twenty years. The campaign itself had been waged under increasingly spartan conditions, and Lucullus, while an able and resourceful commander, was sadly wanting in that human touch which distinguishes the born leader of men from the dehumanized military technician. In the following spring Lucullus had been forced by the entreaties of his hard-pressed lieutenants and the discontent of his troops to turn his march westward. He came in time to relieve his Armenian garrison, but found Pontus all but lost. His legate, Triarius, had been forced to give battle at Ziela by the clamor of his soldiers, and had lost the pick of his troops in a defeat which led to the capture of the Roman camp. The defection of certain of his subordinate commanders had left the unfortunate Lucullus to confront his enemies at the head of a mutinous, utterly unreliable soldiery. Further advance had been out of the question; indeed, the troops had sullenly retreated into the Province of Asia, leaving Mithridates in undisturbed possession of Pontus. Thus the fruit of the many victories of Lucullus was wasted by the insubordination of his soldiers; all his resourceful generalship could ensure was a safe retreat.

The hour of his country's necessity, however, proved to be Pompey's golden opportunity.

[15] Liddell, *op. cit.*

The command had already been transferred from Lucullus to M. Acilius Glabrio, Consul for 67 B.C. But it was very certain that, where Lucullus had failed, Glabrio could not succeed, and at the beginning of the year 66 B.C. the Tribune Manilius moved that Pompey should be invested with the chief command over all Roman dominions in the East, till he had brought the war with Mithridates to an end. The Senatorial chiefs opposed the law of Manilius, but a new supporter appeared in the person of Cicero, who was now Praetor. The eloquent advocate had never yet addressed the Tribes on any political question, and he could not have found an occasion better suited for the first essay than the praises of Pompey. The task was easy and the audience eager; success was a matter of course. Pompey received by acclamation the most extensive authority ever yet conferred by law upon a Roman citizen, with the exception of the Dictatorial power given to Sulla. He was in fact appointed Dictator of the East, and with the army placed at his command it would have been easy to establish himself as master of the West also. It must be confessed that the Senatorial chiefs had some reason to object to this unlimited authority. Necessity had been the excuse in Sulla's case, for without him there would have been anarchy. But no necessity now existed, for it cannot be doubted that Lucullus, with proper reinforcements, would have brought the war to a speedy conclusion. But the cause of Pompey was identified with the cause of the People, Lucullus was held to be a champion of the Senate, and the popular will prevailed.[16]

Thus the governorships of Pontus-Bithynia and Cilicia, with the troops stationed there, as well as the prosecution of the Pontic-Armenian war, together with authority to make war, peace, or alliance with the dynasts of the East at his discretion, were transferred to Pompey—all of which was extremely unjust to the unfortunate Lucullus, who had kept the flag flying in extremely difficult circumstances, only to fall victim to popular clamor whose choice had fallen on a man of no greater military talent than his own but with a far shrewder sense of publicity.

Very characteristically:

[16] Liddell, *op. cit.*

when Pompey received the letters which notified his high promotion, and his friends, who happened to be by, congratulated him on the occasion, he is said to have knit his brow, smote his thigh, and expressed himself as if he were already overburdened with the weight of power: "Alas! is there no end of my conflicts? How much better it would have been to be one of the undistinguished many than be perpetually engaged in war! Shall I never be able to fly from envy to a rural retreat, to domestic happiness and conjugal endearments?" Even his friends were unable to bear the dissimulation of this speech. They knew that the flame of his native ambition and lust of power was blown up to a greater height by the difference he had with Lucullus, and that he rejoiced the more in the present preference on that account.

His actions soon unmasked the man. He caused public notice to be given in all places within his commission that the Roman troops were to repair to him, as well as the Kings and Princes of their allies. Whereever he went he annulled the acts of Lucullus, remitting the fines he had imposed, and taking away the rewards he had given. In short, he omitted no means to show the partisans of that General that all his authority was gone.[17]

A meeting between the two men led to little more than an exchange of abrasive innuendo, whereafter Lucullus departed for Rome, leaving his rival to hasten preparations for his campaign.

Early in 66 B.C. Pompey pushed forward over the frontier of Pontus in search of Mithridates. The King, anxious to avoid battle, retired towards the sources of the Halys, but being overtaken, was forced to stand his ground on a spot which subsequently became the site of the city of Nicopolis. Mithridates had taken up

a strong position defended by rocks, to which there was access by only one road, which he held with an advance guard of four Cohorts. The Romans put an opposing force on guard there to prevent the King from escaping.

At daybreak both commanders put their forces under arms. The outpost began skirmishing on the slope and

---

[17] Plutarch, *op. cit.*

some of the King's horsemen, without their horses and without orders, went to the assistance of their advance guard. A larger number of the Roman cavalry came up against them, and these horseless soldiers of Mithridates rushed in a body back to the camp to mount their horses and meet the advancing Romans on equal terms. When those who were still arming on the higher ground looked down and saw their own men running towards them with haste and outcries, but did not know the reason, they thought they had been put to flight. They threw down their arms and fled, thinking that their camp had already been captured on either side. As there was no road out of the place, they fell foul of each other in the confusion, until finally they leaped down the precipices. Thus the army of Mithridates perished through the rashness of those who caused a panic by going to the assistance of the advance guard without orders. Pompey was left the easy task of killing and capturing men not yet under arms and shut up in a rocky defile. About ten thousand were slain, and the camp with all its war matériel was taken; [18]

only a few fugitives, with Mithridates at their head, contrived to win clear and cross the Euphrates. There was no refuge for the fleeing King in Armenia, where Tigranes, who with difficulty had repelled the assaults of a Parthian force led by his rebellious son, was only too eager to make his submission to the Roman conqueror and secure his support.

Despairing of reorganizing operations in the East, Mithridates conceived the daring idea of uniting the Sarmatian tribes north of the Black Sea and making a descent on Italy itself. But the support of the wild Scythian and Gaulish warriors he had called to his banner was speedily alienated by the King's willful despotism. Mutiny and desertion rapidly led to open insurrection, with Pharnaces, the King's hitherto most favored son, at the head of the insurgents. Mewed up in his palace, Mithridates begged in vain for the mercy he himself had never shown. At last, in 63 B.C., in the true spirit of Eastern despotism, the baffled potentate resolved to perish with all his house: "His wives and daughters died of the poisoned cup, but the King himself found poison unavailing, and owed his death to the sword of a Gallic attendant. His body was sent by Pharnaces to Pompey in Palestine, and was by his orders laid in the

18 Appian, *op. cit.*

tombs of the Kings at Sinope. The great leader of the East against the West, the man who had proved no unworthy opponent of Sulla, of Lucullus, and of Pompey, was dead, and his death was a greater gain to Rome than many victories." [19]

Pompey had still to establish order in the East, where the ancient Kingdom of the Seleucids had fallen prey to Arab emirs in Syria, robber chiefs in Lebanon, and the desert-bred Nabateans from the wastelands about Petra. The Jewish nation, split between the contending factions of Sadducees and Pharisees as it might be, could not brook the command to renounce the monarchy and conquest won by the Hasmonian Princes, and for three months stubbornly defended the Temple and its environs against the Romans. When at last resistance had been overcome, Pompey exhibited acute political foresight in treating the Temple and the Jewish religion with becoming respect. Judea became a Roman dependency under the immediate rule of the high priests of the Pharisees. A triumphal inscription in Rome recorded that Pompey, the people's General, had in three years captured fifteen hundred cities and had slain, taken, or reduced to submission twelve million human beings. Of all the countries bordering on the Mediterranean, Egypt alone had been left independent; of all the islands only Cyprus. The new provinces were reorganized so that while their respective interiors were left in the hands of dependent rulers, the coasts of Asia Minor came directly under Roman control. At the same time every effort was made to foster city communities, urban civilization, and commerce. To encourage colonization, even the subjugated pirates were permitted to settle—well inland!—in Cilicia, while Pompey's invalided veterans formed the nucleus of the population of Nicopolis. Sinope and Amisus were repopulated; the predominantly Greek cities of Antioch and Seleucia in Syria, like Mitylene, were granted local autonomy. Once again the Romans, with Pompey ostentatiously in the forefront of developments, were intent on cultivating that state of "Unity in Concord" whose realization had been so consistently deferred by their complete inability to engender the needful spirit of *Homonoia* in their own midst.

It is characteristic of far too many politicians that they enjoy the comfort of opinion without having undergone the discomfort of thought. The tireless vendetta of faction must be prosecuted for its own fell sake, no matter how jaded

19 How and Leigh, *op. cit.*

and oscitant the arguments dragged out to try and justify it. To no assemblages has this applied with greater truth than to the Senate and *Comitia* in Rome. Throughout the whole five-year period of Pompey's absence in the East *optimates* and *populares* continued to bicker and snarl at each other with unabating rancor.

But there was no life and reality in the traditional opposition of the democrats to the Senatorial oligarchy. Besides the essential hollowness of the Roman party system, the fate of Rome, as all men felt, lay in the hands of the absent soldier. Neither Caesar nor Cicero, but Pompey, was the man of the hour, the center of the political situation. If Pompey should follow in the footsteps of his master, Sulla, there was no party and no leader at this time who could stand for a moment against him. Accordingly, beneath the open warfare of the parties there ran a dark undercurrent of plot and counterplot. The leaders of both parties were awaiting the return of the great captain with mingled fear and hope—fear that his reorganization of the East might be the prelude of a reconstruction of the central government, and hope that they might be able to turn his notorious irresolution to their own purposes and use his prestige in the interest of a faction. The *populares* in particular were conscious of the fact that the Assembly could not now overthrow the military dictatorship whose aid it had evoked. The democracy had made a monster whose giant strength was utterly beyond its control. Hence throughout these years Caesar and Crassus were engaged in fruitless efforts to win for themselves a power and position that would enable them to meet Pompey on equal terms.[20]

In all the welter of cliques and juntas, only the Senate represented a clear-cut purpose—the maintenance of the *status quo*. Its aims were threefold: to discredit the *populares,* to strengthen its authority, and to afford Pompey no excuse for armed interference. If the Senate numbered within its ranks such extreme conservatives and personal enemies of Pompey as Catulus, Metellus, and the comprehensibly disgruntled Lucullus, impractical independents such as Cato, and moderate constitutionalists like Cicero, the make-up of the *populares* could boast little more in the way of

20 How and Leigh, *op. cit.*

homogeneity. A union of malcontents, at one end of the scale were extremists who virtually qualified as anarchists, balanced by the few remaining democratic idealists, both groups being offset by individualists such as Gaius Caesar, pushing his own interests and policies and followed by the more restless members of the young nobility.

Prominent among the noisier extremists of the "popular" party was a certain ruined and dissolute Patrician, L. Sergius Catilina, a man guilty of murder, incest, and adultery. Even in a city as debauched as Rome his whole licentious way of life had become a byword. An erstwhile creature of Sulla's, with his patron's death Catiline, as he was generally termed, had speedily found himself plunged into an obscurity that was as swiftly matched by the poverty of a man who had recklessly squandered a fortune without thought of its dubious origin or the unlikelihood of its replacement.[21] Boisterous, outwardly jovial, with great charm of manner and a superficial air of forcefulness, Catiline was the natural magnet for all those whom the passing of the Sullan regime had thrown into the discard—soldiers of fortune for the most part, whose prosperous service had ended with the breakup of Sulla's Legions, with a few party hacks and petty officials no longer in a position to batten on the helpless or wax fat on the extortions they had feigned to regard as the legitimate perquisites of office. Always at the beck and call of any agitator were the veterans in precarious tenancy of their allotments, who had never taken kindly to the tilling of the earth, and the landless folk who had been dispossessed for their benefit; the sons of exiled Marians; the idle proletariat of the capital. Further afield, support could be looked for from the Transpadani, eager for full citizenship and urged by Caesar to press their claim; and such of the Transalpine Gauls as misgovernment had rendered discontented and rebellious.

Despite his unsavory reputation, Catiline's standing as a member of the old Patrician *gens* had secured him the post of Praetor in the capital, an assignment which had been followed by his appointment to the Governorship of the Province of Africa, where his term of office had been characterized by the perpetration of every enormity that could be imputed to the ruler of a Roman dependency.

"In the year before Caesar's aedilship (66 B.C.), an indictment was laid against Catiline by the profligate P. Clodius Pulcher. He had intended in that year to offer himself as candidate for the consulship. But in consequence of the pending accusation the Senate forbade him to come forward." [22] Catiline was infuriated at this turn of events, and the election of Autronius Paetus and Cornelius Sulla to the consulate was duly carried.

Two other Patricians, Aurelius Cotta and Manlius Torquatus, had stood against them. The successful competitors were unseated for bribery, Cotta and Torquatus took their places; and, apparently as a natural resource in the existing contempt into which the constitution had fallen, the disappointed candidates formed a plot to kill their rivals' friends in the Senate and to make a revolution. Gneius Piso, a young nobleman of the bluest blood, joined in the conspiracy. Catiline threw himself into it as his natural element, and aristocratic tradition said in later years that Caesar and Crassus were implicated also. It was even said that Crassus was to be made Dictator, with Caesar as his Master of the Horse. Some desperate scheme there certainly was, but the accounts of it are confused: one authority claims that it failed because Catiline gave the signal prematurely; others, that Caesar was to have given the signal and did not do it; others, that Crassus's heart failed him; others, that the Consuls had secret notice given to them and took precautions. [23]

One thing at least is certain, that if such a complot ever had existed, then its execution was definitely postponed. One bewildering sequel to events, however, was Cicero's appearance for the defense in the prosecution of Catiline for his misgovernment in Africa. It was not that he entertained the slightest doubt as to his client's culpability. But Cicero was himself about to stand for the consulship, the object of an almost obsessional ambition, and since Catiline's hope of attaining the *curule* chair appeared extremely promising, prudence counseled that it was better to coalesce with him than to oppose him.

In the outcome the Senate returned Cicero as Consul, their choice for his coadjutor falling not upon Catiline—strongly suspected of being engaged in a new conspiracy—but on C. Antonius, son of the well-remembered orator, and a man possessed of all the aristocratic lineage and associa-

22 Liddell, *op. cit.*
23 Froude, *op. cit.*

tions so conspicuously wanting in his fellow office-holder.

For fervor there is no one to compare with the convert, and from the moment of his election Cicero's adhesion to the Senate would have shamed a limpet; it is from this moment that his increasing alienation from Caesar can be traced. Among those attached to Caesar's party was the Tribune P. Servilius Rullus, the sponsor of an agrarian law for the sale of State property acquired since 88 B.C., whereby to accumulate a capital sum for the purchase of territory in Campania for distribution among needy citizens. The measure was immediately opposed by Cicero, who, with infinite casuistry, contrived to demonstrate that the proposal was nothing less than a subtle plot to curb the power of the absent but highly popular Pompey, who had not been named one of the ten commissioners scheduled to supervise the detailed execution of the scheme. "Even so, Caesar gained something from the proposal. By advocating it he secured favor for himself; by forcing Cicero to take part against it he hoped to deprive the orator of a large portion of his popularity." [24]

The two boyhood friends were now in open rivalry, and if Cicero enjoyed a head start over his competitor, Caesar was rapidly overtaking him, while at the same time gaining in the confidence needful to reveal the hand he proposed to play. In 65 B.C. Caesar had been appointed *Curule Aedile*, having for his colleague the wealthy Plebeian Bibulus. Since the aedilship was a magistracy through which it was necessary to pass in order to reach the consulship, Caesar had accepted the offer despite the heavy personal disbursements involved in its tenure, for it was the Aediles who were responsible for the decoration of the city for the season of games, as it was their task to entertain the idle populace with ever more lavish spectacles; "and if they fell short of public expectation, they need look no further for the suffrages of their many-headed master."

Cicero had slipped through the aedilship, without ruin to himself. Caesar, either more ambitious or less confident in his services, raised a new and costly row of columns in front of the Capitol; built a temple to the *Dioscuri,* and charmed the populace with a show of gladiators unusually extensive.[25] Personally he cared

[24] Liddell, *op. cit.*

[25] It is recorded that he brought three hundred and twenty pairs of gladiators into the arena at the same time, by way of grand finale.

nothing for these sanguinary exhibitions, and he displayed his indifference ostentatiously by reading or writing while the butchery went forward. The noble lords watched him suspiciously, and their uneasiness was not diminished when, not content with having produced the insignia of Marius at his aunt's funeral, he restored the trophies for the victories over the Cimbri and the Teutons, which had been removed by Sulla. The name of Marius was growing every day more dear to the popular party. They forgave, if they had ever resented, his cruelties. His veterans who had fought with him through his campaigns, came forward in tears to salute the honored relics of their once honored commander.

As he felt the ground stronger under his feet, Caesar now began to assume an attitude more peremptorily marked. He had won a reputation in the Forum; he had spoken in the Senate; he had warmly recommended Pompey to his high commands; and he was regarded as a prominent democratic leader. But he had not thrown himself into politics with any absorbing passion; his exertions had been intermittent, and he was chiefly known as a brilliant member of fashionable society, a special favorite with women, and remarkable for his abstinence from the coarse debauchery which disgraced so many of his contemporaries.[26]

His only overt move to secure accelerated advancement for himself was to put up Tribunes to propose for himself an extraordinary military command in Egypt. Pretext was not wanting, for Egypt had been bequeathed to the Romans by its late King, and his unpopular successor had been forced to appeal for aid to Pompey, despite the fact that the Country of the Nile was outside his sphere of authority.

Balked in his attempt to secure an independent military command, Caesar's next public activity was to instigate a certain T. Labienus to launch an assault on the arbitrary powers assumed by the Senate in times of emergency, with particular reference to the suppression of the revolutionary movement headed by the Tribune Saturninus during the sixth consulship of Marius.

Labienus, whose uncle had perished at the side of Saturninus, indicted the aged Senator, C. Rabirius, for having slain the Tribune, and it was manifest that were he to be found guilty, it would follow that all those who there-

26 Froude, *op. cit.*

after obeyed the Senate in taking up arms against seditious persons would lay themselves open to a similar charge. "The cause was tried before the *duumviri,* one of whom was L. Caesar, Consul of the preceding year, the other being Gaius Julius Caesar himself. It seemed almost impossible that Caesar should condemn Rabirius, seeing that Marius himself had led the attack against Saturninus. But Caesar was not troubled by scruples. The *duumviri* found Rabirius guilty." [27] In the outcome, a technicality served to spare the aged Senator actual penalization, but Caesar's purpose had been effectually served: the governing body had been humbled, and their right to place seditious individuals under a sentence of outlawry had been quasi-legally called into question.

Cicero's riposte was to block the proposal to restore to full rights of citizenship the sons of those who had been on the proscribed lists of Sulla, and thus Caesar and his erstwhile friend and comrade played off the debasing game of politics against each other, move and countermove.

"It was later in the year that the office of *Pontifex Maximus* became vacant by the death of old Metellus Pius, and Caesar at once took steps to secure it for himself. The chances in his favor were small, but the prize was a tempting one. Success would place him at the head of the whole Roman religious system. He would have the Vestal Virgins and the *Flamens* under his immediate control; he would be the referee in all matters of religious law, public and private; he would have the superintendence of the calendar, then a matter of the utmost weight in Roman politics." [28] To Caesar, however, the secular power wielded by the incumbent of the post was all that mattered. "Two Patricians, Quintus Catulus and Caesar's old General, Servilius Isauricus, were the Senate's candidates, and vast sums were spent to secure the success of one or other of the two. Caesar offered himself to the *Comitia.* Committed as he was to a contest with the richest men in Rome, he spent money freely. He was in debt already for his expenses as Aedile. He engaged his credit still deeper for this new competition. The story ran that when his mother kissed him as he was leaving home for the Forum on the morning of the election, he told her that he would return as pontiff, or she would never see him more. He was chosen by an overwhelming majority; the votes given for him being larger than the col-

27 Liddell, *op. cit.*
28 Warde Fowler, *op. cit.*

lective numbers of the votes entered for his opponents.

"The election for the pontificate was on the sixth of March, and soon after Caesar received a further evidence of popular favor by being chosen Praetor for the next year." [29]

At the time when Cicero had so scornfully rejected the latifundian law proposed by the Tribune Rullus, "Etruria was full of Sulla's disbanded soldiers, who had squandered their allotments, and were hanging about, unoccupied and starving. Catiline sent down Manlius, their old Officer, to collect as many as he could of them without attracting notice. He himself, as Cicero's year of office was drawing to an end and the election day approached, took up the character of an aristocratic demagogue, and asked for the suffrages of the people as the champion of the poor against the rich, as the friend of the wretched and oppressed; and those who thought themselves wretched and oppressed in Rome were so large a body, and so bitterly hostile were they to all the prosperous classes, that his election was anticipated as a certainty. In the Senate the consulship of Catiline was regarded as no less than an impending national calamity. Marcus Cato, great-grandson of the Censor, then growing into fame by his acrid tongue and narrow republican fanaticism, who had sneered at Pompey's victories as triumphs over women, and had not spared Cicero himself, threatened Catiline in the *Curia*. Catiline answered, in a fully attended house, that if any agitation were kindled against him he would put it out not with water, but with revolution." [30]

Catiline was perfectly open with regard to his intentions. "The State, he said, had two bodies, one weak (the aristocracy), with a weak leader, (Cicero); the other, the great mass of the citizens—strong in themselves, but without a head, and he himself intended to be that head." [31]

When the consular elections eventually took place, the outcome was the return of the government candidates, Silanus and Murena. "Yet Catiline remained in Rome, frankly sustaining the thunders of the Consul, and offering himself for arrest when menaced with prosecution. Even when the war began in Etruria, and the old Centurion Manlius, at Faesulae, raised the standard of revolt and demanded relief for the oppressed debtors, there was no movement at Rome. That

29 Froude, *op. cit.*
30 *Ibid.* Cf. Mommsen.
31 Cicero (Marcus Tullius Cicero), *Pro Murena.*

Caesar and Crassus knew that trouble was brewing is certain, but it is improbable that Caesar shared in so shallow and ill-organized a venture"; [32] or that Crassus, the Croesus of the capital, proposed to cancel the many debts owed to him or burn down his own property. Cicero was fully informed of all that was transpiring between Catiline and his lieutenants, Lentulus and Cethegus, owing to the vainglorious confidences made to Fulvia, a woman of quality and a favorite of Roman society.

Her lover, Quintus Curius, who had been expelled from the Senate for many deeds of shame, but was thought fit to share in this plot of Catiline's, told his mistress in a vain and boastful way that he would soon be in a position of great power. By now, too, a rumor of what was transpiring in Italy was getting about. Accordingly, Cicero stationed guards at intervals throughout the city, and sent many of the nobility to the suspected places to watch what was going on. Catiline, since no one had ventured to lay hands on him, forwarded money to Faesulae, and directed his fellow-conspirators to kill Cicero and set the city on fire at a number of different places during the night. Then he departed to join Gaius Manlius, intending to collect additional forces and invade the city while burning. [33]

Forewarned by Curius's inconsequent babbling of the plot against his life, Cicero was easily enabled to foil the would-be assassins. It was at this juncture that the conspirators committed a blunder from which there was no recovery. "Ambassadors of the Allobroges, who were in Rome to make complaint against their magistrates, were solicited to join the conspiracy of Lentulus in order to cause an uprising against the Romans in Gaul. Lentulus sent in company with them, to Catiline, a man of Croton named Vulturcius, who carried letters without signatures. The Allobroges, being in doubt, communicated the matter to Fabius Sanga, the patron of their State; for it was the custom of all the subject States to have patrons at Rome. Sanga communicated the facts to Cicero, who arrested the Allobroges and Vulturcius on their journey and brought them straightway before the Senate. They confessed to their understanding with Lentulus's agents. . . . When they had testified, the Senate de-

32 How and Leigh, *op. cit.*
33 Appian, *op. cit.*

prived Lentulus of his office. Cicero put each of the conspirators under arrest at the houses of the Praetors, and returned
directly to take the vote of the Senate concerning them." [34]

Two of the arrested men had been given into the custody
of Caesar and Crassus, doubtless in order to compel them
either to act with the government or openly to proclaim
themselves on the side of the rebels. With the Senate in session, Cicero demanded what penalty should be meted out
to the apostates from their order, whose treason had been
so starkly demonstrated. The vote was for immediate execution, although Caesar entered a strong and eloquent plea
that to pass a death sentence without trial by legal process
was both immoral and unconstitutional. "You do not propose
to scourge these men," he said, "presumably because the law
forbids it; why, then, do you propose to put them to death?
Both penalties are equally illegal. You should remember also
the precedent your action will create. Once place such a
power as you claim in the hands of a government, and
you cannot put a limit to its use; it may, and will, be used
against good and bad alike." [35]

But the wrought-up, panicky Senate were not in a fit state
to perceive that no legislative assembly can override the
laws without risking the recoil of their lawlessness on their
own heads. Thus "Cato and Catulus carried it for death.
Cato, in a severe speech against the opinion of Caesar,
scrupled not to declare his suspicions of him; and this, with
other arguments, had so much weight, that the conspirators
were delivered to the executioner," [36] led away to the State
dungeon beneath the Capitol, and there strangled. For his
spirited appeal to reason and legality, Caesar was so out of
the favor of his colleagues that he barely escaped with his
life in returning from the Senate to his own house. "The
young Knights who had been present as a Senatorial guard,
rushed at him with their drawn swords. A few friends
protected him with their cloaks, and he left the precincts of
the *Curia*, not to enter it again for the rest of the year." [37]

In Rome, Cicero's brisk handling of the situation so cowed
the mob that it raised no protest when the Consul was hailed
as the savior of his country. But if the conspirators in the
capital had been ignominiously snuffed out,

[34] Appian, *op. cit.*

[35] The whole of Caesar's lengthy oration is given by Sallust in his
Catilina.

[36] Plutarch, *op. cit.*

[37] Froude, *op. cit.* Cf. Warde Fowler.

Catiline met a death more honorable. He had mustered to his standard a motley crew of 10,000 ill-equipped men, whose numbers sank rapidly when the news from Rome leaked out. At length he found himself near Pistoia, at the head of a poor 6,000 followers, cooped up between the armies of Q. Metellus Celer on his line of retreat to Gaul, and C. Antonius pressing on his rear. In a narrow mountain valley he turned at bay. Antonius had the grace to shirk the execution of his former allies, and gave up the command to his lieutenant, M. Petreius. A fierce struggle ensued; quarter was neither given nor taken. At last Petreius with his guard broke through the rebels' center and decided the battle. The rebels fell in their ranks as they had fought; and Catiline sought and found a soldier's death.[38]

Catiline had never been truly formidable, but the ignominious collapse of his badly bungled conspiracy played perfectly into Cicero's hands. In their fall, the anarchic extremists dragged down the moderate democrats, whom public opinion accused of complicity in the complot, and who, even if not actually guilty of the attempt, were regarded as being entirely sympathetic to it. Very cannily, Cicero resisted the temptation to implicate any of them—even Caesar—by false or true testimony. It was sufficient to have baffled them. The net result was to drive the propertied classes into the arms of the administration, and to discredit the party of reform by associating it with the rabble dedicated to red-handed revolution.

By mid-62 B.C. the last mutterings of insurrection were swamped by the news that at long last the all-conquering Pompey was on his way home. "In the East he had already received regal honors; in Italy all was prepared for the erection of a throne. The pitiful weakness of the Senate and the base intrigues of the democrats had fatally discredited the republican form of government. Men saw at last that they had to choose between monarchy and anarchy, and were ready to accept the great conqueror as the ruler of the world." [39]

Politically opportunist as it behooved him to be, Caesar was alert to trim his sails to the prevailing wind. "On

[38] How and Leigh, *op. cit.* Cf. Appian.
[39] How and Leigh, *op. cit.*

the first day of his praetorship (January 1, 62 B.C.), he proposed to transfer the rebuilding and dedication of the Capitoline temple from Catulus to Pompey, and by this stroke of policy at once set Pompey and the aristocrats at variance. To inscribe his name on Rome's proudest temple was just the kind of honor to delight the great soldier and bring him back to the side of his ancient allies." [40] Such was the general feeling, although it was in no wise shared by the Senate. "That they were unscrupulous in removing persons whom they disliked they had shown in a hundred instances, and Pompey naturally enough hesitated to trust himself among them without security. He requested the protection of office, and he had sent forward one of his most distinguished Officers, Metellus Nepos, to prepare the way and demand the consulship for him. Metellus, to strengthen his hands, had stood for tribuneship; and, in spite of the utmost efforts of the aristocracy, had been elected." [41]

On the same day that Caesar submitted his proposal with regard to the dedication of the temple,

Metellus Nepos, as Tribune, silenced Cicero when he wished to address the people on the glories of his consulship saying that he who had condemned citizens unheard should not himself have a hearing. Nepos was also supported by Caesar in pressing his bill appointing Pompey to a military command in Italy, on the excuse that it was necessary to quell the troubles consequent on the insurrection of Catiline. The measure was brought before the people, but vetoed by Cato, and after a scene of riot and disorder the Assembly broke up. The Senate replied by proclaiming martial law and suspending Caesar and Nepos from their offices. Both protested against this illegal step, Nepos taking refuge in his protector's camp, while Caesar retired to his own house until the Senate withdrew its interdict.[42]

It was not lost on the Senate, however, that Caesar had been escorted home by a boisterously applauding crowd; that, once his praetorial court had been closed down, "the mob refused to be comforted. They gathered day after day. They cried to Caesar to place himself at their head, that they might tear down the Senate-house and turn the caitiffs

40 How and Leigh, *op. cit.*
41 Froude, *op. cit.*
42 How and Leigh, *op. cit.*

into the street. Caesar neither then nor ever lent himself to popular excesses. He reminded the citizens that if others broke the law, they must themselves set an example by obeying it, and he bade them return to their homes." [43]

"Terrified at the state of the city, and penitent for their injustice to Caesar, the Senate hurriedly revoked their decree of deposition, sent a deputation to him to apologize, and invited him to resume his place among them. The extreme Patrician section remained irreconcilable. Caesar complied, but only to find himself denounced again with passionate pertinacity as having been an accomplice of Catiline. Witnesses were produced, who swore to having seen his signature to a treasonable bond. Curius, Cicero's spy, declared that Catiline himself had told him that Caesar was one of the conspirators. Caesar treated the charge with indignant disdain. He appealed to Cicero's conscience, and Cicero was obliged to say that he had derived his earliest and most important information from Caesar himself. The most violent of his accusers were placed under arrest. The informers, after a near escape from being massacred by the crowd, were thrown into prison, and for a moment the furious heats were able to cool." [44]

It was in such an atmosphere of emotional instability that the Senate and the people learned of Pompey's imminent appearance in Rome—with all that might portend.

With considerable acumen, Pompey had gone a very long way towards disarming criticism by speedily disbanding the army with which he had gained his triumphs in the East. At this immediate juncture, "he had no mind to found a military monarchy. He aimed at the position of universal reference, in power if not in office, the protector of the Roman Commonwealth. He wished to be the first citizen in a free State, and to find in the goodwill of the citizens, not the swords of the Legionaries, the foundations of his power." [45]

For the moment, however, there was the manner of his official return to the capital to be taken into careful consideration. "As the law did not permit him to enter the city before his 'triumph,' he desired the Senate to defer the election of Consuls on his account, that he might by his presence support the interest of Piso. But Cato opposed it, and the motion miscarried. Pompey, admiring the liberty and firmness with which Cato maintained the rights and customs of his

[43] How and Leigh, *op. cit.*
[44] Froude, *op. cit.* Cf. Plutarch and Appian.
[45] How and Leigh, *op. cit.*

country, at a time when no other man would appear so openly for them, determined to gain him if possible; and as Cato
had two nieces, he offered to marry the one,[46] and asked
the other for his son. Cato, however, suspected the bait, and
looked upon the proposed alliance as a means intended to
corrupt his integrity. He therefore refused it." [47]

The maneuver had certainly lacked subtlety, and Pompey's support of the candidature of his other protégé, Afranius, for the consulship was even cruder. "He distributed
money for that purpose among the Tribes, and the voters
went to receive it in Pompey's own gardens. The thing was
so public that Pompey was much censured for making that
office venal which he had obtained by his great actions, and
opening a way to the highest honor in the State to those who
had money but wanted merit." [48]

Caesar, meanwhile, had been embroiled in a domestic
scandal at once painful and embarrassing. A prominent member of the more dissolute element in Roman society was a
certain Clodius, who had served with Lucullus in Asia and
had been largely responsible for fostering the mutiny which
had reduced that commander to impotence.

> Connected by blood and marriage with the proudest
> members of the aristocracy, he had graduated even
> while a boy in every form of vice, natural and unnatural.
> He was bold, clever, unprincipled, and unscrupulous,
> with a slender diminutive figure and a delicate woman's
> face. . . . Between this promising young man and Cae-
> sar's wife Pompeia there had sprung up an acquaintance,
> which Clodius was anxious to press to further extremes.
> Pompeia was difficult of access, her mother-in-law Aure-
> lia keeping a strict watch over her; and Clodius, who was
> afraid of nothing, took advantage of the *Bona Dea* [49]
> festival to make his way into Caesar's house dressed as
> a woman. Unfortunately for him, his disguise was de-
> tected. The insulted Vestals and other ladies who were
> present flew upon him like the dogs of Actaeon, tore his
> borrowed garments from him, and drove him into the
> street naked and wounded. The adventure became known.
> It was mentioned in the Senate, and the College of

[46] Pompey had divorced his first wife, Antistia, to marry Aemilia,
daughter-in-law of Sulla, who died in childbed.

[47] Plutarch, *op. cit.*

[48] *Ibid.*

[49] A religious festival to which women only were admitted.

Priests was ordered to hold an inquiry. The College found that Clodius had committed sacrilege, and the regular course in such cases was to send the offender to trial. There was general unwillingness, however, to treat the matter seriously. Clodius had many friends in the Senate, and even Cicero, who was inclined at first to be severe, took on reflection a more lenient view. Clodius had a sister, a light lady who, weary of her conquests over her fashionable admirers, had tried her fascinations on the great orator. He had escaped complete subjugation, but he had been flattered by the attentions of the seductive beauty, and was ready to help her brother out of his difficulty. Clodius was not yet the dangerous desperado he afterwards became; and Caesar himself did not press for punishment. As President of the College, he had acquiesced in their decision; and he had divorced the unfortunate Pompeia. But he expressed no opinion as to the extent of her criminality, and gave as his reason for separating from her, not that she was guilty, but that Caesar's wife must be above suspicion.[50]

Clodius was put on trial, not for an affront to Caesar's honor, but for having technically committed sacrilege.

In the circumstances, Caesar can have been nothing but relieved at the prospect of turning his back on Rome for a while to proceed to Further Spain, where, following the expiration of his praetorship, he had been appointed Governor. "But his circumstances were so indifferent and his creditors so clamorous and troublesome when he was preparing for his departure, that he was forced to apply to Crassus, the richest man in Rome, who stood in need of Caesar's warmth and vigor to keep up the balance against Pompey. Crassus, therefore, took upon him to answer the most inexorable of his creditors, and engaged for eight hundred and thirty talents; which procured him liberty to set out for his province." [51]

Pompey's official "triumph" was something of which Rome spoke with bated breath for many a long day after it was all over. Indeed,

the "triumph" was so great, that though it was divided

[50] Froude, *op. cit.* Cf. Appian and Plutarch.
[51] Plutarch, *op. cit.*

into two days, the time was far from being sufficient for displaying what was prepared to be carried in procession; there remained still enough to adorn another "triumph." At the head of the show appeared the titles of the conquered nations: Pontus, Armenia, Cappadocia, Paphlagonia, Media, Colchis, the Iberians, the Albanians, Syria, Cilicia, Mesopotamia, Phoenicia, Palestine, Judea, Arabia; the pirates subdued both by sea and land. In these countries, it was mentioned that there were not less than a thousand castles, and near nine hundred cities taken; eight hundred galleys taken from the pirates, and thirty-nine desolate cities repopulated. On the face of the tablets it appeared besides, that whereas the revenues of the Roman empire before these conquests amounted but to fifty millions of drachmas, by the new acquisitions they had advanced to eighty-five millions. . . . But the most honorable circumstance, and what no other Roman could boast, was that his third triumph was over the third quarter of the world, after his former triumphs had been over the other two; for his first triumph had been over Africa, his second over Europe, and his third over Asia; so that the three seemed to declare him conqueror of the world.[52]

Yet beneath all the smooth smiles and orotund words of praise, there was no dearth of envy and distrust. When the conqueror had once more set foot on Italian soil, many had expected "to see all parties annihilated and Rome at the mercy of a dictator. But no sooner had he landed than Pompey had dismissed the veteran Legions, renounced all idea of a military monarchy, and proceeded slowly to Rome only to claim his 'triumph.' . . . This act of renunciation was a marvel rather of stupidity than of self-denial," [53] and extremely puzzling as well. But in politics nothing arouses more uneasy suspicion than the inexplicable.

Every Praetor, when his year of office was over, became a Propraetor and the Governor of a province. The province which fell to Caesar's lot was the same as that in which he had served as Quaestor—Further Spain. There were more enticing governorships to be had, and nearer home. But so long as Pompey's intentions were in doubt, Caesar regarded it as more prudent, for the moment, "to follow in Sertorius's footsteps, and make once more of this distant terri-

52 Plutarch, *op. cit.*
53 Warde Fowler, *op. cit.*

tory a civilized Roman home for the oppressed democracy. When Pompey's impending absolutism was renounced, such a plan was no longer necessary; it was, in fact, rather inconvenient than otherwise to have to go so far from home at a time when the utmost vigilance was necessary to prevent Pompey from falling under the influence of the Senatorial party and Cicero." [54] But Caesar was committed, and there was no drawing back.

It was not, however, until the late spring of 61 B.C. that the new Propraetor took up his governorship, even then turning his back on Rome before the conclusion of the profligate Clodius's trial.

Portugal [Lusitania] and Galicia were still unsubdued. Bands of robbers lay everywhere in the fastnesses of the mountain ranges. Caesar was already favorably known in Spain for his service as Quaestor. He now completed the conquest of the Peninsula. He put down the *banditti*. He reorganized the administration with the rapid skill which always so remarkably distinguished him. He sent home large sums of money to the treasury. His work was done quickly, but it was done completely. He nowhere left an unsound spot unprobed. He never contented himself with the superficial healing of a wound which would break out again when he was gone. What he began he finished, and left it in need of no further surgery.[55]

Spain also afforded Caesar his first taste of independent military command, and on a comprehensive scale.

Having added ten new Cohorts to the twenty he received there, he marched against the Callaecians and Lusitanians, defeated them and penetrated to the ocean, reducing nations by the way that had not felt the Roman yoke. His conduct in peace was not inferior to that in war. He restored harmony among the cities, and removed the occasions of quarrel between debtors and creditors; for he ordered that the creditor should have two-thirds of the debtor's income, and the debtor the remaining third, till the whole was paid. By these means he was to leave the province with great reputation, though he filled his own coffers, and enriched his soldiers with

54 Warde Fowler, *op. cit.*
55 Froude, *op. cit.*

booty, who, upon one of his victories, saluted him *Imperator*.[56]

Yet no one realized more clearly than the practical hard-headed Caesar that the bestowal of the title was altogether premature. Brooding over a life of Alexander the Great which formed his favorite reading, "he was so much affected with it, that he sat pensive a long time, and at last burst out into tears. As his friends were wondering what might be the reason, he said, 'Do you think I have not sufficient cause for concern, when Alexander at my age reigned over so many conquered countries, and I have not one glorious achievement to boast?' " [57]

But events were in the making in Rome which were very materially to affect Caesar's future. To begin with, the outcome of the trial of Clodius had been nothing short of a public scandal. "Though his defense—an alibi—had broken down through the evidence of Cicero, profuse bribery had secured an acquittal from the jury. The course and result of the trial had demonstrated the weakness of the aristocratic party, sowed the seeds of disunion between the Senate and the Knights, and intensified the hatred of Clodius for Cicero." [58] As Cicero himself wrote despairingly to his friend and confidante Atticus, "Thirty Romans have been found to trample justice underfoot for a bribe, and to declare an act not to have been committed, about which not only not a man, but not a beast in the field, can entertain the smallest doubt." [59]

For his part Clodius was busy reviving the charge that Cicero had done away with the Catiline conspirators without legal trial. On the other hand, "instigated by Pompey's opponents, the Senate had refused to ratify *en bloc* his arrangements in the East; it failed to furnish his veterans with the lands promised them by their General; it discouraged his expectations of a second consulship. This folly it crowned by provoking a rupture of the Knights. Following the honest but stupid guidance of Cato, it refused to revise, in the interest of the tax-gatherers, the contracts for the taxes of Asia.[60] At the same time it attempted to make Knights as well as Senators amenable to penalties for judicial corrup-

56 Plutarch, *op. cit.*

57 *Ibid.*

58 Appian, *op. cit.* Cf. Plutarch, Froude.

59 Cicero, *op. cit.*

60 Where the taxes were farmed.

tion. The union of the orders, on which Cicero rested his policy, had vanished like a dream." [61]

It was to this scene of tangled interests, vindictive cross-purposes, and personal vendetta, that Caesar returned in the late spring of 60 B.C., arriving in Rome before the consular elections for that year; for it was his intention to present himself as a candidate.

But he claimed a "triumph," and therefore applied to the Senate for leave to sue for the consulship without appearing personally in the city. The Senate was disposed to grant this request, but Cato adjourned the question by speaking against time; and Caesar, who scorned the appearance in comparison with the reality of power, relinquished his "triumph" and entered the city. As he had reason to expect, he found Pompey in high dudgeon, and entered into secret negotiations with him; and, to strengthen their hands still further, Caesar proposed to include Crassus in their political union. The advances made by Crassus to Cicero and to the Senate had been ill-received, and he lent a ready ear to the overtures of the dexterous negotiator who now addressed him. Pompey, at the instance of Caesar, relinquished the old enmity which he bore to Crassus; and thus was formed that famous cabal which is commonly, though improperly,[62] called the First Triumvirate.

Thus supported secretly by the power of Pompey and the wealth of Crassus, Caesar was elected to the consulship by acclamation. But the Senatorial chiefs exhausted every art of intrigue and bribery to secure the return of M. Calpurnius Bibulus, known to be a man of unflinching resolution, as his colleague. He was son-in-law to Cato, who to obtain a political advantage did not hesitate to sanction the corrupt practices which on other occasions he loudly denounced. Bibulus was elected; and from the antagonism of the two Consuls, the approaching year loomed big with danger.[63]

And not only the immediate twelvemonth, but the future for well over a decade—"for it was not the disagreement be-

[61] How and Leigh, *op. cit.*

[62] Improperly, because it was a *secret* combination, not an open assumption of power, such as the Romans understood by the word *Triumvirate.*

[63] Liddell, *op. cit.*

tween Caesar and Pompey that produced the civil wars, but rather their union; they first combined to ruin the authority of the Senate, and when that had been effected, they parted to pursue each his own designs." [64] Fortunately for the future destiny of Rome, it was Caesar's "designs" that ultimately prevailed.

CHAPTER X

THE CRUCIBLE OF POWER

"Man's desires are more complex than any pattern he can invent to lend them form and dignity."

—Osbert Burdett

Caesar had been chosen Consul without overt opposition. "His party was so powerful that it seemed at one time as if he could name his colleague, but the Senate succeeded with desperate efforts in securing the second place. They subscribed money profusely, the immaculate Cato prominent among them. The machinery of corruption was well in order. The great nobles commanded the votes of their clients, and they succeeded in giving Caesar the same companion who had accompanied him through the aedileship and the praetorship, Marcus Bibulus, a dull, obstinate fool, who could be relied on, if for nothing else, for dogged resistance to every step which the Senate disapproved." [1]

Immediately following the election of the Consuls, it was customary to determine the provinces to which they would be appointed when the consular term of office should have expired. The decision lay with the Senate, and either in petty spite or to ensure that no armed force should come under his command, they sought to fob off Caesar with the Department of Lands and Forests! [2]

[64] Plutarch, op. cit.
[1] Froude, op. cit.
[2] Silvae callesque.

Patrician by birth though he might be, as he was the nephew of Marius and the erstwhile son-in-law of Cinna, it was inevitable that the members of the old oligarchy should hold him in disapprobation and distrust, as one who had reneged on his own class to curry popular favor. Had they only possessed the wit to realize it, "the consulship of Caesar was the last chance for the Roman aristocracy. He was not a revolutionist. Revolutions are the last desperate remedy when all else has failed. They may create as many evils as they cure; and wise men always hate them. But if revolution were to be escaped, reform was inevitable, and it was for the Senate to choose between the alternatives. Could the noble lords have remembered that, as the rulers of the civilized world, they had duties which the eternal order of nature would exact from their hands, the shaken constitution might have regained its stability, and the forms and even the reality of the Republic might have continued for another century. It was not to be." [3] The ailing body-politic had declined so desperately that only Caesar's rough surgery could avail to cure its wasting sickness.

In the task he had set himself, the army and the moneyed interests, as represented by Pompey and Crassus, were already with him. If his attempt to win over Cicero and the landed aristocracy he represented was less successful, the orator's sulky withdrawal to his country estate at least spared the Senate the interminable drone of his relentless speechifying. As far as that assembly was concerned, there was far less excuse than heretofore to employ words as a substitute for thought; particularly since, by Caesar's order, proceedings in the Chamber were punctually reported in the *Acta Diurna,* a factual daily journal that served as a healthy corrective to rumor's more irresponsible flights of fancy.

Caesar's first major reform consisted of an Agrarian law for which he had been careful to secure Cicero's support.

Had he meant to be defiant, like the Gracci, he might have offered it at once to the people. Instead of doing so, he laid it before the Senate, inviting them to amend his suggestions, and promising any reasonable concessions if they would cooperate. No wrong was to be done to any existing occupiers. No right of property was to be violated which was any real right at all. Large tracts in Campania which belonged to the State were currently held on the usual easy terms by great landed proprie-

[3] Froude, *op. cit.*

tors. These Caesar proposed to buy out, and settle on the ground twenty thousand of Pompey's veterans. There was money enough and to spare in the treasury, which they had themselves brought home. Out of the large funds which would still remain, land might be purchased in other parts of Italy for the rest, and for a few thousand of the unemployed population which was crowded into Rome.[4]

Not only did the measure keep Pompey in good countenance by implementing the pledge he had given to his veterans, but it was in itself both equitable and moderate. But the very name of an Agrarian law stank in the nostrils of the plutocratic property-owners. "The public lands they had shared conveniently among themselves from immemorial time. The public treasure was their treasure, to be laid out as they might think proper. The bill meant in the end the spoilation and division of property, and the first step would bring others after it."[5] Opposition to the measure was immediate and violent, with Cato storming on and on for an entire day.

Entirely unmoved by harangues that did little more than bear witness to the validity of the searching comment, "Where politics are concerned, take eloquence and wring its neck,"[6] Caesar went on to confirm Pompey's arrangements in Asia and to remit a third of the sum payable by the aggrieved taxpayers. It was his hope that the sheer reasonableness of his proposals would be apparent enough to avert recourse to extremities.

Only when the Senate refused even to discuss the measures laid before it, and took refuge in simple negation or barefaced obstruction, did Caesar fall back on a direct appeal to the people. Such an appeal was perfectly legal; but the inconvenience of bringing complicated measures before the Assembly, where discussion and amendment were alike impossible, might well make a statesman pause. Yet Caesar had no alternative, and he was not the man to turn back when once he had put his hand to the plow. In vain did a Tribune interpose his veto; in vain did Bibulus attempt to interfere with the actions of his colleague. He was driven from the Forum by Pompey's veterans, and shut himself up in his house

4 Froude, *op. cit.*
5 *Ibid.*
6 Jean Arthur Rimbaud.

for eight months; his absence from affairs scarcely noticed by the man in the street, who would cheerfully remark that Rome still had two Consuls—"Julius" and "Caesar"! Caesar went on his way entirely unmoved. He added to his original Agrarian law a proposal for the foundation of a settlement at Capua, which would have the effect of removing the disabilities imposed upon it for its disloyalty during the Hannibalic War, and restoring it to the status of a *colonia,* with its own municipal rights. An appended clause compelled all Senators and candidates for office to swear to treat its provisions as valid and so secured it for a time from attack in the Senate.[7]

Doubtless Crassus accorded the new legislation his approval on the score that his money-spinner's resourcefulness perceived sufficient loopholes in it for him to turn it to profitable account. Pompey approved it virtually without reservation, since it removed from the capital a large number of disgruntled veterans who had been hanging idly about its streets for the best part of two years, and in so doing relieved the drain on subsidized corn.

Pompey's association with the Consul soon assumed even greater intimacy. "Caesar's daughter Julia was betrothed to Servilius Caepio, but, notwithstanding that engagement, he gave her to Pompey; and told Servilius he should have Pompey's daughter, whose hand was not properly at liberty, for she was promised to Faustus the son of Sulla. Soon after this Caesar married Calpurnia, the daughter of Piso, and procured the consulship for Piso for the year ensuing."[8] Cato immediately "exclaimed loudly against these proceedings, and called both gods and men to witness how unsupportable it was, that the first dignities of the State should be prostituted by marriages, and that this traffic of women should gain them what governments and forces they pleased."[9]

Cato's self-righteous diatribes were easily ignored by a man as busily employed as Caesar, who was hard at work promoting his much-needed law against official extortion in the provinces. For "extortion had become a habit and almost a necessity with the Governors of Provinces;[10] they spent

---

[7] How and Leigh, *op. cit.*

[8] Plutarch, *op. cit.*

[9] *Ibid.*

[10] A standing commission had been at work since 149 B.C. on the examination of offenses that came under the heading of extortion, but with singularly scant result.

so much on bribery in their efforts to rise to high office that they looked on their propraetorship or proconsulship as a perfectly fair chance of recouping themselves. The two great evils of the day worked together—corruption at home, and cruelty in the provinces; and there was a continual drain on the exhausted provincials to supply the exorbitant demands of the greedy Roman voter. And it was not only the Governor himself who was guilty; with him went a numerous staff, all eager to be let loose on the province." [11]

Doggedly Caesar pushed through legislation which imposed a drastic check on all the abuses hitherto so widely practiced: illegal taxes and tolls, the sale of privileges, the acceptance of anything but the most modest of gifts, the employment of Roman soldiery—for a "consideration"—to help in the recovery of debts. The Governor and the whole of his entourage were to be held accountable; and the penalties to be meted out to those found guilty were exemplary—expulsion from the Senate and restitution to the tune of four times the amount extorted being among the mildest of them. On the other hand Caesar was not above employing somewhat guileful methods for raising money for his own and his associates' purposes. For two-and-twenty years Rome had hesitated whether or not to assert her claims under the will of Alexander and annex Egypt. The *Triumvirs* now agreed to accept a "tribute" of six thousand talents in return for recognizing Ptolemy Auletes as Egypt's legitimate Monarch.

A whole corpus of other enactments went to make up the *Leges Juliae*; there was a law affirming the inviolability of magistrates during their term of office; [12] laws for the protection of the subjects from violence, public or private; a law to deal with judges who accepted bribes; laws against defrauders of the revenue, debasers of coin, against corrupt State contracts, against bribery at elections. There was even a law for the punishment of adultery, a singularly disinterested piece of legislation if popular accounts of Caesar's own habits had in them as much truth as malice.

Swiftly the months went by, and it became highly necessary to plan the steps to be taken when Caesar's twelvemonth of consular office should have run its course. The three leaders were fully aware that it was essential to secure their position for some years ahead. Should the Senatorial party come again into power, their legislation would at once be declared

11 Warde Fowler, *op. cit.*

12 A law obviously reflecting back on the murder of Saturninus, and referring by implication to the killing of Lentulus.

null and void; Caesar himself would be open to attack in the law courts;

> the Legions and the provinces would be given to Senatorial incapables; and by abundant bribery, the city population might be persuaded to restore the Sullan constitution. In fact, the battle was by no means at an end, although for the moment the Senate was beaten all along the line.

It was necessary in the first place to put Caesar not only out of danger, but in a position whence he could continue to watch over Italy and Rome, and give his weaker allies both moral and material support. In the previous year, the Senate, using a constitutional right secured to them by Gaius Graccus himself, had set apart for both Consuls of 59 B.C., as soon as their year of office should expire, the duty of attending to the internal condition of Italy; and if this arrangement held good, Caesar's "province" as Proconsul would have meant no more than the supervision of roads, forests and public works, without Legions, without freedom, and without adventure.[13]

This prospect was not to be entertained. So "the Tribune Vatinius, his creature, proposed a law by which Caesar was specially invested, as Proconsul, with the government of Cisalpine Gaul and Illyricum; and this government was conferred on him for the extraordinary term of five years. No doubt his purpose in obtaining this province was to remain as near Rome as possible, and by means of the troops under his orders to assume a commanding position with regard to Roman politics. Circumstances unexpectedly enlarged his sphere of action, and enabled him to add to his political successes the character of a triumphant General." [14]

But before Caesar could hand over the home government to Pompey and take his departure for Gaul, Cicero and Cato, the chief opponents of the coalition, had to be rendered harmless. As the first-named could not be cajoled into abandoning his hostile attitude, other means had to be found to dispose of him; and in the circumstances the Triumvirate could not afford to be too nice in their choice of instrument to bring about the orator's undoing.

The ineffable Clodius "had never forgiven Cicero for bearing witness against him, and was now able to gratify his malice. With the support of Caesar and the connivance of

---

13 Warde Fowler, *op. cit.*
14 Liddell, *op. cit.*

Pompey, he had gone through the form of adoption into a Plebeian family, and subsequently secured his election to the tribunate," wherein he speedily finessed and bribed his way to a position of considerable authority.

In his proceedings against Cicero, Clodius proposed in the Tribal Assembly a measure in general terms interdicting fire and water to any man who had put a citizen to death without trial before the people. The bill was obviously aimed at the Consul who had, on the advice of the Senate, executed the accomplices of Catiline. Cicero and his friends went into mourning, and appealed to the compassion of the people. The Senators and Knights showed their sympathy for the unfortunate orator, who had, so unwisely, fixed the cap on his own head. But Clodius had at his back the mob of the Forum, and boasted that he was but the agent of the *Triumvirs*. Cicero was not prepared to fight a pitched battle, and after a last piteous appeal to Pompey, he left Rome in a panic. On the very day of his departure, Clodius's measure was carried, and by a later resolution declared to apply to Cicero, whose flight was treated as a confession of guilt.[15]

The *Triumvirs* made use of the same serviceable tool in dealing with Cato. Nominated by Clodius to proceed to Cyprus, depose the reigning Ptolemy—whose title had not been recognized by the *Triumvirs*—and secure the royal treasure, Cato took counsel of his warrantable fears and discreetly accepted the commission, thankful that no greater penance had been imposed upon him. The last champions of the old disorderly, wrangling, faction-ridden mode of conducting the nation's business having been disposed of, Caesar could turn from the complexities of domestic politics to the onerous task that awaited him in Gaul.

For some time past there had been threatening movements in Transalpine Gaul. The Allobrogians, who had been treated with little consideration after the Catilinarian conspiracy, had endeavored to redress their grievances by a resort to arms, and had been subdued by Pomptinus, one of the Praetors employed by Cicero at the Mulvian Bridge. German tribes were threatening inroads which revived the memory

---

[15] How and Leigh, *op. cit.* Cf. Mommsen.

of the Cimbric and Teutonic times; and the Helvetians were moving uneasily within their narrow borders." [16] An able and active commander was sorely needed to deal with these various dangers, and there were not wanting members of the Senate to nurture the private hope that by removing Caesar to a distant, perilous, and uncertain war they might expose him to the risk of failure and the consequent diminishment of his prestige. They therefore added the Province of Narbo [17] to his other commitment, with a fourth Legion to supplement the three properly under his command.

Caesar found his first antagonists in the Helvetii, who were on the move, like some huge tidal wave, to seek new habitations for themselves in more rewarding territory. Central Gaul was their objective, and to avoid passing over the Jura they headed for Geneva, with the purpose of crossing the Rhône at that point and forcing their way through the Roman province of Transalpine Gaul. A hardy, resolute race of mountaineers and herdsmen, so determined were they to establish themselves in "fresh woods and pastures new," that in order that "they might not make a grant of their abandoned huts to the Germans and might render their own return impossible, they had burnt their towns and villages; and their long train of wagons, laden with women, children, and the best part of their movables, arrived at all sides of the Leman lake, where they had fixed their rendezvous." [18] With twelve of their townships and four hundred villages reduced to ashes, there was no turning back for the 300,000 members of the tribes, of whom some 90,000 were warriors, headed by the warlike Tigurini clan. Clearly, if this predatory horde were permitted to migrate as it intended, the repercussions among the Gallic people on the Roman frontier might well set the whole of the borderlands afire. For Rome was distinctly out of favor with the two Gaulish tribes of the Aedui and the Sequani, whom the Senate had entirely failed to support in their efforts to check the incursions of the German chieftain Ariovistus and his swarming Suebi. It was possible, therefore, that the two Gaulish communities would make no effort to repel the Helvetii, with the result that the country vacated by them would be immediately occupied by the Suebi, who would thereby be brought into immediate contact with the Roman frontier at Geneva. The Helvetii must be turned back, to serve

16 Liddell, *op. cit.*

17 Or Narbonensis, west of the Rhône, with Narbo and Massilia as its principal ports.

18 Mommsen, *op. cit.*

as a buffer beween the Transalpine province and the German barbarians.

To confront this formidable host of fighting men Caesar had under his command his four Legions—7th, 8th, 9th, and 10th—brought up to their full strength of 24,000, with a few cavalry and lightly-armed auxiliaries, such as Spanish Horse, Numidian and Cretan archers, and Balearic slingers. Among the Generalissimo's principal lieutenants were some exceptionally promising officers, men such as Publius Crassus, the younger son of Caesar's old political ally, and Titus Labienus, as courageous as he was personally devoted. In addition, a number of fashionable young men had deserted the attractions of Rome to serve as *optios*, or Staff "learners." "But of Caesar's four Legions three were stationed at Aquileia; and although he called out in haste the militia of the Transalpine province, it seemed scarcely possible with so small a force to hinder the innumerable enemy host from crossing the Rhône, between its exit from the Leman lake at Geneva and the point of its breaking through the mountains, over a distance of more than fourteen miles." [19]

Marching swiftly, Caesar arrived at Geneva and immediately ordered the river bridge to be broken down. Certain negotiations, opened by the Helvetii on the pretext that all they sought was a peaceful passage through the province, served usefully to delay matters until all the Legions had been concentrated. In the interim, "with the Legion which he had with him and the soldiers who had assembled from the province, he carried along for nineteen [Roman] miles [20] a wall, to a height of sixteen feet, and a trench, from the lake of Geneva, which flows into the river Rhône, to Mount Jura, which separates the territories of the Sequani from those of the Helvetii. When that work was finished, he distributed garrisons and closely fortified redoubts, in order that he might more easily intercept them, if they should attempt to cross over against his will." [21] With all his troops finally mustered, Caesar was in a position to return a curt refusal to the petition for leave to pass through the province, whereupon it became plainly evident that the Helvetii had every intention of forcing a passage by a resort to arms.

Leaving Labienus to guard the fortified works, Caesar marched at the head of three Legions to attack the Tigurini

[19] Mommsen, *op. cit.*

[20] Not quite eighteen miles.

[21] Julius Caesar, *The Commentaries* (*The War in Gaul*).

in their passage over the Arar.[22] Routing them, he was in turn suddenly assailed by the main body of the tribe, while on the march to Bibracte [23] in search of supplies of which he was running dangerously short.

He gained, however, a strong post for his troops, notwithstanding the surprise; and when he had drawn them up, his horse was brought him. Upon which he said, "when I have won the battle I shall want my horse for the pursuit; at present let us march as we are against the enemy." He sent back his horse, and the rest followed his example. This was to prevent all hopes of a retreat as well as to show his troops that he would take his share of all the danger. He then charged with great vigor on foot.

It cost him a long and severe conflict to drive their army out of the field; but he found the greatest difficulty when he came to their rampart of tumbrels; for not only the men made the most obstinate stand there, but the very women and children fought till they were cut to pieces; insomuch that the battle did not end before midnight.

To this great action he added a still greater. He collected the barbarians who had escaped out of the battle, to the number of a hundred thousand and upwards, and obliged them to resettle in the country they had relinquished, and to rebuild the cities they had burned. This he did in fear that if the country were left without inhabitants, the Germanii would pass the Rhine and seize it.[24]

The Helvetii having been faithfully dealt with, Caesar was free to turn his attention to his major task—the unification and defense of Gaul. The three Gallic tribes encompassing the Roman frontier were the Arverni, beyond the Cevennes to the northwest, who had once been the most powerful tribe in the land; the Aedui to the north, on the west bank of the Saône; and the Sequani in the rich plains between the Rhône and the Saône.[25]

[22] Saône.
[23] Autun.
[24] Plutarch, *op. cit.*
[25] A territory subsequently known as Burgundy.

The Arverni had been in conflict with Rome, and had been partially subdued; with the Sequani the Romans had had no direct dealings of importance. But the Aedui, as lying between these two formidable peoples, and because they could be successfully played off against the beaten but dangerous Arverni, had been taken into close alliance and "friendship," and, backed by Roman influence, had attained a power beyond their natural strength, and claimed now to be the leading State in Gaul.

The result was just what might have been expected. The Arverni, ever jealous of the Aedui, allied with the Sequani to crush them, and called in the aid of the Suebi, which, under Ariovistus, had already crossed the Rhine, and was seeking a settlement to the southward. If the Roman government had been as energetic as the German chief, they would have succored their clients the Aedui, and either declared war on Ariovistus, or at least strengthened their own defenses in that direction. As it was, they left their allies in the lurch, the Aedui were conquered, and the province was practically open to invasion at any moment by a combination of Gauls and Germans.[26]

As it transpired, however, the Sequani elected to appeal to Rome for help in expelling Ariovistus from their territory, from which he defiantly refused to remove himself. To insure against any hostile combination between his unwilling hosts and the Aedui, the Suebian chieftain had taken a number of children of the latter tribe and held them as hostages.

Ariovistus was obviously the next object of Caesar's attention.

He found, however, his officers, particularly those of the young nobility, afraid of this expedition; for they had entered into Caesar's service only in the hopes of living luxuriously and making their fortunes. He therefore called them together, and told them, before the whole army, that they were at liberty to retire, and need not hazard their persons against their inclination, since they were so unmanly and spiritless. For his part, he would march with the Tenth Legion only against these barbarians; for they were neither better men than the Cimbrians, nor was he a worse General than Marius. Upon this some of the Tenth Legion deputed some of their

26 Warde Fowler, *op. cit.*

corps to thank him. The other Legions laid the whole blame upon their officers, and all followed him with great spirit and alacrity.[27]

It was a perfect example of the subtle manner in which Caesar went to work to ensure the devotion of the troops to himself as an individual, rather than to the State, in whose service all of them, from latest-joined recruit to the Generalissimo himself, were ostensibly under arms.

Caesar's opening gambit, a ritual concession to the demands of protocol, was to send an embassy to Ariovistus, to demand "first, that he do not any more bring any body of men across the Rhine into Gaul; in the next place, that he restore the hostages which he had from the Aedui . . . and that he neither provoke the Aedui by outrage, nor make war upon them or their allies." [28]

To this Ariovistus returned the somewhat searching rejoinder that "the right of war was, that they who had conquered should govern those whom they had conquered, in what manner they pleased; that in that way the Roman people were wont to govern the nations which they had conquered, not according to the dictation of any other, but according to their own discretion!" [29]

With this uncompromising home thrust, it was clear that the time had arrived for words to give place to deeds, a resolve in no way weakened by a personal meeting and abrasive exchange of views between Caesar and his self-confident opponent. The atmosphere was scarcely sweetened by the Suebian chieftain's revelation that "certain members of the Roman aristocracy had sent him messages to say that if he killed Caesar they would hold it a good service done, and would hold him their friend forever." [30] The rencontre ended on a note of attempted treachery, when some of the Suebian horsemen stole round to where the Roman escort was drawn up "and supposing they had Gauls to deal with, sought to surround and disarm them. The men of the Tenth Legion stood firm; Caesar fell back and joined them, and, contenting themselves with simply driving off the enemy, they rode back to the camp." [31]

The Roman troops were all eagerness to get at their op-

[27] Plutarch, *op. cit.*

[28] Caesar, *op. cit.*

[29] *Ibid.*

[30] Froude, *op. cit.*

[31] *Ibid.*

ponents, but Ariovistus rather unaccountably struck camp and marched off six miles distant from Caesar's cantonments. The day following, a flank march screened by thick forests brought the Suebians to a point two miles south of the Romans, in a position to cut Caesar's line of communications with his supply base. For five days further, activities were confined to skirmishes between rival groups of scouts and foragers.

Unable to provoke Ariovistus into sallying out from his fortified camp to offer battle, Caesar drew up the six Legions, now under command, into three parallel columns, ready to form the line of battle, and marched to reopen the route along which his convoys were wont to travel. Yet it was not until the third day following that Ariovistus accepted the challenge, his men drawing up their wains and tumbrels in laager formation as a refuge for their womenfolk and children.

Caesar himself began the battle at the head of the right wing, because he had observed that part of the enemy to be the least strong. Accordingly our men, upon the signal being given, vigorously made an attack upon the enemy, and the enemy so suddenly and rapidly rushed forward, that there was no time for the casting of javelins at them. Throwing aside, therefore, their javelins, they fought with swords hand to hand. But the Germans, according to their custom, rapidly forming a phalanx, sustained the attack of the swordsmen. There were found very many of the Roman soldiers who leaped upon the phalanx, and with their hands tore away the shields, and wounded the enemy from above. Although the army of the enemy was routed on the left wing and put to flight, they still pressed heavily on the men from the ring wing, by the great number of their troops. On observing which, P. Crassus, a young man who commanded the cavalry —as he was more disengaged than those who were engaged closer in the fight—sent the third line to the relief of the men who were in distress.

Thereupon the engagement was renewed, and all the enemy turned their backs, nor did they cease to flee until they arrived at the river Rhine, about fifty miles from that place. There some few, either relying on their strength, endeavored to swim over, or, finding boats, procured their safety. Among the latter was Ariovistus, who meeting with a small vessel tied to the bank, escaped in it: our Horse pursued and slew all the rest of them.[32]

Both of Ariovistus's wives perished in the general slaughter, as did one of his daughters, the other being taken captive. An eminent Roman prisoner of the Suebians, C. Valerius Procillus,[33] "as he was being dragged by his guards in flight, bound with a triple chain, fell into the hands of Caesar himself, as he was pursuing the enemy with his cavalry. . . . Caesar, having concluded two very important wars in one campaign, conducted his army into winter quarters among the Sequani, a little earlier than the season of the year required. He appointed Labienus over the winter quarters, and set out in person for Hither Gaul to hold the assizes." [34] This he did in order to keep a close eye on whatever might be transpiring in Rome, for only the river Rubicon—momentous stream!—"parts the rest of Italy from Cisalpine Gaul. During his stay there [35] he carried on a variety of State intrigues. Great numbers came from Rome to pay their respects to him, and he sent them all away satisfied; some laden with presents, others happy in hope. In the same manner in all his wars, without Pompey observing it, he was conquering his enemies by the arms of Roman citizens, and gaining the citizens by the money of his enemies." [36]

News of Caesar's military successes, and the continued presence of his troops in the country of the Sequani, "aroused the jealousy of the Belgic tribes to the north of the Seine, and a powerful confederacy was formed to bar any designs entertained by Caesar for extending the dominion of Rome in Gaul. Caesar did not wait to be attacked. He raised two new Legions without waiting for the authority of the Senate, and early in the next year (57 B.C.) entered the Belgic territory, which was bounded southward by the Seine and Marne."[37] His line of communications was safeguarded to a certain extent by the fact that the Remi, situated about Rheims, had resolved to adopt the Roman side, as had the Aedui in the south.

[32] Caesar, *op. cit.*

[33] He was a Romanized Gaul who had carried Caesar's last message to Ariovistus.

[34] Caesar, *op. cit.*

[35] At Luca.

[36] Plutarch, *op. cit.*

[37] *Ibid.*

Credible reports that came into Caesar's Intelligence section all spoke of the enemy massing in formidable numbers; "the Bellovaci from the mouth of the Seine had sent 60,000; the Suessiones from Soissons, 50,000; the Nervii, between the Sambre and the Scheldt, 50,000; Arras and Amiens, 25,000; the coast tribes, 36,000; and the tribes between the Ardennes and the Rhine, called collectively Germani, 40,000 more. This irregular host was gathered in the forests between Laon and Soissons.

Caesar did not wait for them to move. He advanced at once to Rheims, where he called the Senate together and encouraged them to be constant to the Roman alliance. He sent a party of the Aedui down the Seine to harass the territory of the Bellovaci and recall them to their own defense; and he went on himself to the Aisne, which he crossed by a bridge already existing at Berry-au-Bac. There, with the bridge and river at his back, he formed an entrenched camp of extraordinary strength, with a wall twelve feet high and a fosse twenty-two feet deep.[38]

The Belgae came forward without hesitation and encamped on Caesar's front, their watch fires at night stretching for eight miles across the countryside.

Caesar, after feeling his way with his cavalry, found a rounded ridge projecting like a promontory into the plain where the Belgian host was lying. On this he advanced his Legions, protecting his flanks with continuous trenches and earthworks, on which were placed heavy cross-bows.[39] Between these lines, if he attacked the enemy and failed, he had a secure retreat. A marsh lay between the armies, and each waited for the other to cross. The Belgians, impatient of delay, flung themselves suddenly on one side and began to pour across the river, intending to destroy the cohorts on the other bank, to cut the bridge, and burn and plunder among the Remi. Caesar calmly sent back his cavalry and his archers and slingers. They caught the enemy in the water, or struggling out of it in confusion. All who had got over were killed; multitudes were slaughtered in the river; others,

---

[38] Froude, *op. cit.*
[39] *Onager*, see Chapter IV.

trying to cross on the bodies of their comrades, were driven back.[40]

The Legionaries plied their swords until their arms wearied of the work of killing. It was a veritable battue, with the slain in such prodigious number that "the lakes and rivers were filled with the dead, and bridges were formed of their bodies." [41] With Labienus and his horsemen in hot pursuit of such fugitives as had managed to leave the stricken field, it was plain that the confederacy, shattered in a single encounter, would never again come together.

Soissons, Breteuil, and Amiens surrendered in their turn as the Bellovaci sent in their submission, the leaders of the war party having fled to Britain. "Caesar treated them all with scrupulous forbearance, demanding nothing more than hostages for their future good behavior. At this juncture it was not his intention to annex the country, but to settle it in quasi-independence under Aeduan supervision."

The strongest member of the confederacy, however, was still unsubdued. The defiant Nervii could put sixty thousand fighting men in the field—men brought up to a Spartan way of life, with battle and the chase the be-all and end-all of existence, in that "There was no access for merchants to them; that they suffered no wine and other things tending to luxury to be imported, because they thought that by their use the mind is enervated, the courage impaired; that they were a savage people of great bravery; that they openly declared that they would neither send ambassadors, nor accept any conditions of peace." [42]

A people of the dense forest-lands of Haimault and Cambrésis, the Nervii—like their allies the Atrebates—were particularly adept at laying an ambush, and it was into just such a trap that the Romans were caught by their reprehensible neglect of proper reconnaissance. The surprise attack was launched in densely wooded country on the Upper Sambre. On one side of the stream Caesar's six veteran Legions were in process of pitching camp, while on the further bank the cavalry and a few light-armed auxiliaries were somewhat perfunctorily exploring the thick belt of trees stretching away into infinity.

With the bulk of the Romans busy about the task of settling into their bivouac, the whole force of the enemy

[40] Froude, *op. cit.*
[41] Plutarch, *op. cit.*
[42] Caesar, *op. cit.*

swept in from all quarters, brushing aside the cavalry patrols to rush across the stream and fall on the main body of the Legions. Surprise was complete; and although the veteran Tenth, stoutly supported by the Ninth, refused to give ground, the two Legions on the right wing were in imminent danger of being rolled up and cut to pieces in detail. "As this attack was unexpected, Caesar had, in a manner, everything to do at the same instant. The banner was to be erected, the charge sounded, the soldiers at a distance recalled, the army drawn up, and the signal given. In this surprise he ran from place to place, exhorting his men to remember their former valor; and having drawn them up in the best manner he could, caused the signal to be given. The Legionaries made a vigorous resistance; but as the enemy seemed to conquer or die, the success was different in different places. In the left wing the Ninth and Tenth Legions did wonders, drove the Atrebates into a neighboring river, and made a great slaughter of them. In another place the Eighth and Eleventh Legions repulsed the Vermandui,[43] and drove them before them. But in the right wing the Seventh and Twelfth Legions suffered severely. They were entirely surrounded by the Nervii, all the Centurions of the fourth Cohort being slain and most of the other officers wounded. In this extremity Caesar seized a buckler from one of the private men, put himself at the head of his broken wing, and, being joined by the two Legions which he had left to guard the baggage, fell upon the Nervii, already fatigued, with fresh vigor, and made a dreadful havoc of them." [44] The swift recovery of disciplined troops and the timely employment of the reserves to launch a counterattack, had served to extricate Caesar from a desperate situation which far too casual a method of penetrating enemy territory had openly invited. "But though, encouraged by Caesar's personal example, the Legionaries fought with a spirit above their strength, they were not able to make the Nervii turn their backs. These brave men maintained their ground, and were hewed to pieces upon the spot. It was said that out of sixty thousand not above five hundred were saved, and out of four hundred Nervian Senators not above three." [45] The total of the Roman casualties does not emerge, but they cannot have been light.

Yet, as 57 B.C. hardened into winter and the men of the Legions settled down in quarters on the Upper Loire, it was

[43] Another tribe allied to the Nervii.
[44] Plutarch, *op. cit.*
[45] *Ibid.* Cf. Caesar's *Commentaries.*

clear that the defeat and subjugation of the Nervii and their allies had secured the supremacy of Rome among the principal Belgic clans.

There were, however, a number of lesser tribes still to bring to heel. So,

in the following year (56 B.C.) Caesar built a fleet, and quickly reduced the amphibious people of Brittany, who had defied his power and insulted his Officers. He next received the submission of the Aquitanians in the extreme south, through his young lieutenant P. Crassus, son of the *Triumvir*; and himself chastized the wild tribes occupying the coast-land which now forms Picardy, Artois, and French Flanders, the Menapii and the Morini—"remotest of mankind." [46] He attempted also to occupy a post at Martigny in the Valais, for the purpose of commanding the pass of the Pennine Alp (Great St. Bernard). In this last enterprise he failed. But still, in three campaigns, he seemed to have conquered the whole of Gaul, from the Rhine and Mount Jura to the Western Ocean. [47]

While Caesar in Gaul was winning fame and power, Pompey was left at home to rule the capital. But to keep order in a city still seething with revolution required what Pompey had not—the iron hand in the velvet glove. He was without police or soldiers to suppress by force the bands of blackguards, led by adventurers, whose type and chief was to be seen in the Tribune P. Clodius. The mob under his leadership ran riot in the streets of Rome; murder and arson became crimes of daily occurrence, and anarchy arrogated to herself the sacred name of liberty. Pompey attempted to meet Clodius with his own weapons, but in this warfare of the street the *Triumvir* was no match for the Tribune, and after a time he shut himself up in his house, in fear of assassination. [48]

With Pompey seeking to gain the balance of advantage by promoting the recall of Cicero, and Clodius retaliating by endeavoring to set up Crassus against Pompey, for months on end Rome was the scene of violent clashes between rival gangs of partisans.

[46] "*Extremique hominum Morini,*" Vergil, *The Aeneid*.

[47] Liddell, *op. cit.*

[48] How and Leigh, *op. cit.*

Deceived by the superficial acclaim accorded him by the fickle mob on his return to Rome, Cicero delusively regarded himself as the key figure in a republican revival. Pompey, fretful that his past military *réclame* should pale before the luster of Caesar's Gallic victories, sought in vain for a military command in Egypt, with the object of restoring Ptolemy Auletes to his throne and in the process winning new glory for himself. The Senate, however, produced oracles which declared that such a mission would prove unpropitious. Then, when Cicero so grossly overrated his strength as to question the validity of the Julian law regarding the allotment of land in Campania, Caesar took advantage of the winter lull in field operations to call Crassus and Pompey into conference at Luca.

"The meeting of the three potentates was attended by many provincial Governors and two hundred Senators. Its result was the reestablishment of the coalition on a firmer basis. Pompey and Crassus were to be given the official position which they coveted. After holding the consulship together for the second time, Pompey was to receive Spain and Crassus Syria for five years, by decree of the people, while Caesar secured the renewal of his own command for the same period, and the reversion of the consulship at its close." [49] There were not wanting those to wonder why Caesar granted such favorable terms to a somewhat discredited Pompey.

But the army assigned to Crassus for the invasion of Parthia formed a counterpoise to the Spanish Legions of Pompey; and neither Caesar nor his soldiers were yet prepared to march on Italy. Caesar was not a deliberate schemer aiming at despotism, but a man whose heart was set on doing the work of the hour, confident in his own ability to rise to the height of future emergencies. With the true spirit of a statesman and soldier, he concentrated himself on the immediate problem to the momentary neglect of other issues. His present purpose was to complete the conquest of Gaul, and for that end he chose to run the risk of strengthening Pompey. The time was not yet ripe for revolution, and Caesar would not bid his army turn its weapons against fellow-citizens while there remained a chance of peaceful reformation of the government. [50]

[49] How and Leigh, *op. cit.*
[50] *Ibid.*

While Crassus, upon the expiration of his consulship, promptly repaired to his Province, Pompey lingered in Italy. Having regard for his craving for power and its outward manifestation, this is well-nigh incredible. But, "remaining in Rome, he opened his theater; and, to make the dedication more magnificent, exhibited a variety of gymnastic games, entertainments of music, and battles with wild beasts, in which were killed five hundred lions; but the battle of elephants afforded the most astonishing spectacle. These things gained him the love and admiration of the public; but he incurred their displeasure again, by leaving his Province and army entirely to his friends and lieutenants, while he roved about Italy with his wife, from one villa to another." [51]

To add to the prevailing atmosphere of tension and unrest in Rome, a Parthian attack on Armenia was followed by an outbreak of trouble in Egypt. Leaving the rival claimants to the Parthian Crown to wrangle over the rights of succession, A. Gabinius, the Governor of Syria, set off to ensure the restoration of Rome's client, Ptolemy, to the Throne of the Pharoahs. The Roman forces promptly proceeded to inflict defeat on the insurgents at Pelusium and on the Nile, and were thus enabled to reestablish the rule of the legitimate King.

"Meanwhile Crassus had taken his departure for the East, and thus destroyed another link in the chain that had hitherto maintained union among the *Triumvirs*. Even before his consulship was ended, he left Rome to supersede Gabinius in the government of Syria. His chief object in seeking this Province was by the conquest of the Parthians to balance the military glory of Pompey and of Caesar." [52]

The Parthians, a wild, hardy people originally to be found in the mountainous territory to the southeast of the Caspian Sea, had, on the death of Alexander the Great, come under the nominal sway of Seleucus and his successors. Waxing ever bolder, by the end of the great Mithridatic War their ruler claimed the title of King of Kings and exercised despotic sway over the countries adjacent to and west of the Euphrates. Strong in lightly armored cavalry, accurate bowmen on foot or on horseback, and trained to disperse like a cloud before solidly advancing regular troops, as they fled they would discharge their arrows at their pursuers with an arresting accuracy. [53]

Under their contemporary King Orodes the whole nation

[51] Plutarch, *op. cit.*

[52] Liddell, *op. cit.*

[53] Hence the phrase, "a Parthian (or parting) shot."

was fully braced for war, as Crassus was very speedily to discover.

"Caesar, at his return to his army in Gaul, found another furious war lighted up in the country; the Usipetes and the Teuchteri,[54] two great German nations, having crossed the Rhine to make conquests." [55] Having drifted over the country-side for some time in search of a territory they could usurp, "they came to the Rhine, to districts which the Menapii inhabited, and where they had lands, houses and villages on either side of the river. The latter people, alarmed at the arrival of so great a multitude, removed from those houses they had on the other side of the river, and having placed guards on this side of the Rhine, proceeded to hinder the Germans from crossing." [56] Having, by a ruse, surprised the Menapii scouts, the invaders slaughtered all the local inhabitants they found on their side of the stream, seized all their river craft, and proceeded to cross the water-way in force. Hearing of these matters, Caesar resolved to intervene on behalf of the hapless Menapii. "These barbarians sent deputies to him then to propose a suspension of arms, which was granted them. Nevertheless they attacked him as he was making an excursion. With only eight hundred Horse, however, who were not prepared for an engagement, he beat their cavalry, which consisted of five thousand. Next day they sent other deputies to apologize for what had happened, but without any other intention than that of deceiving him again. These agents of theirs he detained, and marched immediately against them; thinking it absurd to stand upon honor with such perfidious men, who had not scrupled to violate the truce." [57] Having determined his course of action, Caesar set about carrying it out with his usual dispatch. After an eight-mile approach march went undetected, the Roman attack was launched with all the advantage accruing from the employment of the element of surprise. "The enemy's consternation being made apparent by their noise and tumult," Caesar recorded,

> our soldiers rushed into the camp: such of them as could readily get their arms for a short time withstood our men, and gave battle among their carts and baggage-

54 The people of the *March* and of Westphalia, and those of Münster and Cleves.

55 Plutarch, *op. cit.*

56 Caesar, *op. cit.*

57 Plutarch, *op. cit.*

wagons; but the rest of the people consisting of boys and women, (for they had left their country and crossed the Rhine with all their families), began to fly in all directions, in pursuit of whom Caesar sent the cavalry.

The Germans when, upon hearing a noise behind them, they looked and saw their families being slain, throwing away their arms and abandoning their standards, fled out of the camp; and when they arrived at the confluence of the Meuse and the Rhine, the survivors despairing of further escape, as a great number of their countrymen had been killed, threw themselves into the river and there perished, overcome by fear, fatigue, and the violence of the stream. . . . Caesar granted those whom he had detained in the camp liberty of departing. They however, dreading revenge and torture from the Gauls, whose lands they had harassed, said they desired to remain with him. Caesar granted them permission.[58]

Caesar followed up his outstanding victory by accomplishing the difficult feat of bridging the Rhine. "His army passed over it without opposition, the Suevi and Sicambri, the most warlike nations in Germany, having retired into the heart of their forest, and concealed themselves in cavities overhung with wood. He laid waste the enemy's country with fire, and confirmed the better disposed Germans [59] in the interest of Rome; after which he returned into Gaul, having spent no more than eighteen days in Germany." [60]

With the German tribes reduced, at least temporarily, to impotence, Caesar could turn his mind to the furtherance of another project he had long been maturing—the invasion and subjugation of that exiguous island of Britain, whose continued freedom constituted a perennial menace on the flank of his mainland conquests. Moreover, these rude islanders had had the temerity to intervene in Caesar's 56 B.C. campaign against the coastal Veneti and Aquitani; and there were, moreover, merchant-venturers' tales of rich stores of gold, silver, and pearls, which should handsomely repay the cost of the enterprise.

In late August of 55 B.C., therefore, "the men of the Seventh and Tenth Legions were embarked in eighty vessels; crossing the Channel at its narrowest on a course laid from Gersoriacum (Boulogne) to a point near what is now the

[58] Caesar, *op. cit.*

[59] The Ubii, who dwelt about Cologne.

[60] Plutarch, *op. cit.*

town of Dover. A first-class cavalry contingent embarked
further up the coast in eighteen craft, under orders to follow
in support of the initial assault. Caesar's first landfall was a
rockbound strip of coast, whose bordering cliffs were crowned
with a swarm of tribal warriors who watched his every movement lynx-eyed. Probing for a more favorable beachhead,
the Proconsul finally gave orders to force a landing near
the site of the present-day town of Deal.

As the galleys neared the shore, a swarm of
charioteers in their scythed war-carts streamed on to the
beach, heading a press of tribesmen who yelled defiance
and brandished their weapons with such unbridled ferocity that even the veteran Legionaries quailed a little
at the prospect of going in to the assault. It was not until
the Standard-bearer of the Tenth Legion leaped boldly
into the shoal water that his comrades tumbled from
their boats to form up in the shallows. . . . The struggle
was fierce and bloody, but as the Roman swordsmen
gained a footing their discipline and trained skill in arms
slowly won the advantage and their adversaries fell back
in considerable confusion. Had the cavalry been
promptly landed, the tribesmen's retreat could have been
turned into a rout. As it was, Caesar was content to
establish his camp hard by the shore, and to receive the
submission of those of the natives who came forward
with offers of surrender.[61]

Constant assaults on the narrow Roman bridgehead kept
the Legions perpetually at the stretch, but it was the disrup-
tion of his sensitive line of communications which finally
persuaded Caesar to reconsider his position. Accustomed to
the tideless Mediterranean, his shipmen had no comprehension of the mischief that could be worked by the vicious
rips and races, the vagaries of the tides, along the Channel
shore. Having secured their craft far too casually, "on the
fourth night ashore a violent gale aggravated the normal
swell to such an extent that the vessels which had been
hauled up onto the shingle were filled with water, while many
of the anchored transports parted their cables and were
wrecked along the shore." [62] With winter looming ahead
and his antagonists still full of fight, Caesar realized that for
the moment the only thing to do was to pull out, the better

61 Reginald Hargreaves, *The Narrow Seas*.
62 *Ibid*.

to reorganize elsewhere for another descent on this obdurate island, where even the weather conditions conspired with the barbaric inhabitants to repel the would-be invader.

If in the first instance Caesar had underestimated the task of securing a firm grip on Britain, he did not fall into similar error with his second venture, in 54 B.C. With the spring a force of no less than five Legions, with supporting Horse, battled its way through a typical Channel storm to make its landfall not far from the mound which was later to be crowned by Richborough Castle. The Catauvellauni were the first opponents to be encountered, and hard-fighting, dogged foes they proved to be; their chieftain, Cassivelaunus, employed a "scorched-earth" policy that greatly hampered the invaders' success in supplementing their own by local supplies.

"At length, Cassivelaunus was persuaded to sue for peace. Caesar, who feared the approach of the equinox and all its arrival portended, willingly subscribed to a treaty as insubstantial as the show of goodwill with which it was concluded." [63] Theoretically, Caesar had accomplished the mission on which he had set forth, although there was remarkably little to show for it—an empty promise of regular tribute, a little tin, a smaller quantity of gold and silver, and a handful of pearls with which the conqueror ornamented a breastplate hopefully dedicated to the goddess Venus.[64]

It was on his return to Gaul that Caesar "received letters by which his friends in Rome informed him that his daughter, the wife of Pompey, had lately died in childbed. This was a great affliction both to Pompey and Caesar," but one that tended less to draw them together than to increase their growing estrangement. Their association had never been founded upon anything warmer than community of interest; their intimacy had been rather one of wary watchfulness than of even modified friendship. Nonetheless, there can be no question that Julia had done much temporarily to disarm the feeling of mutual distrust with which each man regarded the other. With her untimely death and the waning of her meliorating influence, the latent hostility, the girding sense

[63] Hargreaves, *op. cit.* For nearly a hundred years the island people retained their freedom, and it was not until the Emperor Claudius sent the experienced Aulus Plautius to Britain in A.D. 43 that the country finally came under Roman sway.

[64] Suetonius.

of rivalry, which had always formed the background to their relationship was released from the restraint hitherto imposed upon it. Nor can it have sweetened Pompey's regard for a father-in-law who was his junior only in years when, "preparing to bury his dead wife near his seat at Alba, the people seized the corpse and interred it in the *Campus Martius*. This they did more out of regard for the young woman than either Pompey or Caesar; yet in the honor they did her remains, their attachment to Caesar, though at a distance, had a greater share than any respect for Pompey, who was on the spot." [65]

Yet another link between the two men was destined very shortly to be sundered. On taking over command from Gabinius in Syria, Crassus was determined to demonstrate that in military talent he was in no way the inferior of Pompey and Caesar. For the first year of his proconsulship he was content to confine himself to somewhat desultory operations against the Parthians in Mesopotamia. But early in the next spring he advanced in strength from the Euphrates, intent on penetrating into Parthia. "Artavasdes, the contemporary King of Armenia, who through fear of the Parthian Monarch took part with Rome, wished the Proconsul to take his country as the basis of his operations, and by descending the valley of the Tigris to avoid the open plains, where the Parthian horsemen, seconded by the heat of summer, would act against him at terrible advantage. C. Cassius Longinus, the most experienced officer of the Proconsul, preferred the route of the Euphrates. But Crassus neglected both warning and advice. The Parthians, avoiding a general battle, drew on the Romans into the northern plains of Mesopotamia, until the Legionaries, faint with heat and hunger, found themselves confronted by a vast host of Parthian and Arabian horsemen; and about thirty miles south of Carrhae, the first battle was fought. The Romans were utterly defeated; and young Crassus, the friend of Cicero, to escape capture caused himself to be slain." [66]

During the night Crassus made good his retreat to Carrhae, leaving his wounded to be slaughtered with every circumstance of barbarity. Thereafter, he did not "stand upon the order of his going," but beat a hasty retreat, halting only when within a short march of the fortress of Sinnaca.

[65] Plutarch, *op. cit.*

[66] Liddell, *op. cit.* To provide the Parthian army with sustained fire power, improvised ammunition dumps were instituted, supplied by as many as a thousand camels.

There the Vizier rode in front of the Roman camp to offer, in the name of his King, peace and friendship to the Romans, and to propose a personal conference between the two Generals. The Roman army, demoralized as it was, adjured and indeed compelled its leader to accept the offer. The Vizier received the Proconsul and his Staff with the usual honor, and offered anew to conclude a compact of friendship, but demanded that it should be immediately reduced to writing. A richly-adorned horse was produced; it was a present from the King to the Roman Commander-in-Chief; the servants of the Vizier crowded round Crassus, zealous to mount him on the steed. It seemed to the Roman Officers as if there were a design to seize the person of the Commander-in-Chief; Octavius,[67] unarmed as he was, pulled the sword of one of the Parthians from its sheath and stabbed the groom. In the tumult which thereupon arose, the Roman officers were all put to death; the gray-haired Commander-in-Chief also. The multitude left behind in the camp without a leader were partly taken prisoners, partly dispersed. The army of the Euphrates was no more. And, so far as Asia was concerned, the prestige of Rome had never been at lower ebb.[68]

With enough near-defeat to season the savory fare of his many victories with caution, by 53 B.C. Caesar had mastered the art of generalship, and had evolved an admirable staff system by which to support it. To the standard distribution of responsibilities, he had added a secretariat presided over by Lucius Cornelius Balbus, before his Romanization a prominent citizen of Gades (Cadiz). A trained engineer and confidential scribe of unwearying industry and impeccable discretion, he was as devoted to his patron as Caesar was trustful of him. It was Balbus who dealt with the Pronconsul's political correspondence, enciphering and deciphering the confidential communications that an admirable courier service carried at speed to and from the capital, along the magnificent roads which everywhere veined the countryside where Roman arms held sway. The advantage of receiving the earliest intelligence, and of keeping in close touch both with the capital and outlying garrisons, had counseled the establishment of a chain of posts throughout the whole of the Roman dominions. In due course, "houses were everywhere

[67] One of Crassus's principal subordinates.
[68] Mommsen, *op. cit.*

erected at the distance of only five or six miles; each of them constantly provided with forty horses, and, by the help of these relays, it was easy to travel a hundred miles in a day along the Roman roads." [69]

Caesar himself was a prodigious worker; "when he slept, it was commonly upon a march, either in a chariot or a litter, that rest might be no hindrance to business." [70] Frugal and sparing in his diet, "no common soldier was more careless of hardships than Caesar. His chief luxury was a favorite horse, which would allow no one but Caesar to mount him—a horse which had been bred in his own stables, and, from the peculiarity of a divided hoof, had led the augurs to foretell wonders for the riders of it." [71] Determined to familiarize himself with every detail of his command, "in the daytime he visited the castles, cities and fortified camps, with a servant at his side [Balbus], whom he employed on such occasions to write for him, and with a soldier behind, who carried his sword. He also accustomed himself to dictate letters as he rode on horseback," [72] which can have done little to maintain the clarity of Balbus's calligraphy, as he jogged along, scribbling furiously, at his master's side!

Caesar was singularly fortunate, of course, in the exceptionally high quality of the fighting force he commanded. "The Roman Legionaries were no longer yeomen taken (temporarily) from the plough or shopkeepers from the street. They were men more completely trained in every variety of accomplishment than have perhaps ever followed a General in the field before or since. It was not enough that they could use sword and spear. The campaigns on which Caesar entered were fought with spade and pick and ax and hatchet. Corps of engineers he may have had; but if the engineers designed the work, the execution lay with the army." [73] Moreover, the force was virtually self-supporting. "There were no stores sent from Italy to supply the daily waste of material. The men had to mend and perhaps make their own clothes and shoes, and repair their own arms. . . . Men and instruments were as excellent in their kind as honesty and skill could make them; and however degenerate the patricians and corrupt the legislature, there was plainly sound

[69] Procopius, *Historia Arcana*. Cf. Gibbon.

[70] Plutarch, *op. cit.*

[71] Froude, *op. cit.*

[72] Plutarch, *op. cit.*

[73] Froude, *op. cit.*

stuff somewhere in the Roman constitution" [74]—and the best of it was concentrated in Gaul, as events were speedily to demonstrate.

The summer of 54 B.C. had been meteorologically unkind, with so poor a harvest that, on his return from Britain, Caesar deemed it more expedient to distribute the eight Legions of his command over a far wider area than was militarily advisable, as the best means of ensuring the necessary supplies of grain without subjecting any one region to undue strain. Throughout the entire countryside there was a hostile restlessness and air of nervous tension which could scarcely be accounted for, although undoubtedly aggravated by the general shortage of foodstuffs and the prospect of a pinch-gut winter. Caesar himself was at Samarobriva (Amiens) having one Legion with him and three within call. In the most distant camp of all, at Aduatuca, the *Legatti* Sabinus and Cotta had one Legion of recruits, stiffened by five Cohorts of veterans. "This corps was furiously assailed in its new winter quarters by the Eburones [75] under Ambiorix, but might easily have held its entrenchments. In a weak moment Sabinus listened to the treacherous tale told by Ambiorix of a general assault on the scattered Legions, and accepted his offer of a safe conduct for his soldiers to the camp of Labienus. The little force was decoyed into a trap by the wily chief, and Sabinus, who attempted to make terms, was murdered with many of his Officers. Cotta fought bravely to the last, till the unequal struggle ended in the total annihilation of the Roman division.

Flushed with victory and reinforced from the neighboring cantons, the insurgents flung themselves at the camp of Q. Cicero. But that officer met their attack with coolness, and doggedly refused to treat with an armed enemy. Messenger after messenger was seized on his way to Caesar, yet at length a loyal Gallic horseman reached Amiens. Caesar started next morning with but two Legions to rescue his lieutenant. Within five days the smoke of burning villages announced his coming and drew off the hosts of the enemy. Caesar kept within his camp as though in fear, and then by a sudden sally dispersed the Gauls in confusion.

But the insurrection could not be stamped out in winter. As spring drew on, Indutiomarus, the chief of

[74] Froude, *op. cit.*
[75] A tribe that dwelt between the Maas and the Rhine.

the Treveri, attacked Labienus, but fell in a cavalry skirmish. His tribesmen summoned the Germans to their aid, but a feigned retreat drew them in hot pursuit after Labienus, and led to their destruction before their German allies had come up. Caesar, who had already reduced to subjection, besides the Senones and Carnutes, the fierce Nervii and the hitherto unconquered Menapii, now followed up the easy victory of his lieutenant by a second military promenade across the Rhine. The only task left was the punishment of the guilty Eburones, who were hunted down with merciless severity. By the end of the summer of 53 B.C. Northern Gaul had been terrified into the peace of despair.[76]

"Gaul being tranquil, Caesar, as he had determined, set out for Italy to hold the provincial assizes. There he received intelligence of the death of Clodius." [77] The faction fights between Clodius and T. Annius Milo—who had put himself forward for office in opposition to the interests of the remaining members of the Triumvirate—had ended in the murder of the former in a chance scuffle on the Appian way. "The dregs of the Roman populace were gathered together by his surviving lieutenants to weep over their lost leader's body. After some wild speeches in the Forum a riot broke out, and the venerable Senate House of Rome was used as the funeral pile of the dead demagogue. Milo was besieged in his house, and Pompey saluted as dictator by the excited mob." [78]

For Caesar, this was a development of the gravest import, and it is unquestionable that he would have embarked on some immediate countermove but for the fact that an equally demanding crisis arose even nearer at hand, to demand all his energy, skill, and attention. For the disaffection he had extinguished in the north broke out again with far greater obstinacy in the central and southern tribes. "A real leader at last appeared; a man who had doubtless learnt much from the Romans, and who knew the hopelessness of rebellion without discipline and organization. Vercingetorix was a young Avernian of a noble family, whose father had held the chieftainship of the whole of Gaul. Though the fatal jealousy of his countrymen had caused the father's death, his prestige descended to the son." [79]

---

[76] How and Leigh, *op. cit.*
[77] Caesar, *op. cit.*
[78] How and Leigh, *op. cit.*
[79] Warde Fowler, *op. cit.*

Vercingetorix, therefore, experienced little difficulty in rallying his own tribe and arousing the ardor of those of the west—Senones, Parisii, Pictones, Cadurci, Turoni, Aulerci, and Lemovices—until he found himself at the head of a representative and ever-expanding host of fighting men in whom he had managed to instill something of the stern Roman discipline. "The insurrection of the last winter had failed only through Caesar himself appearing on the scene of action; now he was at a distance, detained on the Po by the imminence of civil war, and the Gallic army, which was collected on the Upper Seine, was far separated from its dreaded leader. If a general insurrection now broke out in Central Gaul, the Roman army might be surrounded, and the almost undefended old Roman Province be overrun, before Caesar reappeared from beyond the Alps; even if the Italian complications did not altogether prevent him from further concerning himself about Gaul." [80]

But Caesar defeated these machinations by his extraordinary rapidity of movement.

Cutting his way through the snows of the Cervennes in the depth of winter, he drew Vercingetorix off to the defense of his own clansmen, and then with a handful of cavalry dashed through the land of the Aedui to the camps of his Legions. Vercingetorix fell back on the plan of starving out the enemy. The country was to be laid waste, the towns and stores burnt, and the Romans prevented from foraging by the fine Gallic cavalry. Only Avaricum (Bourges), the chief town of the Bituriges, was spared. Round that devoted city the war now centered. The Gallic infantry lay secure in impassable morasses; the cavalry cut off Caesar's communications. Still his famished Legions refused to raise the siege, and at length triumphed over the heroic garrison. The town was stormed and the inhabitants massacred by the maddened soldiery. [81]

Caesar then proceeded to dispatch Labienus with four Legions northwards to hold in check the Carnutes and Senones, while he himself turned south against the Arverni. Labienus, however, made little progress on the Seine, and Caesar found his advance arrested by the forbidding fortress of Gergovia.

80 Mommsen, *op. cit.*
81 How and Leigh, *op. cit.*

The town of Gergovia stood on a high plateau. The sides of the hill are steep, and only accessible at a very few places, and the surrounding neighborhood is broken with rocky valleys. Vercingetorix lay in force outside, but in a position where he could not be attacked except at disadvantage, and with his communication with the fortress secured. He was departing again from his general plan for the campaign in allowing Gergovia to be defended, and the result showed that he was right in believing it to be impregnable. Caesar saw that it was too strong to be stormed, and that it could only be taken after long operations. After a few skirmishes he seized a spur of the plateau, which cut off the garrison from their readiest water-supply. He was studying the rest of the problem when bad news came that the recently regenerated Aedui were again wavering. The ten thousand men had been raised among them as he had ordered, but on their way to join him they had murdered the Roman officers in charge of them, and were preparing to go over to Vercingetorix. Leaving two Legions to guard his works, he intercepted the Aeduan contingent, took them prisoners, and protected their lives. In his absence Vercingetorix attacked the camp with determined fury. The fighting had been desperate, and Caesar only returned in time to save the situation. The reports from the Aedui were worse and worse. The patriotic faction had the upper hand, and had massacred every Roman in their territory. It was no time for delaying over a tedious siege: Caesar was on the point of raising it, when accident brought on a battle under the walls. An opportunity seemed to offer itself of capturing the place by escalade, which part of the army attempted contrary to orders. They fought with more than their usual gallantry. The whole scene was visible from the adjoining hills, the Celtic women, with long streaming hair, gesticulating on the walls. The Romans were driven back with worse loss than they had yet met with in Gaul. Forty-six officers and seven hundred men had been killed.[82]

This was a severe setback, but Caesar accepted it with complete imperturbability, although it proved the signal for the defection of the fickle Aedui and risings among the effervescent Belgae. In slight recompense, Labienus succeeded

[82] Froude, *op. cit.*

in fighting his way out of the country of the Seine, and joined his Commander-in-Chief at Agedincum. The united army now moved southward to protect the Province. On the borders of the Sequani territory Vercingetorix, fresh from his election as the warrior-chief of all the Gauls, came up with the Roman army. To his infinite astonishment his cavalry was met and soundly beaten by Caesar's newly-raised German Horse, who chased their bewildered quarry for fifty miles over hill and dale into Alice St. Reine (Alesia).[83]

"Caesar followed close behind, driving Vercingetorix within the lines of the fortress; and the siege of Alesia, one of the most remarkable exploits in all military history, was at once undertaken." [84] All unwittingly, Vercingetorix had shut the trap on himself.

The town itself was situated on the top of a hill, in a very lofty position, so that it did not appear likely to be taken, except by a regular siege. Two rivers, on two different sides, washed the foot of the hill. Before the town lay a plain of about three miles in length; on every other side hills at a moderate distance, and of an equal degree of height, surrounded the town. The army of the Gauls had filled all the space under the wall, and had drawn in front a trench and a stone wall six feet high. The circuit of the fortification which was commenced by the Romans, comprised eleven miles.[85] The Roman camp was pitched in a strong position, and twenty-three redoubts were raised in it, in which sentinels were placed by day, lest any attempt should be made suddenly; and by night the same were occupied by strong guards.[86]

The weakest point in the besieger's lines was on the north side, beyond the river Ose, where the works were not only incomplete, but were awkwardly situated on the forward slope of the hills descending to the stream.

To man his line of circumvallation Caesar had a force of 50,000; penned within the town limits, in addition to the indigenous inhabitants, were the 80,000 warriors who had rallied to the Gaulish leader's banner. With careful hoarding, there was food for a maximum of thirty days.

[83] The present-day Auxois.
[84] Froude, *op. cit.*
[85] Subsequently extended to fourteen miles.
[86] Caesar, *op. cit.*

Vercingetorix had looked on for a time, not understanding what was happening to him. When he did understand it, he made desperate efforts on his side to break the net before it closed about him. But he could do nothing. The Gauls could not face the Roman entrenchments. Their cavalry were cut to pieces by the German Horse. The only hope was in help from without, and before the lines were entirely finished horsemen were sent out to ride for their lives into every district in Gaul and raise the entire nation. The horsemen sped away like the bearers of the fiery cross. Caesar learnt from deserters that they had gone out, and understood the message which they carried. Already he was besieging an army far outnumbering his own. If he persevered, he knew he might count with certainty on being attacked by a second army immeasurably larger. But the time allowed for the collection of so many men might serve also to prepare for their reception. . . . Fortifications the same in kind as those which prevented the besieged from breaking out would serve equally well to keep the assailants off. His plan was to make a second line of works—an exterior line as well as an interior line.[87]

With their enormous industry, the Legions set about creating a series of redoubts and barriers which would enable them, if needed, to fight off a simultaneous attack on front and rear. Dry and wet ditches, fronted by extensive abbatis, a generous sprinkling of *cervi*,[88] a liberal sowing of *stimuli*[89] concealed beneath branches or lurking at the bottom of camouflaged pits deep enough to engulf horse and rider—every lethal contrivance that ingenuity could devise and unremitting toil carry into execution, was employed to strengthen the defense against the coming trial of strength. In the interim, sorties on the part of the beleaguered garrison were beaten back with comparative ease.

Within the hungry township, as the weeks went by and there were no signs of deliverance, the mood of the defenders reached such a point of desperation that an Auvergnois chieftain actually proposed that sooner than yield, they

[87] Froude, *op. cit.*

[88] Pronged instruments like the branching horns of a stag.

[89] Barbed spikes. It has been calculated that in the course of erecting their field works the Legionaries shifted two million meters of earth. (*Revue des Deux Mondes*, May 1, 1858.)

should kill and eat those who were useless for fighting. "Vercingetorix, to prevent the adoption of so horrible an expedient, ordered the peaceful inhabitants, with their wives and children, to leave the town. Caesar forbade them to pass his lines" [90]—the inevitable reaction of a siege commander, who must look upon famine as one of his most potent weapons.

But the day of expected deliverance dawned at last. Five miles beyond the Brenne stream the dust-clouds of the approaching host were seen, and then the glitter of their lances and their waving pennons. They swam the river. They filled the plain below the town. From the heights of Alesia the whole scene lay spread under the feet of the besieged. Vercingetorix came down on the slope to the edge of the first trench, prepared to cross when the turn of the battle should give him the chance. Caesar sent out his German Horse, and stood himself watching and directing from the spur of an adjoining hill. The Gauls had brought innumerable archers with them. The Horse flinched slightly under the shower of arrows, and shouts of triumph rose from the lines of the town; but the Germans rallied again, sent the cavalry of the Gauls flying, and hewed down the protecting archers.[91]

With this preliminary setback the relief force—numbering, in all, some 250,000—drew off until nightfall, when another attack was beaten back with heavy loss to the assailants. The supporting sortie by the Alesia garrison was not only badly timed but found it impossible to pass the besiegers' moat and the trench system beyond it.

There was a lull throughout the early hours of the day following. But the relieving force had marked down the weak spot in the line of circumvallation beyond the Ose. "Sixty thousand men had left the Gauls' camp before dawn; they stole round by a distant route, and remained concealed in a valley till the middle of the day. At noon they came over the ridge at the Romans' back; and they had the best of the position, being able to attack from above. Their appearance was the signal for a general assault on all sides, and for a determined sally by Vercingetorix from within. Thus before,

90 Froude, *op. cit.*
91 *Ibid.*

behind, and everywhere, the Legions were assailed at the same moment." [92]

For the Romans it was a situation of the gravest peril, particularly on the slopes above the Ose, where the defenders were forced out of their works and were fighting back to back as Vercingetorix and his men fell on them from the direction of the town. To the rescue

Caesar sends at first young Brutus, with six Cohorts, and afterwards Caius Fabius, his lieutenant, with seven others: finally, as they fought more obstinately, he leads up fresh men to the assistance of his soldiers. After renewing the action, and repulsing the enemy, he marches in the direction in which he had sent Labienus, drafts four Cohorts from the nearest redoubt, and orders part of the cavalry to follow him, and part to make the circuit of the external fortifications and attack the enemy in the rear. Labienus, when neither the ramparts nor ditches could check the onset of the enemy, informs Caesar by messengers of what he intended to do. Caesar hastens to share in the action.

His arrival being known by the color of his robe, and the troops of cavalry, and the Cohorts which he had ordered to follow him being seen, the enemy join battle. A shout being raised by both sides, it was succeeded by a general shout along the ramparts and whole line of fortifications. Our troops, laying aside their javelins, carry on the engagement with their swords. The cavalry is suddenly seen in the rear of the Gauls; the other Cohorts advance rapidly; the enemy turn their backs; the cavalry intercept them in their flight, and a great slaughter ensues. [93]

Had the men of the Legions been other than utterly worn out, scarcely a tithe of the enemy would have escaped. As it was, the cavalry sent in pursuit broke up the whole barbarian force, capturing seventy-four standards, together with a host of prisoners.

"Next day Vercingetorix called a council of chieftains, and proposed submission as a sheer necessity. 'I myself,' he added, 'have not been fighting for my own ends, but for my country. My work is now over, and I offer myself as a victim to appease Caesar's wrath. Kill me, or surrender me—which-

92 Froude, *op. cit.*
93 Caesar, *op. cit.*

ever you will.' They decided that he should surrender himself, and appeal for them to Caesar's well-known clemency. But to Roman eyes things had gone too far for mercy." [94] On the day following, Caesar "seated himself at the head of the lines in front of the camp, the Gallic chieftains were brought before him. They surrender Vercingetorix and lay down their arms. Reserving the Aedui and Arverni, to try if he could gain them over, he distributed one of the remaining captives to each soldier, throughout the entire army, as plunder." [95] Vercingetorix himself was reserved in custody to be paraded in triumph before the populace—and to find an unknown grave in one of Rome's rubble-tips.

Caesar passed the winter at Bibrachte, receiving the submission of the chiefs of the Aedui and of the Auvergne. With him, whenever possible, retribution was wisely restrained by magnanimity. "His high aim was, not to enslave the Gauls, but to incorporate them in the Empire with the full privileges of Roman citizens. The war being over, he punished no one. He was gracious and considerate to all, and he so impressed the central tribes by his judgment and his moderation that they served him faithfully in all his coming troubles, and never more, even in the severest temptation, made an effort to recover their independence." [96] To a singular degree Caesar possessed the faculty of concentrating upon and dealing thoroughly with one task at a time. But with his hardheaded sense of realism, it is impossible that he should not have realized that stupendous as his labors may have been in Gaul, with Pompey riding the whirlwind of power as sole Consul, even sterner work lay ahead.

[94] Warde Fowler, *op. cit.*
[95] Caesar, *op. cit.*
[96] Froude, *op. cit.*

CHAPTER XI

"THE DIE IS CAST"

"Two stars keep not their motion in one sphere."
—Shakespeare

The art of politics consists of knowing when to stop, and then venturing a little further. This, however, demands a very nice sense of timing; and in this particular Caesar was at considerable advantage over Pompey. Moreover, while Pompey was content to take into view the contour of events, Caesar was at infinite pains to examine their texture.

In Gaul Caesar had learned to look at the narrow politics of the Forum from outside, and to estimate aright their pettiness and folly. Trained in the hard school of toil and anxiety, and breathing the free air of a provincial command, he rose above the shibboleths of a partisan creed, and kept his mind fixed on the duties of Rome to her empire. Gradually the conviction was forced upon him that the sovereign State would never make the welfare of her subjects her first object until her own constitution had been remodeled. Caesar was not selfishly anxious to force on this necessary reform; but he possessed naturally the power of inspiring devotion in his followers, and had acquired the insight, the patience, and the perseverance needed for the proper use of his power. The man was ready to take up the great task of reconstruction, when the destined hour came.[1]

But that hour had not yet struck, despite the fret and fury of faction, the riot and lawlessness of the idle and disso-

[1] How and Leigh, *op. cit.*

lute, of which Rome was the daily witness. There were still matters which demanded attention in his own Province, and Caesar was not the man to leave loose ends untied.

By his victory over the Nervii Caesar had almost extinguished the Belgian confederacy—almost, but not quite. The Carnutes of the Eure and Loire, and the Bituriges had to be given another lesson and brought to acceptance of the fact that opposition to the Romans only led to their own downfall. Furthermore,

the German Aduatuci remained to be brought to submission. They had been on their way to join their countrymen; they were too late for the battle, and returned and shut themselves up in Namur, the strongest position in the Low Countries. Caesar, after a short rest, pushed on and came under their walls. The Aduatuci were a race of giants, and were at first defiant. When they saw the Roman siege towers in preparation they could not believe that men so small could move such vast machines. When the towers began to approach, they lost heart and sued for terms. Caesar promised to spare their lives and properties if they surrendered immediately, but he refused to grant conditions. They had prayed to be allowed to keep their arms, affecting to believe, like the Nervii, that they would be in danger from the Gauls if they were unable to defend themselves. Caesar undertook that they should have no hurt, but he insisted that their arms must be given up. They affected obedience. They flung their swords and lances over the walls till the ditch was filled with them. They opened their gates; the Romans occupied them, but were forbidden to enter, that there might be no plundering. It seems that there had been a faction among the Aduatuci who had been for fighting to extremity. A third of the arms had been secretly reserved, and after midnight the tribe sallied forth with all their force, hoping to catch the Romans sleeping. Caesar was not to be surprised a second time. Expecting that some such attempt might be made, he had prepared piles of faggots in convenient places. These bonfires were set blazing in an instant. By their red light the Legions formed; and, after a desperate and unequal combat, the Germans were driven into the town again, leaving four thousand dead. In the morning the gates were broken down, and Namur was taken without more resistance. Caesar's usual practice was gentleness. He honored brave men,

and never punished bold and open opposition. Of treachery he made a severe example. Namur was condemned.
The Aduatuci within its walls were sold into slavery,
and the contractors who followed the army returned
the number of prisoners whom they had purchased at
53,000.[2]

The Belgae were crushed as absolutely as the Gauls had
been the previous year, while the coastal tribes of Brittany
made voluntary surrender. All in all, the Roman leader "had
taken by storm above eight hundred towns, subdued three
hundred States, and of the three millions of men, who made
up the gross sum of those with whom at several times he
engaged, he had killed one million and captured a second." [3] So great was the impression made by Caesar's overwhelming conquests, indeed, that the Germans beyond the
Rhine sent envoys with offers of submission. Distributing his
troops strategically at Chartres, Orleans, and Blois, Caesar
returned once more to his winter quarters in Italy. So far as
his conquests were concerned, his sole object was, "while
making use of the existing dynastic, feudalist, and hegemonic
divisions, to arrange matters in the interest of Rome, and to
bring everywhere into power the men favorably disposed to
foreign rule. Caesar spared no pains to form a Roman
party in Gaul; extensive rewards in money and especially
in confiscated estates were bestowed on his adherents, and
places in the Common Council and the first offices of State
in their cantons were procured for them by Caesar's influence." [4] In his absence, it was for the individuals whose
own prosperity and power depended on Rome's patronage, to
ensure the dependencies' continued loyalty to their suzerain.
As his ten-year tour of duty in the province of Gaul drew
to an end, it was essential for Caesar to ensure complete freedom to turn his attention to matters concerning not only his
own future, but also that of Rome and her empire.

With the murder of Clodius and the destruction of the
Senate House to furnish him with a funeral pyre, sheer
unbridled anarchy broke loose and held high revel. "For
the moment there was nowhere at Rome any power of resistance in any sort of government, nowhere a real authority.
Men were living in an interregnum between the ruin of the

2 Froude, op. cit.
3 Plutarch, op. cit.
4 Mommsen, op. cit.

aristocratic, and the rise of the military, rule," [5] with the shiftless components of "that worst of tyrants, a usurping crowd," as the lords of misrule, whom no one possessed the means or the resolution to bring to order—an unemployed, indigent, and vicious proletariat brought into being largely by the enormous influx of slave labor into the country. Reveling in the communistic orgies of the Dionysia, dependent for their sustenance and for their diversion upon freshly bestowed *"panem et circenses,"* electorally they were at the disposal of whatever faction—the handful of enervated, timorous Patricians still to be found in the Senate, or the solid phalanx of usurers and bankers—was prepared to offer the larger bribe. And they were always ready to enforce their partisanship with violence—yahoos and degenerates for whom liberty spelt license, "with freedom free to slay herself, and dying while they shout her name." "To be poor was not merely the sorest disgrace and the worst crime, but the only disgrace and the only crime; for money the statesmen sold the State, and the burgess sold his freedom; the post of the officer and the vote of the juryman were to be had for money; for money the lady of quality sold her person as well as the common courtesan; falsifying of documents and perjuries had become so common that in a popular poet of this age an oath is called 'a plaster for debts.' Men had forgotten what honesty was; a person who refused a bribe was regarded not as an upright man, but as a personal foe; for it was not in the contemporary Roman ethos to recognize and accept that 'where money is the measure's-worth, the wrong people are always upper-most.' " In the prevailing circumstances, as Appian duly noted, "good men abstained from office; and the disorder was such that at one time the Republic was without Consuls for eight months, Pompey conniving at the state of affairs in order that there might be need of a dictator." Salvation could only come through the intervention of a man of high purpose and indomitable will, with a dispassionate mind guiding a firm hand—a contemporary Alexander the Great. Since he was the nearest to hand, and still retained some of the effulgence begotten of his early conquests, the Senate turned to Pompey in the hope that he would be able to restore some semblance of order.

It is probable that he would have been appointed Dictator at once, had not Caesar been in Cisalpine Gaul, watching for a false move of the party opposed to

---

[5] Mommsen, *op. cit.*

him. To avoid a direct collision, Cato and Bibulus recommended that Pompey should be named as sole Consul.[6] Milo was soon after brought to trial for the
death of Clodius, and Cicero exerted himself to the utmost to prepare a speech in justification of Milo. But
Pompey was anxious to get rid of a citizen as troublesome on one side as Clodius had been on the other;
and he placed soldiers at every avenue of the Court
for the purpose, as he said, of preserving order. This
unwonted sight, and the fear of popular violence,
robbed Cicero of his eloquence. Milo was condemned
and fled to Massilia.[7]

In something of a huff, Cicero left Rome to assume the
Governorship of Cilicia.

Pompey had now reached the height of his ambition.
He was virtually Dictator, without being bound to any
party; and from this time he seems to have made up
his mind to break with Caesar. He married Cornelia,
the widow of Crassus and daughter of Metellus Scipio,
a leading member of the aristocracy, and on the first
of August associated his new father-in-law in the consulship with himself.[8]

For all practical purposes the days of a constitutional republic were over.
Hastily repealing some of the ultra-democratic measures
sponsored by the unlamented Clodius, he bent all his energies on framing a series of enactments whose object was to
balk Caesar at every turn. One of these measures decreed
that all candidates for office should give in their names in
person, which would have had the effect of putting the victor
of Alesia entirely at his unscrupulous rival's mercy should
he, unprotected by virtue of his office,[9] appear in Rome
after the imminent expiration of his term as Proconsul in
Transalpine Gaul. "At the same time Pompey put himself
above the law by procuring a vote according to which his
own government of Spain was prolonged for five years. . . .
By this law Pompey calculated that he should be able to

---

[6] Actually, a Consul without a colleague with whom to consult is
a contradiction in terms.

[7] Liddell, *op. cit.*

[8] *Ibid.*

[9] He could, for instance, be tried on a trumped-up charge of high
treason or extortion.

keep his own army on foot after the Gallic conqueror had disbanded his. In anticipation of Caesar's seeking a second consulship, he revised a decree that no one should hold a province till five years had elapsed from his [previous] tenure of office." [10]

Caesar was not, of course, without his own following in Rome; neither did his agents in the capital fail to keep him fully informed of what transpired. The legislation aimed at Caesar's supersession was due for final debate on March first, 50 B.C., "but when the day arrived, nothing was done; so well did Caesar's agents do their work, and so halfhearted was Pompeius in his opposition to them, that after two or three adjournments the question was again allowed to drop. And even up to the last day of that year no definite resolution had been taken.

"But if the Senate had taken no decisive step, the political current was setting strongly towards civil war. It was becoming every day plainer that the question was one, not so much between Caesar and the Senate, as between Caesar and Pompeius";[11] between the proponent of a *democratie royale* and the defender of a policy of *laissez faire* which left him cock of the dungheap.

In the summer of 50 B.C. Caesar let it be known in the Senate, through a fickle but able Tribune (C. Curio) who had lately come into his pay, that he was willing to resign his army and Province if Pompeius would simultaneously do the same, and the Senate voted a resolution in this sense by a majority of 370 to 22. The Consul Marcellus broke up the meeting in anger, crying out that they were voting for Caesar to be their master. About this time, or earlier, a scheme was suggested for sending Pompeius to the East, and so ridding themselves of him. In view of this Caesar was required to send home a Legion which he had some time previously borrowed from Pompeius to help in the Gallic rebellion. He at once obeyed the order,[12] but the Legions were detained by Pompeius in Italy and the Parthian war project was quietly dropped. These two facts—the vote in the Senate and the retention of the Legion—show plainly enough that the Senate was afraid of both the rivals, and that it was entirely at the mercy of the one whom it least dreaded.

[10] Liddell, *op. cit.*

[11] Warde Fowler, *op. cit.*

[12] Having bestowed two hundred and fifty drachmas on every man before sending the formation on its way.

So the year wore on, and the actual crisis was still delayed. The consular elections were hostile to Caesar, though, on the other hand, two of his Officers, M. Antonius and Q. Cassius, were elected Tribunes of the people. On Lentulus Crus and Claudius Marcellus, the new Consuls, must rest the immediate blame of the Civil War. No sooner had they entered on office on January first, 49 B.C., than it became obvious that the difficulty would shortly come to a head. On that day Curio once more presented proposals from Caesar, in the form of a letter to be read before the Senate by the new Consuls. In essence, the message affirmed Caesar's readiness to give up the Transalpine province and eight of his Legions, in return for the Senate's sanction for his retention of Cisalpine Gaul with two Legions, or that Province and Illyria with one only; the arrangement to continue until after his election as Consul.[13]

Thereafter, he would resign everything, even if this left him open to his enemies during the last months of the year.

When Caesar's letter was delivered to the Consuls, they were with great difficulty, and a hard struggle of the Tribunes, prevailed upon to suffer it to be read in the Senate; but the Tribunes could not prevail, that any question should be put to the Senate on the subject of the letter. The Consuls put the question on the regulation of the State. Lucius Lentulus the Consul promises that he will not fail the Senate and the Republic, "if they declared their sentiments boldly and resolutely, but if they turned their regard to Caesar, and courted his favor, as they did on former occasions, he would adopt a plan for himself, and not submit to the authority of the Senate: that he too had a means of regaining Caesar's favor and friendship." Metellus Scipio spoke to the same purpose, "that it was Pompey's intention not to abandon the Republic, if the Senate would support him; but if they should hesitate and act without energy, they would in vain implore his aid, if they should require it hereafter."[14]

It was clear that the time for procrastination and time-wasting formulae was over. In October C. Marcellus, on the strength of an entirely mendacious report that Caesar, without

---

[13] Warde Fowler, *op. cit.*
[14] Caesar, *Commentaries* (*The Civil War*, Book I).

awaiting official sanction, had transferred four Legions to Cisalpine Gaul, moved in the Senate that he be declared a public enemy,[15] and that Pompey be ordered to march against him with the Legions concentrated at Capua—which included the troops mustered for the projected war with Parthia that had come to nothing, and thus left two Legions under arms additional to the eight Pompey could speedily put on a war footing. With the country declared to be in danger, the whole of the burgesses were called to arms and the magistrates instructed to form them into Legions; a panic-measure that could bring little influence to bear on the immediate course of events. With this, the Caesarian Tribunes, Antonius and Cassius, accompanied by his principal supporters, Curio and M. Rufus Caelius, fled in disguise to Caesar's quarters. In declaring a state of war, appointing successors as Proconsuls of the Gallic Provinces, and ordering fresh levies and supplies, the Senate sealed its own fate—its end as inglorious as its record of greed, corruption, incompetence, and pusillanimity.

At this juncture Pompey, whose command Headquarters were at Capua, had available seven veteran Legions in Spain, ten in Italy—of which, however, only two were actually on a war footing—and many more on call in Sicily, Macedonia, Syria, Asia, and Africa; their free movement was assured by virtue of the fact that their Generalissimo had complete control of the sea. Moreover, he had learned from officers he had sent to take over the Legion lent for the Gaulish campaign that "Caesar's army was wasted by protracted service, that the soldiers longed for their homes and would change to the side of Pompey as soon as they should cross the Alps. They spoke in this way from ignorance or because they were corrupted. In fact, every soldier was strongly attached to Caesar and labored zealously for him, under the force of discipline and the influence of the gain which war usually brings to victors and which they received from Caesar also; for he gave with a lavish hand in order to mold them to his design. They knew what his designs were, but they stood by him nevertheless. Pompey, however, believed what was reported to him and collected neither soldiers nor apparatus suitable for so great a contest."[16] When it came to

[15] The Consuls invoked the Ciceronian law by which he had put to death the Catiline conspirators.

[16] Appian, *The Civil War* (Book II).

that point, "the soldiers whom Pompey supposed disaffected declared with enthusiasm that they would support their commander and the Tribunes. They offered to serve without pay. Officers and men volunteered contributions for the expenses of the war. In all the army one officer alone proved false. Labienus kept his word to Pompey and stole away to Capua. He left his effects behind, and Caesar sent them after him untouched." [17]

Caesar's only immediate handicap was shortage of numbers. At Ravenna, he had at most 300 Horse and 5,000 Legionaries; of his remaining forces, half were on the Saône and Loire and half in Belgia. Opposed to him at Luceria (Lucera) Pompey's lieutenant, Appius Claudius, had under immediate command two Legions, 7,000 strong. Strategically, however, Caesar was in a very advantageous position, for not only did the province of Cisalpine Gaul flank the entire north of Italy, but southern France (Gallia Transalpina), garrisoned with troops loyal to the conqueror of Alesia, cut across Pompey's land communications between Italy and Spain, thus isolating the forces of his Iberian command. The Senate, of course, indulged in the usual grandiose but empty gestures beloved by politicians in moments of crisis, authorizing Pompey to mobilize veterans and recruit "as many able-bodied men as possible from the neighboring provinces; and voted him for the war all the money in the public treasury, and their own private fortunes in addition, if they should be needed for the pay of the soldiers." [18] But with his amazing speed of thought and movement, Caesar had already seized the initiative.

Luceria and Ravenna are almost equidistant from Rome —by road, some two hundred forty miles. Relying on Pompey's well-known lethargy, Caesar was determined not only to get in the first blow, but to deliver a thrust that would frustrate the concentration of hostile force in overwhelming strength. Having dispatched couriers to hasten the arrival of his own reinforcements from Gaul, "he sent forward the Centurions with a few of their bravest troops in peaceful garb to go inside the walls of Ariminum and take it by surprise. This was the first town in Italy after leaving Cisalpine Gaul. Toward evening Caesar himself rose from a banquet on a plea of indisposition, leaving his friends still feasting. He mounted his chariot and drove toward Ariminum, his cavalry following at a short distance. When his

[17] Froude, *op. cit.*
[18] Appian, *op. cit.*

course brought him to the river Rubicon, he stopped and, while gazing at the stream, revolved in his mind the evils that would result, should he cross the river in arms." [19] Halted there, sunk in deepest meditation,

the General saw a vision of his distressed country. Her mighty image was clearly seen in the darkness of the night; her face expressed deep sorrow, and from her head the white hair streamed abroad; she stood beside him with tresses torn and arms bare, and her speech was broken by sobs: "Whither do ye march further, and whither do ye bear my standards, ye warriors? If ye come as law-abiding citizens, here must ye stop!" Then trembling smote the leader's limbs, a faintness stopped his motion and fettered his feet on the river-bank. But soon he spoke: "O God of thunder, who from the Tarpeian Rock, lookest out of the walls of the great city; O ye Trojan gods of the House of Iulus, and mysteries of Quirinus snatched from earth; O Jupiter of Latium, who dwellest on Alba's height, and ye fires of Vesta; and thou, O Rome, as sacred a name as any, smile on my enterprise. I do not attack thee in frantic warfare; behold me here, Caesar, a conqueror by land and sea and everywhere thy champion, as I would be now also! [20]

Beyond the Rubicon lay the chance of death or the hope of vindication in the birth of a Rome more worthy of the high destiny he could shape for it. His resolution steeled for whatever fate held in store for him, "he crossed the stream with a rush like one inspired, calling to his followers, 'The die is cast: so let it be!'

"Then he resumed his hasty journey and took possession of Ariminum about daybreak, advanced beyond it, stationed guards at the commanding positions, and, either by force or by kindness, mastered all whom he fell in with." [21]

The qualms of the Senate, and Pompey's prudent desire not to invite a blemish on his military repute by risking a trial of arms with a leader of Caesar's proven capacity, led to yet another attempt to come to terms. "Lucius Caesar, a distant kinsman, and the Praetor Roscius arrived, as they said, with a private message from Pompey. The mes-

[19] Appian, *op. cit.*
[20] Lucan, (M. Annaeus Lucanus), *The Civil War*.
[21] Appian, *op. cit.*

sage was nothing. The object was no more than to gain time. But Caesar had no wish for war, and would not throw away a chance of avoiding it. He bade his kinsman tell Pompey that it was for him to compose the difficulties which had arisen." [22] Recapitulating the injuries he had suffered, the pledges which had not been kept, "he affirmed his unaltered readiness to make peace." Let Pompey depart to Spain. His own troops should then be dismissed. The elections could be held freely, and Senate and people would be restored to their joint authority. If this were not enough, they two might meet and relieve each other's alarms and suspicions in a personal interview.

With this answer the envoys went, and Caesar paused at Rimini. Meanwhile the report reached Rome that Caesar had crossed the Rubicon. The ruling caste had nursed the pleasant belief that his heart would fail him, or that his army would desert him. His heart had not failed, his army had not deserted; and, in their terror, they saw him already in their midst like an avenging Marius. He was coming! His Horse had been seen on the Apennines. Flight, instant flight, was the only safety. Up they rose, Consuls, Praetors, Senators, leaving wives and children and property to their fate, not halting even to take the money out of the treasury, but contenting themselves with leaving it locked. On foot, on horseback, in litters, in carriages, they fled for their lives to find safety under Pompey's wing in Capua. In this forlorn company went Cicero, filled with contempt for what was round him.

"You ask what Pompey means to do," he wrote to Atticus. "I do not think he knows himself. Certainly none of us know. It is all panic and blunder. We are uncertain whether he will make a stand or leave Italy. If he stays, I fear his army is unreliable. If not, where will he go, and what are his plans? I am afraid that Caesar will be at Phalaris,[23] and that we may expect the very worst." [24]

Caesar was certainly on the move, recruiting as he went. For the purpose of blocking any attempt to cut his line of communications with Gaul, his lieutenant, Mark Antony, was sent to occupy Arretium. With this township, Iguvium,

[22] Froude, *op. cit.*
[23] A notorious tyrant of Agrigentum.
[24] Froude, *op. cit.*

and Ancona in his hands, he had established a firm base
line, securely protecting Gaul and putting an end to any
danger to his rear. This done, he moved rapidly on Corfinium, where Pompey's representative, Domitius, had been
sent to mobilize the reserve troops called up from the surrounding district. Although Pompey was doubtful of the
readiness of the men recalled to the ranks to serve against
Caesar, it was clear to the latter that it would be the worst
of folly to leave in his rear a potentially hostile force which
would be in a position to cut off his Legions on their march
from Gaul to join up with him.

Caesar's resolution was justified, though it cost him
a delay of seven days, which had other serious consequences. Corfinium was invested, and the conduct of
Domitius's troops showed that Pompeius had rightly
judged the situation. Believing that their commander
was about to make his escape alone, on February twen-
tieth they opened the gates; the next day the Senators
and *Equites* who had gathered there surrendered to
Caesar, who after a short speech released them all un-
conditionally. He protected them from all insult, and
returned to Domitius a large sum of money which had
been entrusted to him for military purposes. The captured troops enlisted in his ranks, and took the oath
of obedience to him.[25]

"The capture of Corfinium and the desertion of the garrison made an end of hesitation. Pompey and the Consuls
thought only of instant flight, and hurried to Brundusium,
where ships were waiting for them; and Caesar, hoping that
the evident feeling of Italy would have its effect with the
reasonable part of the Senate, sent Cornelius Balbus, who
was on intimate terms with many of them, to assure them
of his eagerness for peace, and to tell Cicero especially that
he would be well contented to live under Pompey's rule if
he could have a guarantee for his personal safety." [26]

How far Caesar was sincere in this avowal can only be a
matter for conjecture. Suffice it to record that in the
absence of any response on the lines he had demanded,
Caesar marched on Rome without further loss of time.
"When he was in possession of the city, he behaved with
great moderation in many respects, and composed, in a

25 Warde Fowler, *op. cit.*
26 Froude, *op. cit.*

good measure, the minds of its remaining inhabitants. Only when Metellus, one of the Tribunes of the people, forbade him to touch the money in the public treasury, he threatened him with death, adding an expression more terrible than the threat itself, 'That it was easier for him to do it than to say it.' Metellus being thus frightened off, Caesar took the sums he wanted, and then went in pursuit of Pompey." [27] Moving eastward to Luceria, from that point he took the highway leading to Brundusium.

> Pompey, who was master of Brundusium, and had a sufficient number of transports, desired the Consuls to embark without loss of time, and sent them before him with thirty Cohorts to Dyrrhachium. But at the same time he sent his father-in-law, Scipio, and his son Gnaeus into Syria to provide ships of war. He had well secured the gates of the city, and planted the lightest of his slingers and archers upon the walls; and having now ordered the Brundusians to keep within doors, he caused a number of trenches to be cut, and sharp stakes driven into them, and then covered with earth, in all the streets, except two that led down to the sea. In three days all his other troops were embarked without interruption, and then he suddenly gave the signal to those who guarded the walls; in consequence of which they ran swiftly down to the harbor and got on board. Thus having his whole complement, he set sail, and crossed the sea to Dyrrhachium.[28]

With Brundusium evacuated, Caesar was master of Italy, for what that was worth. By splitting his forces into two main groups, one in Epirus and one in Spain, Pompey had in no sense weakened his hand, for with his command of the sea it should be possible to crush Caesar between them. The crucial factor was the element of time. Perfectly cognizant of this, Caesar decided to hold Brundusium and then, at all speed, move on Spain, where Pompey's main strength was to be found. Meanwhile, to forestall an economic attack on Italy, he sent one Legion to Sicily and a second to Sardinia, to act as guardians over the corn supply. This done, orders were dispatched that would assemble nine of the best Legions in Gaul, together with 6,000 Horse and a body of archers, in the vicinity of Massilia.

It could be argued that the moment to strike at Pompey

[27] Plutarch, *op. cit.*
[28] *Ibid.*

was before he could muster his resources at their maximum strength, that Caesar's Legions could have marched on Pompey through Illyricum and dealt with him before any real threat from the seven Pompeian Legions in Spain would develop. Caesar's own explanation for coming to the decision he did was somewhat cryptically summed up by the entry in his *Commentaries,* "I am setting forth to fight an army without a leader so as by and by to fight a leader without an army."

With all his arrangements made and the troop movements in train, by March twenty-ninth Caesar was back in Rome, where he ordered the construction of two fleets, one in the Adriatic and the other in the Tyrrhenian Sea.

As Caesar marched along the coast he heard that Massilia had collected all the corn from the vicinity and fortified the town, and that Pompey's adherents had roused the citizens in his favor. They had also procured the aid of the Albici, nearby mountain tribes of the western Alps. So soon as he reached the place, Caesar invited some of the principal citizens of Massilia to come to him, and endeavored to talk them over to his cause. But for once his eloquence proved vain. The magistrates claimed that they had received equal reassurances from Pompey as from Caesar, and could in good faith give allegiance to neither, nor admit the forces of either to their town or harbor.[29]

Nonetheless, when Pompey's lieutenant, Domitius, arrived off the harbor with a squadron of seven rowing galleys, he was immediately admitted and made Governor of the place, Caesar, without ships, having had no means of challenging his entry into the haven.

Domitius at once set about fitting out a fleet. He seized upon all the merchantmen which were in the harbor or in the vicinity, and confiscated their cargoes, mostly corn, which was laid up for a siege. Caesar, incensed that a town in the Province should thus turn against him, as well as all but compromised by its treachery—for Massilia, with the aid of the Albici, might cut at Aquae Sextiae the road from Italy to Spain—began to provide means for besieging the place. He could not leave it in his rear without at least a blockade,

[29] Colonel Theodore Ayrault Dodge, *Caesar* (Vol. II).

for it was one of the most important towns on the Mediterranean, and its example might prove disastrous. He himself began the construction of contravallation.

Caesar sent word to Antony to hurry up the Eighth, Twelfth, and Thirteenth Legions, already on the march, and diverted them from Gaul towards Spain. Meanwhile he dispatched Fabius into Spain, with the three Legions at Narbo, to occupy the passes in the Pyrenees, in advance of his own coming. Fabius marched with speed enough to dislodge a small party of Pompey's adherents (part of the forces under L. Afranius) from the passes in the Pyrenees, and descended into Spain. It had been the purpose of Afranius and Petreius to occupy the Pyrenees, but Fabius anticipated them.[30]

It was perfectly clear to Caesar, of course, that a protracted campaign in Transalpine Gaul and Spain would be fatal to his chances. Pompey would return to Italy, and there find no one of real metal to oppose him. The Spanish army had to be destroyed or captured with the minimum of delay. Yet Afranius and Petreius were already over the Ebro with thirty thousand Legionaries and twice that number of Iberian auxiliaries. But Pompey's lieutenants had failed to secure the passes, and in consequence had fallen back, and were "lying at Ilerda (Lérida), in Catalonia, at the junction of the Segre and the Naguera, with the Ebro behind them, and with a mountain range, the Sierra de Llena, on their right flank. Their position was impregnable to direct attack. From their rear they drew inexhaustible supplies. The country in front had been laid waste to the Pyrenees, and everything that Caesar required had to be brought to him from Gaul." [31]

It was Afranius's strategy to refuse battle, if possible, throughout the campaigning season, in order not to risk a defeat that would free his opponent to proceed elsewhere. Equally, it was Caesar's overriding purpose to bring matters to a decisive issue with as little delay as possible.

The first phase of the campaign opened with Caesar's arrival before Ilerda on June twenty-third. The town stood on the right, or western, bank of the Segre on a hill close to the river, commanding the main road from the Pyrenees to the Ebro. Afranius and Petreius were encamped on another hill somewhat to the southwest-

[30] Dodge, op. cit.
[31] Froude, *op. cit.*

ward, and between them and the town was another,
lower, eminence. At Ilerda there was a bridge, so that
by holding the town they could command both banks of
the river, and gather supplies in every direction except
to the north. Caesar also had two bridges, four miles
apart, made by his officer Fabius before his arrival; one
of these had been broken by a storm. As soon as it was
repaired Caesar offered battle, but it was declined, and
he set to work to fortify a camp in the plain near to
that of the enemy, in order to watch his opportunity.

On the twenty-seventh, seeing the importance of the
little hill which lay between Ilerda and the enemy's
camp, he determined to seize it, and so to cut him off
from the town and its bridge, and from communication
from the left bank of the river. But the attempt was a
signal failure, though made with picked men; the enemy's troops reached the hill first, and fighting in loose
skirmishing order, drove the Caesarians before them,
and compelled the whole Legion to which the attacking party belonged to retreat to the nearest high ground.
The surprising result disheartened the whole army. The
Ninth Legion was sent to the rescue, but only succeeded
in making matters worse. They at first repulsed the
enemy, but in pursuing them up to the city wall, were
stopped by a sudden steep rise in the slope they were
following, from the top of which rise the enemy would
discharge missiles on them at leisure. This slope and
the sharp rise at the upper part of it were enclosed
between two rocky spurs or ridges, which projected
from this southern side of the hill at a considerable
angle. The farther Caesar's men pressed up the ascent, the more closely were they hemmed in between
the steep walls of these spurs; and when they were
stopped by the sudden rise they found themselves
crowded in a narrow space where they could no longer
advance or maneuver, or retreat without bringing the
enemy down on them with headlong force. The attacking column was now worse than useless, for it blocked
up the way for supports, which could not reach it on
the flanks owing to the steep sides of the ridges between
which it was wedged. The column, however, stood its
ground bravely, though severely handled by the enemy
above; and Caesar contrived to keep it there during five
hours by sending fresh troops to take the place of the
wounded and fatigued. At last when all the missiles
were spent, the men drew their swords and rushed up the

steep rise above them, driving the enemy under the
city wall and thus making a free space for their own
retreat. This was further secured by the valor of the
cavalry, which pushed up under the steep sides of the
ridge, and interposed themselves between the retreating column and the enemy. The day's work cost Caesar
heavy loss,[32]

and there can be no question that the Caesarians had the
worst of the encounter. Yet even grimmer times were to
follow.

The river Segre had risen and overflowed its bank, and
the two bridges built by Fabius had been carried away,
while the high stone bridge at Ilerda stood firm. Caesar
was cut off from the left bank, while Afranius could always cross to it and prevent any new bridge from being
constructed. Another river, thirty miles to the west, was also
in flood and impassable; so that Caesar was penned in a
narrow area where all supplies had already been exhausted
and the growing corn was still green in the ear. Ilerda, on
the other hand, was amply supplied, while the Pompeians
were free to forage on the left bank of the Segre and with
their numerous Horse, to cut off Caesar's foragers or intercept any convoys destined for his camp. Caesar's troops
were already on remarkably short commons, and unless the
situation were alleviated a disastrous retreat into Gaul would
become inevitable, such as would utterly destroy Caesar's
prestige throughout the Empire.

In this crisis news reached Afranius of a large convoy of supplies which was on its way to Caesar from
Gaul, and was unable to cross the river so as to reach
him; it was protected by Gallic archers and cavalry, but
was heavily encumbered and without discipline. He made
a vigorous effort to capture it and end the war, and
Caesar saw clearly that he must save it or succumb.

The expedient by which he extricated himself from
such peril shows the immense advantage possessed by
a General whose troops are trained to turn their hands
to all kinds of work. He set his men to work to build
boats of timber, wattles, and skins, such as they had
seen in Britain. These were conveyed by night, each on
two carts, twenty miles up the river, so as to be as far
as possible out of the enemy's reach; a few soldiers
crossed in them and fortified a position on the other

[32] Warde Fowler, *op. cit.*

bank. Then a bridge was begun, and finished in two days; the convoy was brought across to the right bank, Caesar's cavalry began to scour the left bank and to cut off Afranius's foraging parties, and the tables were completely turned on the enemy.[33]

It was now the turn of Afranius and his colleagues to think gloomily of retreat, and orders were given for the construction of a bridge over the Ebro to secure their escape to central Spain. They were impelled on this course

by another device of Caesar's. He had ditches dug, thirty feet wide, from one channel of the river to another,[34] about a mile above Ilerda, and so reduced the volume of water in the main stream as to render it fordable at least for his cavalry, which had been compelled each day to go round by his recently constructed distant bridge. The enemy crossed at Ilerda and began his retreat on July twenty-fifth. The left bank was of course chosen, because Caesar could only operate on it in force with cavalry, and because supplies were still to be had there. His cavalry at once began to hang on the retreating foe, but the infantry were detained by the depth of the ford. The men could not endure this, and clamored to be allowed to risk the passage. Caesar could not resist their ardor. He left all the weaker men behind, and the rest got over with trifling loss and overtook the enemy by a forced march. The armies encamped face to face that night. At earliest dawn both Generals reconnoitered and found themselves but a few miles from the rocky hills which here close in from the north upon the valley of the Ebro; it was obvious that whichever army could reach the defiles first would be able to stop the progress of the other.[35]

It was Caesar's men who won the race, and the Pompeians found their way blocked in front and their rear under constant harassment from their enemy's ubiquitous Horse. "Caesar had given up the idea of forcing a battle on the Pompeians. He saw that it would be better, if it were possible, to conquer Afranius and Petreius without destroying the Roman Legions opposed to him. His hope was to bring these Legions, or at least many of the men, over to his

[33] Warde Fowler, *op. cit.*
[34] In this area the Segre flows in three channels.
[35] Warde Fowler, *op. cit.*

cause. What would have been vacillation in many of his movements may really be ascribed to sound military motive. He wished to win by maneuvering rather than by fighting." [36]

By adroit use of ground Caesar eventually succeeded in penning Afranius in a position lying midway between the mouth of the defile for which he had been heading and the nearest substantial water supply.

> Beset on all sides, having no fodder, water, wood, or corn, seeing no chance of exit, and lacking resolution to cut their way out, Afranius and Petreius asked for a private conference. This Caesar refused, but granted the Pompeians a public conference to be held in the presence of both armies. The latter took place. Afranius spoke humbly and asked for easy terms; Caesar spoke in his usual persuasive manner, complimenting Afranius and Petreius and their Legions for avoiding battle to save Roman life, though reproaching them for massacring his soldiers in their camp,[37] paying them a tribute to the high quality of the troops, and promising his good offices to all, but yet with a clear hint that the terms stated were his ultimatum. He knew full well when to be diplomatically generous. As a result of the meeting it was agreed that the Legions of the enemy should be discharged from service and sent back to their homes, and that Afranius and Petreius should evacuate Spain and Gaul.[38]

The Spanish troops were discharged forthwith; the men of Afranius's Legions were marched, under escort, to the confines of Italy, where those who did not volunteer to serve under Caesar's banner were sent to their homes. Pompey's extraordinary inactivity where support for his lieutenants in Spain was concerned, had cost him the continuing services of seven admirable Legions, while Caesar was further encouraged by the naval victory won by Decimus Brutus in an encounter with a numerically superior armament commanded by Domitius, fought out in the waters lying between Massilia and the offshore island that was to acquire the name of Rattonneaux.

With Spain no longer a problem, Caesar was free to take over from Gaius Trebonius the task of reducing Massilia

---

[36] Dodge, *op. cit.*
[37] The captives of earlier encounters.
[38] Dodge, *op. cit.*

itself, and thither he made his way towards the end of September.

Massilia's siege had witnessed much hard fighting, both on land and at sea. After Domitius's defeat by the clumsy but well-handled Caesarian vessels,

Pompey had sent a second squadron to help him, and this had fared no better. It had fled after a single battle, and never reappeared. The land-works had been assailed with ingenuity and courage. The *agger* had been burnt and the siege-towers destroyed. But they had been repaired instantly by the industry of the Legions, and Massilia was at the last extremity when Caesar arrived. He had wished to spare the townspeople, and had sent orders that the place was not to be stormed. On his appearance the keys of the gates were brought to him without conditions. Again he pardoned everyone; more, he said, for the reputation of the colony than for the merits of its inhabitants. Domitius had fled in a gale of wind, and once more escaped.

Two Legions were left in charge of Massilia; others returned to their quarters in Gaul. Well as the tribes had behaved, it was unsafe to presume too much on their fidelity, and Caesar was not a partisan chief but the guardian of the Roman Empire. With the rest of his army he returned to Rome at the beginning of winter. All had been quiet since the news of the capitulation of Ilerda. . . . Spain, Gaul and Italy, Sicily and Sardinia were entirely his own. Elsewhere and away from his own eye, things had gone less well for him. An attempt to make a naval force in the Adriatic had failed; and young Curio who had done Caesar such good service as Tribune had met with a still graver disaster. After recovering Sicily, Curio had been directed to cross to Africa and expel Pompey's garrisons from the Province. His troops were inferior, consisting chiefly of the garrison which had surrendered at Corfinium. Through military inexperience Curio had fallen into a trap laid for him by Juba, King of Mauretania, and had been killed.

Caesar regretted Curio personally. The African misfortune was not considerable in itself, but it encouraged hopes and involved consequences which he probably foresaw. There was no present leisure, however, to attend to Juba. On arriving at the city he was named Dictator. As Dictator he held the consular elections, and, with Servilius Isauricus for a colleague, he was chosen Consul for the year which had been promised to him, though under circumstances so strangely changed.

Civil affairs were in the wildest confusion. The Senate had fled; the administration had been left to Antony, whose knowledge of business was not of a high order; and over the whole of Italy hung the terror of Pompey's fleet and of an Asiatic invasion. Public credit was shaken. Debts had not been paid since the civil war began. Moneylenders had charged usurious interest for default, and debtors were crying for *novae tabulae,* and hoped to clear themselves by bankruptcy. Caesar had but small leisure for such matters. Pompey had been allowed too long a respite, and unless he sought Pompey in Greece, Pompey would be seeking him at home, and the horrid scenes of Sulla's wars would be enacted over again.[39]

Eleven days were all that Caesar could afford to Rome. Accounts must be settled with Pompey while it was still winter, and before his preparations for the invasion of Italy could be completed. It was almost a twelvemonth since Caesar had crossed the Rubicon, and the force now under his command amounted nominally to twelve Legions. Battle casualties had appreciably thinned the ranks, however, which had further been depleted by the troops' transfer from the dry climate of Spain and Southern Gaul to a wet Italian autumn. It is doubtful, therefore, if Caesar could have counted on more than thirty thousand effectives.

On the other hand, Pompey's army, cantoned opposite Brundusium at Dyrrhachium (Durazzo), had all its nine Legions up to full strength, while two more completed Legionary formations were on their way, under Metellus Scipio, from Syria. In addition, Pompey could call on auxiliaries from the allied Princes in the East, from Greece and Asia Minor, on slingers and archers from Crete and the islands. Of money, stores, and reserve weapons there was abundance, Pompey having deflected all the year's income from the East into his own coffers. But his greatest asset— and one that Caesar was in no position to offset—lay in his possession of a naval armament of one hundred and thirty warships, with a full complement of supporting storeships and transports. Distributed all along the shores of Illyricum, Macedonia, and Epirus, with headquarters at Corfu, the sole purpose of the armada was to prevent Caesar's passage across the Adriatic.

The best that Caesar could muster in the way of a fighting marine consisted of twelve combatant triremes, all that remained of his purported Adriatic fleet. It was a force too small to risk in an encounter with Pompey's armada, while the available transport could only give passage across the Adriatic to half of Caesar's army in a single trip. The obvious course was for Caesar to keep his Legions together and proceed round the head of the Adriatic and continue his approach march through Illyricum. But it was difficult country to traverse at any time; in winter it would be very easy to get thoroughly entangled in it, leaving Pompey free in the meantime to invade Italy and overrun his opponent's base. Moreover, many of Caesar's victories had been won by his doing something other than what had been expected of him, and once again he determined on a move the sheer surprise of which should go a long way towards confounding his opponents.

Dyrrhachium, which Pompey had organized as his base, was but a day's sail from the Italian coast. An attack on the port from seaward was the last thing the Pompeians would be likely to foresee, especially in the prevailing blustery weather. Indeed, so little did Pompey anticipate such a move that at this particular juncture he was reported as being absent from Dyrrhachium on a recruiting drive in Macedonia.

Once again, as at the Rubicon, the die was cast.

Although there were transports for only seven of his Legions, Caesar mustered all twelve of them at Brundusium, where

he made a speech to the soldiers: "That since they were now almost arrived at the termination of their toils and dangers, they should patiently submit to leave their slaves and baggage in Italy, and to embark without baggage, that a greater number of men might be put aboard; that they might expect everything from victory and his liberality." They cried out with one voice, he "might give what orders he pleased, that they would cheerfully fulfill them." He accordingly set sail with seven Legions on board. The next day he reached land between the Ceraunian rocks and other dangerous places; meeting with a safe road for his shipping to ride in, and dreading all other ports which he imagined were in possession of the enemy, he landed his men without loss of a single vessel.[40]

Some 15,000 Foot and 500 Horse were put ashore at Acroceraunia—now Cape Linguetta—on the eastern shore of the Straits of Otranto, approximately one hundred miles from Dyrrhachium. From the heights of Corfu his old enemy Bibulus saw Caesar's convoy pass, and put to sea—too late to intercept the outgoing passage, but in time to fall in with the returning transports, whose masters had failed to take advantage of the darkness for their return trip and so were overtaken. Bibulus captured thirty of them, and in a fury at having missed them while they were heading for Acroceraunia, slaughtered everyone he found on board.

Ignorant of this misfortune, and expecting that Antony would follow him in a day or two with the remainder of the army, Caesar advanced at once toward Dyrrhachium, occupied Apollonia, and entrenched himself on the left bank of the river Apsus. The country, as he had anticipated, was well-disposed and furnished him with ample supplies. He still hoped Pompey would come to terms with him. He trusted, perhaps not unreasonably, that the generosity with which he had treated Massilia and the Spanish Legions might have produced an effect; and he appealed once more to Pompey's wiser judgment. Vibullius Rufus, who had been taken at Corfinium, and a second time on the Lerida (Ilerda), had since remained with Caesar. Rufus, being personally known as an ardent member of the Pompeian party, was sent forward to Dyrrhachium with a message of peace.[41]

To this overture there was no immediate response, since at the time of its delivery Pompey was still in Macedonia. Hearing of his rival's successful landing, however, he immediately took the road to Dyrrhachium. "Caesar's landing had produced a panic in Pompey's camp. Men and Officers were looking anxiously in each other's faces. So great was the alarm, so general the distrust, that Labienus had sworn in the presence of the army that he would stand faithfully by Pompey. Generals, Centurions, and Tribunes had sworn after him. They had then moved up to the Apsus and encamped

[40] Caesar, *op. cit.*
[41] Froude, *op. cit.*

on the opposite side of the river, waiting for Pompey to come up.

There was now a pause on both sides. Antony was unable to leave Brundusium, Bibulus being on the watch day and night. A single vessel attempted the passage. It was taken, and everyone on board was massacred. The weather was still wild, and both sides suffered. If Caesar's transports could not put to sea, Bibulus's crews could not land either for fuel or water anywhere south of Apollonia. Bibulus held on obstinately till he died of exposure to wet and cold, so ending his useless life; but his death did not affect the situation favorably for Caesar; his command fell into abler hands.

At length Pompey arrived. Vibullius Rufus delivered his message. Pompey would not hear him to the end. "What care I," he said, "for life or country if I am to hold both by favor of Caesar? All men will think thus of me if I make peace now: I left Italy. Men will say that Caesar brought me back."

In the Legions opinion was different. The two armies were divided only by a narrow river. Friends met and talked. They asked each other for what purpose so desperate a war had been undertaken. The regular troops all idolized Caesar. Deputations from both sides were chosen to converse and consult, with Caesar's warmest approval. Some arrangement might have followed. But Pompey's lieutenant interposed. He appeared at the meeting as if to join in the conference; he was talking in apparent friendliness to Cicero's acquaintance, Publius Vatinius, who was serving with Caesar. Suddenly a shower of darts were hurled at Vatinius. His men flung themselves in front of him and covered his body; but most of them were wounded, and the assembly broke up in confusion, Labienus shouting, "Leave your talk of composition; there can be no peace till you bring us Caesar's head." [42]

Success in warfare depends upon the opportune employment of strength, and in tactics timing is absolutely fundamental to success. And in an apposite sense of timing Pompey was singularly wanting. Vastly superior to Caesar in numbers and engines of war, for two whole months he remained in position opposite his opponent without making the slightest attempt to overwhelm him by sheer weight of men and *matériel*.

[42] Froude, *op. cit.*

A bold offensive at this moment might have been fatal to Caesar. He had but half Pompey's forces. The rest were still at Brundusium, and might indefinitely be kept there by weather and Pompey's fleet; for the latter was well equipped and by good management ought to control the Adriatic. Now was the time, if ever, for Pompey to crush his adversary. A lucky circumstance might any day enable Calenus to bring over Caesar's other Legions. Nor were opportunities wanting. Holding as he did the entire coast, Pompey by a simple forward movement of his right, with reasonable precautions, could scarcely have failed to force Caesar into the interior of Epirus, thus dividing his forces beyond a hope of junction. Moreover, Caesar was placed where victualing his army was already a serious task and might be made all but impossible. For he had no fleet; [43]

and L. Scribonius Libo, Bibulus's successor, had occupied the small island off Brundusium, thus effectively blockading the haven. It was a move that Antony very shrewdly countered by constantly patrolling the foreshore to cut off Libo from his water supplies, thus compelling him to raise the blockade and return to his base.

But time was speeding by, and there were not wanting those in Rome, in anxious doubt as to Caesar's ability to get the better of his more amply furnished opponent, who began to brood on the possible wisdom of changing sides. To no one more than Caesar was the need for action more starkly apparent.

He wrote to Antony sharply. The Legions, true as steel, were ready for any risks sooner than leave their commander in danger. A south wind came at last, and they sailed. They were seen in mid-channel, and closely pursued. Night fell, and in the darkness they were swept past Dyrrhachium, to which Pompey had again withdrawn, with the Pompeian squadron in full chase behind them. They ran into the harbor of Nymphaea, three miles north of Lissa, and were fortunate in entering it safely. Sixteen of the pursuers ran upon the rocks, and the crews owed their lives to Caesar's troops, who saved them. . . . Two only of the transports which had left Brundusium were missing in the morning. They had gone by mistake into Lissa, and were surrounded by the boats

of the enemy, who promised they should not be injured
if they surrendered. One of the vessels had two hundréd
and twenty young soldiers aboard, the other two hundred
veterans. The recruits were seasick and frightened. They
trusted the enemy's fair words, and were immediately
murdered. The others forced their pilot to run the ship
ashore. They cut their way through a band of Pompey's
cavalry, and joined their comrades without the loss of a
man.[44]

Antony's men were speedily concentrated, but there was no
burking the fact that their situation was extremely critical,
for Pompey's army lay between them and the main body
under Caesar. Antony, of course,

> sent messages to Caesar with great dispatch, to inform him
> in which part of the country he had landed his army, and
> what number of troops he had brought over with him.

> Caesar and Pompey received the intelligence almost
> at the same time; for they had seen the ships sail past
> Apollonia and Dyrrhachium. They directed their march
> after them by land; but at first they were ignorant to
> what part they had been carried; but when they had been
> informed of it, they each adopted a different plan; Cac-
> sar to form a junction with Antonius as soon as possible;
> Pompey to oppose Antonius's forces on their march to
> Caesar, and, if possible, to fall upon them unexpectedly
> from ambush. And the same day they both led out their
> armies from their winter encampment along the river
> Apsus; Pompey, privately by night; Caesar, openly by
> day. But Caesar had to march a longer circuit up the
> river to find a ford. Pompey's route being easy, because
> he was not obliged to cross the river, he advanced rapidly
> and by forced marches against Antonius, and being in-
> formed of his approach, chose a convenient situation,
> where he posted his forces; and kept his men close with-
> in camp, and forbade fires to be kindled, that his arrival
> might be the more secret. An account of this was im-
> mediately carried to Antonius by the Greeks. He dis-
> patched messengers to Caesar, and confined himself in
> his camp for one day. The next day Caesar came up with
> him. On learning of his arrival, Pompey, to prevent his
> being hemmed in between two armies, quitted his posi-
> tion, and went with all his forces to Asparagium, in the

[44] Froude, *op. cit.*

territory of Dyrrhachium, and there encamped in a convenient situation.[45]

Slow-witted and lethargic, Pompey, lying hopefully in an ambuscade that had little chance of snaring so alert a prey, had permitted that junction of Caesar's forces which he should have been at the utmost pains to prevent. Firmly entrenched at Asparagium, he ignored all Caesar's attempts to tease him into giving battle, despite his awareness of the fact that his opponent had deliberately reduced his strength by sending a considerable number of troops and a body of cavalry on detached duty. Five Cohorts and 200 Horse had been dispatched under Lucius Cassius Longinus to Thessaly and Aetolia in search of supplies. Two Legions and 500 Horse, under Domitius Calvinus, had been given the task of heading off Pompey's lieutenant, Metellus Scipio, who was bringing up reinforcements from Thessalonica (Salonica). Caesar was left, therefore, with a bare 22,000 men under his immediate command, to cope with a force of at least double that number.

In despair of luring Pompey into open combat, Caesar ostentatiously moved off into the hills eastward, "as if bent on exploring the country for supplies. Then turning suddenly to the north, and marching day and night, he swooped down on Dyrrhachium. It was a brilliant maneuver; the city indeed could not be taken, for it lay on a rocky peninsula, and was accessible only by a narrow neck of land between sea and marshes; but this neck was now in Caesar's power, the great road at this point was in his hands, and Pompeius was cut off from his most valuable stores." [46] Pompey's riposte was to occupy the high ground of Petra, some six miles south of the city, where there was a harbor big enough to take small vessels, by the use of which he could still bring in victuals from his main depot in Dyrrhachium. Thus if Caesar was of a mind to besiege the city, he could do so only at the risk of being called upon to turn and deal with a mobile enemy in his rear. Indeed, in many respects the situation resembled that which had developed at Alesia. In the event, Caesar, while maintaining his blockade on the neck of land leading to Dyrrhachium, constructed a fortified line enclosing Pompey's entrenched camp, of no less than fifteen miles in length. This was done "with these views: as he had but a small quantity of corn, and Pompey was strong in cavalry,[47] that he

[45] Caesar, op. cit.

[46] Warde Fowler, op. cit.

[47] Who might, in effect, interfere with Caesar's countrywide round-up of supplies.

might furnish his army with corn and other necessities from all sides with less danger; secondly, to prevent Pompey from foraging, and thereby render his Horse ineffectual in the operations of the war; and thirdly, to lessen his reputation, on which he saw he depended greatly, among foreign nations, when a report should have spread throughout the world that he was blockaded by Caesar, and dare not hazard a battle." [48]

At the outset Caesar's Legionaries had constructed some forty strongpoints in a circuit about the Pompeian camp, and to join them up to make a continuous line of contravallation involved tremendously fatiguing work, the local soil being heavy clay. Moreover, for toiling, hungry men there was a shortage of those nourishing rations that would have gone a long way towards offsetting the physical strain to which everyone was subjected. Illyricum was not a grain-bearing terrain; it was impossible to get supplies from Italy, since Pompey's warships commanded the local waters. But if corn was in short supply, "the soldiers found great relief from a root in the adjoining fields, which they prepared in milk.[49] Sometimes they made it into bread, and going up to the enemy's advanced guards, threw it in among them and declared 'that as long as the earth produced such roots, they would certainly besiege Pompey.' " [50]

Pompey likewise was not without his difficulties over supplies. Comestibles could be furnished from Italy by way of Dyrrhachium and the small haven below Petra. But it was a different matter where forage and water were concerned, particularly the latter. "For Caesar had either turned the course of all the rivers and streams which ran to the sea, or had dammed them up with strong works," [51] until conditions grew so precarious that it became incumbent on Pompey either to withdraw to Italy or to put his fortune to the arbitrament of the sword. The first course he could not pursue, since all his war *matériel*—reserve of weaponry, siege engines, and the like—was stored in Dyrrhachium. Moreover, the blow to his prestige that such a move would entail would be certain to shake the confidence of his Eastern allies and lukewarm supporters in Italy as potently as it would hearten those who had put their faith in Caesar. With whatever reluctance, Pompey decided on a vigorous resort to arms.

---

[48] Caesar, *op. cit.*

[49] This root was called *claera*. Many of Caesar's men who had served in Sardinia, where the root grew freely, had learned to make bread from it.

[50] Plutarch, *op. cit.*

[51] Caesar, *op. cit.*

Skirmishing between outposts had been constant, and at one point had developed into a serious affray. Work on a particular height where Caesar wished to extend his left to the sea had been consistently subjected to showers of darts and flights of arrows. In the circumstances, Caesar

found it necessary to retire the Ninth [Legion] from the place, and Pompey followed up his opponent's Legionaries vigorously and inflicted some losses on them. The retreat was down the rugged slope to the east, and gradually became difficult. . . . At this setback Caesar became uneasy, for his veterans were exhibiting unusual lack of nerve. Hurdles were brought, and under their cover a trench was dug and the ends fortified with redoubts. The stand thus made was maintained for a period, and later, slingers and archers were thrown out so as to cover a further retreat. The Legionary Cohorts were then ordered to file off, but Pompey's men "boldly and tauntingly pursued and chased" Caesar's, leveling the hurdles and passing the trench. Fearing that this might be the cause of serious demoralization in the army, and that retreat might degenerate into stampede, Caesar ordered Antony, who was in command, when in his withdrawal he reached a given place, to turn and charge. This was gallantly done. At the trumpet signal, the Ninth Legion came to a right-about, closed their files—they were evidently still well in hand—paused but to cast their javelins, and then rushed upon the enemy with the sword. Though as at Ilerda they were charging up a steep incline, they drove everything before them, and Pompey's men "turned their backs," retired in confusion, and with no little loss, for the hurdles and trench lay in the path of their retreat and tripped up many. Five Legionaries of Caesar's were killed; of Pompey's many more. Another hill was selected and fortified, Pompey retaining the one from which he had driven Caesar. The loss of this hill was the first step in the disaster which was bound to result from Caesar's overconfident undertaking in thus enclosing Pompey in siege lines. It enabled Pompey to occupy a larger extent of ground than Caesar had hoped to confine him to, and obliged Caesar to make his own the greater by nearly a half; and moreover it compelled him to close his left by a long line across an extended plain, where later Pompey found his weak spot.[52]

[52] Dodge, *op. cit.*

Pompey might have been hemmed in, but that very fact endowed him with the advantage of working from interior lines, a concentrated position; whereas Caesar's strung-out circumvallation dangerously attenuated the limited number of troops at his disposal, while denying him anything like an adequate reserve to bolster up the defense at any point singled out for mass assault, or to hold in hand for the purposes of counterattack.

It was probably false information, carefully relayed at Pompey's instigation, that persuaded Caesar to stage an attempt to capture Dyrrhachium itself. At all events,

> at the head of a sufficient body of troops he advanced on the city, crossed the narrows at the south end of the lagoon, and advanced with a small escort towards the walls. But his hopes were not realized. Instead of meeting a friendly reception from the party who had (ostensibly) agreed to act with him, the Dyrrhachium garrison issued from the gates suddenly and with hostile intent. A part took ship and sailed around to the narrows to cut him off. Another party moved around his right to prevent his making his way up to the north end of the lagoons. A third party attacked him in front. Caesar quickly rallied his men, met these three detachments with his forces, and a smart combat began with each body. The combat was without result. Fighting in his rear compelled Caesar to retreat, which he did without meeting any particular difficulty.[53]

But it was a disheartening outcome to a venture which had held out such fair, if delusive, promise.

With Antony in control on the sensitive left flank, command of the main camp had been entrusted to Publius Sulla, nephew of Sulla the Dictator. It was he who had to bear the brunt of an assault launched by Pompey to coincide with Caesar's absence to supervise the attempt of Dyrrhachium.

> He [Pompey] organized three attacks on Caesar's siege lines. These were so nearly simultaneous to the ones opposite Dyrrhachium that it looks as if Pompey purposely led Caesar into an ambush, by himself dictating the false promise of opening the gates of that city.
> The attacks were all against redoubts, and were so

managed as to time, numbers and localities, as to make it probable that no reinforcements would be sent from one part of the line to the others. They were at points that lay east of Pompey's camp. There were two columns of four Legions in all. Arrived on the high ground, the Legions divided into three columns. By two of these columns attacks were only partially delivered. In one of the assaults, three of Caesar's Cohorts under Volcatius Tullus easily beat back a Legion which formed one column; and in another, the German auxiliaries made a sally from the lines, defeated another Legion with much loss, and retired safely. These were but demonstrations on Pompey's part.

The third or main assault was severe. Pompey's third column of two Legions had attacked in force at one of the forts which was held by the second Cohort of the Sixth Legion—three hundred men under the Centurion Manucius. The Legionaries resisted the assault with great stubbornness. Pompey's troops had scaling ladders, mural hooks and a ram. They assaulted the towers of the *castellum*, tried to set fire to the hurdles, filled up the trench, and exhibited the utmost determination to break down the defenses. But the Caesarians held on so stubbornly and for so long a time that Sulla was enabled to gather from adjoining works and to lead up two Legions to drive back the Pompeians. The latter, exhausted by their effort, did not stand the charge, but so soon as the front line was struck yielded ground. Sulla had an excellent chance to bring on a general engagement under auspicious conditions, and was loudly criticized in the army for not having done so. But he deemed that he had no right to deliver battle in Caesar's absence, and was sustained by his chief.[54]

Caesar was never one to reprove a *locum* for exhibiting a proper sense of subordination. But the truth could not be disguised that Sulla had failed to exploit the sort of golden opportunity that battle offers all too seldom. And in warfare the penalty exacted for foregoing opportunity is almost invariably disaster—as it was to be in May of 48 B.C. Moreover, Caesar had not only to contend with an open foe, but with treachery.

There were two young Gauls with Caesar whom he had promoted to important positions. They were reported

54 Dodge, *op. cit.*

to have committed various peculations. Caesar spoke
to them privately. They took offense and deserted. There
was a weak spot in Caesar's lines at a point furthest
removed from the body of the army. The Gauls gave
Pompey notice of it, and on this point Pompey determined to fling himself with his whole strength.[55]

The weak joint in the harness was situated on the extreme
left of the system of redoubts and earthworks, where there
had been a failure to dig any entrenchment between the lines
of circumvallation and contravallation; consequently a landing in between them would take Caesar's left in the rear.

Acting on the accurate and comprehensive information obtained from the two Gaulish deserters, Pompey made use of
the cover of darkness to transfer sixty Cohorts to a position
hard by the vulnerable spot in his opponent's lines, at the
same time transporting his light troops by sea to that part
of the works which was nearest to the coast and farthest
from Caesar's main camp.

The assault was launched at daybreak, and effected complete surprise.

The archers and slingers who attacked from the south
were very active, and poured a galling fire upon the
unprepared defenders, whom they outnumbered six to
eight to one. At the same moment the sixty Legionary
Cohorts made a desperate onslaught from the north, using
their weapons and engines to great advantage, and began
to set up their scaling ladders after filling the ditch with
fascines. The danger was imminent enough, owing to
the front and rear attack; but to make the situation hopeless, a party of light troops discovered the unfinished defenses on Caesar's extreme left, and making a gallant
dash in between the two lines, took the Legionaries of the
Ninth absolutely in flank. The Caesarians appear to have
been slenderly supplied with missiles, for their chief
defense, thus taken unawares, was stones; and the osier-
covered headgear of the Pompeians saved them from the
effect of these.[56]

It had been the weight and persistence of the assailants'
missile action which had been the original defenders' undoing; "about thirty thousand arrows had been discharged

[55] Froude, *op. cit.*
[56] Dodge, *op. cit.*

into the works; and in the shield of the Centurion Scaeva were found two hundred and thirty holes." [57]

Caesar was, of course, fully cognizant of the weak spot in his lines; he knew that the deserters were aware of it. Yet he had neither taken steps to strengthen it nor reinforced the detachment holding it, lulled by the belief that Pompey was so loath to fight that extra precautions were unnecessary; all of which materially enhanced the shock-value of the surprise assault.

In any event, Pompey's well-conceived attack was fully successful. His men came on with such a determined rush that the Caesarians broke and could not be rallied, and such Cohorts as were sent to their relief by Marcellinus, whose camp was near the left, also caught the infection and retired in confusion. The Pompeians pressed on; the Caesarians were suffering serious losses, all the Centurions but one of the leading Cohort being killed. He, happily, was the *Primipilus,* and managed to save the Legionary Eagle. The Pompeians did not stop until they reached the camp of the Ninth Legion. There Antony was met debouching from the line of hills where had been erected the circuit of castella [strongpoints], with a bold front of twelve Cohorts, and his brave stand on the enemy's flank checked the latter's onslaught, drove back the enemy, rallied the runaways, and put an end to the immediate danger. [58]

When Caesar himself arrived, summoned by the smoke of signal fires, he saw at once that the disaster to his lines was irreparable. His enemy had forced him to extend his lines, and the ground he had attempted to cover was too great for the working strength of his army. His intense dislike of renouncing any project to which he had set his hand, had led him for once into serious error. All his work was thrown away, the lines were abandoned, and a camp was constructed that same morning for the whole army near the position taken up by Pompeius.

In the afternoon of the same eventful day, Caesar made an attempt to revive the spirits of his men, and to inflict loss on the enemy, by attacking a Pompeian

---

[57] Caesar, *op. cit.* Scaeva survived the action, and as a reward for his services Caesar presented him with two hundred thousand *sesterces* and promoted him from Centurion of the eighth Cohort to Legion *Primipilus.*

[58] Dodge, *op. cit.*

Legion which had been seen marching to occupy a deserted camp some little distance to the north of both armies. This camp had been made by Caesar's Ninth Legion, and then abandoned; it was next occupied by Pompeius, who had connected it by a ditch and rampart with a stream still farther to the north, in order to secure a water supply for its garrison. He, however, in his turn, had for some reason abandoned it; but now, as it was situated on Caesar's right flank, he thought it worth reoccupying. His Legion took possession of it; but Caesar now attacked it in full force, and with his left wing, which he led in person, broke down the gate and drove the defenders to the rear of the camp, where they endeavored to rally. Meanwhile the right wing, misled by the entrenchment leading to the stream, which they strangely took to be part of the camp, had followed this in search of a gate and became separated from their comrades on the left. Finding their mistake, they made a breach in the entrenchment, and poured through, both infantry and cavalry, only to find a powerful body of the enemy pressing upon them which Pompeius had sent to the rescue. A panic seized them, for the rampart and ditch now cut off their retreat; and the whole wing was put to rout as they tried to scale this obstacle, losing more men by the fall into the ditch than by the sword of the enemy. Panic too now seized the victorious left wing, who seeing from the camp the disaster on the right, thought they would be taken in rear and cut off.[59]

Caesar ran to meet them, and would have rallied the fugitives, but it was not in his power. He laid hold on the ensign staves to stop them, and some left them in his hands, and others threw them upon the ground, insomuch that no less than thirty-two standards were taken. Caesar himself was very near losing his life; for having laid hold of a tall and strong man, to stop him and make him face about, the soldier in his terror and confusion lifted up his sword to strike him; but Caesar's armor-bearer prevented it by a blow which cut off his arm.

Caesar saw his affairs that day in so bad a posture, that after Pompey, either through too much caution, or the caprice of fortune, instead of giving the finishing stroke to so great an action, stopped as soon as he had

59 Warde Fowler, *op. cit.*

shut up his enemy within their entrenchments, and sounded a retreat, he [Caesar] said to his friends as he withdrew, "This day victory would have declared for the enemy, if they had had a General who knew how to conquer," [60]

which was valid enough as criticism, but could not obscure the fundamental fact that Caesar himself had suffered a resounding defeat, a defeat whose extent he openly acknowledged by withdrawing his troops from their untenable position and transferring them by a rapid night march to their former camp at Asparagium, whence he made a second march to Apollonia to shake off the pursuit.

With his troops demoralized and shamefaced, his communications with Italy severed, with three months of the campaigning season expended to no good purpose, with his power to take the offensive at least temporarily stultified, and with time working against him in far more deadly fashion than in the case of his opponent, the tide of Caesar's fortunes had never been at lower ebb.

CHAPTER XII

VICTORY AT PHARSALUS

"It does not suffice to gain a victory,
you must learn to turn it to advantage."
—Napoleon

Politics is the art of knowing where to go next, and after his grievous setback at Dyrrhachium, that was the problem which confronted Caesar—where to march his army, and what countermove to set in train to restore the situation in his favor. Although the speed of his retreat to Apollonia had denied Pompey all immediate chance of exploiting his advantage, there were ample grounds for continuing anxiety.

[60] Plutarch, *op. cit.*

To begin with, "he could not overlook all the acts of cowardice which had been at the root of the Dyrrhachium defeat. He selected those on whom reliance was wont to be placed, but who in this instance had failed in their duty, and punished several of the Standard-bearers by reducing them to the ranks. This sufficed as an example. He then addressed his men in such wise as to rob them of the sting of defeat and inspire them with fresh confidence. Indeed, as soon as Caesar's Legionaries had recovered from their first demoralization, they became themselves and eager for battle. They begged Caesar to lead them against the enemy instead of leaving the region of Dyrrhachium, promising to give a good account of themselves. But Caesar mistrusted not their goodwill but their steadiness," although he was careful to maintain morale by "promising his men a victory the next time they struck the enemy." [1] Caesar could give the pledge with all the greater confidence since he was fully aware of the fact that word had passed through the camp that, after the recent defeat, the renegade Labienus had butchered all the prisoners in cold blood after taunting them with having exhibited a cowardice entirely unworthy of Gallic veterans.

Ruminating on the course of recent events, it did not take Caesar long to realize that, with a numerically inferior force, it had been a mistake to try and beleaguer Pompey in the position he had taken up about Dyrrhachium, where he benefited from far better access to supplies than was the case with the besieging force. The thing to do, therefore, was to lure Pompey inland away from his base, and to rely upon skill of maneuver and the restored fighting quality of the Legions in the final clinch that was bound to eventuate.

As for Caesar's antagonist,

the gleam of victory was the cause of Pompey's ruin. It was unlooked for, and the importance of it exaggerated. Caesar was supposed to be flying with the wreck of an army completely disorganized and disheartened. So sure were the Pompeians that it could never rally again that they regarded the war as over; they made no serious efforts to follow up a success which, if improved, might have been really decisive; and they gave Caesar the one thing which he really needed—time to recover from its effects. After he had placed his sick and wounded in Apollonia, his first object was to rejoin Calvinus, who

[1] Dodge, *op. cit.*

had been sent to watch Scipio, and might now be cut off. Fortune was here favorable. Calvinus, by mere accident, learnt his danger, divined where Caesar would be, and came to meet him. The next thing was to see what Pompey would do. He might embark for Italy. In this case Caesar would have to follow by Illyria and the head of the Adriatic. Cisalpine Gaul was true to him, and could be relied upon to refill his ranks. Or Pompey might pursue him in the hope to make an end of the war in Greece, and an opportunity might offer itself for an engagement under fairer terms. On the whole Caesar considered the second alternative the more likely one, and with this expectation he led his troops into the rich plains of Thessaly for the better feeding which they so much needed.[2]

As the *Commentaries* summarized the sequence of events, "Having stationed a garrison of four Cohorts at Apollonia, one at Lissus, and three at Oricum, besides those who were sick of their wounds, Caesar set forward on his march through Epirus and Arcarnania. Pompey, also, guessing at Caesar's design, determined to hasten to Scipio, that if Caesar should march in that direction, he might be ready to relieve him; but that if Caesar should be unwilling to quit the seacoast and Corcyra, because he expected Legions and cavalry from Italy, he himself might fall on Domitius with all his forces." As it transpired, Metellus Scipio eluded Caesar as successfully as Domitius had evaded Pompey.

Both sides were on the way to being reinforced. Caesar had already formulated plans for the future; only Pompey was still of two minds as to the best course to pursue.

The marine-minded Afranius "advised that they should make use of their naval force, in which they were so much superior, and being masters of the sea, should harass Caesar, who was now wandering and destitute, and that Pompey himself should conduct his infantry with all haste to Italy, which now was well disposed towards him and was free from a hostile army. Having mastered it, together with Gaul and Spain, they could attack Caesar again from their own home, the seat of imperial power."[3] On the other hand,

there were not wanting persons who warned him that Caesar's Legions might be still as dangerous. Both Cicero

[2] Froude, *op. cit.*
[3] Appian, *op. cit.*

and Cato advised him to avoid a battle, to allow Caesar to wander about Greece till his supplies and his army were worn out by marches. Pompey himself inclined to the same opinion. But Pompey could no longer act on his own judgment. The Senators who were with him in the camp considered that in Greece, as in Rome, they were the supreme rulers of the Roman Empire. All along they had held their sessions and their debates, and they had voted resolutions which they expected to see complied with. They had never liked Pompey. If Cicero was right in supposing that Pompey meant to be another Sulla, the Senators had no intention of allowing it. They had gradually wrested his authority out of his hands, and reduced him to the condition of an officer of a Senatorial Directory. These gentlemen, more especially the two late Consuls, Scipio and Lentulus, were persuaded that a single blow would now make an end of Caesar. His army was but half the size of theirs, without counting their Asiatic allies. The men, they were persuaded, were dispirited by defeat and worn out. So sure were they of victory that they were impatient of every day which delayed their return to Italy. They accused Pompey of protracting the war unnecessarily, that he might have the honor of commanding such distinguished persons as themselves. They had arranged everything that was to be done. Caesar and his band of cutthroats were in imagination already dispatched. They had butchered hitherto every one of them who had fallen into their hands, and the same fate was designed for their political allies. They proposed to establish a Senatorial Court after their return to Italy, in which citizens of all kinds who had not actually fought on the Senate's side were to be brought up for trial. Those who should be proved to have been active for Caesar were to be at once killed, and their estates confiscated. Neutrals were to fare almost as badly. . . . The Roman oligarchy were true to their character to the eve of their ruin. It was they, with their idle luxury, their hunger for lands and office and preferment, who had brought all this misery upon the country; and standing, as it were, at the very bar of judgment, with the sentence of destruction about to be pronounced upon them, their thoughts were still bent upon how to secure the largest share of plunder for themselves.[4]

4 Froude, *op. cit.*

Marching with his usual rapidity, Caesar reached the watershed of the rivers Aous and Peneus, and descended to Aeginium in Thessaly on June seventh. With the detachment under Domitius, the force under immediate command consisted of nine Legions, less three Cohorts on detachment—in all, some 24,000 men. In addition there were a handful of light troops, and 1,000 Horse. Fifteen Cohorts under Calenus were within reasonable call.

Exaggerated reports of Caesar's defeat at Dyrrhachium had sped on eagle's wings throughout Macedonia, Epirus, and Thessaly, and many of the States, if not yet actively hostile, were weakening in the allegiance they had hitherto displayed for Caesar's cause. But the first sign of active opposition came when the Caesarian force marched out from Aeginium and took their way to the neighboring township of Gomphi. Here the gates were shut, and local herdsmen reported that help had been solicited from Metellus Scipio, at the moment halted some forty-five miles distant at Larissa.

Caesar having fortified his camp, ordered scaping ladders and penthouses to be made for a sudden assault, and hurdles to be provided. As soon as they were ready, he exhorted his soldiers, and told them of what advantage it would be to assist them with all sorts of necessaries if they made themselves masters of a rich and plentiful town; and, at the same time to strike terror into other States by the example of this, and to effect this with speed, before auxiliaries could arrive. Accordingly, taking advantage of the unusual ardor of the soldiers, he began his assault on the town at a little after three o'clock on the very day on which he arrived, and took it, though defended with very high walls, before sunset, and gave it up to his army to plunder, and immediately decamped before it, and marched to Metropolis, with such rapidity as to outstrip any messenger bearing news of the taking of Gomphi.

The inhabitants of Metropolis, at first influenced by the same rumors, followed the same measures—shut the gates and manned their walls. But when they were made acquainted with the fate of the city of Gomphi by some prisoners whom Caesar had ordered to be brought up to the walls, they threw open their gates. As he preserved them with the greatest care, there was not a State in Thessaly (except Larissa, which was awed by a strong army of Scipio's), but on comparing the fate of Metropolis with the severe treatment of Gomphi, gave admission to Caesar and obeyed his orders. Having chosen a position convenient for procuring corn, which was now almost ripe on the ground, he determined there to await Pompey's arrival, and to make it the center of all his warlike operations.[5]

Although when Gomphi had been handed over to plunder, "the soldiers who had suffered much from hunger, had eaten immoderately and drunk wine to excess, the Germans among them being especially ridiculous under the influence of drink," [6] not a man had been absent from the ranks on the march to Metropolis, which everyone had been ready to assail, should the inhabitants refuse prompt submission. Caesar had every reason, therefore, to be

cheered by the conduct of his men, and he felt that he might again trust to their steady bravery. . . . He therefore headed to the east, crossed the Apidanus at Pyrgo, moved on farther into the level country, and camped north of Pharsalus on the left bank of the Enipeus.

Pompey, when he found that Domitius had escaped him and that Scipio was safe, kept on his course with slow marches, southeast towards Larissa.

The event proved that he would have been wiser to move into Italy. But he not unnaturally looked upon another victory as the certain consequence of his last.

But

The plan and sequence of the campaign were dictated by Caesar's movements. Pompey might, by a diversion in Italy, have had things his own way, but he was too lax and indecisive. Even now he was giving his opponent too much time to recruit.

Pompey joined Scipio on June twenty-first at Larissa and assumed command of both armies. Why Caesar had not attacked Scipio before Pompey's arrival has been frequently asked. But such an act was not in accordance with ancient practice. Larissa was too strong a town to assault, and a siege was not possible at the moment when speed was of the essence. . . . Larissa, with Scipio's two Legions, was a different task from Gomphi with its native population.

At all events, Caesar remained *in situ* and awaited his

[5] Caesar, *The Civil War* (Book III).
[6] Appian, *op. cit.*

enemy. Larissa was but twenty miles distant. The harvest was near at hand. His supplies were now certain, and he was in open country where he could maneuver at will. On the other hand, Pompey was in command of 50,000 Legionaries, 7,000 Horse, and many light troops —a force large enough to justify his belief that Caesar was at his mercy; [7]

the more so as the rumor had reached him that his opponents were suffering that abiding plague of soldiering in all ages —dysentery, than which no more debilitating affliction can be visited on men engaged on active service.

It is true that prior to the capture of Gomphi and the submission of Metropolis, many of Caesar's men had been suffering from what Plutarch delicately refers to as "a contagious distemper." But access to ample, wholesome food and uncontaminated water had heralded swift recovery from the epidemic, and Caesar's troops had never been in finer fettle. They were further encouraged by a report that in the hostile camp "it was being whispered among the Equestrian Order 'that as soon as they had taken off Caesar, they could do nothing better than take off Pompey too.' Some said that this was why he did not employ Cato in any service of importance, but, upon his march against Caesar, sent him to the seacoast to take care of the baggage, lest, after he had destroyed Caesar, Cato should oblige him to lay down his commission." [8] The prospect of a dagger in the back offers a poor incentive for a singleminded attack on the enemy in front!

By unspoken consent, both armies had approached each other, awaiting the opportunity to settle the issue between them once and for all.

Caesar lay to the south of Larissa in the plain—which extends between the hill country of Cynoscephalae and the chain of Othrys and is intersected by a tributary of the Peneius, the Enipeus—on the left bank of the latter stream near the town of Pharsalus; Pompey pitched his camp opposite him on the right bank of the Enipeus along the slope of the heights of Cynoscephalae. The entire army of Pompeius was assembled; Caesar on the other hand still expected the corps of nearly two Legions

[7] Dodge, *op. cit.*
[8] Plutarch, *op. cit.*

formerly detached to Aetolia and Thessaly, now stationed under Quintus Fufius Calenus in Greece, and the two Legions of Cornificius which were sent after him by the land route from Italy and had already arrived in Illyria.[9]

"Nearly all the ancient historians agree that Pompey had 110 Cohorts, Caesar 82 Cohorts, and that each had some auxiliaries. Pompey, whose Cohorts were nearer the normal strength than Caesar's, had not far from 50,000 Legionaries, some 4,000 bowmen, 7,000 cavalry, and a host of auxiliaries —a total certainly exceeding 60,000 men. Caesar's Cohorts were small, scarcely more than 300 men each. They had been much depleted and he had not been able to recruit them up to normal strength. He numbered in all not over 25,000 Legionaries, had but 1,000 mounted men, and fewer auxiliaries than Pompey—a total of some 30,000." [10] In short, Pompey outnumbered Caesar substantially two to one.

The respective camps lay some three and a half miles from each other, and the Enipeus—a small sluggish stream, quite liable to be reduced to a mere trickle in hot weather— could scarcely be regarded as an obstacle to free movement across the floor of the valley.

Pompey was still hesitant about initiating the clash, but Scipio, Afranius, and others "continued loud and tumultuous in their demands of a battle, and forced Pompey to call a council of war. Labienus, who had the command of the cavalry, rose up first and took an oath 'that he would not return from the battle till he had put the enemy to flight.' All the other officers swore the same." It was one of those moments when "the same foolish clamors, the same petty competition and quarreling, which his rival had escaped for ten years in Gaul, distracted Pompey now and induced him to offer fight against his better judgment." [11]

"The night following, Pompey had this dream. He thought 'he entered his own theater, and was received with loud plaudits; after which he adorned the temple of Venus the Victorious with many spoils.' This vision, on one side, encouraged him, and on the other alarmed him. He was afraid that Caesar, who was a descendant of Venus, would be aggrandized at his expense. Besides, a panic fear ran through the camp, the noise of which awakened him. And about the

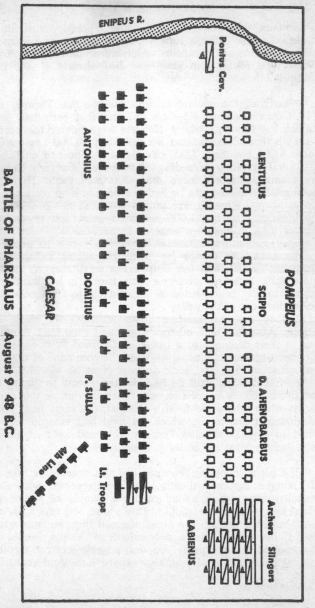

BATTLE OF PHARSALUS   August 9   48 B.C.

morning watch, over Caesar's camp, where everything was perfectly quiet, there suddenly appeared a great light, from which a stream of fire issued in the form of a torch, and fell upon that of Pompey. Caesar himself saw it going his rounds." [12]

Caesar was preparing, at break of day, to march to Scotussa; his soldiers were striking their tents, and the servants and beasts of burden were already in motion, when his scouts brought intelligence that they had seen arms handed about in the enemy's camp, and perceived a noise and bustle which indicated an approaching battle. After this, others came and assured him that the first ranks were drawn up.

Upon this Caesar said, "The long-wished day is come, on which we shall fight with men and not with want and famine." Then he immediately ordered the red mantle to be put up before his pavilion, which, among the Romans, is the signal for battle. The soldiers no sooner beheld it than they left their tents as they were, and ran to arms with loud shouts and every expression of joy. And when the officers began to put them in order of battle, each man fell into his proper rank as quietly, and with as much skill and ease, as a chorus in a tragedy. [13]

Caesar then proceeded to address the customary, and expected, exhortation to his troops—a carefully calculated harangue in which an appeal to valor was astutely supported by the rehearsal of legitimate grievances.

"My comrades," he said, "this day will decide everything. Remember what you promised me at Dyrrhachium. Remember how you swore to each other in my presence that you would never leave the field except as conquerors. These men, fellow soldiers, are the same that we have come to meet from the Pillars of Hercules, the same men who gave us the slip from Italy. They are the same who sought to disband us without honors, without a triumph, without rewards, after the toils and struggles of ten years, after we had finished those great wars, after innumerable victories, and after having added four hundred nations in Spain, Gaul, and Britain to our country's sway. I have not been able to pre-

[12] Appian, *op. cit.*
[13] Plutarch, *op. cit.*

vail upon them by offering fair terms, nor to win them by benefits. . . . Recall all these facts to your minds today, and if you have any experience of me recall also my care for you, my good faith, and the generosity of my gifts to you."

Caesar then went on to point out,

"Nor is it difficult for hardy and veteran soldiers to overcome new recruits who are without experience in war, and who, moreover, like boys, spurn the rules of discipline and of obedience to their commander. I learn that he was afraid and unwilling to come to an engagement," the speaker went on to assure his attentive auditors. "His star has already passed its zenith; he has become slow and hesitating in all his acts, and no longer commands, but obeys the orders of others. I say these things of his Italian forces only. As for his allies, do not think about them, pay no attention to them, do not fight with them at all. They are Syrian, Phrygian, and Lydian slaves, always ready for flight or servitude. Give your attention to the Italians only, even when those allies come running around you like dogs trying to frighten you." [14]

Then with characteristic foresight and prudence, Caesar admonished his men, " 'When you have put the enemy to flight, let us spare the Italians as being our own kindred, but slaughter the allies in order to strike terror into the others.' Finally, to emphasize the supreme importance of the coming trial of arms, he sternly concluded, 'Before all else, in order that I may know that you are mindful of your promise to choose victory or death, throw down the walls of your camp as you go out to battle, so that we may have no place of refuge if we do not conquer, and so that the enemy may see that we have no camp and know that we are compelled to camp in theirs.' The men's response was voiced by Crastinus, a Centurion, of the Tenth Legion, already known to Caesar for his gallantry, who called out, 'Follow me, my comrades, and strike, and strike home for your General. This one battle remains to be fought, and he will have his rights and we our liberty. General,' he said, looking at Caesar, 'I shall earn your thanks this day, dead or alive.' "

Grimly but with the veteran's unhurried assurance, the Legionaries set about their final preparations for a contest in

[14] Appian, *op. cit*. Cf. Caesar, *op. cit*.

which the whole future of the known world trembled in the balance. For never, perhaps,

> have the contending forces in a worldwide revolution been so exactly focused in two armies on a single battlefield. On the one side the disunion, selfishness, and pride of the last survivors of an ancient oligarchy, speculating before the event on the wealth or office that victory was to bring them; on the other the absolute command of a single man, whose clear mental vision was entirely occupied with the facts and issues that lay before him that day. For one host was composed in great part by a motley crowd from Greece and the East, representing that spurious Hellenic civilization that for a century had sapped the vigor of Roman life; the other was chiefly drawn from the Gallic populations of Italy and the West, fresh, vigorous, intelligent, and united in devotion and loyalty to a leader whom not even defeat could dishearten. With Pompeius was the spirit of the past, and his failure did but answer to the failure of a decaying world; with Caesar the spirit of the future; and his victory marks the moment when humanity could once more start hopefully upon a new line of progress.[15]

Caesar's disparaging comments upon the enemy cavalry were entirely for the purpose of reassuring and heartening his men. In his own mind he was perfectly well aware of the nature of the threat they embodied, and he was careful to take the necessary steps to countervail it.

For "after he had spoken Caesar detailed two thousand of his oldest men to guard the tents. The rest, as they passed out, demolished their fortifications in the profoundest silence and filled up the ditch with the debris. When Pompey saw this, although some of his friends thought that it was a preparation for flight, he knew it was an exhibition of daring, and groaned in spirit, to think that they were now coming to grips with wild beasts." [16]

The movements in Caesar's camp had drawn Pompey's forces down into the plain. As the troops deployed it could be seen that

> on the left wing were the two Legions delivered over by Caesar at the beginning of the disputes in compliance with the Senate's decree, one of which was called the

15 Warde Fowler, *op. cit.*
16 Appian, *op. cit.*

First and the other the Third. Here Pompey commanded in person. Scipio with the Syrian Legions commanded the center. The Cilician Legion, in conjunction with the Spanish Cohorts brought over by Afranius, were disposed on the right wing. These Pompey considered his steadiest troops. The rest he had dispersed between the center and the wing, and he had 110 complete Cohorts; these amounted to 45,000 men. He had besides two Cohorts of volunteers, who having received favors from him in former wars, flocked to his Standard; these were dispersed through his whole army. The seven remaining Cohorts he had disposed to protect his camp and the neighboring forts [earthworks]. His right wing was secured by a river with steep banks [the Enipeus], for which reason he placed all his cavalry, archers, and slingers on his left wing.

Caesar, observing his former custom, had placed the Tenth Legion on the right, the Ninth on the left, although it was very much weakened by the battles of Dyrrhachium. He placed the Eighth Legion so close to the Ninth, as almost to make one of the two, and ordered them to support one another. He drew up on the field eighty Cohorts, making a total of 22,000 men. He left two Cohorts to guard the camp. He gave the command of the left wing to Antonius, of the right to P. Sulla, and of the center to Cn. Domitius; he himself took his post opposite Pompey. At the same time, fearing from the disposition of the enemy lest his right wing might be surrounded by their numerous cavalry, he rapidly drafted a single Cohort from each of the Legions composing the third line, formed of them a fourth line, and disposed them to be ready to meet Pompey's cavalry, and acquainting them of his wishes, admonished them that the success of the day depended upon their courage. At the same time he ordered the third line, and the entire army, not to charge without his command; that he would give the signal whenever he wished them to do so.[17]

And in that is to be found the clue to all that subsequently transpired. "The defect in Pompey's army was the lack of one head, one purpose to control events. Caesar, on the other hand, *was* his army. The whole body was instinct with

[17] Caesar, *op. cit.*

his purpose. From low to high, all worked on his own method. He controlled its every mood and act. He was the mainspring and the balance wheel alike." [18]

"Pompey had vauntingly declared to his men that he would make Caesar's Legions fly before their [i.e., his own] infantry came to action, and was unwise enough to explain to them how he proposed to do it. His plan was to place his heavy body of cavalry on his own left wing and have it sally out and envelop Caesar's right and rear, and charge in on the uncovered side—of which all Romans had a dread—before Caesar's Legions could reach his line of Foot." [19] In this, Pompey was guilty of two cardinal errors, one psychological and the other tactical. In the first place, to promise troops an easy fight is to put a premium on their taking it too casually. Secondly, to employ a tactic your adversary is expecting you to adopt, without seeking to distract and confuse him by some sort of preliminary feint, is to forfeit the invaluable element of surprise.

There was space enough between the armies for each to advance part way upon the other, as was the usual manner in ancient battles. But Pompey had ordered his Legions to await Caesar's onset and to strike when the enemy should reach them tired with the rapid charge and with ranks presumably disordered. Pompey thought "that the javelins would fall with less force if the soldiers were kept on their ground, than if they met them in their course; at the same time he trusted that Caesar's soldiers, after running over double the usual ground, would become weary and exhausted by the fatigue." But Caesar knew well the value, moral and physsical, of impetus. "There is a certain impetuosity of spirit and an alacrity implanted by nature in the hearts of all men, which is inflamed by a desire to meet the foe. This a General should endeavor not to repress, but to increase; nor was it a vain institution of our ancestors, that the trumpets should sound on all sides, and a general shout be raised, by which they imagined that the enemy were struck with terror, and their own army inspired with courage." Caesar knew that his men could endure the fatigue and that they would be the more inspired by Pompey's line awaiting their attack, as if from fear.

[18] Dodge, *op. cit.*
[19] Froude, *op. cit.*

The Caesarians rushed forth with great bravery. It was Crastinus, with one hundred and twenty chosen volunteers, on the right, who charged first. This was the place of honor, given to such men who, having discharged to the State all their military obligations, still preferred the career of arms. The Caesarians, perceiving that Pompey's men did not advance of their own accord, and with the experience bred of many battles, paused as with one consent midway, lest they should reach the enemy out of breath. After a short respite, they again advanced. When within distance they paused to let the front-rank men cast their javelins, "instantly drew their swords as Caesar had ordered them," and again sent their battlecry resounding to the clouds and rushed upon their foemen with cold steel. Pompey's Legions received them manfully and with unbroken ranks, hurling their *pila* and quickly drawing swords. The battle was engaged with staunchness on either side. The two lines mixed in one, each intent on breaking down the other's guard, and swayed to and fro in the deadly struggle, neither able to wrest from the other an advantage which foretold success.[20]

True to his vow, Crastinus was the foremost in the fight, "and many followed to support him. He charged into the midst of the enemy. They soon took to their swords, and numbers were slain; but as Crastinus was making his way forward and cutting down all before him, one of Pompey's men stood to receive him, and pushed his sword in at his mouth with such force that it went through the nape of his neck. Crastinus thus killed, the fight was maintained with equal advantage on both sides." [21]

At the instant of the crash of meeting Legions, the cavalry was launched from Pompey's left upon Caesar's small body of Horse, followed by his whole host of archers and slingers. The effect of the impact was never doubtful. Weight was superior to courage. Caesar's cavalry was borne back, slowly but surely. It fought well, remembering the many fields on which it held its own; but it soon began to lose formation, to melt into a disorganized mass, and finally broke up. The

20 Dodge, *op. cit.*
21 Plutarch, *op. cit.*

enemy, believing success within their grasp, commenced to file off in small troops to get in the rear of the army. The moment was critical.

The foresight of Caesar now proved his salvation. His fourth line of six Cohorts, hitherto held behind the other three, now came into play." [22]

Thrusting forward at an oblique angle to the line of advance taken earlier by their fellow Legionaries,

they did not, according to custom, attempt to annoy the enemy with their javelins at a distance, nor strike at the legs and thighs when they came nearer, but aimed at their eyes, and wounded them in the face agreeable to the orders they had received. For Caesar hoped that these young cavaliers, who had not been used to war and wounds, and who set a great value upon their beauty, would avoid, above all things, a stroke in that part, and immediately give way, as well on account of the present danger as the future deformity. The event answered his expectation. They could not bear the spears pointed against their faces or the steel gleaming upon their eyes, but turned away their faces and covered them with their hands. This caused such confusion that at last they fled in the most infamous manner, and ruined the whole cause. For the Cohorts which had beaten them off, surrounded their infantry, and charging them in the rear as well as the front, soon cut them to pieces. [23]

For "Caesar ordered his third line to advance, which till then had not been engaged, but had kept their post. Thus, new and fresh troops having come to the assistance of the fatigued, and others having made an attack on their rear, Pompey's men were not able to maintain their ground, but all fled. Nor was Caesar deceived in his opinion that the victory, as he had declared in his speech to his soldiers, must have its beginning in those six Cohorts which he had placed as a fourth line to oppose the Horse. For by them the cavalry were routed; by them the archers and slingers were cut to pieces; by them the left wing of Pompey's army was surrounded, and obliged to be the first to flee." [24]

Pharsalus had been fought and won. In something under

22 Dodge, *op. cit.*
23 Plutarch, *op. cit.*
24 Caesar, *op. cit.*

ninety minutes the whole future of the known world had been steered onto a new and more hopeful course.

By the great dust that was raised, Pompey conjectured the fate of his cavalry; and it is hard to say what passed in his mind at that moment. He appeared like a man moonstruck and distracted; and without considering that he was Pompey the Great, or speaking to anyone, he quitted the ranks, and retired step by step towards his camp:

> Amazed he stood with terrors not his own,
> O'er his broad back his moony shield he threw,
> And glaring round, by tardy steps withdrew.[25]

"The stream of fugitives pouring in told him only too surely what the issue had been. He mounted his horse and rode off in despair. His Legions were rushing back in confusion. Caesar, swift always at the right moment, gave the enemy no leisure to re-form, and fell at once upon the camp." [26] Determined to exploit the success already won, "Caesar ran hither and thither among his troops and besought them to continue their exertions till they should capture Pompey's camp, telling them that if they allowed the enemy to rally they would be the victors for only a single day, whereas if they should take the enemy's camp they would finish the war with this one blow. He stretched out his hands to them and took the lead in person. Although they were weary in body, the words and example of their commander lightened their spirits," [27] and resolutely they braced themselves for the final effort.

It was noon, and the morning had been sultry; but heat and weariness were forgotten in the enthusiasm of a triumph which all then believed must conclude the war. A few companies of Thracians, who had been left on guard, made a brief resistance, but they were soon borne down. The beaten army, which a few hours before were sharing in imagination the lands and offices of their conquerors, fled out through the opposite gates, throwing away their arms, flinging down their standards, and racing, officers and men, for the rocky

25 Plutarch, *op. cit;* Homer, *trans.* Pope.
26 Appian, *op. cit.*
27 Caesar, *op. cit.*

hills which at a mile's distance, promised them shelter.

The camp itself was a singular picture. Houses of turf had been built for the luxurious Patricians, with ivy trained over the entrances to shade their delicate faces from the summer sun; couches had been laid out for them to repose on after their expected victory; tables were spread with plate and wines, and the daintiest preparations of Roman cookery. Caesar commented on the scene with mournful irony. "And these men," he said, "accused my patient, suffering army, which had not even common necessaries, of dissoluteness and profligacy."

Two hundred only of Caesar's men had fallen. The officers had suffered most. . . . The Pompeians, after the first shock, had been cut down unresisting. Fifteen thousand of them lay scattered dead about the ground.[28]

The Legionaries' swords bit deep, and the proportion of dead to wounded was correspondingly heavy. Especial honors were reserved for Crastinus, one of the first of the thirty Centurions to be slain. "When sought for he was found among the dead, and Caesar bestowed military honors on his body and buried it, and erected a special tomb for him near the burial place of the others." [29]

Caesar's object "was to stamp out the fire on the spot, that it might never kindle again. More than half the Pompeians had reached the hills and were making for Larissa. Leaving part of his Legions in the camp to rest, Caesar took the freshest the same evening, and by a rapid march cut off their retreat. The hills were waterless, the heat suffocating. A few of the guiltiest of the Pompeian leaders—Labienus, Lentulus, Afranius, Petreius, and Metellus Scipio (Cicero and Cato had been left at Dyrrhachium)—contrived to escape in the night. The rest, twenty-four thousand of them, surrendered at daylight. They came down praying for mercy which they had never shown, sobbing out their entreaties on their knees, that the measure which they had dealt to others might not be meted out to them. Then and always Caesar hated unnecessary cruelty, and never, if he could help it, allowed executions in cold blood. He bade them rise, said a few gentle words to relieve their fears, and sent them back to the camp. Domitius

[28] Froude, *op. cit.*
[29] Appian, *op. cit.*

Ahenobarbus, believing that for him at least there could be no forgiveness, tried to escape, and was killed. The rest were pardoned." [30] Among those who made submission and were forgiven was M. Junius Brutus, whom history was to reveal as an ingrate to take rank with Judas.

As the Centurions gathered in the hundred and eighty captured Standards and all the Eagles of Pompey's Legions, Caesar turned to the examination of his defeated enemy's own quarters. "In Pompey's own tent was found his secret correspondence, implicating persons, perhaps, whom Caesar had never suspected, revealing the mysteries of the past three years. Curiosity and even prudence might have tempted him to look into it. His only wish was that the past should be forgotten: he burned the whole mass of papers unread." [31]

Pompey had not only been beaten but—at least temporarily—rendered incapable of further action. But as long as he continued at large he would remain a potential source of trouble. And Pompey had not only won free, but still possessed a formidable fleet and the liberty of movement and opportunity for the recovery of the initiative with which command of this powerful armament endowed him.

Pompey had ridden from the battlefield direct to the sea, attended by a handful of Horse. He had gone aboard a grain vessel which carried him to Amphipolis. At Amphipolis he had stayed but a single night and had sailed for Mitylene, where he had left his wife and his sons. The last accounts which the poor lady had heard of him had been such as reached Lesbos after the affair at Dyrrhachium. Young Patricians had brought her word that her husband had gained a glorious victory, that he had joined her father, Metellus Scipio, and that together they were pursuing Caesar with the certainty of overwhelming him. Rumor, cruel as usual,

Had brought smooth comforts false, worse than true wrongs.

Rumor had told Cornelia that Caesar had "stooped his head" before Pompey's rage. Pompey came in person to inform her of the miserable reality. At Mitylene Pompey's family were no longer welcome guests. They joined him on board his ship to share his fortunes, but what those fortunes were to be was all uncertain. Asia had seemed devoted to him. To what part of it

30 Froude, *op. cit.*
31 *Ibid.*

should he go? To Cilicia? To Syria? To Armenia? To Parthia? (For even Parthia was thought of.) Unhappily, the report of Pharsala had flown before him, and the vein of sentiment had everywhere veered round.

Such is the invariable way of things: a leader once discredited, all his deeds, whether good or bad, tell against him. Thus

the Aegean islands begged Pompey politely not to compromise them by his presence. He touched at Rhodes. Lentulus, flying from the battlefield, had tried Rhodes before him, and had been requested to pass on upon his way. Lentulus was said to have gone to Egypt. Polite to Pompey the Rhodians were, but perhaps he was generously unwilling to involve them in trouble in his behalf. He went on to Cilicia, the scene of his old glory in the pirate wars. There he had meant to land and take refuge either with the Parthians or with one of the allied Princes. But in Cilicia he heard that Antioch had declared for Caesar. Allies and subjects, so far as he could learn, were all for Caesar. Egypt, whither Lentulus had gone, appeared the only place where he could surely calculate on being welcome. Ptolemy the Piper, the occasion of so much scandal, was no longer living, but he owed the recovery of his Throne to Pompey. Gabinius had left a few thousand of Pompey's old soldiers at Alexandria to protect him [Ptolemy] against his subjects. These men had married Egyptian wives and had adopted Egyptian habits, but they could not have forgotten their old General. They were acting as guards at present to Ptolemy's four children, two girls, Cleopatra and Arsinöe, and two boys, each called Ptolemy. The father had bequeathed the Crown to the two elder ones, Cleopatra, who was turned sixteen, and a brother two years younger. Here at least, among these young Princes and their guardians, who had been their father's friends, their father's greatest benefactor might count with confidence on finding hospitality.[32]

Pompey had contrived to scrape together a somewhat motley following of seafarers and soldiers numbering about two thousand, together with a few vessels in which to transport them. At their head he arrived off Pelusium (the modern

[32] *Ibid.*

Damietta). "When he was informed that his fleet was still entire and that Cato was gone to Africa with a considerable body of men which he had collected after his flight, he lamented to his friends his great error, in suffering himself to be forced into an engagement at land, and making no use of those forces in which he was confessedly stronger: nor even taking care to fight near his fleet, that in case of meeting with a check at land, he might have been supplied from the sea with another army, capable of making head against the enemy. Indeed, we find no greater mistake in Pompey's whole conduct, nor a more remarkable instance of Caesar's generalship, than in removing the scene of action to such a distance from the naval forces." [33]

All battles are wonderfully well fought once they are over; but hindsight is useless unless another opportunity arises to put its lessons into practice. Pompey's problem, as his convoy dropped anchor off Pelusium, was to recruit and concentrate the necessary force and create the opportunity to challenge Caesar in such circumstances as would permit his superiority at sea to be exploited to its full advantage. In the meantime it was necessary to ensure the good graces of a boy of fourteen, and ingratiate himself with his advisers, already distracted with the outbreak of hostilities with the forces put into the field by their charge's sister Cleopatra.

Ptolemy was very young, and Photinus, his Prime Minister, called a council of his ablest Officers, though their advice had no more weight than he was pleased to allow it. He ordered each, however, to give his opinion. But who can, without indignation, consider that the fate of Pompey the Great was determined by Photinus, an eunuch; by Theodotus, a man of Chios, who was hired to teach the Prince rhetoric; and by Achillas, an Egyptian? For amongst the King's chamberlains and tutors, these had the greatest influence over him, and were the persons he most consulted. Pompey lay at anchor at some distance from the place, waiting the determination of this respectable board; but the council was divided in their opinions; some advising the Prince to give an honorable reception; and others to send him an order to depart. But Theodotus, to display his eloquence, insisted that both were wrong. "If you receive him," he said, "you will have Caesar for your enemy,

[33] Plutarch, *op. cit.*

and Pompey for your master. If you order him off, Pompey may one day avenge the affront, and Caesar resent your not having put him in his hands. The best method, therefore, is to send for him and put him to death. By this means you will do Caesar a favor, and have nothing to fear from Pompey." He added with a smile, "Dead men do not bite."

This advice being approved of, the execution of it was committed to Achillas. In consequence of which, he took with him Septimus, who had formerly been one of Pompey's Officers, and Salvius, who had also acted under him as a Centurion, with three or four assistants, and made up to Pompey's ship, where his principal friends and Officers had assembled, to see how the affair went on. When they perceived there was nothing magnificent in their reception, nor suitable to their hopes, but that a few men only in a fishing boat came to wait upon them, such want of respect appeared a suspicious circumstance; and they advised Pompey, while he was out of reach of missile weapons, to get out to the main sea.

Meantime, the boat approaching, Septimus spoke first, addressing Pompey in Latin, by the title of *Imperator*, Then Achillas saluted him in Greek and desired him to come into the boat, because the water was very shallow towards the shore, and a galley must strike upon the sands. At the same time they saw several of the King's ships getting ready, and the shore covered with troops, so that if they would have changed their minds, it was then too late; besides, their distrust would have furnished the assassins with a pretence for their injustice. Pompey therefore embraced Cornelia, who lamented his sad exit before it happened, and ordered two Centurions, one of his manumitted slaves, named Philip, and a servant called Scenes, to get into the boat before him. When Achillas had hold of his hand, and he was going to step in himself, he turned to his wife and son, and repeated the lines of Sophocles,

"Seek'st thou a tyrant's door? then farewell freedom!
Though free as air before?" [34]

But the presence of Septimus, an old comrade-in-arms, gave Pompey false confidence, although the veteran had ac-

[34] Plutarch, *op. cit.*

knowledged his erstwhile General's greeting with no more
than a curt nod.

When they approached the shore, Cornelia, with her
friends in the galley, watched the event with great
anxiety. She was a little encouraged when she saw a
number of the King's Great Officers coming down to the
strand, in all appearance to receive her husband and do
him honor. But the moment Pompey took hold of Philip's
hand to raise himself with more ease, Septimus came
behind and ran him through the body; after which
Salvius and Achillas also drew their swords. Pompey
took his robe in both hands and covered his face;
and without saying or doing the least thing unworthy
of him, submitted to his fate; only uttering a groan
while they dispatched him with many blows. He was
just fifty-three years old, for he was killed the day after
his birthday.[35]

With the weeping Cornelia still with her eyes fixed on the
shore, the Roman galley put hastily to sea, a brisk gale
discouraging the Egyptians from pursuit.

The murderers having cut off Pompey's head, threw
the body out of the boat naked, and left it exposed to
all who were desirous of such a sight. Philip stayed until their curiosity was satisfied, and then washed the
body with seawater and wrapped it in one of his own
garments, because he had nothing else at hand. The next
thing was to look out for wood for a funeral pile, and
casting his eye over the shore, he spied the remains
of an old fishing boat; which, though not large, would
make a sufficient pyre for a poor naked body that was
not quite entire.[36]

The devoted freedman was presently joined in his pious task
by a veteran of the dead Generalissimo's early conquests,
and the twain brought their labors to an end with the erection
of a monument, on which the words were roughly traced,

"How pitiful a tomb for one so rich in temples." [37]

35 *Ibid.*

36 *Ibid.*

37 Appian, *op. cit.* This was to credit Pompey with possession of the
temples in the territories he had conquered.

Thus perished in obscurity a man whose whole life had been passed in the glare of public attention. A leader's genius for generalship must be judged by the degree of battle-worthiness characterizing his opponents; which method of appraisal reveals Pompey as exceedingly fortunate. Confronted by antagonists whose resources were never on a par with his own, and whose troops were no match for the thoroughly trained and sternly disciplined Roman Legions, Pompey must rate as a lucky rather than as an outstanding commander. As an administrator of captured or dependent territories, however, his honesty and lack of that insatiable greed which befouled the reputation of so many of his contemporaries, put him in a class apart. Unfortunately for him, a combination of circumstances had conspired to enhance his rather negative virtues, until he had been elevated above his natural level; and his egoism misled him into sadly overrating his capabilities. "So long as he stood by Caesar he had maintained his honor and his authority. But he had allowed men more cunning than himself to play upon his vanity, and Pompey fell—fell amidst the ruins of a Constitution which had been undermined by the villainies of its representatives . . . a weak good man, whom accident had thrust into a place to which he was unequal." [38]

Pharsalus was the turning point in the struggle against the Pompeians, but it did not put an end to the conflict.

Having set free his Thessalian allies and pardoned the suppliant Athenians with the mordant comment, "How often will the glory of your ancestors save you from self-destruction?" Caesar set out in pursuit of his beaten but still potentially dangerous rivals. For Cato and Scipio had made good their escape, together with many others of the Senatorial party, and a junction between them and the fugitive Pompey could easily end in the mustering of another army and a second attempt to crush the Caesarians by force of arms. For with the fleet at their disposal, they held command of the sea and could strike at their enemy where and when it best suited them.

Having learned that Pompey had fled eastward, Caesar followed hard on his heels, essaying to cross the Hellespont in any sort of craft on which he could lay his hands. "Here Cassius came upon him in midstream with a part of his fleet, as he was hastening to Pharnaces. Although he might

[38] Froude, *op. cit.*

have mastered the small boats with his numerous triremes, he was panic-stricken by Caesar's astounding success, which was then heralded with consternation everywhere, and he thought that Caesar had sailed purposely against him. So he extended his hands in entreaty from his trireme towards the skiff, begged for pardon, and surrendered the fleet. So great was the power of Caesar's prestige." [39]

With a mere four thousand Legionaries to support him, Caesar arrived in Egypt to learn of Pompey's death and the manner of it; "and when Theodotus presented the head to him, he turned from the sight of it with great abhorrence. The signet of that General was the only thing he took, and on taking it he wept. As often as any of Pompey's friends and companions were taken, wandering about the country, by Ptolemy and brought to Caesar, he loaded them with favors and took them into his own service. He wrote to his friends at Rome 'that the chief enjoyment [he] had of his victory was in saving every day one or other of his fellow citizens who had borne arms against him.' " [40] It was not for nothing that Caesar had studied the writings of Alexander the Great, which extolled in such fervent terms the overriding virtues of *Homonoia*.

It is not without irony that Caesar should have gone to Alexandria in pursuit of Pompey and stayed on there in pursuit of Cleopatra—one of those seductive incarnations of youthful vitality to which middle-aged men are so apt to surrender in the hope of recapturing something of their own vanished youth. It was an infatuation, moreover, which inevitably embroiled him in Egyptian politics, when prior attention should patently have been given to the consolidation of his position in Italy. As the quintessence of the overriding might of Rome, Caesar was indubitably responsible for settling the vexed question of the disputed succession to the Egyptian throne. Yet it was clear that Achillas and his colleagues were in no mind to surrender their importance by agreeing to a compromise between the young King, their nominal master, and his sister. Moreover,

> the turbulent mob of Alexandria was moved to fury by the sight of a Roman calmly awarding the Crown of Egypt, and even the half-Roman army of Ptolemy was stung into resistance by the disdainful pride of

[39] This is Appian's version of events, which differs from that of the other chroniclers.

[40] Plutarch, *op. cit.*

Caesar's handful of Legionaries. For months Caesar was besieged in the eastern quarter of the town, and kept his communications open only by the desperate tenacity with which he clung to the lighthouse island [of Pharos] and its eastern harbor. At last Mithridates of Pergamum [41] brought up an army of relief through Pelusium and Memphis. Ptolemy, who had put himself at the head of the insurgents, marched off to meet him, but failing to prevent his junction with Caesar, was utterly defeated on the Nile and drowned in the river. Caesar assigned the Throne to Cleopatra and her younger brother, but installed a garrison of two Legions to ensure the obedience of Monarch and people alike to Roman rule.[42]

After dallying a further three months in Egypt, Caesar suddenly emerged from the sensuous trance to which he had so long surrendered, to journey through Syria and Cilicia, regulating the affairs of rulers and ruled, cities and palaces, with his customary speed and efficiency. In his absence Pharnaces had boldly asserted his right to his father's kingdoms of Pontus and Lesser Armenia. He had defeated the Galatian and Pontic levies of Caesar's lieutenant, Domitius Calvinus, and now ventured to defy Caesar himself. Caesar demanded instant submission, and when it was not forthcoming, proceeded to inflict crushing defeat on his rash opponent in the battle of Ziela, in a whirlwind five-day campaign which Caesar himself summed up in the immortal phrase *"Veni, vidi, vici."*

But there was ample work waiting to be attended to elsewhere.

After Pharsalus, Cato had retired from Dyrrhachium to Corcyra, where he was joined by Gnaeus, the eldest son of Pompey, with Cicero, Labienus, Afranius, and others. He offered the chief command to Cicero, but the orator declined a post for which he had neither aptitude or inclination, and returned to Italy. A considerable fleet was now assembled at Corcyra. Cato and the rest embarked with the troops that they had rallied, and sailed for Cyrene in the hope of learning news of their chief. Here they fell in with Cornelia and young Sextus, full of the tragic scene which they had just witnessed on the beach at Pelusium. Cato remained at

[41] A reputed son of the great Mithridates.
[42] How and Leigh, *op. cit.*

Cyrene, while the fleet, with Labienus and the greater part of the troops, pursued its course across the Syrtis to the Province of Africa, where the Pompeian cause was upheld by Varus and King Juba. Cato joined them after an arduous march across the desert, and by the beginning of next year all the Pompeian leaders were assembled in Africa.[43]

Metellus Scipio was appointed to command the troops, but it was the obdurate Cato who kept the spirit of opposition to Caesar alive and ready for action. And for the nonce there was no counter-action on which Caesar could embark. His lieutenant in Further Spain, Q. Cassius Longinus, had been given orders to invade Africa and suppress the Pompeians, but had made himself so unpopular in his Province that C. Trebonius had to be sent in all haste to supersede him and restore order. There was, therefore, no immediate support to be looked for from the troops in Further Spain.

With Caesar's own return to Italy, his plans to deal with the Pompeians in Africa were again delayed by mutiny on the part of his troops cantoned in Campania. "Enervated by a year's ease, they refused to embark for Africa, and marching to Rome, tumultuously demanded their discharge. Caesar at once granted their request, and promised that they should nevertheless share in the substantial rewards, though not the honors, of his coming triumph; and when he addressed them no longer as comrades but as mere citizens,[44] the veterans broke down and begged to be received again into his service. After a politic delay Caesar granted their prayer, and at once set out for Africa." [45]

With six Legions and 2,000 Horse, Caesar led his expeditionary force to their first staging area in Sicily. Here, "to prevent his Officers from entertaining any hopes of having the expedition delayed, he pitched his own tent almost within the wash of the sea; and a favorable wind springing up, he re-embarked with 3,000 Foot and a small body of Horse. After he landed them privately and safely on the African coast, he set sail again in quest of the remaining part of his troops, whose numbers were more considerable, and for whom he was under great concern. He found them, however, on their way at sea, and conducted them all to his African camp." [46]

[43] Liddell, *op. cit.*

[44] Employment of this term was tantamount to cashiering them.

[45] How and Leigh, *op. cit.*

[46] Plutarch, *op. cit.*

Constantly harassed by the enemy's far more numerous Numidian cavalry, who seriously curtailed the activities of Caesar's foragers, the Legions were often on painfully reduced rations. Indeed, "he was obliged to give his horses the very seaweed, only washing out the salt and mixing a little grass with it to make it go down." [47] In such poor trim were Caesar's mounted troops, in fact, that they were worsted in several brushes with the Numidians, with a consequent lowering of their morale which their commander found it difficult to restore.

Scipio, flushed with these successful preludes, was desirous to come to a decisive action. Therefore, leaving Afranius and Juba in their respective camps, which were at no great distance, he went in person to the camp above the lake, in the neighborhood of Thapsus, to raise a fortification for a place of arms and occasional retreat.[48] While Scipio was constructing his walls and ramparts, Caesar, with incredible dispatch, made his way through a country almost impracticable, by reason of its woods and difficult passes, and coming suddenly upon him, attacked one part of his army in the rear, another in the front, and put the whole to flight. Then making the best of his opportunity and of the favor of fortune, with one tide of success he took the camp of Afranius and destroyed that of the Numidians, Juba, their King, being glad to save himself by flight. Thus, in a small part of one day, he made himself master of three camps, and killed 50,000 of the enemy, with the loss only of fifty men.[49]

The battle of Thapsus sounded the death knell of the Pompeian cause. Of the leaders only Labienus and the two sons of Pompey made good their escape. Afranius was cut down and killed by Caesar's Legionaries; Scipio, Petreius, and King Juba chose to die by their own hands rather than to fall captive to the conqueror; while no longer would

> Cato give his little Senate laws,
> And sit attentive to his own applause.

Realizing that his course was run, he stabbed himself to

[47] *Ibid.*
[48] I.e., rest camp.
[49] Plutarch, *op. cit.*

death, rather than seek clemency from a man he had been forced to acknowledge as bigger than himself.

"After the victory of Thapsus, Caesar was able to give some months to the work of reorganizing the empire. He celebrated a well-earned 'triumph,' in which Gaul and Egypt, Pontus and Numidia, attested the worldwide prowess of the conqueror; but no single Roman captive was led behind his chariot. Caesar only triumphed over the foes of Rome, not over personal opponents." [50] Those it was always his design to try and reconcile. The distribution of war bonuses to his soldiery and largesse to the citizenry, pageants, games, the erection of a temple to the conqueror's ancestress Venus, the inauguration of a Forum, not for purposes of commerce but for the transaction of public business—all these activities were carried through with that combination of painstaking thoroughness and lively imagination which was Caesar's particular secret.

Nominated Dictator for a period of ten years, with the right to name the individuals whom the people were to choose for their Praetors and Consuls, Caesar labored tirelessly to root out the clubs and caucuses, the bribery of the Tribes and intimidation of electors, the organized bands of voters, which had made such a shameful mockery of constitutional government. "The Courts of Law were purified. No more judges were to be bought with money or with fouler temptations. The *Leges Juliae* became a practical reality";[51] and there was even a long overdue and highly necessary reform of the calendar.

Caesar's unending round of toil in Rome was interrupted, however, by news of the worsening state of affairs in Spain, where the last of the Pompeians, led by Labienus and young Gnaeus Pompeius, had sought a refuge. One way and another, Gnaeus had managed to rake together a considerable army, "composed of soldiers from Pharsalus and Africa itself, who had come hither with their leaders, of Spaniards and Celtiberians, a strong and warlike race. There were also a great number of emancipated slaves in Pompeius's camp, who had all been under discipline four years and were ready to fight with desperation." [52] Despite the fact that winter was not far off, Caesar marched rapidly westward, reaching Saguntum in twenty-seven days. In his train marched his most trusted Officer, Decimus Brutus—nominated for the future Governor-

50 How and Leigh, *op. cit.*

51 Froude, *op. cit.*

52 Appian, *op. cit.*

ship of Cisalpine Gaul—and his sister's seventeen-year-old grandson, Octavius. Himself childless,[53] Caesar had adopted the youth and trained him carefully to assume a successor's responsibilities when the day should come to transfer the reins of power to younger hands.

With his arrival in Spain, Caesar speedily discovered that "the winter season did not bring to him its usual advantages, for the whole peninsula had revolted, and Gnaeus Pompey and Labienus could shelter their troops in the towns, while Caesar was obliged to keep the field. Attempts here and there to capture detached positions led to no results. On both sides now the war was carried on upon the principles which the Senate had adopted from the first. Prisoners from the revolted Legions were instantly executed, and Gnaeus Pompey murdered the provincials whom he suspected of an inclination to Caesar. Attagona was at last taken. Caesar moved on to Cordova, and Pompey, fearing that the important cities might seek their own security by coming separately to terms, found it necessary to risk a battle.

The scene of the conflict which ended the civil war was the plain of Munda on the Guadalquivir, so near to Cordova that the remains of the beaten army found shelter within its walls after the battle, which was one of the most desperate in which Caesar had ever been engaged. The numbers were nearly equal, the *matériel* on both sides equally good. Pompey's army was composed of revolted soldiers. In arms, in discipline, in stubborn fierceness, there was no difference. The Pompeians had the advantage of situation, the village of Munda, with the hill on which it stood, being in the center of their lines. The Moorish and Spanish auxiliaries, of whom there were large bodies on either side, stood apart when the Legions closed, having no further interest in the matter than in siding with the conqueror when fortune had decided who the conqueror was to be. There were no maneuvers, no scientific evolutions. The Pompeians knew there was no hope for them if they were defeated. Caesar's men, weary and savage at the protraction of the war, were determined to make an end of it, and the two armies fought hand-to-hand with their short swords, with set teeth and pressed lips, opened only with a sharp cry as an enemy fell dead. So equal was the struggle, so doubtful at one moment the issue of it, that Caesar

[53] That is to say, without legitimate offspring.

himself sprang from his horse, seized a standard, and rallied a wavering Legion. It seemed as if the men meant all to stand and kill or be killed as long as daylight lasted. The ill fate of Labienus decided the victory. He had seen, as he supposed, some movement which alarmed him among Caesar's Moorish auxiliaries, and had galloped conspicuously across the field to lead a division to check them. A shout arose, "He flies—he flies!" A panic ran along the Pompeian lines. They gave way, and Caesar's Legions forced a road between their ranks. One wing broke off, and made for Cordova; the rest plunged wildly within the ditch and walls of Munda, the avenging sword smiting behind into the huddled mass of fugitives. Scarcely a prisoner was taken. Thirty thousand fell on the field, among them the last remains of the haughty youths who had threatened Caesar with their swords in the Senate House and had hacked Clodius's mob in the Forum. Among them was slain Labienus—his desertion of his General, his insults and his cruelties to his comrades, expiated at last in his own blood. Attius Varus was killed also, who had been with Juba when he destroyed Curio. The tragedy was being knitted up in the deaths of the last actors in it.[54]

Gnaeus Pompey and his brother fled on horseback; Sextus vanished into the fastness of the Sierra Morena; the elder struggled to reach Gibraltar, where he hoped to find a friendly squadron to afford him refuge.

"Munda was at once blockaded, the enclosing wall—savage evidence of the temper of the conquerors—being built of dead bodies pinned together with lances, and on the top of it a fringe of heads on swords' points, with the faces turned towards the town. A sally was attempted at midnight, and failed. The desperate wretches then fought amongst themselves, till at length the place was surrendered, and fourteen thousand of those who still survived were taken, and spared." [55]

Cordova, which was filled with refugees from the Munda battlefield, continued to hold out with desperate obstinacy. It fell at length, and was given over to pillage and massacre. Thereafter, every town opened its gates, and all Spain submitted to the conqueror. Sextus Pompey vanished tempor-

[54] Froude, *op. cit.*
[55] *Ibid.*

arily out of human ken; his brother was hunted down and slain out of hand.

Thus bloodily ended the Civil War, which the Senate of Rome had undertaken against Caesar, to escape the reforms which were threatened by his second consul-ship. They had involuntarily rendered their country the best service they were capable of conferring upon it, for the attempts Caesar would have made to amend a system too decayed to benefit by the process had been rendered forever impossible by their persistence. The free constitution of the Republic had issued at last in elections which were a mockery of representation, in courts of law which were an insult to justice, and in the conversion of the provinces of the Empire into the feed-ing-ground of a gluttonous oligarchy. In the army alone the Roman character and the Roman honor survived. In the *Imperator,* therefore, as chief of the army, the care of the provinces, the direction of public policy, the sover-eign authority in the last appeal, could alone thencefor-ward reside. The Senate might remain as a Council of State; the magistrates might bear their old names and administer their old functions. But the authority of the executive government lay in the loyalty, the morality, and the patriotism of the Legions to whom the power had been transferred. Fortunately for Rome, the change came before decay had eaten into the bone, and the gen-ius of the Empire had still a refuge from platform ora-tory and Senatorial wrangling in the hearts of her sol-diers.[56]

Caesar did not immediately return to Italy. From open re-volt in any part of the Roman dominions there was nothing more to fear; but there was a tremendous amount of "tidying up" which demanded his personal attention, his administra-tive flair, and his genius for reconciliation. It was not, there-fore, until late in the autumn of 45 B.C. that he re-entered the capital,

honored and feared as no one had ever been before. All kinds of honors were devised for his gratification without stint, even such as were divine—sacrifices, games, statues in all the temples and public places, by every Tribe, by all the provinces, and by Kings in alliance with Rome.

[56] Froude, *op. cit.*

He was proclaimed the Father of his Country and chosen Dictator for life and Consul for ten years, and his person was declared sacred and inviolable. . . . Many temples were decreed to him as a god, and one was dedicated to him and the goddess Clemency, who were represented as clasping hands. Thus while they feared his power they besought his clemency.

There were some who proposed to give him the title of King, but when he learned of their purpose he forbade it with threats.[57]

He was a monarch in all but name by the legitimacy of accomplished fact. The substance of power was already his, its trappings were immaterial. He even "dismissed the Praetorian Cohorts that had served as his bodyguard during the wars and showed himself with the ordinary civil escort only."[58]

"As Consuls for the ensuing year he designated himself and Antony, his Master of Horse, and he appointed Lepidus, who was then Governor of Spain but was administering it by his friends, Master of Horse in place of Antony. Caesar also recalled the exiles, except those who were banished for some very grave offense. He pardoned his enemies and forthwith advanced those who had fought against him to the yearly magistracies, or to the command of Provinces and armies." [59] Gaius Cassius, who would have killed him in Cilicia, was pardoned and advanced. Marcus Brutus, who had fought against him at Pharsalus, was welcomed back to Rome. To the widows and children of his opponents who had fallen in the war he restored the estates and honors of their families. Even the prating, irreconcilable Cicero was pardoned and protected. He made no attempt to retaliate for the past, nor by severity to secure himself for the future. Reconciliation; the best men for the work they best could do; *Homonoia*, "Unity in Concord,"—"this was the dream which absorbed all his energies during the last months of his life." [60] Wearied, aging—he was in his forty-seventh year—plagued by the attacks of epilepsy and "convulsions" whose incidence had become far more frequent, "he resumed the interrupted work of the great Alexander, whose image, we may well believe, was never absent from Caesar's soul." [61]

57 Appian, *op. cit.*

58 Suetonius, *op. cit.*

59 Appian, *op. cit.*

60 G. Ferrero, *The Greatness and Decline of Rome* (Vol. II).

61 Mommsen, *op. cit.*

The program of consolidation and reform was, indeed, virtually illimitable. To begin with, Caesar "increased the number of the Senate to nine hundred, filling its ranks from eminent provincials; introducing even 'barbarian' Gauls, and even *libertini,* the sons of liberated slaves, who had risen to distinction by their own merits. The new members came in slowly, and it is needless to say they were unwillingly received; a private handbill was sent round, recommending the coldest of greetings to them." In the capital "he cut short the corn grants, which nursed the city mob in idleness; and from the impoverished citizens he furnished out masses of colonists to repair the decay of ancient cities. Corinth rose from its ashes under Caesar's care. Eighty thousand Italians were settled down on the site of Carthage," [62] while he made continual efforts to check the hedonism and sybarite self-indulgence and effeminate affectations which, like a canker, were eating into the Roman character.

Where public works were concerned, Caesar projected the draining of the malarial Pomptine marshes, the construction of a great harbor at the mouth of the Tiber, the cutting of a canal through the Isthmus of Corinth, the establishment of Italian colonies in Provence, Lampsacus, Albania, Sinope, Heraclea, and the Black Sea; while he called in the aid of Marcus Varro to help form libraries in the principal towns. He invoked the services of the best juridical authorities to reduce the huge mass of legal enactments and precedents to a coherent digest, or Code of Laws, while encouraging physicians, chirurgeons, and men of science to settle in Rome by offering them the freedom of the city. And all the while he was quietly organizing an expedition he proposed to lead to Parthia, where the local war-leaders had formed an alliance with the last of the Pompeian Generals, Caecilius Bassus.

Without illusions and without fear, Caesar had undertaken a tremendous program of regeneration, and he was determined that it should succeed; for success is the most powerful justification known to history.

"Gratitude," it has been remarked, "is a test that friendship rarely survives." It certainly failed to do so with some of those to whom Caesar had extended not only his clemency but his favor. M. Junius Brutus, for one, had never forgiven the *Imperator* for having had to seek his forgiveness—nor

62 Froude, *op. cit.*

for the further humiliation of having obtained it. And much the same could be said of Cassius, while Cicero went about muttering with sinister ambiguity that "Caesar was but mortal, and that there were many ways in which a man might die."

Steadily the curdling spite of disappointed fanaticism and baffled selfishness hardened into a definite conspiracy to remove the object of the cabal's jealous hatred. "Brutus, once wrought upon, became with Cassius the most ardent in the cause which assumed the aspect of a sacred duty. Behind them were the crowd of Senators of the familiar faction, and others worse than they, who had not even the excuse of having been partisans of the beaten cause; men who had fought at Caesar's side till the war was over, and believed, with Labienus, that to them Caesar owed his fortune, and that he alone ought not to reap the harvest." [63] Trebonius, still smarting under the sense of his own failure in Spain, was another in the complot, as was the favored Lepidus; and as the Ides of March approached the conspirators met and agreed that the act of tyrannicide—as they insisted on terming it—should be consummated in the Senate House on the day following, the fifteenth of the month.

On the morning of the fifteenth,

while Caesar was actually being borne to the Senate, one of his intimates, who had learned of the conspiracy, ran to his house to tell him what he knew. When he arrived there and found only Calpurnia he merely said that he wanted to speak to Caesar about urgent business, and then waited for him to come back from the Senate, because he did not know all the particulars of the affair. . . . A tablet informing him of the conspiracy was put in Caesar's hand by another person while he was sacrificing in front of the Senate, but he went in immediately, and it was found in his hand after his death. Popilius Laena, who a little before had joined his prayers with the party of Crassus, accosted Caesar and engaged him aside in earnest conversation. The sight of this proceeding and especially the length of the conversation struck terror into the hearts of the conspirators, and they made signs to each other that they would kill themselves rather than be captured. As the conversation was prolonged they saw that Laena did not appear to be revealing anything to Caesar, but rather to be urging some peti-

63 Froude, *op. cit.*

tion. They recovered themselves, and when they saw him return thanks to Caesar after the conversation they took new courage. . . . The conspirators had left Trebonius to engage Antony in conversation at the door. The others, with concealed daggers, stood around Caesar like friends as he sat in his chair. Then one of them, Tillius Cimber, came in front of him and petitioned him for the recall of his brother, who had been banished. When Caesar answered that the matter must be deferred, Cimber seized hold of his purple robe, and pulled it away so as to expose his neck, exclaiming, "Friends, what are you waiting for?" Then Casca, who was standing over Caesar's head, drove his dagger at his throat, but swerved and wounded him in the breast. Caesar snatched his toga from Cimber, seized Casca's hand, sprang from his chair, turned around, and hurled Casca with great violence. While he was in this position another one stabbed him with a dagger in the side, which was stretched tense by his strained position. Cassius wounded him in the face, Brutus smote him in his thigh, and Bucolianus in the back. With rage and outcries Caesar turned now upon one and now upon another like a wild animal; but, after receiving another wound from Brutus, he at last despaired and, veiling himself with his robe, composed himself for death and fell at the foot of Pompey's statue. They continued their attack after he had fallen until he had received three-and-twenty wounds.[64]

Such was the apotheosis of Gaius Julius Caesar. But great as he was, the work to which he set his hand was even greater; and Pharsalus was to be justified in the enduring stability which was the victor's gift to Rome.

[64] Appian, *op. cit.*

EPILOGUE

Pax Romana

"The centuries are but morsels of the night."

—The Divan of abu al-Ala

It has been written that "power gravitates naturally to those prepared to make decisions and live with the results." Like all men who have left their mark upon the world, Caesar was always prepared to come to a decision and abide by its consequences. But in one respect, he qualifies for inclusion in even a rarer category. For it has been given to few men to establish a system of governance so sound, so farsighted, and so appropriate to the particular ethos of the governed, as to survive the demise of its progenitor.

It was President Woodrow Wilson who once pointed out that "liberty in itself is not government; in the wrong hands, in hands unpracticed and undisciplined, it is incompatible with government." In short, all effective institutions, determined to endure, are careful to avoid tendentious—or Ciceronian!—debate; they simply lay down the law and see that it is obeyed.

Such was Caesar's method; but at the same time he fully realized that the exercise of power must always be accompanied by some quality which renders power tolerable. His real genius lay, in fact, in his acute appreciation of where to draw the line between the firm but benign exercise of power and its tyrannical abuse; when to be unbending and when to extend the hand of reconciliation. A devout believer in the Alexandrian concept of "Unity in Concord," it was Caesar's abiding design to consummate the reconstruction of the Roman Empire on a rational and humanitarian basis. Moreover, as Wilcken has clearly emphasized, "his policy did not aim at a national Roman *Imperium,* but at an international world-empire which was to embrace the whole world

of Hellenistic-Roman culture." Rome and the Provinces were
to be welded into one entity; Rome itself was to become the
denationalized capital of many nations. The provinces themselves were no longer to be administered by wealth-hungry
Governors and their corrupt, avaricious underlings, but by
men of probity, who had their charges' interests sincerely at
heart; while the prime purpose of colonization was to relieve
the capital and its environs of a seething incubus of idle,
rancorous out-of-works, and ensure their healthy, gainful employment.

With the Senate transformed into an advisory Council of
State, it would be shorn of the hampering powers hitherto
exercised by a self-regarding oligarchy whose members had
very largely made use of their powers to further their own
interests. As a consultative rather than as an executive body,
it could render far better service to the State. The objective,
in short, was a monarchical democracy, with freedom under
discipline instead of license under greed. Or as Mommsen
summed it up, "Caesar resumed the interrupted work of the
great Alexander, whose image, we may well believe, never was
absent from his soul."

Furthermore, the foundations of the design were so well
laid, the structure so firmly erected, that it endured.

Stoutly supported by Antony, Caesar's designated heir,
Octavius, set about extinguishing the embers of the revolt
ignited by Brutus and Cassius, finally establishing his supremacy in the crucial sea encounter of Actium. Elected *Princeps
Senatus*, he was endowed with the semi-divine title of Augus-
tus. Thus by irreversible degrees, what had been a dyarchy
was transformed into the Augustan Dynasty.

This principate persisted, to reach its most outstanding
epoch of peace and prosperity under Trajan (A.D. 56-117), continuing in impressive equilibrium under the brilliant, cos-
mopolitan Hadrian, the able Antonius Pius, and the philos-
opher-statesman Marcus Aurelius Antoninus.

If the dynastic record was temporarily besmirched by such
sorry travesties of majesty as Caracalla, Heliogabalus, and
Nero, its luster was more than adequately restored by Dio-
cletian and Constantine, who strove worthily to preserve their
mighty heritage and to maintain that beneficent Pax Romana
which was its vindication. Thus even Gibbon was brought,
however grudgingly, to allow that "mankind was never so
happy as under the Antonines."

Yet slowly, erosively, Rome was falling victim to her own
wellbeing and prosperity, as to "the cankers of a calm world
and a long peace." Sunk in luxury, enervated by self-in-

dulgence, her people were no longer heedful of the stern demands of military service, which, with incredible rashness, they progressively delegated to alien auxiliaries and hired mercenaries. Thus when Alaric the Goth and his loot-hungry barbarians stormed out of the north, there was neither the spirit nor the strength to repel them; and Rome, with all it stood for, perished almost in a night.

Such is History's inexorable rhythm. The greatest and most ruthless reorganizer is Time. Nations come and nations go, and "the best in this kind are but shadows," their best hope no more than to earn a sympathetic glance over the shoulder from those who come hurrying to fill the niche that once was theirs.

> *Like leaves on trees the race of man is found,*
> *Now green in youth, now withering in the ground:*
> *Another race the following Spring supplies;*
> *They fall successive and successive rise.*

BIBLIOGRAPHY

Adcock, F. E., *The Roman Art of War under the Republic*.
Appian (Appianus Alexandrinus), *The Civil Wars*.
Arrian, Flavius, *Anabasis Alexandron*.
Atticus (Titus Pomponius), *The Epistles*.
Bassett-Lowke, W. J., & Holland, George, *Ships and Men*.
Beesly, A. H., *The Gracci, Marius and Sulla*.
Caesar, Gaius Julius, *The Commentaries*.
Cambridge Ancient History, Vol. IX.
Cassius, Dion, *The History*.
Cicero, Marcus Tullius, *De Officiis*.
———, *Pro Murena*.
Curtius, Quintus, *De Rebus Gestis Alexandri*.
Dio (Dion Cassius), *History of Rome*.
Diodarus, Siculus, *Bibliothéké Historiké*.
Dionysius (Dionysius Helicarnassensis), *The Roman Antiquities*.
Dodge, Colonel Theodore Ayrault, *Caesar*.
Ferraro, G., *The Greatness and Decline of Rome*.
Florus, Lucius Annaeus, *Epitome of Roman History*.
Fowler, W. Warde, *Julius Caesar*.
Froude, James Anthony, *Caesar*.
Fuller, Major-General J. F. C., *Armament and History*.
Gibbon, Edward, *The Decline and Fall of the Roman Empire*. (6 vols.)
Grimal, Pierre, *The Civilization of Rome*.
Grose, Francis, *Military Antiquities*. (2 vols.)
Grote, George, *History of Greece*.
Hargreaves, Reginald, *The Narrow Seas*.
Hittle, Lieutenant Colonel J. D., *The General Staff*.
How, W. W., and Leigh, H. D., *A History of Rome*.
Ihne, Wilhelm, *The History of Rome*.
Isocrates, *Panegyricus*.
Josephus, *De Bellum Judaico*.
Kahler, Heinz, *Rome and Her Empire*.
Lamb, Major A. J. R., *The Story of the Horse*.
Lemprière, John, *Classical Dictionary*.
Liddell, Henry G., *A History of Rome*. (2 vols.)

Livy (Titus Livius), *A History of Rome.*

Lucan (M. Annaeus Lucanus), *The Civil War.*

———, *Pharsalia.*

Mahaffey, J., *The Greek World Under Roman Sway.*

Mahan, Captain A. T., *The Influence of Sea Power Upon History.*

Mommsen, Theodor, *A History of Rome.* (4 vols.)

Montanelli, Indro, *Rome.*

Oman, Sir Charles, *A History of the Art of War.*

———, *A History of Greece.*

Ovid (Publius Ovidius Naso), *The Fasti.*

Payne-Gallwey, Sir Ralph, *Projectile-Throwing Engines of the Ancients.*

Parker, H. M. D., *The Roman Legions.*

Plutarch (Ploutarchos), *Lives.*

Polybius, *The History.*

Preston, R. A., Wise, S. F., and Werner, H. O., *Men in Arms.*

Procopius, *Historia Arcana.*

Rostovetzeff, V., *History of the Ancient World.* (2 vols.)

Sallust (Gaius Sallustius Crispus), *Historiarum Libre Quinque.*

———, *The Jugurthine War.*

Starr, Chester G., *The Roman Navy.*

Strabo, *Geographica.*

Stuart-Jones, H., ed., *The Companion to Roman History.*

Suetonius (C. Suetonius Tranquillus), *The Lives of the Twelve Caesars.*

Tacitus, Cornelius, *The History.*

Tarn, W. W., *Alexander the Great and the Unity of Mankind.*

Vegetius (Flavius Vegetius Renatus), *Military Institutions of the Romans.*

Vaghts, Alfred, *A History of Militarism.*

Watson, G. R., *The Roman Legions.*

Webster, Graham, *The Roman Army.*

Wilcken, Ulrick, *Alexander the Great.*

INDEX

THE NEW AMERICAN LIBRARY *publishers of*
SIGNET, MENTOR, SIGNET CLASSICS & NAL BOOKS

MENTOR
BOOK

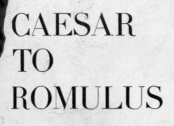

CAESAR
TO
ROMULUS

This is a dynamic history of Rome from the time of its emergence as a tribal community which dominated a sector of the Italian peninsula, to the day when the fate of an empire was decided at Pharsalus in a bitter conflict between Gaius Julius Caesar and his son-in-law Gnaeus Pompeius Magnus (Pompey the Great). Major Hargreaves makes skillful use of the accounts of early Roman historians to reconstruct the foreign battles, the civil strife, the political intrigues and personal rivalries that went into the making of the Roman Empire. Here is a lively interpretation of ancient chronicles, and a rare view of early Rome, by a renowned expert in military history.

MAJOR REGINALD HARGREAVES, M. C., the noted military historian, is the author of Onlooker at War, Red Sun Rising: The Siege of Port Arthur, and The Enemy at the Gates.

DESIGN: HENRY WOLF